SUCCESSION LAW

IN

NORTHERN IRELAND

The Queen's Anniversary Prizes for Higher and Further Education recognise the contribution of universities and colleges to the social, economic, cultural and intellectual life of the nation.

In 1994, the inaugural year of the competition, The Queen's University of Belfast was awarded a prize for the work of Servicing the Legal System.

The prize citation for SLS reads:

> *"This is an outstanding service to overcome the special problems of distributing knowledge about new law inside a small jurisdiction. It is an international exemplar."*

The Servicing The Legal System Programme

This programme was inaugurated in August 1980 in the Faculty of Law at Queen's University, Belfast to promote the publication of commentaries on various aspects of the law and legal system of Northern Ireland. Generous financial and other support for the programme has been provided by the Northern Ireland Court Service, the Inn of Court of Northern Ireland, the Bar Council of Northern Ireland, the Law Society of Northern Ireland and Queen's University. Details of other SLS publications may be obtained from the SLS Office, School of Law, The Queen's University of Belfast, Belfast BT7 1NN.

Succession Law

in

Northern Ireland

Sheena Grattan

Lecturer in Law, The Queen's University of Belfast

SLS Legal Publications (NI)
1996

First published 1996 by SLS Legal Publications (NI),
School of Law, Queen's University, Belfast BT7 1NN.

ISBN 0 85389 657 7

Typeset by SLS Legal Publications (NI)
Printed by Hartnolls, Cornwall

PREFACE

This book is aimed primarily at the Northern Ireland legal profession and is designed to fill, at least partially, a gap which has existed in the practitioner's library for a number of years. It is hoped, however, that it will also be of use to persons who are studying for both academic and professional examinations.

Most people will now be aware that the Wills Act 1837, which has governed the law of wills for so long, has been virtually repealed and replaced by the Wills and Administration Proceedings (NI) Order 1994 (Judge Langton's criticism of the term dependent relative revocation - "overloaded with unnecessary polysyllables" - springs to mind). This legislation, which became effective on 1 January 1995, has made a number of significant amendments to the law of wills. These generally aim to assimilate the law in Northern Ireland with that in England and Wales, where amendments were made to the Wills Act 1837 by the Administration of Justice Act 1982, in order to implement recommendations made in the Twenty-Second Report of the Law Reform Committee on the Making and Revocation of Wills (Cmnd 7902, 1980). The net effect of the 1994 Order is thus a drastic reduction in the number of divergences between the two jurisdictions. However, a complete assimilation has not been achieved and a handful of differences still exist. Appendix A contains a noter-up of the new Order, which should illustrate at a glance both the amendments and also where the law remains different in Northern Ireland.

The draft Succession (NI) Order 1996, which is expected to become effective no later than the beginning of 1997, was published on 21 March. This legislation, which proposes that a 28 day survivorship clause apply between spouses on intestate deaths, that the doctrine of hotchpot be abolished and that automatic *locus standi* under the Inheritance (Provision for Family and Dependants) (NI) Order 1979 be granted to cohabitants of two years standing, has been incorporated into the existing paragraph structure.

The award of an SLS-funded Research Fellowship in the Autumn of 1994 enabled work on the manuscript to enter the home stretch and I gratefully acknowledge this assistance. In addition, I would like to record my thanks to a number of people who helped with the writing and publication of this book. I am particularly indebted to Mr Alastair Rankin, Cleaver, Fulton and Rankin Solicitors, who took time to read the entire manuscript and gave it the benefit of his immense knowledge and experience in the field. Both Master R Millar and

Mr Leslie Millar, of the Probate and Matrimonial Office, read and commented on the chapter dealing with the procedures for obtaining a grant of representation. The responsibility for any errors remains, of course, my own. Thanks also to Mrs Sara Gamble, Publications Editor of SLS Legal Publications who prepared the Tables of Cases, Legislation and Rules, made many helpful suggestions on the layout of the text and personally handled every stage of the publication, and to Professor Brigid Hadfield of the School of Law, Queen's University who kindly helped to proof read the last draft. The final acknowledgment is reserved for George, whose enthusiasm for this project never faltered, and who provided much practical assistance with proofing and indexing.

Sheena Grattan
31 August 1996

CONTENTS

TABLE OF CASES

TABLE OF LEGISLATION AND RULES

KEY TO ABBREVIATIONS

"1837 Act"   -   Wills Act 1837

"1954 Act"   -   Wills Act (Amendment) Act (NI) 1954

"1955 Act"   -   Administration of Estates Act (NI) 1955

"1960 Act"   -   Inheritance (Family Provision) Act (NI) 1960

"1967 Act"   -   Administration of Estates (Small Payments) Act
                      (NI) 1967

"1978 Order"   -   Matrimonial Causes (NI) Order 1978

"1979 Order"   -   Inheritance (Provision for Family and Dependants)
                      (NI) Order 1979 (Chapter 8)

                  -   Administration of Estates (NI) Order 1979 (Chapter 11)

"1982 Order"   -   Forfeiture (NI) Order 1982

"1986 Order"   -   Mental Health (NI) Order 1986

"1994 Order"   -   Wills and Administration Proceedings (NI) Order 1994

"NCPR"   -   Non-Contentious Probate Rules

CHAPTER ONE

INTRODUCTION

BASIC TERMINOLOGY

1.01   The law of succession is concerned with the redistribution of property on death.   In the modern[1] British legal system the key vehicle[2] in this redistribution is undoubtedly the *will* - the state confers on virtually all adult citizens the freedom to make an effective declaration which determines the ownership of most of their property[3] on death. A person who has exercised this right (ie a *testator* or, if female, a *testatrix*)[4] and dies having made a valid will is said to die *testate*. All other persons, that is, those who have not made an effective will, die *intestate* and the law prescribes how their estate is to be distributed between spouse and next-of-kin. The traditional view of the law of succession is that it consists solely of these complementary twin pillars; the rules of testate and of intestate succession. For a number of reasons, however, this labelling has become simplistic and inaccurate.

1.02   First, the freedom of testation referred to above is no longer absolute. Since 1960 a mechanism has existed for the distribution of property on death following a judicial arbitration procedure known as family provision. Testators thus remain free to endow the beneficiaries of their choosing, but the court may then set this distribution aside in favour of spouses or other close relatives and dependants. This third pillar of the succession system, transmission of assets by arbitration, is having an increasingly significant impact on the redistribution of property and will be dealt with in Chapter Eight.

---

[1] This was not always the case as wills emerged comparatively late in history. In the early feudal period there was a prohibition on devises of land and it was not until after the enactment of the Tenures Abolition Act (Ir) 1662 that real property became completely alienable by will (subject to a widow's dower and a widower's right of curtesy). Only *part* of the personal estate (one half if deceased had no children, one third if he did) could be disposed of by will until the passing of the Statute of Distributions (Ir) 1695.

[2] Ie, key in the sense of perceived importance. It is not in fact the most important statistically as the majority of persons seem not to make a will - see para 6.01 *post*.

[3] Arts 2(3) and 3 of the Wills and Administration Proceedings (NI) Order 1994 provide that a person may dispose by will of all property to which he is beneficially entitled for an estate or interest not ceasing on death. Property is defined in art 2(2) as including "any estate in land, any chattels, any thing in action, and any rights which are treated commercially as property and also includes any interest in property". A mere life interest (ie not one *pur autre vie*) or a joint tenancy cannot be disposed of by will.

[4] Note that in this work the term "testator" applies *mutatis mutandis* to a testatrix.

1.03   In addition, succession law has a much broader aspect which ought properly to be considered. First, account should be taken of the whole process of transfer of resources from one generation to the next, *post mortem* and *inter vivos* - in one respect the will is but one species of the gift. More importantly, social and economic changes have diminished the significance of both the will and the intestacy code. New property forms such as insurance policies and the growing trend for couples to hold their major asset, the family home, as joint tenants, result in an increasing amount of wealth being transmitted outwith the traditional succession regime. The point having been made, and while a number of these so-called 'will-substitutes' are examined in the course of this book,[5] the emphasis remains primarily on succession law in its narrower sense of redistribution of property through the will and the intestacy code.

THE NATURE OF A WILL

Definition
1.04   There is no statutory definition of a will.[6] Of the variants which have been offered from time to time by the judiciary and academic commentators, the following from the third edition of Halsbury's Laws of England is one of the most comprehensive:[7]

> "A will or testament[8] is the declaration in a prescribed manner of the intention of the person making it with regard to matters which he wishes to take effect upon or after his death."

Dual meaning of the word 'will'
1.05   Even within its limited property law context the word 'will' is used in two distinct ways. A testator is not restricted to making a single testamentary document, but can make any number, provided that each is executed in accordance with the necessary statutory formalities.[9] In one sense the 'will' of a testator who has executed several such documents is the sum of his wishes, the aggregate of *all* the documents:

---

[5] Eg, *donationes mortis causa* at para 1.28 *post*; joint tenancies at para 10.16 *post* and statutory nominations at para 10.08 *post*.

[6] The now repealed interpretation provision of the Wills Act 1837 Act, s 1, simply described a will as including a testament, a codicil and an appointment by will.

[7] 3rd Ed Vol 39 p 157.

[8] In the past a 'will' disposed of a deceased's real property and a 'testament' of his personal property. There is no longer any practical significance in the double terminology and it has become a complete anachronism.

[9] A later document does not automatically revoke an earlier one - see para 4.25 *post*.

"Whether a man leaves one testamentary writing or several testamentary writings, it is the aggregate or the net result that constitutes his will, or, in other words, the expression of his testamentary wishes ... In this sense it is inaccurate to speak of a man leaving two wills; he does leave, and can leave, but one will."[10]

Notwithstanding these reservations it remains common parlance to refer also to *each* of the individual documents as being a 'will'. Moreover, the difficulties with nomenclature are further heightened by the fact that where there is more than one testamentary document it is customary to refer to the principal one as a 'will' and to any supplementary ones as *codicils* to that will.[11] No scientific formula exists to determine when a codicil ceases to be such and becomes a will and it is equally acceptable to refer to all testamentary documents as wills, whatever their length or content.

A will is a public document

1.06 As soon as a will has been proved it becomes a public document.[12] It is open to inspection by anybody, irrespective of whether they can show an interest in the estate.

Secret trusts

1.07 There may be occasions when a testator is keen to benefit a person whose identity he would like to keep secret; for instance, he may wish to support a mistress or an illegitimate child without his family's knowledge. He can achieve his objective by entering into a 'secret trust', a mechanism which involves leaving property in the will to a reliable person (the secret trustee)[13] who enters into an agreement with the testator to hold that property on trust for the undisclosed beneficiary. Lack of space precludes discussion of the law relating to secret trusts here and readers are referred to the standard works on Trust Law.[14]

---

[10]*Per* Lord Robertson in *Douglas-Menzies* v *Umphelby* [1908] AC 224.

[11]Often dubbed a 'postscript to the will'.

[12]In Northern Ireland wills are kept in the Probate Office or District Probate Registry for several years after they have been proved. Members of the public are usually charged a small fee to inspect a will there. Thereafter they are transferred to the Public Records Office where they can be examined free of charge.

[13]It can either be left to the trustee absolutely, with no reference to the trust appearing on the face of the will (a fully secret trust) or it can be left to him upon trust, but with the terms of the trust remaining secret (a half-secret trust).

[14]Note that the law in Ireland as regards the time for communication in *half-secret* trusts may be different to that in England, but this is documented well in English books.

A will is ambulatory

1.08   A will is said to be *ambulatory*, that is, it has no effect whatsoever until the death of the testator. Thus a testator who has made a will leaving Blackacre to his nephew remains free to sell or otherwise dispose of Blackacre before his death.[15] It follows on from this that a testator can revoke or change his will at any time.[16] However, there are times when by revoking his will the testator is in breach of a binding agreement. These circumstances are considered below.[17]

The doctrine of incorporation by reference

1.09   In certain circumstances a document which has not been duly executed by the testator may be incorporated into his will. Once incorporated in this way the document becomes part of the will, and is subject to the usual rules governing testamentary documents, such as the doctrines of ademption and lapse.[18] Further, it will be admitted to probate[19] with the will[20] and is thereafter open to public inspection in the usual way. The doctrine of incorporation does not therefore operate to avoid publicity and if this is what the testator desires he should make a secret trust.[21] The practical benefit is simply that it avoids encumbrancing the will with lengthy or complex detail which it would be more suitable to record elsewhere.

The requirements for operation of the doctrine

1.10   The obvious danger is that the operation of the doctrine will undermine the rationale behind the statutory formalities for the execution of a will. It is therefore unsurprising that the pre-requisites for its application are relatively onerous and have been interpreted strictly by the judiciary. They are as follows:

---

[15] The gift is said to have been "adeemed". Ademption is dealt with at para 7.60 *post*.

[16] See para 4.01 *post*.

[17] Testamentary promises at para 1.14 *post*.

[18] *Bizzy* v *Flight* (1876) 3 Ch D 269.

[19] Unless there are exceptional circumstances which make it impracticable to insist upon filing. Eg in *Re Balme* [1897] P 261 a lengthy library catalogue which had been incorporated was not required to be filed in the Probate Registry. Instead a note was put on the probate stating that the catalogue was in the care and custody of Selwyn College library and could be inspected there.

[20] The oath for executor (see para 11.16 *post*) should refer to the fact that there is a document to be incorporated, and both the document and the will should be labelled separately and referred to as such.

[21] See para 1.07 *supra*.

(a) The document to be incorporated must have already been in existence at the time when the will was executed.[22]

This requirement derives from the fact that a person cannot be allowed to reserve for himself the power to make future, unwitnessed testamentary dispositions. However, if the document has come into existence after the date of the execution of the will but before the execution of a codicil which republishes that will,[23] this requirement[24] is satisfied.[25]

(b) The document must be *referred to in the will* as already being in existence.[26]

Thus when a will refers to instructions "to be found in my notebook which I shall write at some time before my death", the contents of the notebook cannot be incorporated into the will. The situation is the same even if the testator had actually written up his notebook before the execution of the will - the will itself must refer to its existence.[27]

(c) The document must be identified in the will.[28]

A very rigid application of this requirement is found in the Irish case *Re Conwell*,[29] in which the testator referred to the document which it was sought to incorporate as "instructions to [his] executors" which had been "written, signed and sealed" by him. After his death signed instructions to his executors were found, but the court refused to incorporate them because they had not been sealed.

No incorporation

1.11 If the testator has expressly excluded the doctrine it will not operate.[30] A document which has been stated to have been incorporated but which cannot be found has no effect.[31]

---

[22]*Singleton v Tomlinson* (1878) 3 App Cas 404.

[23]For republication or confirmation see paras 4.67 and 4.79 *post*.

[24]Although note that requirement (b) might not be satisfied.

[25]*In the Goods of Lady Truro* (1866) LR 1 P&D 210.

[26]*In the Goods of Sunderland* (1866) LR 1 P&D 198.

[27]*Re Smart's Goods* [1902] P 238. Although see the contrary Irish authority, *In the Goods of Mitchell* (1966) 100 1 LTR 185.

[28]*In the Goods of Garnett* [1894] P 90; *In the Estate of Mardon* [1944] P 109.

[29](1896) 30 1 LTR 23.

[30]*Re Louis* (1916) 32 TLR 313.

[31]*Re Barton, Barton v Bourne* (1932) 48 TLR 205.

Conditional wills

1.12 A testator can make his will[32] *conditional* upon the satisfaction of a specified event; for example, that he survives his wife by 28 days. If the condition is not satisfied the entire will is inoperative.[33] The condition must be apparent on the face of the actual will and cannot be established using extrinsic evidence.[34]

1.13 A constant source of litigation in this area is testators who refer to a future happening as being the reason for making their wills and who then survive this happening to die a different death. In such cases it is a question of construction whether the testator intended the will to be effective *only* if he died as specified (ie the will is conditional), or whether he was simply expressing the motive which had made him consider his own mortality and get his affairs in order (ie unconditional).[35] For example, in *Re Dobson*[36] Lord Penzance held that a will drafted in the following terms "In case of any fatal accident happening to me, being about to travel by railway, I hereby leave ..." was unconditional, and it could take effect when the testator, having survived his railway journey, succumbed to ill health.

TESTAMENTARY PROMISES

Mutual wills

1.14 Two people may wish to make testamentary dispositions which are interdependent; to pool their resources during their lives, yet to ensure that after the death of the survivor what remains goes to specified beneficiaries. Consider a husband and wife who agree to execute wills, each leaving to the other absolutely but with a substitutionary gift to their children.[37] The wills remain unrevoked until the husband dies and his widow duly takes her benefit. A few years later she decides to remarry and executes another will which leaves her

---

[32] This is not to be confused with a conditional *gift* within a will, which he is also at liberty to make. In this case the failure of the condition does not affect the validity of the will itself.

[33] So if it contains a clause revoking a previous will that will remains effective - *In the Goods of Hugo* (1877) 2 PD 73.

[34] *Corbett* v *Newey* [1996] 2 All ER 914 reversing [1995] 1 All ER 570.

[35] Eg *Re Spratt's Goods* [1897] P 28 where a number of the cases are discussed. Also *Re Govier* [1950] P 237 (A joint will by a husband and wife "In the event of our two deaths ..." held by Willmer J to be conditional upon the simultaneous deaths of the testators).

[36] (1866) LR 1 P&D 88.

[37] For illustrations of this type of arrangement, see *Re Green* [1951] Ch 148 and *Re Cleaver* [1981] 1 WLR 939. The other commonly encountered mutual will arrangement is husband and wife leaving reciprocal life interests with remainder over to their children eg *Re Hagger* [1930] 2 Ch 190.

entire estate to her new husband. Yet it has already been observed that by its very nature her will is revocable throughout her life. How can this be reconciled with the conflicting policy that in doing so here she is acting in breach of an agreement she had with her first husband, under whose will she has benefitted? It was to remedy this sort of unconscionable revocation of wills that the Courts of Equity invented the doctrine of mutual wills. The solution is that in keeping with the inherent nature of a will the widow retains the *power* to revoke her will.[38] Further, if she executes a new will before she dies a grant of representation will be made in accordance with this new will rather than with the agreement.[39] However, the agreement then takes effect by way of *trust*; Equity imposes a constructive trust upon the widow's personal representatives to hold her property[40] for the children in accordance with the agreement.

The Law Reform (Husband and Wife) Act (NI) 1964

1.15 In addition to the equitable remedy of the constructive trust, beneficiaries under mutual wills who are the children of at least one of the testators may be able to sue under the contract themselves notwithstanding that they were not parties to it. This is because section 5 of the Law Reform (Husband and Wife) Act (NI) 1964, which extends only to Northern Ireland and has no English counterpart, provides that where a contract is expressed to be for the benefit of, or *by its express terms purports to confer a benefit upon, a third party being the wife, husband or child* of one of the contracting parties, it shall be enforceable by the third party in his or her own name as if he or she were a party to it.[41]

Not a joint will

1.16 Mutual wills, which can be executed in a single document, (although it is advisable to have a separate instrument for each testator), should not be confused with *joint wills*. A joint will is a single document executed by more than one person, which is treated as the separate will of all of them and which is proved on each death. Each person remains free to revoke his will at any time, even after the death of the other(s).

---

[38] Note that in the particular case described the revocation of the widow's will would have been effected automatically by her remarriage. It has recently been confirmed that even revocation by marriage (which is involuntary revocation) breaches the agreement - *Goodchild* v *Goodchild* [1996] 1 All ER 670.

[39] Eg *Stone* v *Hoskins* [1905] P 194 and *Re Heys* [1914] P 192.

[40] See para 1.20 *post* as to the extent of this property.

[41] Thus the *Re Dale* litigation which is discussed below would have been unnecessary in Northern Ireland because the daughter could have sued under the contract made between her parents.

Requirements for mutual wills

There must be an agreement

1.17   The essence of mutual wills is the prior agreement between the testators not to revoke their wills without notice to the other(s). The fact that the parties have executed wills in similar terms at the same time is not in itself sufficient to establish an agreement.[42]   It is advisable that the agreement be recited in the actual wills,[43] since otherwise it has to be proved[44] by extrinsic evidence and in practice proving such an agreement can be very difficult. This is well illustrated by the recent decision of *Goodchild* v *Goodchild*[45] where Carnwath J warned that it is:

> "....difficult to rely on the evidence of lay witnesses, when one is
> dealing with the somewhat technical issues as to whether there
> has been an agreement for mutually binding wills."

There need not be a mutual benefit

1.18   Until recently Equity's intervention in mutual wills cases was grounded in unjust enrichment; that as the survivor had received a benefit under the will of the first to die it was inequitable for him then to revoke his will contrary to the agreement. This theoretical basis has changed following the recent decision in *Re Dale*,[46] in which mutual wills were enforced even though the testators did not receive mutual benefits. Mutual wills are now justified on the more general consideration that it is a fraud on the first to die for the survivor to have allowed him to go to his grave in the belief that the arrangement remained:

> "... there is a binding contract ... it has been performed by T1 on
> the faith of the promise made by T2 and in each case T2 would
> have deceived T1 to the detriment of T1 if he, T2, were
> permitted to go back on his agreement."[47]

---

[42]"The fact that the two wills were made in identical terms does not necessarily connote any agreement beyond that of so making them" - *per* Astbury J in *Re Oldham* [1925] Ch 75 at 88.

[43]Eg as in *Re Hagger* [1930] 2 Ch 190.

[44]On the balance of probabilities - *Re Cleaver* [1981] 1WLR 939.

[45][1996] 1 All ER 670 at 679.

[46][1993] 4 All ER 134 - husband and wife executed wills leaving everything to their children; after husband's death wife changed will substantially reducing the gifts to her daughter. Held to be mutual wills.

[47] *Per* Morrit J in *Re Dale, ibid* at p 142.

When does the trust arise?

1.19   While both testators are still alive either is free to revoke his will, provided that notice is given to the other.   In the past there have been conflicting opinions about when exactly the trust arises.   The decision in *Re Dale* seems to confirm that the survivor is bound as soon as the first party dies.[48]

What property is bound?

1.20   The scope of the trust is not entirely clear.[49]   In the first instance it depends upon the terms of the agreement between the parties and may have been expressly limited to specified property or to part of the estate.[50]   When there are no express terms, a number of possibilities arise.   Does it merely attach to the property received by the survivor from the first to die?   Or does it extend to the property that the survivor himself owned at the date of the first death?   Or is it even wider, covering all property owned by the survivor at his own death, irrespective of how it was acquired?   In *Re Cleaver*[51] the last approach was adopted by Nourse J; the trust attached to all the survivor's assets, including those which she had acquired after the death of the first party. However, the learned judge went on to state that this fiduciary duty to which her property was subject did not crystallise until her death.   During her life she could therefore enjoy her property, and was disabled only from making voluntary dispositions which were calculated to defeat the agreement; there was no objection to ordinary gifts of small value.

A caveat

1.21   It should be evident from the foregoing that mutual wills are far-reaching in effect[52] and should not be entered into lightly.   If testators do wish to make mutual wills, the terms, especially which property is subject to the agreement, should be set out clearly.   Moreover, persons who are making wills in identical terms but who do not intend them to be mutual wills should think of expressly stating that they are not mutual wills in the body of the instrument.

---

[48]Previously a number of judicial dicta supported the view that it did not arise until a benefit was taken - see Mitchell (1951) 14 MLR 136.

[49]See Mitchell, *ibid.*

[50]Eg *Re Green* [1951] Ch 148.

[51][1981] WLR 939.   This approach has recently been adopted in *Goodchild* v *Goodchild* [1996] 1 All ER 670.

[52]In addition, mutual wills sever a joint tenancy; eg if husband and wife execute wills purporting to leave property which they own as joint tenants the tenancy is severed: *Re Heys* [1914] P 192.

Contracts to leave property by will

1.22   A contract in which a testator promises with someone to leave him benefits under his will may be valid.[53]   First, it is subject to the usual contractual requirements: there must be offer, acceptance, intention to create legal relations[54] and consideration, and the arrangement must not be too uncertain to be enforced.[55]   In addition, a contract to leave land by will is not enforceable unless it has been evidenced in writing[56] or there has been satisfaction of the equitable doctrine of part performance.[57]

1.23   Similarly, a contract in which the testator promises *not to revoke* an existing will under which the promisee is due to benefit is also valid.   The recognition of this type of arrangement may seem to contradict the principle discussed earlier[58] that a will can always be revoked.   It does not.   The actual will remains revocable; the testator will not be restrained from revoking it and any substituted testamentary provision will be admitted to probate.   However, the testator or his estate will be liable for breach of contract.

1.24   Generally marriage or remarriage, which effects the automatic revocation of a will irrespective of the testator's actual intention, does not breach a contract not to revoke a will.   For example, in *Re Marsland*[59] the wording of the covenant, "not to revoke", was held on its true construction to be limited to voluntary revocation under section 20 of the Wills Act 1837.[60]

---

[53]Thus a contract under which the deceased promised to make a will leaving a house to the woman he intended to marry was upheld in *Synge* v *Synge* [1894] 1 QB 466. Similarly a contract to leave a house to a couple if they acted as housekeepers for the testator was upheld in *Parker* v *Clark* [1960] 1 All ER 93.

[54]The contract must not be merely an informal family arrangement. For an example of this see *Re Fickus* [1900] 1 Ch 331.

[55]Eg *MacPhail* v *Torrance* (1909) 25 TLR 810 where a promise to "make ample provision" was held to be too vague. Note also that even if the testamentary promise is not enforceable as part of a binding contract, the promisee may find a remedy in the doctrine of proprietary estoppel - eg *Re Basham* [1987] 1 All ER 405. For further information see, Pettit, *Equity and the Law of Trusts* (7th ed, 1993) from p 183.

[56]Statute of Frauds (Ir) 1695, s 2. See, eg *Parker* v *Clark* [1960] 1 All ER 93 in which a letter written from testator to promisee was held to be a sufficient note.

[57]*Lowry* v *Reid* [1927] NI 142; *Wakeham* v *Mackenzie* [1968] 1 WLR 1175; compare *Maddison* v *Alderson* (1883) 8 App Cas 467. In England the doctrine of part performance has been abolished by s 2 of the Law of Property (Miscellaneous Provisions) Act 1989. Corresponding legislation has been recommended for NI by the Land Law Working Group.

[58]See para 1.08 *supra*.

[59][1939] Ch 820.

[60]In Northern Ireland now art 12 of the 1994 Order. Although compare the wording "not to do or commit any act, deed, matter or thing by means whereof the said will so to be made by

1.25 Prior to 1979 property which was subject to a contract to devise was not available for making a family provision award.[61] Article 13 of the Inheritance (Provision for Family and Dependants) (NI) Order 1979 empowers the court to claw such property back into the net estate in any case where it was contracted to be disposed of by will with the intention of defeating a family provision claim.[62]

Time of breach

1.26 The time of breach is generally the date of the testator's death. Where, however, the testator's promise is to leave *specific* property which he then purports to alienate *inter vivos* to a third party, the testator has committed an anticipatory breach of the contract and can be sued immediately.[63] The position where the testator has contracted to leave the entire estate or the residue is less clear, but it seems that in such circumstances the testator is not under an obligation to refrain from disposing of any of his assets during his lifetime.[64]

Remedies for breach

1.27 The basic remedy for breach of contract is damages, but in appropriate circumstances the court may order specific performance[65] or an injunction.[66] Where damages are awarded they will not necessarily equal the value of the property to be left in the will. For example, in the case of an anticipatory breach the amount awarded will usually be subject to a reduction for the acceleration of the benefit, and, if the benefit is personal to the promisee, a reduction to cover the contingency of him failing to survive the testator.[67]

DONATIONES MORTIS CAUSA

Definition

1.28 A *donatio mortis causa*[68] is a peculiar type of gratuitous transfer which is hybrid in nature between a lifetime gift and a testamentary gift,

---

her should be revoked, annulled, cancelled or affected in any matter whatsoever", held in *Robinson* v *Ommaney* (1883) 23 Ch 285 to include revocation by marriage.

[61]*Schaefer* v *Schuhmann* [1972] AC 572.

[62]See para 8.96 *post*.

[63]*Synge* v *Synge* [1894] 1 QB 466; *Schaefer* v *Schuhmann* [1972] AC 572.

[64]Unless the contract contained an express term to the contrary - *Palmer* v *Bank of New South Wales* [1973] 2 NSWLR 244.

[65]Eg *Synge* v *Synge* [1894] 1 QB 466.

[66]Eg an injunction may be granted to prevent the testator disposing during his lifetime of specific property which he contracted to will - provided, of course, that a purchaser for value has not obtained an interest in it - *Synge* v *Synge ibid*.

[67]*Schaefer* v *Schuhmann* [1972] AC 572 at 586.

[68] Gift in the face of death.

differing from both in fundamental respects, yet sharing characteristics with each. In an oft-quoted dictum, Buckley LJ described it as :

> "... a singular form of gift. It may be said to be amphibious in nature, being a gift which is neither entirely *inter vivos* nor testamentary. It is an act *inter vivos* by which the donee is to have the absolute title to the subject of the gift not at once but when the donor dies. If the donor dies the title becomes absolute and not under but as against his executor. In order to make the gift valid it must be made so as to take effect on the donor's death."[69]

In short, it is a gift made during a donor's lifetime with the intention that it should not take effect until his death. By way of illustration consider Maud, who before going into hospital for a triple bypass gives her nephew George a brown envelope containing five £100 notes, with the request "keep it if I don't make it". Maud dies on the operating table. Her death makes the gift to George fully effective and he is entitled to keep the £500. If, on the other hand, Maud had survived the operation, George would have to return the money.

Effect of a *donatio mortis causa*

1.29   The point has been made that a *donatio mortis causa* does not devolve on the personal representatives. It is, however, part of the donor's estate for inheritance tax[70] purposes and is liable for the payment of the donor's debts if all the assets of the estate have been exhausted.[71] Moreover, following the enactment of the Inheritance (Provision for Family and Dependants) (NI) Order 1979[72] a *donatio* is automatically part of the "net estate", that is, the property out of which an award may be made.[73]

Requirements for an effective *donatio*

1.30   In *Cain* v *Moon*[74] Lord Russell CJ set down the following requirements which must be satisfied to establish a *donatio mortis causa*:

    (a)   the gift must be made by the donor in contemplation, although not necessarily in expectation, of death;

---

[69]*Re Beaumont* [1902] 1 Ch 889 at 892.

[70]Inheritance Tax Act 1984, ss 4(1), 5(1).

[71]*Re Korvine's Trust* [1921] 1 Ch 343. But for a contrary view see Warnock-Smith [1978] Conv 130.

[72]Art 10.

[73]See para 8.93 *post*.

[74][1896] 2 QB 283 at 286.

(b)   the gift must be conditional on death, so that if the donor recovers from the contemplated cause of death, the gift is revoked;

(c)   before the donor dies he must part with dominion over the subject-matter of the gift.

In addition, there is a fourth condition which derives from this last requirement:

(d)   the subject-matter must be of the type that is capable of passing as a *donatio mortis causa*.

Each requirement will be considered in turn.[75]

Contemplation of death

1.31   There must be some relatively immediate threat to the donor's life; in practice, most effective *donationes* have been made by persons who are terminally ill. The contemplation need not be express but may be inferred from the circumstances. It is not enough that the donor was merely contemplating death in the general sense that it is the inevitable lot of all. However, if the donor contemplates death resulting from one particular cause and dies from another while the gift is unrevoked, the *donatio* will still take effect. For example, if Maud in the illustration above died the night before her operation because she fell out of bed and sustained head injuries the *donatio* remains valid.[76]

1.32   A gift cannot be made in contemplation of death by suicide.[77]

Conditional on death

1.33   The donor need not expressly manifest his intention that the gift is conditional upon death and it may be inferred from the surrounding circumstances.[78] If the donor really intended to make a *lifetime* gift the court will not allow it to be perfected by treating it as a *donatio*.

---

[75]Points (c) and (d) are considered together.

[76]*Wilkes* v *Allington* [1931] 2 Ch 104 - terminally ill donor caught a chill and died of pneumonia.

[77]*Agnew* v *Belfast Banking Co* [1896] 2 IR 204; *Re Dudman* [1925] Ch 553 (distinguished in *Mills* v *Shields* [1948] IR 367).

[78]*Re Lillingston* [1952] 2 All ER 184.

Part with dominion

1.34 Satisfaction of this requirement usually needs delivery of the subject-matter of the *donatio* to the donee or the donee's agent. Moreover, the delivery must be with the intention of parting with dominion; for example, delivery for safe custody will not suffice.[79]

1.35 Obviously it is not difficult to "part with dominion" when the subject-matter of a *donatio* is tangible, moveable property which is capable of manual delivery. What is the position where the nature of the property (land, choses in action, bulky chattels) defies delivery in this sense? Two extensions of the word "delivery" have widened the type of property which can constitute the subject-matter of a *donatio*.

1.36 First, the donor may be taken to have parted with dominion if the donee has been put in possession of the means of getting to the property; for instance, he has been given the keys to where it is kept.[80] Secondly, rather than deliver the subject-matter itself, it may be enough to deliver a document which is "the essential indicia or evidence of title, possession or production of which entitles the possessor to the money or property purported to be given".[81] For example, the contents of bank and building society accounts have been held to be capable of passing as a *donatio* where the passbooks were delivered to the donee.[82] At one time it was thought that land was incapable of being the subject-matter of a *donatio* because of the difficulties of delivery,[83] but it was recently held by the Court of Appeal that there could be an effective *donatio* of unregistered land by delivery of the title deeds.[84] It has yet to be determined conclusively whether company shares can form the subject-matter of a *donatio*, dominion over which can be parted by delivery of the share certificates.[85]

---

[79]If, however, the donor delivers the subject-matter for safe keeping but then changes his mind and manifests an intention to part with dominion this is effective.

[80]*Re Wasserberg* [1915] 1 Ch 195; *Re Cole* [1964] Ch 175. Although it seems there is no parting with dominion if the donor retained a second key - *Re Craven's Estate* [1937] Ch 423 and *Sen v Headley* [1991] 2 All ER 636.

[81]*Per* Evershed MR in *Birch v Treasury Solicitors* [1951] Ch 298 at 311. Note that where delivery of the "indicia" of ownership gives the donee an *equitable* title only, Equity will nevertheless perfect an imperfect gift and compel the personal representatives to transfer the legal title.

[82]*Ibid.* This is subject to the passbooks being all that is needed to withdraw money.

[83]*Duffield v Elwes* (1827) 1 Bli NS 497.

[84]*Sen v Headley* [1991] 2 All ER 636.

[85]*Moore v Moore* (1874) LR 18 Eq 474 and *Mill v Shields* (No2) [1950] IR 21 (they cannot). Compare *Staniland v Willott* (1852) 3 Mac & G 664 and *Re Craven's Estate* [1937] Ch 423 (they can).

Revocation of a *donatio*

1.37 As has been seen, a *donatio* is automatically revoked if the danger which caused the donor to contemplate death passes. In addition, it can be revoked at any time during the donor's life. However, as a *donatio* becomes fully effective at the moment of death, it seems that it cannot be revoked by will.[86]

THE FUNCTIONS OF A WILL

1.38 The primary and most important function of a will is the disposition of the testator's property on his death. A will may also, or indeed only, express the testator's wishes on other matters, such as the appointment of executors or testamentary guardians for his minor children, or his wishes about funeral arrangements.

Burial requests and other instructions regarding the testator's body

1.39 It is well-established that the law does not recognise any property in a dead body. A testator cannot therefore dispose of his mortal remains by will [87]and burial instructions are not legally binding.[88]

1.40 In the usual circumstances, where for example there is no suspicion of a crime,[89] the personal representatives are entitled to the custody and possession of the body and they are under a duty to lawfully dispose of it in a manner suitable to the estate which the deceased left.[90]

---

[86]Which, of course, has no effect until the moment of death.

[87]*Williams* v *Williams* (1882) 20 Ch D 659. However, some wishes expressed by a testator during his lifetime do have legal effect. By virtue of the Human Tissue Act (NI) 1962 if a person, either in writing at any time or orally during his last illness, requests his body or some specified part of it to be used after his death for therapeutic purposes or for the purposes of medical education or research, the person lawfully in possession of his body after his death may authorise this.

[88]Sometimes testators are happy to insert directions for the disposal of their bodies in their wills, simply as a non-binding statement of their wishes. It is questionable if a will is a sensible forum for the expression of such wishes - time will obviously be of the essence and it is submitted that burial requests should be left in a letter which is to be opened immediately after death. The testator should ensure that a trusted relative is informed of the existence and whereabouts of this letter.

[89]For the circumstances in which the coroner has an interest, see the Coroners Act (NI) 1959, ss 7 and 8.

[90]2 Blackstone Commentaries at 508, quoted in *Williams* v *Williams* (1882) 20 Ch D 659.

Appointment of guardians

1.41 Currently, the mother of both a legitimate and an illegitimate child may, by will, appoint one or more guardians of the child.[91] A father may do so in the case of a legitimate child, but in the case of an illegitimate child only if he was entitled to the legal custody of the child under an order in force immediately before his death.[92] This position will change once the Children (NI) Order 1995 becomes effective on 1 October 1996. By virtue of article 160 of this Order any person who has "parental responsibility" for a child may appoint a guardian for that child by will. This appointment is revoked if the parent of the child appoints his or her spouse as guardian (ie the child's step-parent) and the marriage to that person is then terminated.[93]

A second change introduced by the 1995 Order relates to the time at which appointments of guardians become effective. At present, while a will is usually so worded that a guardian only acts if both parents are dead, where this is not the case the guardian acts jointly with the surviving parent and can seek a court order if the parent objects. Article 161(5) of the 1995 Order provides that, subject to a contrary intention, an appointment only takes effect when there is nobody else with parental responsibility for the child. In other words, an appointment which has been made by the first parent to die is deferred until the death of the surviving parent.

SOLICITOR'S DUTY OF CARE WHEN PREPARING A WILL

1.42 It is well-established that a solicitor owes a duty of care in tort to a client for whom he is preparing a will. This, of course, is in addition to the contractual obligation which he owes his client. The difficulty is that the inherent nature of the work involved means that breaches of either sort do not usually come to light until after the testator's death; the *testator's estate* has suffered no loss and damages will at best be nominal. Whether those who have suffered loss, that is, the disappointed beneficiaries, should be allowed to seek redress is an issue which has generated much debate about our law of obligations. The recent landmark decision of the House of Lords in *White* v *Jones* [94] confirmed[95] the principle first enunciated in *Ross* v *Caunters*[96] that

---

[91] Guardianship of Infants Act 1886, s 3.

[92] *Re D* (1978) 76 LGR 653.

[93] Art 161 (5).

[94] [1995] 1 All ER 691.

[95] By a three to two majority: Lord Goff, Lord Nolan, Lord Browne-Wilkinson; Lord Keith and Lord Mustill dissenting.

solicitors owe a duty of care to the prospective beneficiaries under their clients' wills. The facts were as follows. The testator, having quarrelled with his two daughters, the plaintiffs, executed a will under which they received no benefit. Later, family differences having been settled, he wrote to his solicitors instructing them to prepare a new will under which the daughters were to take gifts of £9,000 each. For a combination of reasons the solicitors took no action for a couple of months and by the time they got round to seeking an appointment with the testator he had been dead for three days.

1.43 It is interesting that no member of the Lords was prepared to circumvent the doctrine of privity and craft a solution from the realms of contract. On this point the relevance of the Law Reform (Husband and Wife) Act (NI) 1964, a piece of legislation peculiar to this jurisdiction, must be noted. Section 5 of this Act provides that where a contract is expressed to be for the benefit of, or by its express terms purports to confer a benefit upon, a third party being the wife, husband or child of one of the contracting parties, it shall be enforceable by the third party in his or her own name as if he or she were a party to it. In Northern Ireland therefore disappointed beneficiaries who are the spouse or children of the testator (as in *White* v *Jones* itself) can themselves sue under the contract between the solicitor and the testator.

1.44 Returning to the actual decision in *White*, the majority in the Lords found in favour of the plaintiffs by extending the "assumption of responsibility" principle found in *Hedley Byrne* v *Heller*;[97] a solicitor not only assumes responsibility towards his client, but also towards an intended beneficiary who was reasonably foreseeably deprived of his intended legacy as a result of the solicitor's negligence.[98] This decision raises a number of theoretical issues on the scope of our law of obligations which are beyond this work.[99] On its narrowest level it is a salutory reminder, if one were needed, that the execution of a will is an area of practice where expedition is imperative. The message should be clear: draftsmen, procrastinate at your peril.

---

[96] [1979] 3 All ER 580. In this case the solicitor omitted to warn the testator that a beneficiary or his spouse was not able to witness the will which had been sent to him for execution.

[97] [1963] 2 All ER 575.

[98] Inherent in the nature of such liability is the fact that it does not extend to cases in which the defect in the will comes to light before the death of the testator, and the testator either leaves the will as it is or otherwise continues to exclude the previously intended beneficiary from the relevant benefit.

[99] Practitioners should note that the decision does *not* establish that a general duty is owed to third-party clients other than beneficiaries under a will. Eg their Lordships made it clear that it does not extend to third parties in a conveyancing transaction.

FOREIGN ELEMENTS

1.45   There are two main ways in which a succession lawyer practising in this jurisdiction can encounter a conflicts of laws issue:

>   (a)   the testator / deceased has domicile outside Northern Ireland, or;
>
>   (b)   the testator / deceased owned property outside Northern Ireland.

A deceased who had property or domicile in another part of the British Isles is governed by the same general principles for determining the appropriate law to apply as a deceased with property or domicile in, for example, Australia. It should immediately be evident that the potential for 'conflicts' issues in succession matters is considerable. However, two factors ease the burden when administering such an estate.

1.46   First, the fact that the law in Northern Ireland is broadly similar to that in England and Wales, and the Republic of Ireland, certainly reduces the potential problems. That having been said, the relatively minor differences which do remain can be significant and the fact that the Scottish system is fundamentally different,[100] mean that difficulties can and do arise.[101] Secondly, many of the procedural difficulties in administering the estate where a deceased with Northern Ireland domicile had assets elsewhere in the United Kingdom have been removed by the Administration of Estates Act 1971 which provides for the reciprocal recognition of grants.[102]

Conflicts of laws - the basic principles
1.47   Different rules govern "moveable" and "immoveable" property. It should be remembered that this   classification is not interchangeable with personalty/realty.[103]

---

[100] Throughout this book attention has been drawn to the differences between Northern Ireland and England. Scottish law is so different it would be impracticable to do the same and readers are referred to D R MacDonald, *Succession* (2nd ed, 1994).

[101] For an excellent article on the Conflicts problems in 'domestic' situations see Morris (1969) 85 LQR 339.

[102] See para 11.99 *post*.

[103] Although there is a broad overlap, 'immoveables' include interests in land such as leaseholds which are personalty rather than realty.

1.48　The common law rule is that succession to moveables is governed by the law of the deceased's domicile (the *lex domicili*), while the succession to immoveables is governed by the law of the country in which the property is situated (the *lex situs*). Therefore if a client with Northern Ireland domicile owns land in Spain which he wishes to leave by will, the position is governed by the law of Spain and further advice should be sought.[104] A point of great practical significance is that a number of continental jurisdictions prohibit or at least restrict freedom of testation and require land within the jurisdiction to devolve on certain members of the deceased's family.

1.49　This common law position has been extended as regards the requirements for the formal validity of a will by the Wills Act 1963, which applies to deaths on or after 1 January 1964. Previously, as above, in the case of moveables the formal requirements for validity were those of the law of the country where the deceased was domiciled; in the case of immoveables, those of the country where they were situated. Section 1 of the Wills Act 1963 provides that "a will shall be treated as properly executed" if its execution conforms with the internal law in force in any one of the following territories:

(a)　the territory where the will was executed - irrespective of the duration of the testator's visit;

(b)　the territory where the testator was domiciled either at the time of making the will or at death;

(c)　the territory where the testator was habitually resident either at the time of making the will or at death;

(d)　the state of which the testator, either at the time of making the will or at death, was a national.

International wills

1.50　Sections 27 and 28 of the Administration of Justice Act 1982, which are the only substantive provisions of this Act to extend to Northern Ireland, make provision for "international wills" made in accordance with the requirements of the Washington Convention on International Wills.[105] No date has yet been set for these sections to come into force. When they do, an international will will

---

[104]It is probably most prudent to contact a firm with branches in the country in question. Reference might also be made to Pugh, *The Administration of Foreign Estates* (2nd ed 1995).

[105]These are set out in Sch 2 to the 1982 Act which is reproduced in Appendix F.

be valid in the United Kingdom and in all other contracting states, irrespective of the place of execution or of the nationality or domicile of the testator.

CHAPTER TWO

CREATION OF A WILL - THE MENTAL ELEMENTS

GENERAL

2.01 This chapter examines those aspects of creating a will which could loosely be described as relating to the 'mind' of the testator, or to the *substantial* as opposed to the *formal*[1] validity of the will. This involves the testator having the mental capacity necessary to make a will; having knowledge and approval of its contents; having the intention of making a testamentary disposition and, in doing so, having exercised his genuine free choice.

2.02 In the past those denied the power to make a valid will included married women[2] and certain criminals. Today the only two classes of person who do not have the capacity to make a will are unmarried minors and those who lack "sound disposing mind".

Minors

2.03 The general rule is that no person under the age of 18, or 21 if the will was made before 1 January 1970,[3] can make a valid will. There are two exceptions, one longstanding and the other recently introduced by the Wills and Administration Proceedings (NI) Order 1994.

Privileged wills

2.04 Minors who satisfy the qualifying criteria can make a privileged will.[4] The age limit is 14 years for a male and 12 years for a female.

Married minors

2.05 Married minors, or minors who *have* been married, can now make a valid will. This exception was introduced by article 4 of the 1994 Order, on the basis that it was unreasonable to deny someone who had taken on the

---

[1] The requirements for the formal validity of a will are dealt with in Chapter Three.

[2] For removal of restrictions on married women, see Married Women's Property Act 1893, s 3 and Law Reform (Miscellaneous Provisions) Act (NI) 1937, s 9(a).

[3] 1994 Order, art 4(2); formerly Age of Majority Act (NI) 1969, s 2(1)(a).

[4] See para 3.64 *post*.

responsibilities of marriage the capacity to make a will, condemning them to remain intestate for up to two more years. It adopts the position in the Republic of Ireland[5] rather than that in England, where married minors are still unable to make wills.

Article 4 is not retrospective. Wills made by minors before 1 January 1995 are still invalid, even if the minor was married at the time.

SOUND DISPOSING MIND

2.06   To put it simply, a testator must be of sound mind, memory and understanding.   The very nature of the problem, however, means that the practical application of this concept is rarely simple.   In the words of Lord Cranworth:

> "On the first head the difficulty to be grappled with arises from the circumstance that the question is almost always one of degree. There is no difficulty with the case of a raving madman or drivelling idiot in saying that he is a person incapable of disposing of property; but between such an extreme case and that of a man of perfectly sound and vigorous understanding, there is every shade of intellect, every degree of mental capacity. There is no mistaking midnight for noon, but at what precise moment twilight becomes darkness, is hard to determine."[6]

What constitutes sound disposing mind?

2.07   The classic test as to the validity of a will where doubt has been cast on the testator's mental capacity emanates from the judgment of Cockburn CJ in *Banks* v *Goodfellow*:[7]

> "It is essential ... that a testator *shall understand the nature of the act and its effects; shall understand the extent of the property of which he is disposing; shall be able to comprehend and appreciate the claims to which he ought to give effect*; and, with a view to the latter object, that no disorder of the mind shall poison his affections, pervert his sense of right, or prevent the exercise of his natural faculties - that no insane delusion shall influence his will in disposing of his property and bring about a disposition of it which, if the mind had been sound, would not have been made."

---

[5] Where s 77(1)(a) of the Succession Act 1965 empowers married minors to make wills.

[6] In *Boyse* v *Rossborough* (1857) 6 HLC 2 at 45.

[7] (1870) L R 5 QB 549 at 565, emphasis added.

Thus there are three things in particular which the testator must comprehend:

(a) The nature of the act and its effects

> It is not necessary that the testator is aware that he is actually executing a *will*. Nor is it necessary that he should view the document with "the eye of a lawyer", and comprehend its provisions in their legal form.[8]

(b) The extent of the property of which he is disposing

> The testator is not required to give a detailed inventory of all that he owns. Rather, he must have "a recollection of the property he means to dispose of"[9] and know "generally the state of his property and what it consists of".[10] In short, he must have some idea of "how much he is worth", and the amount of detail required will obviously vary with the amount of wealth involved. A testator of plentiful means will not be expected to recall every single share holding, whereas someone who possesses only a couple of bank accounts will need to be aware of them both.

(c) The claims to which he ought to give effect

> The testator must "not only be able to understand that he is by his will giving the whole of his property to one or more objects of his regard... he must also have the capacity to comprehend... the nature of the claims of others whom, by his will, he is excluding from all participation in that property." This necessity to appreciate claims which one is *excluding* is probably the single most difficult hurdle in the threefold test for mental capacity. Testators who are perfectly aware of the nature of their property and of the persons whom they are benefitting with it, may not be aware that they are effectively disinheriting other members of their family.[11]

2.08   It should be clear that only a very limited overlap exists between what constitutes unsoundness of mind for the purposes of will-making and what is

---

[8] *Ibid* at p 567.

[9] *Ibid.*

[10] *Waters* v *Waters* (1848) 2 De G & Sm 591, 621.

[11] See *Re Beaney* [1978] 1 WLR 770, which although concerning an *inter vivos* gift is instructive, in that Mr Martin, sitting as a Deputy High Court Judge, held that the degree of mental capacity needed to make a complicated lifetime transfer was the same as that needed to make a will.

classed as a "mental abnormality" to bring the sufferer within the scope of the Mental Health (NI) Order 1986.[12] Some patients detained under that Order will still have the capacity to make a will, while others who have never been near a mental institution do not. Neither is it conclusive to "sound disposing mind" that the testator was capable of understanding complicated business or following his professional calling.[13] Mere eccentricity or irrationality are not, in themselves, enough to deprive someone of the ability to make a valid will. It is still the case, family provision claims apart,[14] that "every testator is free to adopt his own nonsense",[15] and sound mind does *not* mean "a perfectly balanced mind". This last remark was the observation of Sir J Hannen in *Broughton and Marson v Knight*[16] who went on to add "if so, which of us would be competent to make a will!" Eccentricity or irrationality *may*, however, be evidence of a further problem.

Delusions

2.09   A delusion is a belief on a subject which no rational person could hold, and which cannot be permanently eradicated from the mind of the sufferer by reasoning with him.[17] The existence of delusions does not in itself deprive the sufferer of testamentary capacity and the court does not seek to knock down rational dispositions for the sake of it:

> "The law is founded on the assumption that a rational will is a
> better disposition than any that can be made by the law itself."[18]

2.10   The key issue in such cases is therefore whether or not the delusion had any *influence* on the testator when he was making his will. For instance, in *Banks v Goodfellow*[19] the testator suffered two recurring delusions; that he was being chased and molested by a man long since dead, and that he was being pursued by evil spirits. Neither had any effect on his will which benefitted the persons which one would have reasonably expected, and it was upheld as valid. It would be different if the delusion had an effect on the testamentary

---

[12] See para 2.17 *post*.

[13] *Smee v Smee* (1879) 5 PD 84, where the testator, amongst other notable achievements, was the author of a number of pamphlets.

[14] See Chapter Eight.

[15] *Per* Shadwell VC in *Vaughan v Marquis of Headfort* (1840) 10 Sim 639 at 641.

[16] (1873) LR 3 P & D 64 at p 66.

[17] *Dew v Clark* (1826) 3 Add 79.

[18] Cockburn CJ in *Banks v Goodfellow* (1870) LR 5 QB 549 at 565.

[19] *Ibid*.

disposition,[20] say if the testator's delusion was that he was being persecuted by his daughter and in consequence he cut her out of his will. It may be the case that a parent has formed an unduly harsh assessment of his offspring's character, which has nothing to do with a delusion, and the parent still remains free to exclude that child from his bounty (subject now to family provision claims). Eventually, however, the point is reached where repulsion and aversion to one's children are in themselves evidence of unsoundness of mind.[21]

Delusions affecting only part of a will

2.11 If a testator was not of sound disposing mind at the time the will was executed[22] the will is void. There is, however, one reported first instance decision in which *part only* of a will was struck out and the remainder admitted to probate. *In the Estate of Bohrmann*[23] the testator was suffering from the delusion that London County Council was persecuting him (in fact, the Council had been trying to dispossess him from his house) and in consequence he altered a single clause in one of the four codicils to his will, substituting "United States" for "England". This was the only clause affected by the delusion and Langton J took the novel step of declaring in favour of the testamentary disposition subject to the deletion of the one offending clause. In doing so the learned judge proceeded by analogy with the well-known practice of striking out those parts of a will of which the testator did not have knowledge and approval.[24] The amount of reliance which can be placed upon this authority is, however, questionable.

When must the testator have sound disposing mind?

2.12 Generally, of course, the material time is the *execution* of the will, and it is then that the testator should satisfy the test of sound disposing mind. There is one concession to this, known as the rule in *Parker* v *Felgate*.[25] If a person's faculties are declining rapidly, it might be the case that when he gives instructions to his solicitor he satisfies the test of mental capacity, but he no longer does so by the time the will has been drafted and presented to him for execution. In these circumstances, it may be sufficient if it can be shown that the testator understood that he was engaged in executing a will for which he had

---

[20] Eg *Dew* v *Clark* (1826) 3 Add 79.

[21] *Broughton and Marson* v *Knight* (1873) LR 3 P & D 64.

[22] Or if the rule in *Parker* v *Felgate* applies, when instructions were given, see para 2.12 *post*.

[23] [1938] 1 All ER 271.

[24] See para 2.50 *post*.

[25] (1883) 8 PD 171 - approved by Privy Council in *Perera* v *Perera* [1901] AC 354, and in *Re Flynn* [1982] 1 All ER 882 at 890.

previously given instructions and that *when the instructions were given* he had sound disposing mind. In *Parker* v *Felgate* itself the testatrix had fallen into a coma after she had given instructions for her will to her solicitor. During the coma she was capable of being roused from time to time and at one stage she had replied "yes" to the question asking her if she wanted her will executed, a fact which could be corroborated by eye-witnesses. Her will was upheld.

2.13   The rule in *Parker* v *Felgate* demonstrates a relatively lenient spirit by the judiciary. However, the opportunities for abuse are obvious, and it ought not to be applied if any suspicious circumstances exist. In *Battan Singh* v *Armichand*[26] the Privy Council expressed grave reservations about applying the rule when the testator himself does not give the instructions to the solicitor who draws up the will, but to a lay intermediary who then repeats them to the solicitor. If such is the case, the court ought to be strictly satisfied that there is no ground for suspicion, and that the instructions given to the intermediary were unambiguous and clearly understood, faithfully reported by him and rightly appended by the solicitor. In *Battan Singh* itself the Privy Council refused to apply the rule.

2.14   Of course, it need hardly be emphasised that the execution of a client's will is one area of professional practice where there should be no delay.[27]

Burden of proof
2.15   The *legal* burden of proving that a testator was of sound disposing mind is on the person propounding the will. The *evidential* burden may, however, shift in the course of a case.

The following rebuttable presumptions apply:

(a)   If a will is rational on its face, there is a presumption that the testator had testamentary capacity. This can be rebutted by evidence to the contrary.

(b)   If there is evidence of prior mental illness or unsoundness of mind, there is a presumption that this state was continuing when the will was executed.[28] This presumption is rebutted if it can be established

---

[26] [1948] AC 161.
[27] *White* v *Jones* [1995] 1 All ER , see para 1.42 *supra*.
[28] *Banks* v *Goodfellow* (1870) LR 5 QB 549.

that the will was executed in a period of continuing lucidity or after recovery from illness.[29]

Some practical points if mental capacity is in doubt

2.16 In instances where there is some doubt about the mental capacity of the testator, it is prudent for legal advisers to seek the opinion of a medical practitioner (preferably one experienced in the field) and, if the practitioner is satisfied that the person does have the requisite capacity, he should act as one of the attesting witnesses. This practice has received judicial support,[30] although proposals to put it on a statutory footing and make medical evidence conclusive in the absence of fraud or interest, were rejected by the Law Reform Committee.[31]

In any situation where there is reason to suspect that the mental capacity test has not been satisfied, a full memorandum of the facts should be prepared by the solicitor responsible for the execution of the will.

Mental patients - statutory wills

2.17 Where an order is in force in respect of a person under the Mental Health (NI) Order 1986 (hereafter in this chapter "the 1986 Order"), an application can be made to the High Court for the execution of a "statutory will" for that patient.[32] This is the only way in which a will can be executed for someone lacking mental capacity, since enduring powers of attorney do not extend to the making of wills.

The jurisdiction

2.18 Under Part VIII of the 1986 Order the court is given wide powers to manage a patient's property and affairs, including, in article 99(1)(e), the power to execute for him:

> "....a will making any provision (whether by way of disposing of property or otherwise) which could be made by a will executed by the patient if he were not mentally disordered."

---

[29]*Chambers and Yatman* v *Queen's Proctor* (1840) 2 Curt 415.

[30]From Templeman J, first in *Kenward* v *Adams* [1975] CLY 3591 and again in *Re Simpson* (1977) 121 Sol J 224.

[31]*The Making and Revocation of Wills*, Cmnd 7902 (1980) para 2.17. The main reason for the rejection of the idea was the potential prejudice to the confidential relationship between solicitor and client.

[32]In England the equivalent jurisdiction is that of the Court of Protection under the Mental Health Act 1983.

2.19   Before a statutory will is made, however, it is not enough that the court is satisfied that the person is incapable by reason of a mental disorder of managing and administering his own affairs (the qualifying requirement for intervention with any of the powers contained in the 1986 Order).[33] It must also have reason to believe that *the patient is incapable of making a valid will for himself.*[34]

2.20   The making of a statutory will under article 99(1)(e), like the exercise of any of the other powers under Part VIII of the 1986 Order, must be justified under one or other of the pre-requisites contained in article 98;[35] that is, the execution of the will must be:

>   (a)   for the maintenance and benefit of the patient, or;
>
>   (b)   for the maintenance and benefit of members of the patient's family, or;
>
>   (c)   for making provision for other persons or purposes for whom or which the patient might be expected to provide if he were not mentally disordered, or;
>
>   (d)   for otherwise administering the patient's affairs.

In addition, it is expressly provided that the first priority must be the requirements of the patient.[36]

Minors
2.21   A statutory will cannot be made for a patient who is a minor.[37]

Approach of the court
2.22   A number of useful (non-exhaustive) guidelines on the court's approach to statutory wills were given by Sir Robert Megarry VC in the Court of Protection in *Re D (J)*.[38] First, the court must assume that the patient is having a brief lucid interval at the time the will is made, during which he is assumed to have full knowledge of the past and full realisation that, as soon as the will is

---

[33] Art 97(1).
[34] Art 99(4)(b).
[35] *Re C* [1991] 3 All ER 866.
[36] Art 98(2).
[37] Art 99(4)(a).
[38] [1982] Ch 237.

implemented, he will relapse into the mental state which previously existed. Secondly, the test is *subjective* rather than objective. It is neither a hypothetical patient nor a reasonable patient, but the *actual* patient, charged with all the antipathies and affections which he had while of full capacity, and seeking to make the will which he, acting reasonably, would make. Lastly, the patient is envisaged as being advised by a competent solicitor (at least one who knows something of ademption and lapse!) and normally as taking the 'broad brush' to the claims on his bounty, rather than the 'accountant's pen'.

2.23 This subjective approach in *Re D(J)* departed from the earlier, objective approach of *Re Davey*.[39] However, the fact that it is the *actual* patient who should be considered has since been confirmed in *Re C*.[40] The latter case is illustrative of how the court exercises its powers in the difficult situation in which the patient has been incapable since birth and where his personality and preferences are consequently a complete blank. The patient in question, a 75 year old blind woman, who was unable even to dress or undress herself, had lived in a mental hospital for many years. She had no close family, barely knew her relatives, and her only friend appeared to be a voluntary worker with a mental health charity who took her on outings from time to time. Having inherited money from both her father and her mother, the patient was worth over £1.6 million. Proposals were put to the Court of Protection that some sort of balance between giving to mental institutions and charities on the one hand, and to members of the family, on the other, would be appropriate. Hoffmann J held that in such circumstances the court must assume that she was a normal, decent person acting in accordance with contemporary standards of morality. As such, she would have been influenced by two considerations: first, that she had spent her life in hospital, relying on the National Health Service and mental health charities; secondly, that she derived her fortune as a child of a family. It was therefore appropriate to benefit the various charities/hospitals and relatives equally, a task which was to be achieved by a combination of *inter vivos* gifts and a statutory will. Some reservations were expressed about the desirability of giving away the patient's assets during her lifetime when the future was unforeseeable, especially in light of the fact that the primary concern was the requirements of the patient. While Hoffmann J agreed that nothing should be done to put the comfort of the patient at risk, he was of the opinion that this was not a danger in the case in question, in view of the large amount of money involved. Moreover, in the circumstances it was not unreasonable that the family should avail of the financial benefit from the large inheritance tax

---

[39] [1980] 3 All ER 342.
[40] [1991] 3 All ER 866.

savings by making *inter vivos* gifts. In determining the actual proportions by which the relatives were to benefit, it was felt undesirable to depart from the distribution laid down by the intestacy rules, save for some measure of special provision being made for the Down's Syndrome child of one of the patient's cousins.

Re C represents one type of case where the power to make a statutory will is beneficial, that is, the patient is of considerable means and a distribution solely by the intestacy code is inappropriate. It is also particularly useful where the patient already has a will, but it has been outdated to his needs or circumstances.

The procedure for applications

2.24   Applications for the power to execute a statutory will to be exercised on behalf of a patient must follow one of the procedures laid down in the Patient's Affairs Rules.[41] Order 109, rule 14 provides that only the following persons can make an application for a statutory will:

(a)   the controller for the patient;

(b)   any person who has made an application for the appointment of a controller which has not yet been determined;

(c)   any person, who under any known will of the patient or under his intestacy, may become entitled to any property of the patient, or any interest therein;

(d)   any person for whom the patient might reasonably be expected to provide if not mentally disordered;

(e)   any other person whom the court may authorise.

2.25   The application, which includes a draft of the proposed statutory will, is normally heard by the Master in Chambers, although a solicitor is usually required to be present. Generally evidence is by way of affidavit,[42] although unsworn evidence, written or oral, may be taken into account.[43] Proof of the incapacity of the patient to make a will must be provided by a recent medical

---

[41]RSC, O 109.
[42]R 22.
[43]R 23.

certificate and evidence must be adduced of the family tree, the current ages of relatives, the assets of the patient, the needs of the patient (both present and future), and any tax implications of the draft will.

Emergency applications

2.26 In cases where time is of the essence, making it inappropriate to comply with the normal requirements listed above, the emergency provisions contained in article 97(2) of the 1986 Order can be used.[44]

Formalities

2.27 The normal formalities relating to the execution of a will do not apply. Statutory wills must instead be executed in accordance with article 100(1)(a) and (b) of the 1986 Order, as amended by the Wills and Administration Proceedings (NI) Order 1994. The statutory will must be signed by the authorised person, with the name of the patient and with his own name, in the presence of at least two witnesses who are present at the same time. The witnesses must then subscribe and attest their signatures in the presence of the authorised person.

KNOWLEDGE AND APPROVAL

2.28 A testator must know and approve the contents of his will, a requirement which derives from the fact that a person's will must be the act of his own intelligence and volition. To delegate *completely* to another the task of making a will is not permitted;[45] for instance, the request "draw up the will which you think is most suitable for me and I will sign it without reading it". It is, of course, possible to delegate the role of drafting to give effect to the testator's wishes, and a person can be taken to know and approve the contents of his will, even though he is ignorant of their legal effect. The introduction of the third-party draftsman opens the possibility of insertions or omissions of which the testator was not truly aware. This often vexed question of the extent to which the testator is bound by such mistakes is dealt with in some detail below.[46]

---

[44]For an example of an important application made in haste see *Re Davey* [1980] 3 All ER 342.

[45]*Hastilow* v *Stobie* (1865) 1 P & D 64.

[46]See para 2.37 *post*.

2.29   A statutory will is the only exception to the knowledge and approval rule.[47]

Burden of proof

2.30   The burden of proving that a testator knew and approved the contents of his will is on the person propounding it.[48] There is a rebuttable presumption that if the testator was of sound capacity and the will appeared to be duly executed by him, he had knowledge and approval of its contents.[49] However, the presumption does not apply if there is anything in the circumstances surrounding the execution of the will which raises a suspicion that the testator did not know and approve the contents. Likewise it does not apply if the testator is deaf and dumb, blind or illiterate,[50] or if the will has been signed by someone other than the testator on his behalf.

2.31   The Non-Contentious Probate Rules[51] require the Master, before admitting a will to probate in certain circumstances, to satisfy himself (by affidavits from the attesting witnesses or other eye-witnesses) that the testator knew and approved its contents. This requirement applies in the following circumstances:

      (a)   In any case where it appears that the will was signed by a blind or illiterate person;

      (b)   In any case where it appears that the will was signed by another person at the direction of the testator;

      (c)   In any other case where the existence of knowledge and approval is in doubt.[52]

Establishing knowledge and approval

2.32   The evidence required to prove knowledge and approval, where it is necessary to do this, varies with the circumstances of the case.[53] One obvious

---

[47]See para 2.17 *supra*.

[48]*Cleare* v *Cleare* (1869) 1 P & D 655.

[49]*Barry* v *Butlin* (1838) 2 Moo PC 480.

[50]*In the Goods of Owston* (1862) 2 Sw & Tr 461; *In the Goods of Geale* (1864) 3 Sw & Tr 431 - in both these cases the court required additional proof of the type of signs made by deaf and dumb testators.

[51]RSC O 76.

[52]*Ibid* r 10

[53]*Wintle* v *Nye* [1959] 1 WLR 284.

form of proof is to establish that the will was read over to or by the testator when he executed it. However, 'reading over' must be more than a mere literal, physical fact of reading; it must affect the "consciousness of the testator".[54] Even if the will was not read over to the testator, it may still be possible to establish that he was acquainted with the contents.[55]

Cases in which lack of knowledge and approval is alleged generally fall into two broad categories; suspicious circumstances and mistake.

Suspicious circumstances

2.33   It has already been noted that the usual presumption that the testator had knowledge and approval of his will does not apply if any suspicion as to the execution of the will exists. Whenever a will is prepared and executed under circumstances which raise the suspicion of the court, that will ought not to be proved unless the person propounding it adduces evidence to remove the suspicion and satsifies the court that the testator knew and approved it.[56] The most obvious 'suspicious circumstances' arise when a person instrumental in the execution of a will takes a benefit under it:

> "If a party writes or prepares a will, under which he takes a benefit, that is a circumstance that ought generally to excite the suspicion of the court, and calls upon it to be vigilant and jealous in examining the evidence in support of the instrument, in favour of which it ought not to pronounce unless the suspicion is removed."[57]

2.34   The rule extends beyond cases where the will was prepared or its execution procured by a person taking a benefit under it. It also applies to any case in which the circumstances attending the preparation or execution of the will excite the suspicion of the court. For example, in *Tyrell* v *Painton*[58] the will was prepared by the son of the person to benefit under it. The suspicious circumstances do, however, have to attend or be relevant to the *preparation or execution* of the will itself. In *Re Musgrove*[59] the Court of Appeal overturned the decision at first instance of Hill J, who pronounced against a will on the ground that suspicion was raised by the circumstance that the executrix knew

---

[54] *Re Morris* [1971] P 62 at 77. Also *Re Begley* [1939] IR 479.

[55] *Fincham* v *Edwards* (1842) 3 Curt 63 - testatrix nearly blind.

[56] *Tyrrell* v *Painton* [1894] P 151.

[57] *Barry* v *Butlin* (1838) 2 Moo P C 480 at 482, followed by the House of Lords in *Fulton* v *Andrew* (1875) LR 7 HL 448 and in *Wintle* v *Nye* [1959] 1 WLR 284.

[58] [1894] P 151.

[59] [1927] P 264.

of the will for 16 years before she sought to prove it (nearly 20 years after the testatrix's death), yet the executrix's own daughter was to receive large benefits under it. It was held that any suspicion which did attach only arose *subsequent* to the execution, thus the presumption that the will was duly executed and that the testatrix knew and approved its contents applied.[60]

2.35   The problem of solicitors receiving benefits under wills which they execute was discussed at length by the House of Lords in *Wintle* v *Nye*.[61] The testatrix in question, a 66 year old spinster, had approached the defendant, the family solicitor, to draw up a will for her. A number of interviews between the defendant and the testatrix followed. The defendant claimed that he had told the testatrix to take independent legal advice, but she refused to do so, and the solicitor was named as sole executor. In addition he took the residue which amounted to the bulk of the testatrix's large estate. Viscount Simonds stated the position as follows:

> "It is not the law that in no circumstances can a solicitor or other person who has prepared a will for a testator take a benefit under it. But that fact creates a suspicion that must be removed by the person propounding the will. In all cases the court must be vigilant and jealous. The degree of suspicion will vary with the circumstances. It may be slight and easily dispelled. It may, on the other hand, be so grave that it can hardly be removed. In the present case the circumstances were such as to impose on the respondent as heavy a burden as can be imagined."[62]

2.36   Solicitors in whose favour clients wish to make legacies should encourage them to be separately advised. If the client refuses to do so the solicitor should decline to act.[63]

Mistake

Mistake as to the document
2.37   If the testator or his draftsman get their papers mixed up, with the result that the testator signs a document which is not *his* will at all, that document will not be admitted to probate. In particular, *sisters* for whom nearly identical wills are being drafted should read carefully before executing,

---

[60]See also *Re R (dec'd)* [1951] P 10.

[61][1959] 1 WLR 284.

[62]*Ibid* at p 291.

[63]See *Re A Solicitor* [1975] QB 475.

as the evidence indicates that they are particularly prone to sign each other's instruments![64]

Mistake as to the legal effect of the meaning of the will

2.38   If a testator executes a will knowing and approving the words used, those words cannot later be struck out because he has taken a view as to their legal effect which turns out to be mistaken.[65]   Similarly, the testator is taken to have adopted a mistake of his draftsman as to the legal effect. Thus in *Collins* v *Elstone*[66] the testatrix realised that a revocation clause had been included in a testamentary document and asked her adviser to remove it because the will in question only dealt with the proceeds of a small insurance policy. She was assured, inaccurately, that the will would be invalid without such a clause and that it would not actually effect the revocation of her earlier will. With regret, the President was forced to conclude that she had known and approved the contents of her will.

Mistakes inserted "per incuriam"

Deaths before 1 January 1995

2.39   Traditionally it was the case that if the testator was of the requisite mental capacity, had the will read over to him or otherwise had notice of its contents at the time of execution, then, in the absence of fraud, he was taken to have known and approved the document and any evidence to the contrary could not be regarded. It did not matter that something had been inserted or omitted by himself or his draftsman *per incuriam* (ie, inadvertently). By the mid-nineteenth century the absolute nature of this rule had been established by Lord Penzance in *Guardhouse* v *Blackburn*.[67]   Gradually, however, it was progressively eroded by the judiciary, starting with the decision of the House of Lords in *Fulton* v *Andrew*:[68]

> "There is no unyielding rule of law ... that, when it has been proved that a testator, competent in mind, has had a will read over to him, and has thereupon executed it, all further inquiry is shut out."

---

[64]*In the Goods of Hunt* (1875) 3 P & D 250; *In the Goods of Meyer* [1908] P 353.

[65]*In the Estate of Beech* [1923] P 46.

[66][1893] P 1.

[67](1866) LR 1 P&D 109.

[68](1875) LR 7 HL 448.

By 1971 Latey J in his judgment in *Re Morris*[69] was content to declare, following a review of the authorities:

> "[the rule in *Guardhouse* v *Blackburn*] does not survive in any shape or form."[70]

2.40 It has already been noted that legal phraseology chosen deliberately by the draftsman, who has put his mind to such, will bind the testator. Knowledge and approval in such cases is imputed to the testator. However, the demise of the *Guardhouse* v *Blackburn* rule meant that certain other mistakes inserted inadvertently by the draftsman could now be deleted on the basis that the testator did not truly have "knowledge and approval" of them.

2.41 Examples of cases where mistakes introduced *per incuriam* have been deleted include *Re Morrell*,[71] in which the number "40" preceded the word "shares" throughout the testator's will, when in fact he owned "400" shares and it had been his intention that *all* his shares should go to a named beneficiary. Probate was ordered with the number "40" deleted throughout. Similarly, in *Re Walkeley*[72] when the numbers of the testator's houses caused the draftsman some confusion, resulting in him mentioning number "103" twice but not mentioning number "105" at all, probate was ordered with the second reference to house "103" struck out.[73] In Northern Ireland this type of approach was commended by the High Court in *Re Murphy*,[74] a case which involved the deletion of a revocation clause and which is discussed in more detail below.[75]

2.42 However, the rectification of wills was limited to this judicially created power to *delete* from probate words or phrases which had been *inserted* inadvertently. In all the above cases the only option available to the court was to strike offending clauses out and grant probate "in blank" (ie with a blank space in place of the words which had been deleted). If the inadvertence had resulted in words being unintentionally omitted from the will they could not be inserted, on the basis that to do such would contravene the requirement that a

---

[69] [1971] P 62.

[70] At p 79.

[71] (1882) 7 PD 68.

[72] (1893) 69 LT 419.

[73] See also *Re Swords* [1952] 2 All ER 281 (testatrix approved will from draft, whereas will she executed contained an extra clause, which put her one number out when she attempted to revoke a particular clause).

[74] (1980) 3 NIJB.

[75] See para 4.28 *post*.

will must be in writing. For instance, in *Re Morris*[76] a solicitor revoked "cl 7" instead of "cl 7(iv)" of a previous codicil. The numeral "iv" could not be added and the only, albeit not ideal, solution was to order deletion of the expression "cl 7".

2.43   One limitation to this power to delete words was that the omission must not alter the meaning of the remaining part of the will. Put another way, the part to be deleted must be 'self-contained'. In *Re Horrocks*[77] the residuary estate was left for "charitable *or* benevolent purposes", a formula which is void for uncertainty.[78] It was argued that the insertion of the word "or" was a typist's error and that the word "and" had been on the instructions, although the evidence of this was not accepted. The court refused to delete the word "or" because to further qualify the word "charitable" by the word "benevolent" was considered tantamount to writing a new will for the testator, a process which went far beyond its powers.

Deaths on or after 1 January 1995

2.44   Article 29(1) of the Wills and Administration Proceedings (NI) Order 1994 empowers the court to order the rectification of a will so as to bring it into accord with the testator's intentions where it is satisfied that the will as expressed fails to carry out those intentions either in consequence of:

(a)   a clerical error, or;

(b)   a failure to understand the testator's instructions.[79]

2.45   No distinction is made between inserting or deleting words and the court may order the insertion of words omitted inadvertently as well as ordering the deletion of words so inserted. Thus the situation in *Re Morris*[80] which was discussed earlier, could now be remedied by the insertion of the numerals "(iv)" after cl 7. Likewise in *Re Walkeley*[81] the number of the house which had been omitted, "105", could be inserted. In both of these cases the problem was

---

[76][1971] P 162.

[77][1939] P 198.

[78]*Re Diplock* [1951] AC 251.

[79]This corresponds to s 20 of the Administration of Justice Act 1982 which implemented the recommendations of the Nineteenth Report of the Law Reform Committee on the Execution of Wills (1973) Cmnd 5301.

[80][1971] P 162.

[81](1893) 69 LT 419.

caused by a slip of the draftsman which is clearly within the scope of a "clerical error".

2.46   In *Wordingham* v *Royal Exchange Trust*[82] the High Court applied the English equivalent of article 29 of the 1994 Order (s 20(1)(a) of the Administration of Justice Act 1982) to insert the exercise of a power of appointment, which had been omitted from a testatrix's most recent will, but contained in her two previous ones. Her instructions to her solicitor were clear that the earlier will was to be altered in certain defined respects only and the exclusion of the power of appointment was not one of the alterations. Mr Evans-Lombe QC, sitting as a deputy High Court Judge, gave the following definition of "clerical error":

> "[the words 'clerical error'] are to be construed as meaning an
> error made in the process of recording the intended words of the
> testator in the drafting or transcription of his will."[83]

2.47   Article 29(1)(b) allows for rectification of mistakes which have arisen out of a failure to understand the testator's intentions; say communications have broken down in some way, so that the testator wants to do "x" but the draftsman thinks that he wants to do "y". However, the rectification of errors which have arisen because the draftsman is mistaken as to the legal effect of the words which he has used is outside the scope of article 29[84] and the position is still that words cannot be deleted or inserted to remedy this type of mistake.

2.48   Applications for rectification under article 29 of the 1994 Order must be made within six months from the date on which representation with respect to the estate of the deceased is first taken out,[85] although the court does have a discretion to allow out of time applications. This is similar to the time limit in the Inheritance (Provision for Family and Dependants) (NI) Order 1979. Until

---

[82][1992] Ch 412.

[83]*Ibid* at p 419. See also the definition of "clerical error" contained in art 2(2) of the Rates (NI) Order 1977 in which it "includes an arithmetical error, the transposition of figures, a typographical error or any similar type of error, and also includes any erroneous insertion or omission or any misdescription". There is also considerable case law on the meaning to be attributed to "clerical errors" in the context of patent law - see eg *Re Sharp's Patent, ex p Wordsworth* (1840) 3 Beav 245, referred to in *Wordingham*.

[84]*Wordingham* [1992] Ch 412 at 419.

[85]Art 29(2). In considering when representation with respect to the estate of a deceased person was first taken out, grants limited to settled land or to trust property are to be left out of account, and a grant limited to real estate or to personal estate is to be left out of account unless a grant limited to the remainder of the estate has previously been made or is made at the same time - art 29(4).

some judicial guidance has been given on the exercise of the discretion in relation to requests for rectification, the cases decided under the 1979 Order and its English counterpart[86] may be useful.[87]

2.49   After this period of six months has elapsed the personal representatives are protected from any personal liability for distributing the estate. They are not therefore expected to take into account the possibility of the court allowing an out of time application for rectification.[88]

The effect of lack of knowledge and approval
2.50   If it is established that the testator did not know and approve any of the contents of his will then the entire will is invalid.[89]   Where he had knowledge and approval of part only of the contents the consequences depend upon whether he died before or after 1 January 1995.   This has already been discussed above.

UNDUE INFLUENCE OR FRAUD

Undue influence
2.51   A will must not be made as a result of the undue influence of another person. The doctrine of undue influence in the Probate Court is much narrower than that developed by the Courts of Equity to protect the parties in an *inter vivos* transaction.   Most significantly, undue influence in relation to a will *cannot be presumed* because a special relationship exists between the testator and the beneficiary (such as doctor, patient; solicitor, client and confessor, penitent).[90]   In short, undue influence essentially means coercion in relation to wills. Persuasion, however immoral on the part of the persuader, is not enough:

> "Influence may be degrading and pernicious, and yet not undue influence in the eye of the law."[91]

Consider a foolish and profligate young man "caught up in the toils of a harlot" and persuaded by this ladyfriend to make a will solely in her favour at the expense of his relatives.[92]   Such conduct, however "morally reprehensible", does

---

[86]Inheritance (Provision for Family and Dependants) Act 1975.

[87]See para 8.17 *post*.

[88]Art 29(3).

[89]*In the Goods of Hunt* (1875) 3 P & D 250; *In the Goods of Meyer* [1908] P 353.

[90]*Boyce* v *Rossborough* (1857) 6 HLC at 49; *Parfitt* v *Lawless* (1872) LR 2 P & D 462.

[91]*Per* Lord Macnaghten in *Baudains* v *Richardson* [1906] AC 169 at 184.

[92]*Per* Sir J Hannen in *Wingrove* v *Wingrove* (1885) 11 PD 81 at 82.

not amount to undue influence unless the testator would have said of his will: "this is not my wish but I must do it."

2.52   Coercion may take a number of forms, ranging from violence, threats of violence or imprisonment at one end of the spectrum, to the incessant talking to a person, already so weakened in the last hours of his life that very little pressure would bring about the desired result, at the other:

> "Importunity or threats, such as the testator has not the courage to resist, moral command asserted and yielded to for the sake of peace and quiet, or of escaping from distress of mind or social discomfort, these, if carried to a degree in which the free play of the testator's judgment, discretion or wishes, is overborne, will constitute undue influence, though no force is either used or threatened. In a word, a testator may be led but not driven: and his will must be the offspring of his own volition, and not the record of someone else's."[93]

Burden of proof
2.53   The burden of proving undue influence is on the person alleging it. It is not sufficient to show that a person has the *power* to unduly overbear the will of the testator; it must be shown that the power was actually exercised and that the execution of the will was obtained by it.[94]

Fraud
2.54   In practice fraud arises very rarely in connection with wills. Purporting to prove a forgery would clearly amount to fraud, as would a false representation concerning the character of a beneficiary which was made to induce the testator to revoke the bequest in his favour.[95] If a testator attributes a false character to a legatee, the will is invalidated only if the false character was acquired by a fraud which deceived the testator. For instance, if a testator leaves his entire estate "to my *wife* Rose" when, in fact Rose was not his wife because she was already married to a third party at the time of her marriage to the testator, the misdescription does not invalidate the will if the testator knew of her bigamy and was not therefore deceived by it.[96]

---

[93] *Per* Sir J P Wilde in *Hall* v *Hall* (1868) LR 1 P & D 481.

[94] *Wingrove* v *Wingrove* (1885) 11 PD 81, approved by Privy Council in *Craig* v *Lamoureux* [1920] AC 349.

[95] *Allen* v *McPherson* (1847) 1 HLC 191,207.

[96] *Giles* v *Giles* (1836) 1 Keen 685; *In the Estate of Posner* [1953] P 277.

Burden of proof

2.55   The burden of proving fraud is on the person alleging it. The normal civil standard (the balance of probabilities) applies, but because of the serious nature of the allegation, a high degree of probability within that standard is required.[97]

Consequences of fraud or undue influence

2.56   The normal consequence of both fraud and undue influence is that the will in its entirety is invalid. If, however, only *part* of the will was affected by the fraud or undue influence, that part alone will be deleted and probate granted to the remainder of the will.[98]

---

[97]*Hornal* v *Neuberger Products* [1957] 1 QB 247.
[98]*Allen* v *McPherson* (1847) 1 HLC 191.

CHAPTER THREE

CREATION OF A WILL - FORMAL VALIDITY

3.01   The preceding chapter examined the various elements concerning the 'mind' of the testator which must be present before a valid will can be executed. This chapter is primarily concerned with the *formalities* which must be observed in order to execute a valid will.

FORMAL WILLS

3.02   Several reasons have been advanced to justify the existence of the very technical formalities which must be observed when executing a valid will:

> "The formalities of executing a will are useful ones.   They impress the testator with the solemnity of his acts; they ensure a standard written document; they eliminate most of the dangers of forgery or fraud; they encourage the use of middlemen (lawyers) who can help plan a rational, trouble-free disposition of assets."[1]

3.03   Of these, avoidance of fraud is clearly the paramount consideration and while there is some merit in the so-called 'channelling' functions, realistically they are merely incidental benefits.   The British and Irish judiciary have generally interpreted these formalities literally and rigidly, on several occasions reluctantly going against the obvious intention of the testator, notwithstanding that fraud was not alleged.[2]   In a number of Commonwealth jurisdictions dispensing provisions, which empower courts to disregard the absence of strict observance of the formalities if there has been "substantial compliance" and there is no allegation of fraud, have gained momentum.[3]   However, the extension of comparable provisions to British jurisdictions has been expressly

---

[1]   Friedman "The Law of the Living, the Law of the Dead: Property, Succession and Society" [1966] Wisconsin L R 340 at 367.

[2]   Eg *Re Colling (dec'd)* [1972] 3 All ER 729 and *Re Groffmann* [1969] 1 WLR 733.

[3]   For a review and comparison of such provisions see J G Miller "Substantial Compliance and the Execution of Wills" [1987] 36 ICLQ 559.

rejected.[4] It is thus imperative that the prescribed formalities are followed exactly.[5]

The relevant statutory provisions

3.04   The main statutory provision relating to the execution of wills is now article 5 of the Wills and Administration Proceedings (NI) Order 1994, which re-enacts, with substantial amendments, section 9 of the Wills Act 1837. In England and Wales the original section 9 of the 1837 Act was amended by section 17 of the Administration of Justice Act 1982,[6] and the 1994 Order essentially mirrors the amended English section 9. Useful reference can thus be made to English case law decided under the new provisions.

3.05   The amendments introduced by the 1994 Order are not retrospective and apply only to *wills made on or after* 1 January 1995.[7] The former law will therefore remain relevant for many years. For this reason both article 5 and its predecessor are dealt with in this chapter.

Article 5 of the 1994 Order is as follows:

> "(1) No will is valid unless it is in writing and is executed in accordance with the following requirements, that is to say, -
>
> (a) it is signed by the testator, or by some other person in his presence and by his direction; and
>
> (b) it appears from the will or is shown that the testator intended by his signature to give effect to the will; and
>
> (c) the signature is made or acknowledged by the testator in the presence of two or more witnesses present at the same time; and
>
> (d) each witness, in the presence of the testator (but not necessarily in the presence of any other witness),either-
>
> > (i) attests the testator's signature or the testator's acknow-ledgment of his signature and signs the will;or
> >
> > (ii) acknowledges his signature.

---

[4] Law Reform Committee, 22nd Report, *The Making and Revocation of Wills*, Cmnd 7902 (1980), pp 3-4.

[5] This statement is perhaps qualified by a more liberal approach to the validity of 'home-made' wills evident in a couple of recent decisions, discussed at para 3.26 *post*. Reliance upon this from the outset, however, is hardly prudent.

[6] The amended section extends only to wills of testators who die on or after 1 January 1983.

[7] Sch 1, paras 2,3. Compare the English provisions, which apply to wills of testators who *die* on or after commencement, ie 1 January 1983.

(2) No form of attestation or acknowledgment is necessary."

Section 9, as originally enacted, was as follows:

> "No will shall be valid unless it shall be in writing and executed
> in manner hereinafter mentioned; (that is to say), it shall be
> signed at the foot or end thereof by the testator, or by some other
> person in his presence and by his direction, and such signature
> shall be made or acknowledged by the testator in the presence of
> two or more witnesses, present at the same time, and such
> witnesses shall attest and subscribe the will in the presence of
> the testator, but no form of attestation shall be necessary."

The effect of the 1994 Order - relaxation of the formalities

3.06   Article 5 of the 1994 Order has made two changes of substance from
section 9 of the 1837 Act. First, the removal of the prescription on the location
of the testator's signature and secondly, the introduction of the facility for the
witnesses simply to acknowledge their signatures after the testator has either
made or acknowledged his.   Both are discussed in detail in the following
paragraphs.

3.07   This reduction in the extent of the formalities should undoubtedly
validate a small number of home-made wills which would previously have been
ineffective.   In addition, there is some evidence that the similar provisions
introduced in England by the Administration of Justice Act 1982 have
encouraged the judiciary there to interpret those formalities which do remain
with more leniency of spirit, again aiding the non-professionally drafted will.[8]
However, the changes introduced by the 1994 Order will not affect prudent
professional practice when executing a will.

A caveat - the gap between the minimum required by statute and sensible practice

(When reading the following pages, the warning contained below should always
be borne in mind.)

3.08   Compliance with the formalities described hereafter, some of which
have been interpreted relatively leniently (although many more have not),
should ensure that the executed will is accepted for probate.   The difficulty,
however, is that any person who is propounding a will has the burden of
proving that it was properly executed. It would be administratively unworkable
for the Probate Office to demand supplementary evidence from eye-witnesses in
every application for probate, and its task in this regard has been facilitated by

---

[8]   See para 3.26 *post*.

two matters. The first is the presumption *omnia praesumuntur rite esse acta* (everything is presumed to have been done correctly), which essentially means that if nothing irregular appears on the face of the will it is presumed that it was properly executed and the contrary has to be shown. Secondly, there are various provisions contained in the Non-Contentious Probate Rules.[9] Together, these make it of the utmost importance that a will is executed as regularly and with as few 'quirks' as possible. Of course, failure to do so will not necessarily sound the death-knell for the will, but at the very best it will put the estate to unnecessary delay and expense.

In writing

3.09   Every will must be in *writing*.[10] Video firms which have now added wills to their existing repertoire of births, deaths and marriages are thus restricted to providing a visual supplement to a properly executed written document. The statutory requirement is merely that the will be in writing and there are no restrictions on either the nature of the material upon which it appears[11] or the language used.[12]   The will may be typed or printed in pen or pencil.[13] A *holograph* (a will written in the testator's own handwriting) is valid, provided that the requisite formalities have been observed.[14]

No prescribed form

3.10   The legislation does not prescribe any particular form for a will; neither is legal phraseology a pre-requisite for a valid will.   If the Probate Office is satisfied that a will was executed in accordance with the law it will accept it for probate, whatever the actual lay-out or drafting, provided that the meaning of the contents is clear.   For example, probably the shortest will ever proved consisted of the three words "all for mother".[15]

3.11   The Lord Chief Justice is given power by virtue of section 42 of the Administration of Estates Act (NI) 1955 to prescribe forms, reference to which

---

[9]   For more detail on both of these, see para 3.58 *post*.

[10] Art 5 of the 1994 Order which re-enacts s 9 of the 1837 Act on this point.

[11] *Hodson* v *Barnes* (1926) 43 TLR 71, will written on an egg-shell.

[12] *Whiting* v *Turner* [1903] 89 LT 71 (French); *Lewis* v *Lewis* [1908] P 1 (Welsh); *Re Berger* [1989] 2 WLR 147 (Hebrew).

[13] For the presumption when a will appears in a mixture of pen and pencil, see para 4.59 *post*.

[14] In some jurisdictions which derive from Roman Law (eg Scotland) unattested holograph wills are valid.

[15] *Thorn* v *Dickens* [1906] W N 54.

would automatically incorporate them into the will. However, no such regulations have ever been made.[16]

3.12   Ready-made printed forms can be bought from newsagents, but it is recommended that caution be exercised in their use.[17]   This caveat was particularly pertinent in this jurisdiction prior to the enactment of the 1994 Order because the forms were invariably published in England, where the law was then different in small but significant respects.[18]   Even though the law is now effectively the same, it is submitted that attempting to draft one's own will is a false economy for the vast majority of the public.

Signature
3.13   Article 5 requires that the will either:

    (a)   be signed by the testator himself, or

    (b)   be signed on his behalf, by someone else, in his presence and at his direction

This re-enacts, without amendment, the former position under section 9 of the 1837 Act.

What constitutes a signature
3.14   The counsel of perfection must be that the testator sign, for *himself*, as he has been described in the body of the will. A testator described as 'John William Smith' should sign in full 'John William Smith' - even if that is not his normal signature. Omitting his middle name, or even simply using the initial, will require the discrepancy to be recited in the Oath for Executor,[19] and if this is overlooked the papers will be returned by the Probate Office for amendment.

3.15   However, a signature by way of a thumbprint,[20] initials,[21] or a mark, or made by a stamp[22] may also be valid. The test in every case is whether the

---

[16] In England such forms were issued under the equivalent s 179 of the Law of Property Act 1925 - see SR & O 1925 No 780. It appears, however, that they are rarely used.

[17] In a three-month period during 1978 (ie before the law was changed), the Law Reform Committee carried out a survey in England of wills submitted to probate in one of the probate registries. Only 4.2% were rejected, but over 90% of these were 'home-made'.

[18] For instance, one such will form examined at random contained the instruction that the *best* place for the testator to sign was at the foot or end of the will (rather than the *only* place).

[19] See para 11.18 *post*.

[20] *In the Estate of Finn* (1935) 105 LJP 36.

[21] *In the Goods of Ernest Kieran* [1933] 1 IR 222.   Ftnt [22] see overleaf.

purported signature was made *animo testandi*, that is, with the intention of representing the testator's signature. In *Re Colling*[23] a hospital patient started to sign his will in the presence of two witnesses, but had only managed "Coll..." when one, a nurse, was called away. He completed his name in her absence, but it was held that the mere partial signing done, as required by section 9 of the 1837 Act,[24] in the presence of *both* witnesses, could not represent the testator's signature. By contrast, in a case distinguished in the judgment,[25] "E.Chal" (instead of E.Chalcraft) was intended to represent the signature of a feeble, dying testatrix who was unable to complete her full name.

3.16   Once this intention to represent the testator's signature has been established, it does not matter that the testator signed under an assumed name,[26] or chose to identify himself with some other form of words such as "your loving mother".[27]

3.17   If signature has been by a mark there is no need to prove inability to write[28] and the mark need not be of the traditional cross shape.[29]   There is conflicting authority as to whether affixing a seal can be classed as making a signature.[30]

Directed signature

3.18   A testator can have made his own signature even if he has been assisted by someone else; if, for example, another person has helped him to support his pen. However, there must be some *active physical contribution* from the testator himself which is sufficient to indicate an intention to execute his will personally. Mere passive conduct is insufficient.[31]

---

[22]*Re Bulloch* [1968] NI 96.

[23][1972] 3 All ER 729.

[24]This aspect of the decision has not been changed by the amendments introduced by the Administration of Justice Act 1982.

[25]*Re Chalcraft (dec'd)* [1948] 1 All ER 700.

[26]*In the Goods of Charlotte Redding (dec'd)* (1850) 2 Rob Ecc 339.

[27]*In the Estate of Cook (dec'd)* [1960] 1 WLR 353.

[28]*Baker* v *Dening* (1838) 8 A & E 94, Coleridge J holding that the inconvenience of seeking proof in every case outweighed the obvious increased possibility of fraud.

[29]*In the Goods of Ernest Kieran* [1933] 1 IR 222 - an aborted attempt at making initials resulting in "two undecipherable scrawls."

[30]*In the Goods of Emerson* (1882) 9 LR Ir 443 a seal containing the testator's initials and put on with the words "this is my hand and seal" was held to be sufficient. Similarly, *Re Bulloch* [1968] NI 96 would suggest the same, *obiter*. There is considerable older authority, however, which disputes that the mere affixing of a seal can constitute a signature.

[31]*Fulton* v *Kee* [1961] NI 1.

3.19   It has already been noted that article 5 of the 1994 Order[32] provides the facility for a testator *to direct another to sign on his behalf*, in his presence. This facility is very useful in situations where the testator is suffering from physical weakness or a disability which affects his ability to write.   The direction may be express, but can also be by conduct, including an implication from a negative rather than a positive attitude on the part of the testator.[33]

3.20   A *directed* signature should not be confused with the aforementioned *assisted direct* signature.   However, there is clearly a potential overlap between the two concepts, for although conduct of the testator which is completely passive to that of the assistor cannot be a direct signature, that same conduct may constitute an *implied* direction to the assistor to sign on the testator's behalf.[34]

The position of the signature
(The law on this point has been changed by the 1994 Order with regard to wills made on or after 1 January 1995.)

Wills made before 1 January 1995
3.21   It has already been noted that section 9 of the 1837 Act, as originally enacted, required the signature to be "at the foot or end" of the will. Dissatisfaction with the rigid interpretation given to this section in its early years, for instance, in refusing probate to the will of a testatrix, who, to accommodate a lengthy attestation clause, opted to sign her will on a new page rather than on the 0.8" left blank below the end of the dispositive contents on the preceding page,[35] led to its amendment by section 1(1) of the Wills Act Amendment Act 1852.   Its key provisions can be summarised as follows:

(a)   A testator was given a wider berth as to *where* to place his signature. The former "foot or end" of the will was extended to "at or after, or following, or under, or beside or opposite to" the end of the will. This was qualified by the fact that it had to be apparent *on the face of the will* that the testator intended that the signature give effect as such to his will.

---

[32] As did s 9 of the 1837 Act.

[33] *Fulton v Kee*, [1961] NI 1 - testator did not object as the solicitor's clerk moved his hand.

[34] See the comments made in *Fulton v Kee ibid,* that in many borderline cases this distinction would be fine and often blurred.

[35] *Smee v Bryer* (1848) 1 Rob Ecc 616.

(b)   A will was not invalidated by the fact that either:

  (i)   there was a blank space between the end of the will and the signature, or,

  (ii) that the testator's signature was after the attestation clause, or beside the names of the witnesses, or

  (iii) that the signature appeared on a sheet on which there were no dispositive   contents - even if the space on the previous sheet would have accommodated the signature.

(c)   The 1852 Act did not alter the general principle that a signature was not operative to give effect to dispositive clauses which either:

  (i)   appeared below or following it, or

  (ii) which were inserted after it was made.

Notwithstanding the apparently unambiguous language of section 1(1) of the 1852 Act, which clearly prohibits signatures at the *top* of the will, the point has been litigated as far as the Court of Appeal, which, not surprisingly, confirmed:

> "Though [section 1] gives a wide geographical liberty as to where a signature could be placed, the liberty does not go so far as to say that a signature may be placed at the beginning. In fact, the last four lines provide that no signature should be operative to give effect to any disposition which is underneath or follows it."[36]

3.22   A series of cases with more equivocal fact situations have, however, stretched the language of the section considerably. In *Re Roberts*,[37] the testator, having completed the substantive contents of his will and reached the end of the sheet, turned it sideways and both he and his witnesses signed at right angles to the other writing. Had he signed opposite to the attestation clause, it would clearly have come within the 1852 Act. As it was, however, he left this space for the witnesses, and made his own signature on what was, in effect, the top of the will, albeit at right angles. The court held the will to be valid. The facts of

---

[36]*Per* Lord Hanworth MR in *Re Stalman* [1931] All ER 193.
[37][1934] P 102.

Re Hornby[38] are even more extreme. The testator ruled out a small box in advance around the middle of his single page will and, when executing the document, duly placed his signature there. Wallington J conceded that the will must fail if the statute was to be applied strictly. However, it was held that the signature should be regarded as being, in the intention of the testator, at the end of the will.[39] A narrower construction was applied by the Northern Ireland Court of Appeal in *Re Martin*.[40] There a will was prepared on a ready-made printed form, in the usual style of a large sheet folded vertically to give four smaller pages. The dispositive contents appeared on pages one and two, and the signatures and attestation clause at the bottom of the latter. A substantial residue clause appeared at the top of page three, which was clearly after the signature if the will was read, in book fashion, as four separate pages. The court rejected the ingenious construction of counsel that pages two and three should properly be regarded as one single page which, if folded horizontally instead of vertically, had been duly executed. Andrews LJ cited with approval the "sound advice" once given by Lord Penzance:

> "It does not become the court in a laudable anxiety to give effect to the document to twist or distort the plain meaning of the statute by ingenious construction, and virtually break the law to amend the testator's blunder."[41]

3.23 On occasions, the courts have also taken a broad view in cases where the will consists of several pages which, if read in their *apparent* order,[42] contain a signature that is somewhere in the middle, rather than at the end of the dispositive contents. Where the court was satisfied that the whole document was written before the signature was made, it sometimes treated it as cyclic and read it in the order in which the testator had intended that it be read, thus admitting the entire document to probate, rather than just the part appearing before the signature.[43] However, this approach was not adopted if the part of the contents appearing to come after the signature were, in reality, a mere annexe or schedule to or an expansion of the earlier contents.[44] If, on the other hand, the testator had made it clear that clauses appearing after the signature were to be interpolated in the body of the will, for example, by way of

---

[38] [1946] P 171.

[39] See the criticisms of this in Hodgekiss (1953) 26 ALJR 574.

[40] [1928] NI 138.

[41] In *Sweetland* v *Sweetland* (1865) 4 Sw & Tr 6 cited at p141.

[42] Eg as numbered or found in the envelope.

[43] *In the Goods of Mary Moorhouse Smith* [1931] P 225; *In the Estate of Mabel Amy Long (dec'd)* [1936] P 166.

[44] *In the Estate of Long, ibid; Royle* v *Harris* [1895] P 163.

asterisks[45] or arrows, the court was generally prepared to read the clauses where the testator intended them to be read, and treat the signature as *constructively* at the end of the will. Of course, the interpolated clauses must have been written before the will was executed.

Will made on or after 1 January 1995

3.24   Article 5 of the 1994 Order removes the limitation on the position of the testator's signature. It is no longer necessary that the signature appears in or around the foot or end of the will, provided that "it appears *from the will or is shown* that the testator intended by his signature to give effect to the will". However, the clearest and most effective way of demonstrating this is for the testator to place his signature at the end.

3.25   The amended section 9 of the 1837 Act, which has been operative in England for 13 years, is in the same terms, apart from the fact that it does not contain the emphasised words. This has led to some confusion about whether extrinsic evidence can be relied upon to demonstrate the testator's intention in making his signature. It will be recalled that section 1(1) of the Wills Act Amendment Act 1852 required that the testator's intention be apparent from the *face of the will* and it has been suggested that the omission of this requirement introduces   the admissibility of extrinsic evidence.[46] The drafting of the Northern Ireland legislation makes it clear that the testator's intention can be established from the will itself and/or from extrinsic evidence.

3.26   In *Wood* v *Smith*,[47] the first significant litigation to test the scope of the amended section 9 of the 1837 Act, the Court of Appeal upheld the formal validity[48] of a holograph will which a testator had started with the clause "My will by Percy Winterborne", before he had duly completed the dispositive clauses below it. After the two attesting witnesses had subscribed their signatures, one helpfully pointed out that the testator himself had not signed, to which Mr Winterborne replied that this was no longer necessary, as the will could be signed anywhere. Overturning the first instance decision of Mr David Gilliland QC who, sitting as a Deputy High Court Judge, had held that this execution was ineffective, their Lordships were unanimously of the view that a

---

[45] *In the Goods of Charles Birt* (1871) LR 2 P & D 214, "see over *" written in the body of the will and * and clause on the other side; *Palin* v *Ponting and Another* [1930] P 185, "see other side for completion" and "continuation for other side".

[46] This is now widely accepted to be the case - see, eg *Weatherhill* v *Pearce* [1995] 2 All ER 492, where extrinsic evidence was considered without discussion.

[47] [1992] 3 All ER 556.

[48] Ultimately, however, the will was held invalid because the testator lacked sound disposing mind.

signature could give effect to a will written after it, so long as the signature and the contents of the will were all "one continuous operation".

3.27   This decision is certainly not without difficulties - for example, what is the exact scope of "one continuous operation"? If Mr Winterborne had made his signature in the morning, went for lunch and returned in the afternoon to fill in the dispositive contents, it presumably would not constitute "one continuous operation". However, it takes little imagination to think of more equivocal fact situations. Undoubtedly the point will recur   for further judicial clarification, and in the meantime it is submitted that the decision on the formal validity of Mr Winterborne's will is best seen as correct, but on the ground that his name at the top of the document was a signature which he acknowledged[49] in the presence of the witness *after* the dispositive clauses had been completed.

3.28   These specific difficulties do not, however, detract from the important theme which emerges from the judgments in *Wood* v *Smith*. The tenor is quite clearly of a more generous and robust approach to the interpretation of the will formalities. It is summarised in the following observations made by Scott LJ in the course of his judgment:

> "There can be no doubt that the parliamentary intention in substituting the new section 9 for the original section was to simplify the requirements for the execution and witnessing of a will .... *These requirements demand a practical approach.*"[50]

Signing a will which consists of a number of pages

3.29   If a will consists of a number of pages it is not necessary that each page is separately signed and attested, although this is the practice of some professional draftsmen. At one time it was thought that the individual pages should be physically attached together during signature, at least by the pressing action of the testator's thumb.[51] However, following the decision of the Northern Ireland High Court in *Sterling* v *Bruce*[52] it now seems sufficient if the pages are all in the same room as the testator at the time of execution and

---

[49] "Acknowledgment" is construed widely and no express form of words is needed. See para 3.30 *post.*

[50] [1992] 3 All ER 556, at p 561. Emphasis added. The general approach of *Wood* v *Smith* has recently been endorsed by Kolbert J in *Weatherhill* v *Pearce* [1995] 2 All ER 492 and by Colyer J in *Couser* v *Couser*, *The Times*, 18 March 1996.

[51] *Lewis* v *Lewis* [1908] P 1; see also *Re Little* [1960] 1 All ER 387; although in *In the Goods of Mann (dec'd)* [1942] P 146 the peculiar circumstances of the case persuaded Langton J to depart from a rule he regarded as both "salutory and wise" and uphold a signature on an envelope which had not been touching the other pages during execution.

[52] [1973] NI 255; see also *In the Goods of the Rev John Tiernan* [1942] IR 572.

"under his control". Obviously it remains good practice to have the pages of a will permanently attached during execution, for example, with tape.

Acknowledgment of signature
3.30   Instead of making his signature in the presence of two witnesses, a testator has the option of *acknowledging* his signature in their presence. In this respect article 5 of the 1994 Order has merely re-enacted the former law.

"Acknowledgment" of a testator's signature can be by express words,[53] but acknowledgment by gestures,[54] or by simply placing the will in front of two people with the request that they witness it are also sufficient.[55] However, it is essential that the witness did see, or, at least, *could* have seen the signature; for example, gesturing to a will which is ensconced in a jacket pocket will not do.[56]

Attestation

The formalities

Wills made before 1 January 1995
3.31   It has been noted that section 9 of the 1837 Act required the testator to either make or acknowledge his signature in the presence of two witnesses and required both witnesses to be present when this was done.[57] After the testator had signed or acknowledged his signature in the presence of the witnesses, they then had to sign in his presence. Invariably when wills are executed by professional draftsmen, each of the witnesses will still be present when the other signs, but this was *not* actually required by the section.[58] Thus this scenario produced a valid execution:[59]

> (a)   Tom signs his will in front of two witnesses, Dick and Harry;

> (b)   Dick then signs the will in the presence of both Tom and Harry;

---

[53] "This is my will" - *Brown v Skirrow* [1902] P 3.

[54] *In the Goods of Martha Davies* (1850) 2 Rob Ecc 337.

[55] *Daintree v Butcher and Fasulo* (1888) 13 PD 102; *Weatherhill v Pearce* [1995] 2 ALL ER 492.

[56] *Re Groffmann, (dec'd)* [1969] 1 WLR 733.

[57] *Re Colling* - see para 3.15 *supra*.

[58] Art 5 of the 1994 Order expressly states that the witnesses need not sign in each other's presence.

[59] And still does under art 5 of the 1994 Order.

(c)   Dick leaves;

(d)   Harry signs his own name in Tom's presence.

Of course, the will would not be valid if the testator (Tom) had left with Dick, so that Harry did not subscribe his signature in the presence of the testator.

3.32   The *Colling* case discussed earlier[60] confirmed that the sequence of the events in section 9 of the 1837 Act was mandatory: signature or acknowledgment thereof by the testator *followed by* subscription and attestation by the witnesses. It will be recalled that in the case in question the testator actually made his signature only in part in the presence of *both* witnesses and that this was held insufficient to be his signature. While witness A was still away, witness B had proceeded to subscribe his own name. On the return of witness A, and whilst witness B was still present, the testator *acknowledged* his completed signature, whereupon witness A also signed. It might be thought that this course of events validated the earlier error - the testator had, after all, acknowledged his signature in the presence of *both* the witnesses. However, section 9 was interpreted as requiring the witnesses to attest and subscribe *after* the testator made or acknowledged his signature.[61]   To validate the will in *Colling* a second signature would have been needed from witness B after the testator had acknowledged his full signature. The position has been changed by article 5 of the 1994 Order, so that a *Colling* scenario occurring after 1994 would produce a valid execution.

Wills made on or after 1 January 1995
3.33   Article 5(1)(d) of the 1994 Order requires that each witness, in the presence of the testator (but not necessarily in the presence of each other),[62] either:

(a)   attests the testator's signature or acknowledgment of
         his signature and signs the will; or

(b)   acknowledges his signature.

3.34   A witness can now *either* attest the will and make his signature or he can acknowledge a signature which he has made previously. The provision

---

[60] See para 3.15 *supra*.
[61] See also *Brown v Skirrow* [1902] P 3.
[62] Although this was not expressly mentioned before, it is merely stating what was well-established under s 9 of the 1837 Act.

about acknowledgment is new and rectifies the *Colling* scenario described above. When witness A returned it would now be sufficient that witness B pointed out the signature he had made earlier while alone in the presence of the testator.[63] *Couser* v *Couser*[64] has recently confirmed that the case law which has developed on what constitutes acknowledgment of a testator's signature will be applied by analogy with acknowledgment by witnesses.[65]

3.35   One point which should be noted is that *attestation*, that is, certifying on the will that it has been signed by the proper person as testator, is required only from a person who *signs after* the testator, but not from one who signs beforehand and *acknowledges* his signature after the testator has signed.

What must the witness know?
3.36   Since the role of the witnesses is to witness the testator's signature, it is not necessary that they see the contents of the will. Furthermore it would seem that a witness does not even have to know that he is witnessing a will.[66]

"In the presence of..."
3.37   The phrase "in the presence of" appears twice in article 5 of the 1994 Order.[67] The testator must initially sign or acknowledge his signature in the presence of the witnesses, and they must sign in his presence. When the testator is signing the witnesses must be in a position to actually see him do so. For example, a testatrix, who signed her will whilst standing at one end of a large shop was held not to have been in the presence of a witness who was standing at the other end and was unable to see what was happening.[68]

3.38   "In the presence of" means actual visual presence. When the witnesses are attesting the testator's signature, the testator must not only be physically present but also mentally present.[69]

---

[63] For an example of an execution which would have been ineffective under s 9 of the 1837 Wills Act, but complies with art 5 of the 1994 Order, see *Weatherhill* v *Pearce* [1995] 2 All ER 492 (a decision on the amended s 9 in England).

[64] *The Times*, 18 March 1996.

[65] See also the recent decision in *Weatherhill* v *Pearce*, where the court proceeded on the assumption that no particular form of acknowledgment is required from the witnesses.

[66] *Re Benjamin* [1934] 150 LT 417.

[67] As it did in s 9 of the 1837 Act.

[68] *Brown* v *Skirrow* [1902] P 3. See also *Couser* v *Couser*, *The Times*, 18 March 1996.

[69] *Re Chalcraft (dec'd)* [1948] 1 All ER 700. In this particular case the testatrix had just slipped into unconsciousness on finishing her signature, but the court held that, although clearly a "borderline" case, she was "mentally present to a sufficient degree."

Signature by witness himself

3.39   A witness must sign the will himself and there is no parallel provision to that which enables the testator to direct someone else to sign on his behalf in his presence.   As in the case of the testator's own signature, a witness's signature may be assisted provided that there is an active physical contribution from the witness himself.[70]   Again initials, a mark (including one subscribed with a stamp)[71] or a form of words intended to identify the witness[72] are sufficient.

Position of signatures of witnesses

3.40   Although it is usual for the witnesses to sign immediately below the testator's signature, they can sign anywhere on the will, provided that it is clear that they placed their signatures with the intention of attesting the signature of the testator. This will be most obvious if the witnesses' signatures immediately follow that of the testator.

Restrictions on who can be a witness

3.41   The fact that there are no statutory restrictions on the age[73] or competence of witnesses should be tempered by the possibility of them being asked to give affidavit evidence, and competent, literate persons should be chosen.   In addition, if it is possible, a witness should not be a person with a potential interest under an intestacy.   Giving evidence of the execution of a will is essentially a *visual* matter, a fact which precludes a blind person from acting as a witness.[74]

3.42   A person who has signed the will on behalf of the testator at his direction is not disqualified from also acting as one of the witnesses.[75]

Beneficiaries and their spouses

3.43   The most significant restriction on the identity of the witnesses is article 8 of the 1994 Order, which re-enacts, with amendments, section 15 of the 1837 Act.

---

[70] *Re Bulloch* [1968] NI 96.
[71] *Ibid* but signing in own hand stated to be preferable because it is more easily authenticated.
[72] *In the Goods of Sperling* (1863) 3 Sw & Tr 272 (servant to Mr Sperling).
[73] A minor can be a witness - provided that he is old enough to understand what is going on.
[74] *Re Gibson* [1949] P 434, although Pearce J did suggest, without further elaboration, that there might be "peculiar circumstances" in which a blind person could be a witness.
[75] *Smith* v *Harris* (1845) 1 Rob Ecc 262.

Article 8 provides that any gift in a will to a witness or to a witness's spouse is void. The validity of the signature or the will itself is not affected but the gift in question falls into residue, or if residuary, results in a partial intestacy.

3.44   It is more complex if there are remainders or substitutionary gifts after a gift which is invalidated by article 8. If a testator leaves to "A for life, remainder to A's children" and A is the spouse of an attesting witness, and there are children living at the death of the testator, the gift to them is accelerated.[76] If there are no such children living there is an intestacy during A's life or until such children are born.[77]

3.45   The right of a witness who is a beneficiary or the spouse of a beneficiary to give evidence of the due execution of the will, if required to do so, is expressly preserved.[78]

3.46   The relevant time at which a witness must not have an interest under the will is the *date of execution* of the document. Thus a solicitor witness who, sometime after the execution of the will, replaced one of the original trustees, was held entitled to keep a legacy for his trouble in acting as such.[79] Similarly, a witness who becomes the spouse of a beneficiary some time after the execution of the will is outside the scope of article 8 of the 1994 Order.

3.47   Section 15 of the 1837 Act voided only 'beneficial' interests left to witnesses and their spouses, and it had been well-established that trustees and others who did not take a beneficial interest were outside the section. By contrast, article 8 of the 1994 Order refers simply to persons to whom "property" is given in the will, and "property" is defined sufficiently widely in the interpretation section to include bare legal title.[80] However, it is submitted that this provision should be construed in the light of the previous case law and that those witnesses or spouses of witnesses who take a bare legal title should not be precluded from taking.

---

[76] *Re Clark* (1885) 31 Ch D 72.

[77] *Re Townsend's Estate* (1886) 34 Ch D 357.

[78] Art 8(2) of the 1994 Order.

[79] *In Re Royce's Will Trusts* [1959] Ch 626; also *Re Ray's Will Trusts* [1936] Ch 520.

[80] Art 2(2) defines property as including "any estate in land, any chattels, any thing in action, and any rights which are treated commercially as property and also includes any interest in property".

3.48   The modern basis for secret trusts, which justifies their existence as totally independent of the will, enables a secret beneficiary to take even though he is a witness to the will.[81]

Privileged wills

3.49   An informal will made by a privileged testator need not be witnessed at all.[82] If therefore such a testator makes a written will which he intends to be an informal will, but it is witnessed by a beneficiary or his spouse, the rule does not apply and the gift is valid.[83]

Will confirmed by a codicil

3.50   If a will which is witnessed by a beneficiary or a beneficiary's spouse is subsequently confirmed by a will or codicil *not* so attested, the general rule does not apply and the gift is valid.[84]

Witness to codicil a beneficiary under the will

3.51   If a beneficiary under a will subsequently attests a codicil to that will (though not the will itself) the gifts under the will remain valid.[85] Of course, any benefit to him under the codicil itself would fail.

Supernumerary witnesses

3.52   The requirement in article 5 of the 1994 Order[86] is that the will be attested by at least two witnesses. What if a beneficiary or his spouse were to witness a will when there are already two non-beneficiary witnesses? In *Re Bravda*[87] the English Court of Appeal reluctantly refused to give section 15 of the 1837 Act the "tortuous construction" it thought would be required in order to disregard the signatures of an ill-advised testator's two daughters (the sole beneficiaries), whom he had asked to be witnesses to his will. The will had already been witnessed by the testator's two neighbours, and he had asked his daughters to be witnesses "to make it stronger". There was no allegation of fraud and the testator's intention was clearly defeated,[88] but the court voided the

---

[81] *Re Young (dec'd)* [1951] Ch 344.

[82] See para 3.64 *post*.

[83] *Re Limond* [1915] 2 Ch 240.

[84] *Re Trotter* [1899] 1 Ch 764.

[85] *Re Marcus* (1887) 57 LT 399.

[86] As it was under s 9 of the 1837 Act.

[87] [1968] 1 WLR 479.

[88] This was especially so in the *Bravda* case because the deceased's estranged widow inherited everything under the intestacy; often the 'deprived' supernumerary witnesses will receive at least some of the estate under the intestacy.

gifts to the daughters. Both Russell and Salmon LJJ strongly advocated legislation, and the decision was reversed in England and Wales by section 1 of the Wills Act 1968,[89] which did not extend to Northern Ireland. Article 8(3) of the 1994 Order enacts corresponding provision for this jurisdiction. The witnessing by a person to whom, or to whose spouse, property is given can now be disregarded, provided that the will is duly executed without his signature and without that of any other such person. In short, if there are *two* non-beneficiary witnesses, any gifts to other witnesses will still be able to take effect.

3.53   Article 8(3) is only effective for the wills of persons who die on or after 1 January 1995[90] and the position before this date is still governed by *Re Bravda*. On this point it is worth noting that gifts to supernumerary 'witnesses' will not be voided if it can be shown that they did not sign as witnesses, but, for example, to express agreement with the contents. This argument was unsuccessful in *Bravda* itself because, *inter alia*, the daughters had actually signed below the heading "witnesses".

Charging clauses
3.54   It should be remembered that a clause enabling a solicitor to charge for his professional services in acting as executor is construed as a legacy of that value in his favour. As such it will be void if he also acts as an attesting witness.[91]

FORM OF ATTESTATION AND PROOF OF DUE EXECUTION

Attestation clause
3.55   Article 5 of the 1994 Order expressly provides that no particular form of attestation is required.[92] Put another way, an attestation clause is not necessary. However, in the absence of an attestation clause or if there is an ineffective attestation clause, affidavits as to the manner of execution will be sought by the Probate Office and at best the issuing of the grant will be delayed.

3.56   The following attestation clause is widely used in Northern Ireland and is acceptable to the Probate Office:

---

[89] For deaths after 29 May 1968.
[90] Sch 1, para 5 to the 1994 Order.
[91] *Re Barber* (1886) 31 Ch D 665. Note that employees within a firm of solicitors are not within the ambit of this exclusion, merely a sole trader or partner.
[92] This re-enacts s 9 of the 1837 Act.

> "Signed and acknowledged by the said testator as and for his
> last will in the presence of us both present at the same time who
> at his request in his presence and in the presence of each other
> have hereunto subscribed our names as witnesses."

The equally acceptable shortened form has become increasingly popular in recent times:

> "Signed by the testator in our presence and *then* by us in his."

Prior to the enactment of the 1994 Order the clause was ineffective if the word "then" had been omitted, and the Probate Office required further affidavits of due execution to be submitted. The introduction of the facility for a witness to acknowledge his signature makes its inclusion unnecessary.

3.57 Any 'quirks' in the execution of the will should also be recited in the attestation clause; for example, that the testator's signature was directed, or by way of a mark, that the testator was blind or that the will had been altered before execution.

Proof of due execution

3.58 The burden of proving that a will has been duly executed is on the person propounding its validity and the standard is the balance of probabilities. If a will appears on the face of it to have been duly executed the rebuttable presumption *omnia praesumuntur rite esse acta* (everything is presumed to have been done correctly) applies. The presumption is strengthened by an effective attestation clause and where it does apply, clear evidence of non-compliance with the formalities is needed to rebut it. Furthermore, the mere fact that witnesses cannot actually remember the exact execution and verify its compliance with the statute is not in itself sufficient to rebut the presumption if there is an effective attestation clause.[93]

Additional affidavits

3.59 It has been noted that in some circumstances the Probate Office may require additional affidavits as to proof of due execution. These circumstances are set out in the Non-Contentious Probate Rules,[94] rule 9 of which provides that affidavits as to due execution are required from one or more of the attesting witnesses if there is either -

---

[93] *Wright* v *Sanderson* (1884) 50 LT Rep 769. ·See also the recent application of the maxim in *Weatherhill* v *Pearce* [1995] 2 All ER 492 and *Couser* v *Couser, The Times*, 18 March 1996.
[94] RSC O 97.

(a)   no attestation clause, or

(b)   an insufficient attestation clause, or

(c)   where it appears to the Master that there is some doubt
        about the execution of the will.

The Master thus has a wide discretion to call for affidavits if he is in any way
unhappy about the due execution of a will.

3.60   In the event that the witnesses to the will are not available, any other
eye-witnesses to the execution are required to furnish affidavit evidence. If
there are no available eye-witnesses the Master has a discretion, to be exercised
with regard to "the desirability of protecting the interests of persons prejudiced
by the will", to request affidavits to authenticate the deceased's signature or to
prove anything else which could raise a presumption in favour of due
execution. If, having considered such evidence, the Master is satisfied that the
will was not duly executed, probate shall be refused. However, if he still
retains some doubt he has the discretion to refer the matter to the court which
will decide.

Unusual situations
3.61   Rule 10 of the Non-Contentious Probate Rules requires the Master to
be satisfied that a testator who is blind, illiterate or who directed his signature
had knowledge of the contents of his will. More generally, this duty extends to
wills which have been executed in circumstances that give rise to doubt about
the testator's knowledge of the contents. Proof of these matters may be asked
for by affidavit.[95]

Date of execution
3.62   If there is any doubt about the date of the execution of the will, the
Master may require evidence proving this date, again generally by affidavit. It
is fundamental that a will be dated when executed.

Potential difficulties arising from the 1994 Order
3.63   It has been noted that the 1994 Order does not require witnesses who
merely acknowledge their signatures in the testator's presence to actually attest.
In such cases there will not ordinarily be an attestation clause and presumably

---

[95]R 13.

the Probate Office will need to satisfy itself of due execution by way of affidavit evidence.

INFORMAL WILLS

3.64   It is recognised that there are exceptional circumstances in which it is unreasonable to expect a person to comply with the above formalities. Certain classes of person (generally soldiers, sailors and airmen) have therefore been afforded the facility to make an informal or *privileged* will. Such a will can be oral (ie, a nuncupative will) or, if in writing, it need not be signed by the testator in the presence of at least two witnesses etc.

A valid informal will is effective to revoke an existing formal will.[96]

The statutory authority

3.65   Section 11 of the Wills Act 1837 provides that "any soldier being in actual military service, or any mariner or seaman being at sea, may dispose of his *personal* estate as he might have done before the making of this Act" (ie, without need of formalities). The privilege was subsequently extended to devises of *real* property by the Wills (Soldiers and Sailors) Act 1918.[97] The armed forces of the Crown are an "excepted matter" under the Northern Ireland Constitution Act 1973 and as such cannot be dealt with[98] by an Order in Council under the Northern Ireland Act 1974. It has not therefore been possible to make a special rule applying to servicemen in the 1994 Order and section 11 of the 1837 Act remains in force, the only substantive provision of this legislation not to be repealed.[99]

The extent of the privilege

3.66   Section 11 of the 1837 Act refers to "any soldier being in actual military service, or any mariner or seaman being at sea". The Wills (Soldiers and Sailors) Act 1918 added members of the RAF, if in actual military service,[100] and members of the Navy,[101] not only when at sea, but when so circumstanced that, if soldiers, they would be "in actual military service".

---

[96] *Re Gosage's Estate* [1921] P 194.

[97] S 3(1).

[98] Save in an ancillary way.

[99] Merchant shipping is not an excepted matter, but the Land Law Working Group was of the opinion that the application of privileged wills to merchant seamen should not be split from their application to servicemen.

[100] S 5(2).

[101] S 2.

Soldiers on actual military service

3.67 Under Roman Law soldiers could only make a privileged will if "*in expeditione*"[102] and it seems that this idea influenced the narrow judicial interpretation given to the phrase "in actual military service" in its formative years. Gradually a broader view was taken and it has generally been the case that all the provisions concerned with the scope of privileged wills have been indulged with a leniency of spirit.

3.68 The interpretation of the term "actual military service" has evolved with the changing nature of warfare. For instance, prior to the Second World War a soldier had to be either serving overseas in a campaign or about to do so,[103] but this was extended by cases arising out of the 1939-45 conflict. A landmark decision was *Re Wingham*[104] in which a member of the RAF who died in a flying accident in Canada, where he had been sent for training, was held by a unanimous Court of Appeal, reversing the trial judge, entitled to make a privileged will. Cohen LJ adopted the following test:

> "That the deceased was liable at any time to proceed to some area in order to take part in active warfare and that under these circumstances he was in actual military service."[105]

3.69 A soldier can be on "actual military service" even though war has not been declared and he is acting in aid of the civil power in putting down insurrection. *Re Jones*[106] arose out of the conflict in Northern Ireland: a corporal in the Parachute Regiment was shot by a lone sniper while on patrol, and on his way to hospital said "if I don't make it, make sure Annie [his fiancée] gets all my stuff". It was held that the corporal was "on actual military service" and that the communication constituted a valid nuncupative will, thus revoking a formal will which he had previously made in favour of his mother.

3.70 There is no authority on whether a member of the Royal Ulster Constabulary will be construed as coming within the term "soldier" to enable him to make a valid privileged will.[107]

---

[102] See for instance, *Drummond v Parish* (1843) 3 Curt 522.

[103] *White v Repton* (1844) 3 Curt 818; *Gattward v Knee* [1902] P 99; *Re Booth*, [1926] P 118.

[104] [1949] P 187.

[105] *Ibid* p 194.

[106] [1981] 1 All ER 1.

[107] On the basis of very liberal Australian authority he probably would: *Re White's Application* [1975] 2 NSWLR 125.

Mariners or seamen at sea

3.71 The term "mariner or seaman" applies to any sailor, notwithstanding that he is engaged in a purely civilian capacity. An interesting case arising out of the Lusitania tragedy is *Re Hale*.[108] Sarah Hale, a typist with the Cunard Steamship Company, died on the Lusitania. After her death documents written by her, clearly intended to be testamentary and dated some months before, were found in the house in which she stayed when not at sea. Madden J held that she was a "seaman at sea" within the meaning of section 11 of the 1837 Act.[109]

Duration of a privileged will

3.72 A privileged will made by a testator who satisfies the qualifying criteria remains fully effective until either it is revoked or the testator dies. There is no equivalent to the well-known provision of Roman Law whereby such a will only remained in force for the period of one year after the testator's return from actual military service.

Infants

3.73 A minor who satisfies the qualifying criteria can make a privileged will,[110] although if this is done, and the minor then ceases to qualify, he cannot make a new formal will before reaching his majority or marrying.[111] He can, however, revoke his privileged will before that age.[112]

Revocation of a privileged will

3.74 Revocation of a privileged will is governed by the same rules as revocation of a formal will.[113] In particular, it should be remembered that involuntary revocation (ie revocation on marriage)[114] applies equally to a privileged will.[115]

Alteration of a privileged will

3.75 Privileged wills are not subject to the statutory rules contained in article 11 of the 1994 Order.[116]

---

[108] [1915] 2 IR 362.

[109] See also *In the Goods of Newland* [1952] 1 All ER 841, where it was held that "at sea" includes a time when at home awaiting re-appointment.

[110] S 1 Wills (Soldiers and Sailors) Act 1918.

[111] For the power of married minors to make wills, see para 2.05 *supra*.

[112] Age of Majority Act (NI) 1969, s 2(2).

[113] See para 4.02 *post*.

[114] Art 12 of the 1994 Order, see para 4.05 *post*.

[115] *Re Wardrop* [1917] P 54.

[116] See para 4.54 *post*.

Attesting witness a beneficiary under a privileged will

3.76   An informal will does not need to be witnessed at all. Thus if a testator makes such a will in writing and has it witnessed, the general rule does not apply[117] and any gifts in the will to the witness or his spouse are not void.[118]

Animus testandi

3.77   The deceased must manifest an intention to make a testamentary disposition, even though he did not actually think that he was making a will. An exchange which is intended to be no more than a casual conversation will not suffice.

3.78   The type of communication which is sufficient to create an informal will is illustrated by the Northern Ireland case, *Re Hamilton.*[119]   It had been conceded that the deceased was a "mariner at sea" within the meaning of section 11 of the 1837 Act and the only contentious issue was whether certain communications made by the deceased could be considered to be testamentary. Both the deceased's parents were dead and he had no remaining family.   On visits home to Belfast he stayed with an old friend and visited frequently at the home of a Mrs Down whom he had known for years. While he had been home for his mother's funeral the deceased had told Mrs Down that he was naming her as 'next-of-kin' on his naval papers and that that meant everything would automatically come to her on his death.   In fact this was inaccurate and her nomination was little more than an administrative procedure whereby she would be notified first in the event of his illness or death.   In and around the same time, in a conversation with the friend whom he was staying with, the deceased re-iterated that Mrs Down was to receive his property on death.   The court pronounced that these statements by the deceased amounted to a valid nuncupative will since they were to the clear effect that he wanted all his property to pass to Mrs Down after his death.

---

[117] Ie, that contained in art 8 of the 1994 Order, see para 3.43 *supra*.

[118]See para 3.49 *supra*.

[119][1982] NI 197.

CHAPTER FOUR

REVOCATION, ALTERATION, REVIVAL AND REPUBLICATION OF WILLS

REVOCATION

The right to revoke

4.01   By virtue of its ambulatory nature, which has already been discussed in Chapter One,[1] a testator has the right to revoke his will at any time during his life, subject to him still having the mental capacity required to do so. This is the case even if he has expressly declared his will to be irrevocable,[2] although if he has entered into a *contract* not to revoke his will[3] he will be liable in damages to the aggrieved party if he subsequently does so.[4]

Methods of revocation

4.02   Article 14(1) of the Wills and Administration Proceedings (NI) Order 1994 sets out the *only* ways in which a will can be revoked. These are:

(a)   by the marriage of the testator after the will is executed;

(b)   by another will;

(c)   by a document declaring an intention to revoke the will and executed in the same way as a will;

(d)   by the testator, or some other person in his presence and by his direction, burning, tearing, or otherwise destroying the will with the intention of revoking it.[5]

These provisions of the 1994 Order substantially re-enact the former law, which was contained in sections 18 and 20 of the Wills Act 1837. The only

---

[1] See para 1.08 *supra*.
[2] *Vynior's Case* (1609) 8 Co Rep 81b.
[3] For contracts to leave property by will, see para 1.22 *supra*.
[4] See also mutual wills, para 1.14 *supra*.
[5] In addition, revocation of *part* of the will will be effected where unattested alterations have been made to the will and the original wording is not "apparent"; see para 4.65 *post*.

amendment which has been introduced by the 1994 Order relates to revocation on marriage.

Classification into voluntary and involuntary revocation

4.03   Revocation of a will on marriage happens automatically, independent of the testator's intentions. For this reason it has been termed 'involuntary' revocation in order to distinguish it from the other three methods of revocation, which collectively constitute 'voluntary' revocation.

Mental capacity required for revocation of a will

4.04   Voluntary revocation requires the same mental capacity as that needed to execute a will.[6]

Revocation by the marriage of the testator

General

4.05   Article 12(1) of the 1994 Order[7] states the general rule that a will is revoked if the testator marries after it has been executed, thus achieving the sensible objective that a person should be allowed to start married life with a clean slate:

> "The purpose of the law as to revocation by marriage is to let in the claims of wives and children, and it is reasonable to suppose that their claims are properly protected and adjusted by the law as on intestacy. To maintain a will made before marriage may result in injustice to the children, or even to the wife herself...."[8]

In general this rule has been well-received, and proposals that it should be modified have received little support.[9]

Void and voidable marriages

4.06   A marriage which is voidable[10] under the Matrimonial Causes (NI) Order 1978 is effective for the purposes of article 12(1) and revokes an existing will,[11] even if the marriage is subsequently annulled.[12] In contrast, a void

---

[6] *Re Sabatini* (1969) 114 SJ 35. See para 2.06 *supra*.

[7] Formerly s 18 of the Wills Act 1837.

[8] *Per* Adams J in the New Zealand case *Burton* v *Mc Gregor* [1953] NZLR 487 at 490.

[9] Proposals were put to the Law Reform Committee on the Making and Revocation of Wills, Cmnd 7902 (1982) that either the will should be retained but super-imposed with a statutory legacy in favour of the spouse or children if appropriate, or that the rule be restricted to first marriages. Neither was adopted - see para 3.4 of the Report.

[10] For the grounds on which a marriage is void or voidable, see Appendix D.

[11] *Re Roberts* [1978] 1 WLR 653.

[12] See overleaf.

marriage does not revoke a will which has been made previously by either of the parties.[13]

4.07 A significant change made by the 1978 Order was the re-classification of marriages which lack the consent of one of the parties from void to voidable. One consequence of this is that a marriage which is later annulled on the ground of lack of consent is effective to revoke an earlier will, thus leaving the party who is suffering from a mental disorder without a will, yet probably lacking the mental capacity to execute a new one. In *Re Roberts*[14] Buckley LJ conceded that this situation could lead to anomalies, but in light of the language and construction of the corresponding English legislation, the Matrimonial Causes Act 1973, the learned judge felt that he could not accede to Counsel's submissions to treat marriages which lacked mental capacity in the same way as void marriages. As a result of the reservations raised in *Roberts*, the Law Reform Committee specifically examined the problems posed by such marriages, but change was not recommended.[15]

Solicitor's duty to his client

4.08 A solicitor advising a client whom he has reason to know is contemplating marriage in the near future is under a duty to warn the client about the effect of that marriage on his will. It would seem that this duty extends to situations in which the solicitor is made aware of the client's plans indirectly and not through the client himself, but not if the client merely mentions marriage in a casual or jocular way.[16] Notwithstanding the fact that there is no duty to mention the implications of marriage to clients in general, it would seem eminently prudent to remind all persons making a will of this limitation on its validity.

---

[12] Art 16 of the 1978 Order provides that a decree of annulment is only effective from the date on which it is granted.

[13] *Mette v Mette* (1859) 1 Sw & Tr 416; also see *obiter dictum* in *Re Roberts* [1978] 1 WLR 653.

[14] [1978] 1 WLR 653.

[15] Law Reform Committee, Twenty Second Report, *The Making and Revocation of Wills*, Cmnd 7902, para 3.19. Moreover, the one positive recommendation which was made, that individuals and charities who were denied benefits because of the revocation of such a will should automatically be afforded a family-provision style claim, was not actually implemented. This approach was adopted by the Northern Ireland Land Law Working Group (Final Report, p 16).

[16] *Hall v Meyrick* [1957] 2 QB 455.

Exceptions to the rule that marriage revokes a will

4.09   Two statutory exceptions exist to the general rule that marriage revokes any will made by either party prior to that marriage. The following are not revoked by the subsequent marriage of a testator:

> (a)   Wills made in expectation of a forthcoming marriage;
>
> (b)   Dispositions in a will made in exercise of certain powers of appointment.

Wills made in expectation of marriage

4.10   This exception, the rationale of which is that some people may make wills before they are married with the intention that the will should remain effective after the wedding, is the one aspect of the law of revocation which has been altered in scope by the 1994 Order. Article 12 provides as follows:

> "(3) *Where it appears from a will* that at the time it was made the testator was expecting to be married to a particular person and that he intended that the will should not be revoked by the marriage, the will is not revoked by his marriage to that person.
>
> (4) Where it appears from a will that at the time it was made the testator was expecting to be married to a particular person and that he intended that a disposition in the will should not be revoked by his marriage to that person, -
>
> > (a)   that disposition takes effect notwithstanding the marriage; and
> >
> > (b)   any other disposition in the will also takes effect also, unless it appears from the will that the testator intended the disposition to be revoked by the marriage." [Emphasis added]

4.11   This re-enacted, with very significant amendments, section 1 of the Wills Act (Amendment) Act (NI) 1954:

> "A will expressed to be made in contemplation of a marriage shall ... not be revoked by the solemnisation of the marriage contemplated."[17]

---

[17] This followed exactly the wording of its English counterpart, s 177 of the Law of Property Act 1925. This provision has since been amended by s 18(1) of the Administration of Justice Act 1982. Art 12 of the 1994 Order is in the same terms as s 177 as amended by the 1982 Act.

Article 12(3) and (4) do not apply to wills made before 1 January 1995. Section 1 of the 1954 Act does not apply to wills made before 22 June 1954.

4.12   The first point which should be made about the two provisions is that while the wording of article 12 is much clearer than that of its legislative antecedent, it would seem that 'expectation' of marriage is to be construed as synonymous with 'in contemplation' thereof. The cases in which the phrase "made in contemplation of marriage" was litigated will thus continue to remain relevant to the scope of the new provision. The main principles to have emerged from these cases are as follows.

4.13   A will which contains a clause expressly declaring it to be made in contemplation/in expectation of marriage to a named individual leaves no element of doubt about the operation of the exception. This is obviously the most prudent course for the professional draftsman who has been instructed that his client wants a will to survive his forthcoming marriage. It is clear from the wording of both article 12(3) of the 1994 Order and section 1 of the 1954 Act that it is marriage to a *particular person* which the testator must have in mind and it was confirmed in *Sallis* v *Jones*[18] that a general declaration in the nature of "this will is made in contemplation of marriage" will not suffice.

4.14   Does a reference in a will to a named beneficiary such as 'my fiancée, Flavia' or 'my future husband, Marcus' show that the testator both intended to be married to that person in the future *and* that the will should survive that marriage? This has been the most contentious issue in the past and will undoubtedly continue to arise with the 1994 Order. In *Re Langston*[19] it was held that a will made by a deceased in which he had left his entire estate to a named woman described as "my fiancée" was not revoked when the deceased subsequently married the same lady some ten weeks after the will had been executed. Davies J suggested this to be the proper test: "did the testator express the fact that he was contemplating marriage to a particular person?" In reaching his decision the learned judge relied upon the earliest reported case, *Pilot* v *Gainfort*,[20] in which a testator had described the woman with whom he was living as "my wife" in a will made before he had married her and it had been held that the will should survive the marriage. However, a different approach was evident in *Re Gray*[21] in which Simon P refused to accept that a

---

[18] [1936] P 43.
[19] [1953] P 100.
[20] [1931] P 103.
[21] (1963) 107 SJ 156.

testator calling the woman he was later to marry by his own surname, "Gray", showed a clear intention that he intended to make her his wife.[22]

4.15   The most recent examination of these authorities is contained in the judgment of Megarry J in *Re Coleman*.[23] A testator, before his marriage to a certain Mrs Jeffrey, had executed a will which included the following dispositions, "unto my fiancée, Mrs Murial Jeffrey":

(a)   all his personal chattels

(b)   his stamp collection

(c)   a legacy of £5 000

(d)   his freehold dwelling house.

Mrs Jeffrey was not the only beneficiary under the will since the residue (which was a significant proportion of the estate) had been left between the testator's brother and sister. On the testator's death, Murial who was now Mrs Herbert Coleman, and much better off financially under an intestacy as the surviving spouse,[24] claimed that the will had been revoked on their marriage and that it had not been saved by the exception contained in section 177 of the Law of Property Act 1925. The learned judge was of the view that, unless curtailed by the context, language such as "my fiancée" connoted not only the current state of affairs, but also the "sublimation" of those circumstances into marriage:

> ".... it seems to me that in ordinary parlance a contemplation of marriage is inherent in the very word fiancée."[25]

4.16   Returning to the wording of article 12(3) of the 1994 Order, it will be noted that the testator's intention must be apparent from the will itself. Extrinsic evidence of this intention is not therefore admissible. This confirms what was widely believed to be the case but conveniently removes the last

---

[22] This is similar to the approach of the New Zealand judiciary who have generally been unprepared to accept that references such as "my fiancée [name]" are more than a description of an existing state of affairs. They do not, without more, connote a changing state of affairs: *Burton* v *McGregor* [1953] NZLR 487; *Public Trustee* v *Crawley* [1973] 1 NZLR 695; *Re Whale* [1977] 2 NZLR 1. For a useful review of some of the New Zealand authorities see Edwards and Langstaff "A Will to Survive Marriage" [1975] 39 Conv 121.

[23] [1975] 1 All ER 675.

[24] In fact the spouse's statutory legacy would have exhausted the entire estate, whilst under the will she was entitled to less than half.

[25] At p 680. Note, however, that the Law Reform Committee was of the opinion that the use of the word fiancée should not be conclusive.

vestiges of uncertainty which existed under its predecessor, which had been silent on the matter.[26]

4.17 The substantive change introduced by the 1994 Order is contained in article 12(4). The Wills Act (Amendment) Act (NI) 1954 required the actual will to be made in contemplation of marriage. In contrast, the 1994 Order saves individual gifts within a will if it is clear from the will that those gifts were made in expectation of the marriage. In addition, the other gifts in the will remain effective unless there is a clear intention to the contrary.

4.18 The difference is well illustrated by *Re Coleman*, the facts of which have just been discussed. It will be recalled that in this case there were large gifts of residue which had not been given to Mr Coleman's fiancée, and it was on this basis that Megarry J held that the will had not been made in contemplation of marriage, as was required by s 177 of the Law of Property Act 1925 and that it had thus been revoked on marriage. In doing so the learned judge appeared to substitute a much stricter test for the one adopted by Davies J in *Re Langston* ("did the testator express the fact that he was contemplating marriage to a particular person?"). In *Coleman* this test had clearly been satisfied.

A will similar to that in *Coleman* made on or after 1 January 1995 would not be revoked by the testator's subsequent marriage.

4.19 It should be remembered that a will made "in contemplation of marriage" is not *per se* conditional upon the marriage taking place, although it is possible to execute a will which is conditional upon marriage.[27]

Powers of appointment

4.20 Unlike the previous exception, the provision saving various powers of appointment from revocation on the subsequent marriage of the testator dates from the enactment of the Wills Act 1837.[28] The language has recently been updated by the 1994 Order but no substantive change has been made.

4.21 The rule can be complex and is probably best introduced by considering its rationale. It has been noted that the purpose of the general rule

---

[26] The weight of judicial authority was against allowing evidence of surrounding circumstances to be relied upon - see in particular, Megarry J in *Re Coleman* [1975] 1 All ER 675. Cf *Sallis* v *Jones* [1936] P 43; *Pilot* v *Gainfort* [1931] P 103.

[27] See para 1.12 *supra*.

[28] S 18.

revoking a will on a testator's marriage is the protection of spouses and children. This same principle underlies the exception relating to powers of appointment. If a power of appointment is revoked, it will obviously be those entitled in default who will benefit, provided that the power is not re-exercised by another will. Thus, if the class of person entitled in default is broadly the spouse and the children, the object of the legislature would be achieved by revoking the power of appointment. If, on the other hand, different persons were to benefit on default there would be nothing to be gained from revocation. To this end, section 18 of the 1837 Act provided that an appointment made by will was not revoked by the subsequent marriage of the testator if "the real or personal estate thereby appointed would not in default of appointment pass to his or her heir, customary heir, executor, or administrator, or the person entitled as his or her next-of-kin under the Statute Of Distributions". Only gifts in default to the actual *class* specified revoked the power. The appointment was unrevoked if those entitled in default were *individuals*, even though members of the class.[29]

4.22   When the Statute of Distributions (Ir) 1695 was replaced by the Administration of Estates Act (NI) 1955, it was uncertain whether "next of kin under the Statute of Distributions" was to be considered to be "next of kin under the 1955 Act".[30] Article 12(2) of the 1994 Order now removes this doubt:

> "A disposition in a will in exercise of a power of appointment takes effect notwithstanding the testator's subsequent marriage unless the property so appointed would in default of appointment pass to his personal representatives."

4.23   If the exception in article 12(2) operates it saves only the appointment and not the remainder of the will.[31]

Termination of marriage by divorce or annulment
4.24   The subsequent termination of a testator's marriage does not *revoke* a pre-existing will, but for deaths on or after 1 January 1995 any gifts therein to the former spouse pass as if the former spouse had predeceased the testator. These provisions are discussed in Chapter Seven.

---

[29] *In the Goods of Fitzroy* (1858) 1 Sw & Tr 133 (children); *In the Goods of Russell* (1890) 15 PD 111 (brothers and sisters).

[30] Mitchell, *The Revocation of Testamentary Appointments on Marriage*, (1951) 67 LQR 351 and the contrary view in note by Russell at (1952) 68 LQR 455.

[31] *In the Goods of Russell* (1890) 15 PD 111. As to the form in which probate will be granted, see *Re Poole* [1919] P 10.

Revocation by another will

4.25 The execution of a later will, which either contains an express revocation clause or impliedly revokes the earlier document, is the most common method of voluntary revocation. It should be remembered, however, that execution of a later will does not *per se* revoke an earlier one:

> "The mere fact of making a subsequent testamentary paper does not work a total revocation of a prior one, unless the latter expressly, or in effect, revoke the former, or the two be incapable of standing together."[32]

It has already been noted[33] that the date of the execution of a will must be proved to the satisfaction of the Master before the will can be admitted to probate. The importance of dating all wills should be evident.

Express revocation

4.26 The vast majority of wills contain express clauses revoking all earlier wills and codicils and it is standard practice to insert an express revocation clause, typically along the lines "... and I hereby revoke all former wills and other testamentary dispositions heretofore made by me" near the beginning of a professionally drafted will. No particular form of words is prescribed, but the common declaration that starts a will, "this is the *last* will and testament of ..." is not generally construed as a clause which revokes all former testamentary dispositions.[34] A revocation clause need not be so widely drawn and may merely revoke part of a will or particular clauses within it. This sort of clause is naturally more common in a codicil.

4.27 The rule that a testator must know and approve the contents of his will was discussed in Chapter Two. This rule is not limited to the dispositive clauses but extends to all the contents, including revocation clauses. Indeed, the fact that a disproportionately large number of cases concerning knowledge and approval involve revocation clauses would suggest that a number of persons (including the professional draftsman) fall into the trap of inserting such clauses mechanically.

---

[32] *Per* Lord Penzance in *Lemage* v *Goodban* (1865) 1 P & D 57 at 62.

[33] See para 3.62 *supra*.

[34] *Simpson* v *Foxon* [1907] P 54; "this is the last and only will of me" held by Sir Gorell Barnes P not to constitute an express revocation clause or to effect revocation by implication; followed by Bateson J in *Kitcat* v *King* [1930] P 266.

4.28   A prime illustration which involved pre-printed will forms is *Re Phelan*.[35] A testator mistakenly believed that his various stocks and shares had to be dealt with in separate units, so he promptly executed a separate home-made will for each block; in none of which he managed to strike out the revocation clause. The wills dealt with different stocks and shares and were not inconsistent. Stirling J, relying on *Re Morris*,[36] granted probate to the wills with the revocation clauses deleted. This decision was followed by the Northern Ireland High Court in *Re Murphy*,[37] a case which concerned a professionally drafted will. The testator's first will gave one of his farms to his brother but did not contain a residue clause; his second will left his other farm to his nephew and went on to declare "it is not my wish at present to dispose of the rest of my property". The solicitor who drafted this second document had inserted a standard revocation clause "as a matter of course". Kelly J, as he then was, ordered deletion of the revocation clause, commending the approach of Stirling J as "sensible and realistic ....I look to all the circumstances to find the deceased's intentions".[38]

4.29   It is still the case, however, that a revocation clause raises a presumption of revocation and will not be lightly disregarded.[39]

Implied revocation
4.30   If a subsequent testamentary document is inconsistent, either wholly or partly, with one of an earlier date, then the latter instrument will revoke the former to the extent that they are inconsistent and cannot stand together. Thus if they are totally inconsistent only the later in time will be admitted to probate. If they are only partly inconsistent both will be admitted with the earlier revoked to the extent of the inconsistency. In *Re Bryan*[40] the testatrix's second will, which did not contain an express revocation clause, did not dispose of the residue of her property, whereas an earlier will did. However, because the substance of the two wills varied so much, Sir Gorell Barnes P held that the second was completely inconsistent with the first. The latter was thus revoked and consequently there was an intestacy as to the residue.

---

[35] [1971] 3 All ER 1256.

[36] Discussed at para 2.42 *supra*.

[37] (1980) 3 NIJB.

[38] At p 4. For earlier examples of revocation clauses being omitted see *In the Goods of Oswald* (1874) 3 P & D 162; *In the Goods of Moore* [1892] P 378; *Marklew v Turner* (1900) 17 TLR 10.

[39] Eg, *Collins v Elstone* [1893] P 1, discussed at para 2.38 *supra*.

[40] [1907] P 125.

Revocation by revival of a previously revoked will

4.31   Revival of a previously revoked will has the effect that the revived will is deemed to have been executed at the time of revival.[41] Thus this may have the effect of revoking, impliedly or expressly, a will made after the first execution but before the revival of the revived will.

Revocation declared in a document which has been executed in the same manner as a will

4.32   Article 14(1)(c) of the 1994 Order provides for revocation "by some writing, declaring an intention to revoke the will, executed in the same manner in which a will is required to be executed". This corresponds to section 20 of the Wills Act 1837. For example, the signed and attested words "we are witnesses to the erasure of the above" written below a codicil, the contents of which had been completely obliterated have been held to revoke a will in the above manner.[42] In addition, this provision has been extended judicially to a properly attested request to destroy a testamentary document: "will you please destroy the will already made out", which was sent to the bank manager to whose custody the will had been entrusted.[43]

Revocation by destruction

4.33   Article 14 of the 1994 Order provides that a will may be revoked by the burning, tearing or otherwise destroying of it by the testator or by someone else in his presence and at his direction. This re-enacts, without amendment, the former law which was contained in section 20 of the Wills Act 1837.

"Burning, tearing or otherwise destroying"

4.34   In general, this phrase has been given a restrictive interpretation and its exact terms must be adhered to. In *Stephens* v *Taprell*[44] Sir Herbert Jenner held that "otherwise destroying" should be construed *ejusdem generis*, so that simply striking a pen through the contents of a will would not effect a valid revocation:[45]

> "It appears to me quite impossible to put such a construction upon the Act as to say that cancelling a will, by striking it

---

[41] See para 4.67 *post*.
[42] *In the Goods of Gosling* (1886) 11 PD 79.
[43] *Re Spracklan's Estate* [1938] 2 All ER 345.
[44] (1840) 2 Curt 458.
[45] Under the Statute of Frauds (Ir) 1695 (the predecessor of the Wills Act 1837) "cancelling or obliterating" did revoke a will. Sir Herbert seemed influenced by the fact that the Report of the Commissioners on Real Property had originally retained these words but they were later omitted by the legislature.

through with a pen, is a destruction of the will. When the legislature, after mentioning 'burning' a will, and 'tearing' a will, speak of 'otherwise destroying' a will, they must be understood as intending some mode of destruction *ejusdem generis*, not an act which is *not* destroying in the primary meaning of the word, though it may have the sense metaphorically, as being a destruction of the contents of the will; it never could have been their intention that the cancelling of a will should be a mode of destroying it."[46]

4.35   In another well-known case a testator put his pen through the contents of his will, and wrote on the back "this is revoked". He threw it in a wastepaper basket from where it was rescued by a servant. In due time his executors sought to prove it and it was held that the will had not been revoked in accordance with the section as there had been no *actual* destruction or injury and a mere symbolical destruction was outside the scope of section 20 of the 1837 Act.[47]

4.36   To effect revocation of the entire will it is not necessary to destroy the document completely. It is enough if there has been a destruction of so much as to impair the entirety of the will, so that it may be said that the will does not exist in the manner framed by the testator.[48]   Thus destruction of fundamental parts of the will, such as the signatures of the testator or attesting witnesses, will revoke the whole will. In the words of Sir Herbert Jenner:

> "I consider the name of the testator to be essential to the existence of a will, and that, if that name be removed the essential part of the will is removed and the will is destroyed."[49]

4.37   If, however, the mutilation or destruction of the will is not such as to raise an inference that it was done *animo revocandi* of the *whole* will, probate will be granted to the will in its mutilated state. An example of this is found in the case *Re Everest*,[50] in which a will was found after the testator's death with the lower part of the first page cut away. A number of pages remained and Lane J held that the testator had intended these to be effective. In contrast,

---

[46] *Per* Sir Herbert Jenner at p 465.
[47] *Cheese* v *Lovejoy* (1877) 2 PD 251. It has been suggested that it is reasonable that a testator should have the option of revoking his will by striking it through with a pen. The Law Reform Committee did look at the desirability of such a change in the law but decided against it because of the small number of wills involved (approximately 2 or 3 in 29000) (Cmnd 7902 (1980), para 3.40).
[48] *Reed* v *Harris* (1867) 6 Ad & E 209 followed by Sir Herbert Jenner in *Hobbs* v *Knight* (1838) 1 Curt 768.
[49] *Hobbs* v *Knight* (1838) 1 Curt 768 at p 779. See also *Re Woodward* (1871) LR 2 P&D 206.
[50] [1975] 1 All ER 672.

where a testator had destroyed the first two pages of a five page will, it had the effect of destroying the validity of the whole will because the later pages were practically unintelligible and unworkable as a testamentary document in the absence of the earlier ones.[51]

4.38 The most recent discussion of the scope of "otherwise destroying" was in *Re Adams*[52] in which the above dictum of Sir Herbert Jenner on the removal of the signature was approved. A document which purported to be a will was found after the testatrix's death, heavily over-scored with a ball-point pen. The depth of the over-scoring varied from page to page; some of the dispositive contents remained legible but others did not. Most importantly, the signatures of the testatrix and the attesting witnesses could no longer be read. The first question was whether over-scoring with a pen could amount to an "otherwise destroying", in view of the authorities, which were clear that "cancelling or obliterating" generally did not. If this was answered in the affirmative, the next question was whether the entire will had been revoked by destruction of only part. On the first issue, Mr Francis Ferris QC, sitting as a Deputy High Court Judge, relied on an *obiter dictum* of Sir Herbert Jenner in *Hobbs* v *Knight*:

> "It was said in argument ... that a will cannot now be revoked by obliteration, the term obliteration being advisedly omitted by the legislature; but I am not prepared to say (although I now merely throw this out) that a will may not be revoked in that way, for I see no reason why, if the obliteration amounts to a destruction of the will (that is the name of the testator which is essential to a will, be so obliterated that it cannot be made out) a will may not be revoked in that way as in any other."[53]

4.39 Sir Herbert then proceeded to discuss the relationship between revocation and the provisions for *alteration* contained in section 21 of the Wills Act 1837 (in Northern Ireland now article 11 of the 1994 Order), which provided:

> "No obliteration, interlineation, or other alteration, made in any will after the execution thereof shall be valid, or have any effect, except so far as the words, or effect of the will before such alteration, shall not be apparent."

4.40 If this provision which is couched in the negative is turned around to a positive form, unattested alterations have the effect of *revoking* words which

---

[51] *Leonard* v *Leonard* [1902] P 243.
[52] [1990] 2 WLR 924.
[53] (1838) 1 Curt 768 at 780.

have been obliterated by them and which are no longer apparent. Thus the issue for Mr Ferris in *Adams* had now changed to whether or not the words in question were *apparent*. From the authorities it was clear that words were "apparent" if they could be deciphered by an expert with his naked eye or with the help of a magnifying glass[54] without interfering with the overlaid substance.[55] The testatrix's signature could not be made out in this way, and the entire will was held to be revoked.

By the testator or someone else in his presence and at his direction

4.41   Destruction when the testator is not present will not revoke his will,[56] and it is not possible for a testator later to ratify a destruction of his will carried out either in his absence or without his authority.[57]

4.42   This may create problems for the testator who is abroad and who wishes to revoke his will. By an extension of the provision which allows revocation by a document executed in the same manner as a will, it has been held that it is possible for a testator to 'delegate' revocation of his will in his absence by sending properly signed and attested instructions to a third party directing them to destroy the will.[58] It is, however, preferable for such a person to execute a new will expressly revoking the earlier one.

With the intention that the will should be revoked

4.43   Destruction of a will carried out by mistake or by accident will not revoke it. There must be an intention to revoke (*animo revocandi*):

> "... all the destroying in the world without intention will not revoke a will, nor all the intention in the world without destroying: there must be the two."[59]

Thus probate was granted to a will which had been torn up by the testator when he was under the influence of drink but which he had pasted together again in the cold light of morning.[60] Similarly, a codicil was admitted to probate after

---

[54] *Ffinch* v *Combe* [1894] P 191.

[55] For a fuller discussion of these authorities, see para 4.65 *post*.

[56] *Re Gilliland* [1937] NI 156; also *In the Estate of Kremer* (1965) 110 SJ 18, in which a solicitor who burnt a will while testatrix was on the other side of a telephone line was guilty of a "considerable professional error". See also *In the Goods of Dodds* (1857) Dea & Sw 290, testator in another room, held not to be in his presence.

[57] *Gill* v *Gill* [1909] P 157 (will torn up by the testator's wife after he had irritated her when drunk; in his presence but not by his authority). See also *Mills* v *Millward* (1890) 15 PD 20.

[58] See para 4.32 *supra*.

[59] *Per* James LJ in *Cheese* v *Lovejoy* (1877) 2 PD 251, quoting Dr Deane in the court below.

[60] *In the Goods of Brassington* [1902] P 1.

the testatrix had directed her nieces to tear it up because she mistakenly believed that her mixing up its date (March day of 21st) invalidated it.[61] The destruction must be that which the testator intended; when a testator started to tear up his will, but had only torn it into four pieces when stopped, partly by the apologies of the beneficiary who had been the object of his annoyance, it was held that the will had not been revoked.[62]

4.44 A further factor which is relevant to this issue of intention is the mental capacity of the testator. The mental capacity required to revoke a will is the same as that required to execute one; in *Re Sabatini*[63] Baker J refused to accept that a lesser standard of mental awareness would suffice to destroy a will. For instance, wills destroyed by testators when drunk,[64] or suffering from delirium tremens[65] or softening of the brain[66] have been held not to have been revoked.

Revocation of a will does not effect revocation of a codicil

4.45 Prior to the enactment of the Wills Act 1837, a codicil automatically perished when the will was revoked. The Wills Act reversed this rule and now if the codicil itself has not been revoked in accordance with article 14 of the 1994 Order it will be admitted to probate. Whether or not it will be effective thereafter, without a supporting will, is a matter of construction.[67]

No revocation presumed by change in circumstances

4.46 Article 14(2) of the 1994 Order[68] provides that no will is revoked by any presumption of an intention on the ground of alteration in circumstances. Marriage is thus unique amongst the milestones of life as the only one which effects an automatic revocation of previous wills. The fact that events such as the birth of a first child or accretion of considerable wealth do not have an effect on a person's will, makes it particularly important that wills are reviewed regularly and not considered lifelong.

---

[61] *In the Estate of Thornton* (1889) 14 PD 82 (the solicitor had pasted it together again when it had been sent to him with the instructions to prepare a new draft for execution; the testatrix died before this was executed). See also *Clarkson v Clarkson* (1862) 2 Sw & Tr 497 (will burnt because it was erroneously believed that it had already been revoked).

[62] *Doe'd Perkes v Perkes* (1820) 3 B & Ald 489.

[63] (1969) 114 SJ 35.

[64] *Re Brassington* [1902] P 1.

[65] *Brunt v Brunt* (1873) 3 P & D 37.

[66] *In the Goods of Hine* [1893] P 282.

[67] *In the Goods of Turner* (1872) LR 2 P & D 403.

[68] Formerly Wills Act 1837, s 19.

4.47   Although termination of marriage by divorce or annulment does not revoke a will, provisions introduced by the 1994 Order will cause gifts in a will to a former spouse to fail. This is discussed in more detail at paragraph 7.51 below.

Dependent relative revocation

4.48   The essence of 'voluntary' revocation is that there is an *intention* to revoke. This intention may be absolute or conditional. Where it is conditional, the revocation will not be effective unless the condition is satisfied. If therefore revocation is shown to be conditional upon a particular fact, the revocation is ineffective if the condition is not satisfied and the will remains valid. 'Dependent relative revocation' is the term which has been adopted for this doctrine, although on occasions the simpler 'conditional revocation' has been preferred.[69]

4.49   The doctrine of dependent relative revocation has been employed most frequently where the revocation of a will is conditional upon the validity of a later one. For instance, a testator executes will A and a few years later executes will B. Assuming will B to be valid, he then revokes will A by destruction. In the event will B transpires to be invalid. If the court is satisfied that will A was only revoked *on the condition* that will B would be valid, will A has not actually been revoked.

4.50   In the formative years from its inception[70] the doctrine was limited to the following sequence: making a second will, *followed* by the revocation of the first.[71] By the turn of the twentieth century it had been extended to the situation where a testator had destroyed the old will *before* the new one had been executed.[72] Since then, the doctrine has been further developed so that if the truth of a particular fact is a condition of the revocation, and the fact turns out not to be true, the revocation has not been effective. In *Adams v Southerden*[73] a testator burnt his will under the mistaken belief that his wife would get everything on his intestacy. The English Court of Appeal applied the doctrine, the first time that it had been given consideration in that particular forum.

---

[69] "The name of this doctrine seems to me to be somewhat overloaded with unnecessary polysyllables"; *per* Langton J in *Re Hope-Brown* [1942] P 136. See also Roskill LJ in *Re Jones* [1976] Ch 200 at 212.

[70] The earliest application of the case would appear to be *Onions* v *Tyrer* (1716) 1 P Wms 343.

[71] Although see *Re Appelbee* (1828) 1 Hag Ecc 143.

[72] *Dixon* v *Treasury Solicitor* [1905] P 42.

[73] [1925] P 177.

Similarly, in *Re Carey*[74] it was held that the destruction of a will by the testator because he believed that he had nothing to leave was conditional upon this fact. Thus when the testator later inherited under his sister's intestacy the revocation was held not to be effective.

4.51 Whether the condition has been satisfied depends on the facts of each particular case. In the case of the condition being the validity of a second will, it will be established more readily if both the wills are in the same or very similar terms.[75]

4.52 The intention or *animo revocandi* of the testator is clearly central to the doctrine of dependent relative revocation. Yet on occasions the judiciary have blatantly imputed to testators an intention which was never actually present. For instance, the courts have often applied the doctrine to cases where the purported 'condition' for the revocation of an earlier will was the validity of a later will, simply on the basis that it could be established that the testator had revoked the first will, intending to make a second will.[76] This liberal tide has since been stemmed to a degree in *Re Jones*[77] when the English Court of Appeal held that the trial judge had misdirected himself in asking the following questions:

> "Did she cut her will with the intention of revoking it and dying intestate, or did she do so because she was determined to make some fresh testamentary dispositions?"

All three members of the Court of Appeal agreed that a mere intention to make a new will, however clearly shown, is not enough in itself to make revocation conditional. Goff LJ framed the proper test as:

> "Was the revocation absolute and unqualified, in which case it does not take effect, unless the condition be satisfied?"[78]

4.53 A Northern Ireland illustration of the application of the doctrine is found in *Sterling v Bruce*,[79] a decision of Jones LJ in the Northern Ireland High Court. The testatrix in question, a Miss McCalla, had enjoyed the reputation of prolific will-making throughout her life. Generally she had instructed her

---

[74] (1977) 121 SJ 173.
[75] *Re Faris* [1911] IR 469.
[76] *In the Estate of Bromham* [1951] 2 TLR 1149; *In the Estate of Green* (1962) 106 SJ 1034; *In the Estate of Addison* (1964) 108 SJ 504.
[77] [1976] Ch 200.
[78] *Ibid* at p 216.
[79] [1973] NI 255.

solicitors to do whatever was necessary, but some months before her death she had sent one of her named executors to collect her most recent will from their office. It was never seen again. After her death a sealed envelope was found, containing what obviously purported to be a new will. In the event, however, the learned judge felt unable to find that this document had been validly executed - the writing was of varying quality and the entirety of the bequests was not continuous. However, Jones LJ proceeded to hold that the former will (presumed to be destroyed by burning although a copy did exist from which the contents could be proved) had not been revoked since the condition had not been satisfied:

> "... because she was under the impression that she had made another effective will and that the [earlier] will was destroyed by her, and so revoked, because and only because, she had as she thought substituted for it an effective disposition, namely the [later] will ... in other words her *animus revocandi* had only a conditional existence, the condition being the validity of the paper ... intended to be substituted."[80]

ALTERATION OF WILLS AND CODICILS

4.54   Article 11 of the 1994 Order is the provision which regulates the alteration of wills:

> "No obliteration, interlineation or other alteration made in any will, after its execution, is valid, or has any effect except so far as the words or effect of the will before the alteration are not apparent, unless the alteration is executed in the manner in which a will is required to be executed; but the will, with the alteration as part of it, is duly executed if the signature of the testator and the subscription of the witnesses are made in the margin, or on some other part of the will opposite or near to the alteration, or at the foot or end of or opposite a memorandum referring to the alteration and written at the end of some other part of the will."

This re-enacts, without amendment, section 21 of the Wills Act 1837.

The law can be summarised as follows.

> (a)   If the alteration, interlineation or obliteration has been made *before* the execution of the will it is valid and there is no requirement to comply with the procedures

---

[80] At p 266.

prescribed in article 11. There is a rebuttable presumption, however, that alterations and interlineations were made *after* execution, so there may be some difficulty in proving that they were made beforehand.

(b)   For an alteration, interlineation or obliteration which has been made *after* the execution of the will to take effect as part of the will or codicil, that alteration, interlineation or obliteration must have been intended by the testator to form part of his will and be signed and attested in compliance with article 11.

(c)   An alteration, interlineation or obliteration which is unattested, and which cannot be shown to have been made before the execution of the will, will have no effect and probate will be granted to the original provisions before alteration.   If, however, the unattested alteration or obliteration is such that the original is not "apparent" the original will be taken to have been revoked.   In this case probate is not granted to the unattested alteration but in blank.

4.55   Before these points are discussed in more detail, a couple of practical caveats should be noted.   First, it is generally preferable to execute a new will rather than rely upon the correct method of effecting an alteration.   This is particularly the case if the alteration is anything other than the most minor error in a name or address, or unless the testator is *in extremis*.   Secondly, the difficulties in proving that *alterations* were made before execution should be anticipated, and all alterations, whenever made, should be carried out in accordance with article 11.   The attestation clause should recite this fact.

Need to prove that unattested alterations, interlineations and obliterations were made after execution

4.56   Rule 11(1) of the Non-Contentious Probate Rules[81] provides that where a will contains any obliteration, interlineation, or other alteration which is not authenticated in the requisite manner, the Master shall require evidence to show whether the alteration was present at the time the will was executed.

---

[81]RSC O 97.

Presumption that alterations, interlineations and obliterations were made after execution

4.57   There is a rebuttable presumption that unattested alterations, interlineations and obliterations are made after execution.[82] The presumption can be rebutted by internal evidence from the document itself, or by extrinsic evidence or by a combination of both.[83] For example the presumption has been rebutted where interlineations were made in the same ink and hand as the rest of the will, and gave sense to otherwise unintelligible sentences.[84] The mere fact, however, that the alterations are dated before the will may not be enough.[85] The most obvious external evidence is direct proof from the draftsman or an attesting witness.[86] Declarations of the testator himself before or at the time of execution are admissible.[87]

4.58   The presumption is more easily rebutted if the alterations are 'trifling': in *Re Hindmarsh*[88] Sir J P Wilde held that alterations of no real consequence to the will of a lawyer who presumably was familiar with the statutory forms were made after execution. This proposition is endorsed by the Non-Contentious Probate Rules which provide that the Master need not require evidence to show whether an alteration was present at the time the will was executed if the alteration appears to him to be of 'no practical importance'.[89]

4.59   It will be recalled that a testator is free to write his will in whatever medium he chooses.[90] If, however, a will is written in a mixture of ink and pencil, there is a presumption that the pencil marks are deliberative only.[91]

The effect of republishing a codicil

4.60   A subsequent codicil republishes a will,[92] so if the alterations to a will are made before the execution of the codicil, the will is republished in its altered form. If, however, the codicil does not refer to the alterations, there is a presumption that they were made after the execution of the codicil.[93] It is

---

[82] *Re Adamson* (1875) LR 3 P & D 253.
[83] *In the Goods of Benn* [1938] IR 313.
[84] *In the Goods of Cadge* (1868) LR 1 P & D 543. Also *Birch v Birch* (1848) 1 Rob Ecc 675; *Re Tonge* (1891) 66 LT 60.
[85] *Re Adamson* (1875) LR 3 P & D 253.
[86] *Keigwin v Keigwin* (1843) 3 Curt 607.
[87] *Doe'd Shallcross v Palmer* (1851) 16 QB 747; *In the Goods of Sykes* (1873) LR 3 P & D 26.
[88] (1866) 1 P & D 307.
[89] R 11 (1).
[90] See para 3.09 *supra*.
[91] *In the Goods of Adams* (1872) LR 2 P & D 367.
[92] See para 4.79 *post*.
[93] *Lushington v Onslow* (1848) 6 NC 183.

different if the codicil takes account of the alterations. For instance, in *Re Heath*[94] the testator had originally given his executor a legacy of £10,000, which was increased by a further £1000 by an unattested alteration. In a subsequent codicil he recited the fact that he had given the executor £11,000. Probate was granted to the will with its alteration, as it had been republished as such by the codicil.

Effecting alterations in accordance with article 11

4.61 Article 11 of the 1994 Order requires that the alteration or inter-lineation or obliteration be signed by the testator and subscribed by witnesses, thus following the procedure prescribed for the execution of the will itself.

4.62 It is acceptable for the testator and witnesses merely to initial the alteration, provided that the initials are intended to represent their signatures.[95] By analogy with the cases on what constitutes the testator's signature for the purposes of execution of the will itself, any sort of mark which is intended to represent the signature is adequate.[96]

4.63 The signatures must be placed in the margin or some other part of the will, opposite or near to the alteration. Alternatively, a memorandum may be drafted, either at the end of the will or at some other part of it, which refers to the alteration *and* the signatures of the testator and two witnesses placed at the foot or end or opposite to the memorandum.[97]

4.64 This procedure must be followed exactly. In *Re Shearn*[98] an omission from a will was discovered shortly after execution and corrected by a small interlineation which was initialled by the two witnesses in the margin. The testatrix herself did not initial the insertion, although it was alleged that she had acknowledged her previous signature to the will itself before the witnesses had initialled the alteration. It was held that the interlineation had not been properly executed.[99] This decision has recently been approved by Mr Andrew Park QC, sitting as a Deputy High Court Judge in *Re White*.[100] In *White* a testator purported to alter his will three years after its execution, and as in *Shearn* the witnesses signed the alteration but the testator did not. Clearly the requisite

---

[94] [1892] P 253.
[95] *In the Goods of Blewitt* (1880) 5 PD 116.
[96] See para 3.15 *supra*.
[97] For an example of such, see *In the Goods of Treeby* (1875) LR 3 P & D 242.
[98] (1880) 50 LJP 15.
[99] Although see *In the Goods of Dewell* (1853) 1 Ecc J Ad 103.
[100] [1990] 3 All ER 1.

procedure for validating alterations had not been complied with as the changes had not been signed by the testator. Moreover the novel argument that the alteration of the will and subsequent attesting by the witnesses amounted to the execution of a new will, during which the testator had acknowledged his three year old signature before the witnesses had initialled the document, was rejected.[101]

Unattested alterations, interlineations and obliterations which make the original not "apparent"

4.65   It is now well established that to be "apparent" the original wording of the will must be decipherable by handwriting experts using their naked eyes or scientific instruments such as magnifying glasses or more unorthodox gadgets.[102] If the obliteration has been caused by the will being overlaid with a substance, such as ink or paint, it is not permissible to remove that substance in order to read what is underneath.[103] Likewise paper pasted over the original cannot be removed and if the original words can only be made out by way of infra-red photography they are not apparent.[104]

Privileged wills

4.66   Privileged wills are not subject to the statutory rules contained in article 11 of the 1994 Order. There is a presumption that if alterations or obliterations have been made to a privileged will they were made during the continuance of the military service.[105]

REVIVAL AND REPUBLICATION

Meaning of terms

4.67   "Revival" is the "re-activation" of a will which has previously been revoked. "Republication" (which has now been changed in name to "confirmation") simply confirms a will which is still subsisting. Both revival and republication have in common the fact that they cause the will to have effect as if it had been first executed on the date of revival or republication.

---

[101]But would this argument be different following the decision in *Wood* v *Smith* [1992] 3 All ER 556? See para 3.26 *supra*.

[102]In *Ffinch* v *Combe* [1894] P 171 opaque brown paper was used to border the will which was then held up to a window panel. See also *Re Brasier* [1899] P 36.

[103]*In the Goods of Itter* [1950] P 130; *Re Adams* [1990] 2 WLR 924.

[104]*In the Goods of Itter, ibid.*

[105]*In the Goods of Tweedale* (1874) LR 3 P & D 204; *In the Goods of Newland* [1952] 1 All ER 841.

The term "republication" is something of an anachronism which dates from pre-1837, when one of the formalities required of a testator was the publication of his will.[106] Before 1837 wills of realty were not ambulatory, so bringing a will "forward in time" often had a significant impact. However, republication lost much of its practical utility after the enactment of the 1837 Act. "Confirmation", the term now adopted in the 1994 Order, is much more appropriate at expressing the true effect of republication in modern times.

Revival of a revoked will

4.68   Article 15 of the 1994 Order provides that a revoked will may *only* be revived in the following ways:

(a)   by re-execution of the revoked will, or;

(b)   by a codicil showing an intention to revive the will.

This introduces no changes to the former law as contained in section 22 of the 1837 Act.

4.69   No other method effects a revival. For instance, the revocation of a will which itself revoked a former will, does not revive that earlier will. In *Re Hodgkinson*[107] the testator executed a will leaving all his property to a named beneficiary. A few months later he executed a second will (with no revocation clause) which effectively left all his real property to someone else. He subsequently revoked this second will by cutting off his signature. At first instance it was held that as the second will had been revoked, it was effectively not in existence at all, so the first will was still valid. This was overturned by the Court of Appeal which emphasised that the only methods of revival were the two mentioned in section 22 of the Wills Act 1837. Probate was therefore granted to the first will limited only to personalty.

By a codicil showing an intention to revive the revoked will

4.70   Article 15 of the 1994 Order requires that the codicil show an *intention* to revive the revoked will. Much greater evidence of intention is required than that necessary to confirm or republish a will and a mere reference to the earlier will is not sufficient. However, it is not necessary that the codicil contain *express* words of revival. Rather:

---

[106]Removed by s 13 of the 1837 Act- "every will....shall be valid without any other publication thereof".
[107][1893] P 339.

> "... the intention must appear on the face of the codicil, either by express words referring to a will as revoked and importing an intention to revive the same, or by a disposition of the testator's property inconsistent with any other intention, or by some other expression conveying to the mind of the court with reasonable certainty the existence of intention."[108]

4.71   Merely attaching a codicil to a revoked will with a piece of tape does not show an intention to revive it.[109]

A codicil expressly referring to a revoked will and showing an intention to revive same

4.72   To effect revival before the 1837 Act it was only necessary to show that the codicil was a codicil of the particular will to be revived. There was thus no requirement of *intention*. Since 1837 much litigation has arisen out of variants of the following chronological sequence of events: first will executed by testator; subsequent will executed expressly or impliedly revoking the former will; codicil executed referring to the earlier, now revoked, will:

> "If experience had not shown the fact, it would be almost incredible that mistakes should occur so constantly as they do in so simple a matter as reciting the true date of a will."[110]

4.73   In such cases the question is obviously the extent to which the reference in the codicil to the now revoked will can be taken as indicating an intention to revive it. The general principle is that the courts have been unprepared to impute an intention to revive an earlier will from the fact of its mere mention, and in consequence have treated it as an error of description. The result is that probate is granted to the later will together with the codicil, with the offending words (those reciting the date of the revoked will) omitted. Cases where this approach was adopted include *Rogers* v *Goodenough*,[111] *Re Alfred Reade*,[112] *Re Lady Isabella Gordon*[113] and *Re Steele*.[114]

4.74   It is different, however, if the codicil refers to the contents of the revoked will as well as its date, showing that the draftsman actually applied his mind to it. An interesting illustration is *Re Chilcott*[115] in which the testatrix's

---

[108]*Re Steele* (1868) LR 1 P&D 575, at 580 quoted with approval in *Re Davis* [1952] P 279.
[109]*Marsh* v *Marsh* (1860) 1 Sw & Tr 528.
[110]*Per* Sir J P Wilde in *Re Steele* (1868) LR 1 P & D 575 at 580.
[111](1862) 2 Sw & Tr 342.
[112][1902] P 75.
[113][1892] P 228.
[114](1868) LR 1 P & D 575.
[115][1897] P 223.

1889 will had been revoked by one executed three years later and which had been drafted by a different solicitor. The following year the solicitor who had been responsible for the first will (and who knew nothing of the second) prepared a codicil which purported to be a codicil of the will of 1889 and confirmed the said 1889 will. Sir Gorell Barnes held that, by its language, the codicil revived the earlier will and *both* wills and the codicil were admitted to probate. The learned judge conceded that this did not express the testatrix's true intention, adding that he could only deal with the documents as they stood.

Some other expression conveying to the mind of the court with reasonable certainty the existence of intention

4.75   In *Re Davis*[116] a testator, on learning that his recent marriage had revoked his will, wrote on the envelope which enclosed the document the words "the herein named X is now my lawful wedded wife". The words were signed and attested in the correct manner. Two questions arose for the court:

    (a)   Did the envelope constitute a codicil?

    (b)   Did it show an intention to revive the will?

The first question was answered in the affirmative. As regards the second, the court was of the opinion that the *only* intention which the deceased could have had was to revive the will.

Effect of revival

4.76   A will which has been revived is deemed to have been made at the time of revival[117] and it thus operates as if it had been executed at that time. An exception exists in relation to the status of illegitimate children and this is discussed in the next chapter.[118]

Will revoked in stages

4.77   If a will has been partially revoked, and at a later date revoked completely, a subsequent revival will not revive that part which was revoked first, unless an intention to the contrary can be shown.[119] Revival of the will *prima facie* only negatives the final revocation.

---

[116][1952] P 279.
[117]Art 16 of the 1994 Order provides "(a) every will which is re-executed is made at the time of the re-execution; (b) every will which is ..... revived by codicil is made at the time of the execution of the codicil." (formerly Wills Act 1837, s 34).
[118]See para 5.29 *post*.
[119]1994 Order, art 15(2) - formerly Wills Act 1837, s 22.

Destroyed will no longer in existence

4.78   If the revoked will has been destroyed and is no longer in existence, revival is not possible.[120]

Republication or confirmation of a will

4.79   It has already been noted that the 1994 Order has adopted the word "confirmation" in place of the anachronistic "republication". This term will be used hereafter.

Confirmation of a will can be effected in two ways:

> (a)   by re-execution of the original will,[121] or;

> (b)   by executing a codicil to that will.

4.80   The codicil need not demonstrate an *intention* to confirm the will, in the sense in which an intention *to revive* must be shown. It is enough if the testator describes the codicil as "the codicil to my will",[122] although it is standard practice for a testator expressly to confirm his will with a phrase along the lines of "in all other respects I confirm my will".

4.81   "Confirmation" of a will means the confirmation of the will *together with* all intervening codicils. Any alterations to the will by such codicils (for instance the revocation of a particular legacy) are therefore unaffected.[123]

4.82   The effect of confirmation, in bringing forward in time a will which has throughout remained valid, has already been noted, as has the fact that this process now has little practical impact. Notwithstanding this, the general rule that a confirmed will operates as if it had been executed at the time of confirmation can still raise some interesting questions as to how the confirmation of a will can alter the meaning and effect of phrases therein. Is the will to be read as having a new starting point for the purposes of construction? It has been suggested[124] that the modern trend has been for the

---

[120]*Rogers* v *Goodenough* (1862) 2 Sw & Tr 342, although Sir C Cresswell left open the question where the will was destroyed without the testator's knowledge.

[121]*Dunn* v *Dunn* (1866) LR 1 P & D 277.

[122]*Re Taylor* (1880) 57 LJ Ch 430, 434; also *Re Harvey* [1947] Ch 285. But see *Re Smith* (1890) 45 Ch D 632 (not mentioned in will - Stirling J held that for confirmation to be implied, something had to be found in the second testamentary instrument from which the inference can be drawn that, when making and executing it, the testator "considered the will as his will").

[123]*Re Fraser* [1904] 1 Ch 726.

[124]See Mitchell, "The Present State of Testamentary Republication" [1954] 70 LQR 351.

courts to be generous in allowing confirmation of a will to alter both the objects and the subject-matter of gifts, provided that this can be done without doing violence to the language of the will.

4.83 Thus if a will contains a description of *persons* to benefit, it has been held to relate to those who fit the description at the date of confirmation. For example, in *Re Hardyman*[125] property was left to the wife of the testatrix's cousin. After execution of the will the said wife died. The testatrix later confirmed her will by a codicil. The cousin remarried and it was held that his second wife could benefit. There is a statutory exception to this rule relating to the status of illegitimate children. This is discussed in the next chapter.[126]

4.84 Gifts of *property* are governed by the same principle. In *Re Reeves*[127] the testator bequeathed his interest in his "present lease", which at that time was an unexpired term of under four years. The testator subsequently acquired a new lease for 12 years and later confirmed his will. It was held that the beneficiary was entitled to the unexpired term of this new lease.[128]

4.85 In conclusion the point should be made that this judicial power has generally been intended as beneficient and nowadays a broad view to interpretation is likely to be taken. One Irish judge has described confirmation of a will as:

> "A useful and flexible instrument for effectuating a testator's intentions, by ascertaining them down to the latest date at which they have been expressed."[129]

In keeping with this beneficient approach, it will not be applied to invalidate a gift which was valid at the date of execution.[130]

Remedy of witnessing failure

4.86 The confirmation of a will which has been attested by a beneficiary or his spouse by a codicil which has been attested by different witnesses will

---

[125]*Re Hardyman* [1925] Ch 287.

[126]See para 5.29 *post*.

[127][1928] Ch 351.

[128]See also *Re Champion* [1893] 1 Ch 101 - the devise of certain freehold property "now in my own occupation".

[129]*Per* Barton J in *Re Moore* [1907] 1 IR 315 at 318.

[130]*Re Park* [1910] 2 Ch 322.

validate the gift in the will. Otherwise, of course, the gift would be void under article 8 of the 1994 Order.[131]

---

[131]*Anderson* v *Anderson* (1872) LR 13 Eq 381; *Re Trotter* [1899] 1 Ch 764; *Gurney* v *Gurney* (1885) 3 Drew 208. See para 3.43 *supra*.

CHAPTER FIVE

CONSTRUCTION OF WILLS

5.01   A chapter of this length can at best scratch the surface of this vast and very complex subject. Accordingly its objective is no more ambitious than to highlight the primary rules of construction. In addition, it provides a suitable home for a miscellany of statutory provisions contained in the Wills and Administration Proceedings (NI) Order 1994 which would otherwise have to go unmentioned.

BASIC RULES OF CONSTRUCTION

5.02   To begin with the basics, the Family Division of the High Court (the "probate court") has jurisdiction to determine any questions about the validity of a will or the identity of those entitled to the grant of representation. By contrast, any questions which arise about the interpretation or construction of a testamentary document which has been admitted to probate are dealt with by the Chancery Division of the High Court (the "court of construction").

5.03   It must be emphasised at the outset that it is not the function of the court of construction to write a new will for a testator[1] and the judiciary are confined to interpreting the words actually used by the testator. The statutory requirement that a will be in writing ensures that it is the language of the will itself[2] which provides the primary evidence of the testator's intention, although extrinsic evidence is admissible as an aid to interpretation in limited circumstances. In the famous words of Lord Simon in *Perrin* v *Morgan*:[3]

> "... the fundamental rule in construing the language of a will is
> to put on the words used the meaning which, having regard to
> the terms of the will, the testator intended. The question is not,
> of course, what the testator meant to do when he made his will,
> but what the written words he uses mean in the particular case,
> what are the 'expressed intentions' of the testator."

5.04   While the phrases and expressions employed in wills are almost as infinite in variety as the number of testators themselves, there have been key

---

[1] *Scalé v Rawlins* [1892] AC 342.

[2] For the limited power to rectify a will, see para 2.44 *supra*.

[3] [1943] AC 399 at p 406.

words which have caused recurring difficulties and over the centuries the judiciary have developed certain 'rules of construction' as an aid to interpretation in cases where there is some doubt about the actual language of the will. However, these rules of construction are not rules of law and if the meaning of the will is entirely clear they have no application:

> "A rule of construction is not a rule of law, and so if their application results in attributing to the testator an intention which appears inconsistent with the scheme of the will as a whole, they are not to prevail."[4]

The following are some of the more important non-statutory rules of construction. They are by no means exhaustive.

The will must be read as a whole

5.05   It has been said that the "fundamental and over-riding duty binding the court is to ascertain the intention of the testator as expressed in his will *read as a whole* [Emphasis added]."[5] For instance, it may be the case that an ambiguous or uncertain provision might be clarified by a clause or definition elsewhere in the will.

Words are given their ordinary meaning

5.06   Subject to a contrary intention, words are presumed to bear their 'ordinary meaning', that is "the strict, plain, common meaning of the words themselves."[6] Where the ordinary meaning of a word has changed with time, it is the meaning at the date of the will which is taken.[7]

This presumption can be rebutted in two ways.

(a)   Under the 'dictionary principle'. This principle applies if it is clear from the will as a whole that the testator intended a meaning other than the ordinary one (ie the testator is said to have supplied his own 'dictionary').[8] A testator who wishes to do this would be well-advised to include an actual definition clause in his will.

---

[4] *Per* Ritchie J in *National Trust Co Ltd* v *Fleury* (1965) 53 DLR 700 at 710.

[5] *Per* Ungoed Thomas J in *Macandrew's Will Trusts* [1963] 3 WLR 822,834. See also *Baddeley* v *Leppingwell* (1764) 3 Burr 1533; *Crumpe* v *Crumpe* [1900] AC 127.

[6] *Per* Tindal LCJ in *Shore* v *Wilson* (1842) 9 Cl & F 355, 565.

[7] *Perrin* v *Morgan* [1949] AC 399.

[8] Eg *Re Davidson* [1949] Ch 670.

(b)   If the ordinary meaning does not make sense, but a secondary meaning does.[9]

Technical words

5.07   There is a rebuttable presumption that technical words or legal phrases are given their technical meaning.[10] This presumption is particularly strong where legal phrases appear in a professionally drafted will,[11] but it also extends to 'home-made' wills. For example, in *Re Cook*[12] a testatrix whose estate consisted primarily of real property simply bequeathed "all my personal property". Harman J reluctantly held that this was not effective to pass the realty, which went on intestacy to persons who would not have benefitted under the will:

> "It seems unlikely that she intended to dispose only of the personal estate in the lawyer's sense of the word ... but this is a case where a layman has chosen to use a term of art. The words 'all my personal estate' are words so well-known to lawyers that it must take a very strong context to make them include real estate. Testators may make black mean white if they make the dictionary sufficiently clear, but the testatrix has not done so..."[13]

Falsa demonstratio

5.08   By virtue of the maxim *falsa demonstratio non nocet cum de corpore constat* a description of a person or thing which is partly true but partly false will not fail provided that the part which is true describes the person or thing with sufficient clarity. The false part is ignored and the gift is able to take effect.

5.09   In addition, the doctrine extends to descriptions which are entirely false provided that the context and surrounding circumstances show unambiguously the intention of the testator.[14]

---

[9] *Re Smalley* [1929] 2 Ch 112 - "wife" meant putative wife not legal wife; *Thorn v Dickens* [1906] WN 54 - by "mother" testator meant his wife.

[10] *Re Harcourt* [1921] 2 Ch 491; *Re Cook* [1948] Ch 212; *Falkiner v Commissioner of Stamp Duties* [1973] AC 565.

[11] *Read v Blackhouse* (1831) 2 Russ & M 546; *Hall v Warren* (1861) 9 HL Cas 420.

[12] [1948] Ch 212.

[13] At p 216.

[14] *Re Brockett* [1908] 1 Ch 185; *Ellis v Bartrum* (1857) 25 Beav 110.

Last of contradictory phrases prevails

5.10   Where there are two contradictory phrases in a will there is a rule of construction that the last is to prevail, the rationale being that this is the final expression of the deceased's wishes.[15]   In a deed the opposite rule applies and the first word or phrase prevails. Thus if a testator leaves property to Abigail and Beatrice "jointly and severally", creating the problem whether they take as joint tenants (as indicated by the word "jointly") or as tenants in common (by the word "severally"), the last word, that is, "severally" prevails. Abigail and Beatrice therefore take as tenants in common. It would seem that this rule is now subject to the provisions of article 28 of the 1994 Order which is discussed below.[16]

MISCELLANEOUS STATUTORY RULES OF CONSTRUCTION

A will speaks from death

5.11   It has been stated repeatedly throughout this work that a will is ambulatory and speaks from death. This principle is given statutory effect in relation to the subject-matter of testamentary gifts by article 17 of the 1994 Order, which re-enacts without amendment, section 24 of the Wills Act 1837. Article 17(1) provides as follows:

> "Every will is to be construed with reference to the property referred to in it, to speak and take effect as if it had been executed immediately before the death of the testator, unless a contrary intention appears from the will."

Thus any description of property *prima facie* includes that which satisfies the description at the date of the testator's death, even if he acquired it after he made his will.[17]   For example, a gift of "my shares in Northern Ireland Electricity" will be construed as the shares the testator owns at his death, unless there is a contrary intention.

5.12   A contrary intention can be shown by express words, for example, if the testator refers to "my shares in Northern Ireland Electricity which I own at

---

[15]*Re Potter's Wills Trusts* [1944] Ch 70, where Lord Greene MR described it as "a rule of despair" (at p 77).

[16]See para 5.16 *post*.

[17]*Langdale* v *Briggs* (1856) 8 De G M & G 391. Prior to 1837 a will was not ambulatory as to realty.

the time of the execution of this will."[18] In addition, one can be implied if the testator describes the subject-matter with such precision that it is clear that an object in existence at the date of the will was intended.

5.13   The statutory presumption is limited to the testator's *property* and does not extend to the objects of his bounty. Thus the converse presumption applies to the beneficiaries of the will and *prima facie* a description of a beneficiary refers to the person satisfying that description at the date of execution of the will and not the date of death.[19]

5.14   It will be recalled that confirmation of a will by a later codicil generally has the effect that the will speaks from the date of the codicil. The implications that this has for issues of construction have already been discussed.[20]

The rule in Wild's Case[21]
5.15   It is convenient to deal with the rule in *Wild's Case* at this point although it is non-statutory in nature.

This rule governs a gift of land "to A and his children". If A has no children when the will is executed A takes a fee tail, a position which remains the same even if A has children before the testator's death. By contrast if A does have children when the will is executed the words "and his children" are regarded as words of purchase, so that A will take jointly with all his children who are living at the testator's death.

The law leans against an intestacy
5.16   Article 28 of the 1994 Order provides that if a gift admits of more than one interpretation, then, in cases of doubt, the interpretation to which the gift will be operative is to be preferred. This therefore puts the principle *ut res magis valeat quam pereat* (ie, the law leans against an intestacy) on a statutory footing.

Article 28 is similar to section 99 of the Republic of Ireland Succession Act 1965. No corresponding statutory provision has been enacted in England.

---

[18]Where the language used is 'now' or 'currently' etc it is not conclusive and it remains a question of construction whether this is the date of execution or the date when the will becomes effective, ie that of death - *Re Evans* [1909] 1 Ch 784.

[19]*Re Whorwood* (1887) 34 Ch D 446; *Amyot v Dwarris* [1904] AC 268.

[20]See para 4.82 *supra*.

[21](1599) 6 Co Rep 16a.

Presumption that the fee simple passes

5.17   It will be recalled that to transfer a fee simple of land by deed *inter vivos* words of limitation are required. Article 18 of the 1994 Order[22] provides that, subject to a contrary intention appearing in the will,[23] a *devise* of land passes the fee simple, or other whole estate of which the testator has power to dispose. Words of limitation are therefore unnecessary. For example, if Teresa holds Rosebud Cottage in fee simple and bequeaths it in her will "to Polly", Polly takes the fee simple.

Presumption as to the effect of gifts to spouses

5.18   Article 23 of the 1994 Order introduces the statutory presumption that a testamentary gift to a spouse in absolute terms should be treated as an absolute gift, notwithstanding that it is followed by words purporting to give issue an interest in the same property.   For example, it happens not uncommonly that a 'home-made' will leaves everything to the wife, but after her death to the children, a formula which might in the absence of article 23 have unintentionally created a mere life interest.

This provision, which corresponds to section 22 of the Administration of Justice Act 1982, operates subject to a contrary intention.[24]

Powers of appointment

5.19   Where a testator fails to exercise a *general* power of appointment[25] which can be exercised by will,[26] article 20 of the 1994 Order[27] provides that the property subject to the power passes under a general or residuary gift in the testator's will.[28]

---

[22]Which re-enacts s 28 of the Wills Act 1837.

[23]Art 18(3).

[24]This intention need only be "shown"; hence extrinsic evidence is admissible to do so.

[25]Ie one where no restrictions are placed upon whom he can appoint. In contrast, a *special* power is exercisable only in favour of the persons specified by the donor and a *hybrid* or *intermediate* power is exercisable in favour of anyone other than the persons specified by the testator.

[26]*Re Powell's Trusts* (1869) 39 LJ Ch 188; *Phillips v Cayley* (1890) 43 Ch D 222.

[27]Which re-enacts s 27 of the Wills Act 1837.

[28]Property subject to a special or a hybrid power is not within the scope of art 20, a pre-requisite of which is that the testator had power to appoint "in any manner he thinks proper".

5.20 Article 20 operates subject to a contrary intention, which must be apparent from the will.[29] The burden of showing such an intention is on the persons asserting it[30] and in practice it will rarely be found. For this reason it is suggested that a testator who wishes to exclude the operation of article 20 should make it very clear that the residuary gift is not intended to constitute an exercise of his general power.

"Die without issue"

5.21 At common law a gift by will in the form "to Andrew but if he dies without issue, to Beatrice" was construed as follows:

    (a)   If the gift was of realty Andrew took a fee tail;

    (b)   If the gift was of personalty (which could not be entailed) Andrew took an absolute interest.

5.22 Article 27 of the 1994 Order, which re-enacts section 29 of the Wills Act 1837, provides that words such as these give Andrew an *absolute* interest, whatever the nature of the property, subject to a gift over to Beatrice should Andrew die without issue. This provision, which operates subject to a contrary intention in the will, applies to any words in a gift which import either the want or failure of issue of any person in his lifetime, or at the time of that person's death or indefinitely. Other examples include "have no issue" or "die without leaving issue". Since Andrew could not know for definite during his lifetime whether the gift to Beatrice would take effect (even if he had issue he could not be entirely sure that any of them would survive him) it is expressly provided that Andrew's interest becomes absolute as soon as any of his issue reach 18 or marry.[31]

Article 27 does not apply to an entail.[32]

Illegitimate and adopted children[33]

Illegitimate persons

5.23 At common law words such as "child" or "issue" in a will were presumed to refer to legitimate persons only[34] and the contrary had to be shown.

---

[29]*Re Thirlwell* [1958] Ch 146.

[30]*Re Jarrett* [1919] 1 Ch 366.

[31]Art 27(3).

[32]Art 27(4).

[33]For the treatment of such persons under the intestacy rules, see para 6.26 and para 6.28 *post*.

This principle was reversed by article 4(1) of the Family Law Reform (NI) Order 1977, which governs wills made on or after 1 January 1978 but before 1 July 1995, and provides that the following rules of construction be applied:

(a)   Any reference (express or implied) to the child or children of any person shall be construed as, or as including, a reference to any illegitimate child of that person; and

(b)   any reference (express or implied) to a person or persons related in some other manner to any person shall be construed as, or as including, a reference to anyone who would be so related if he, or some other person through whom the relationship is deduced, had been born legitimate.

Both of these rules operated subject to a contrary intention so, for example, a bequest 'to my legitimate children' excluded any illegitimate children.

5.24   These rules of construction therefore placed illegitimate and legitimate persons on a more or less equal footing for the purposes of identifying beneficiaries under a will.   In this respect they went much further than the corresponding provisions of the 1977 Order which governed intestate succession.   As has been noted in more detail elsewhere, these merely enabled illegitimate children to inherit on the death intestate of either parent as if they had been born legitimate, but did not extend this equality to the wider family circle.   Thus an illegitimate person could not take on the death intestate of his grandparents or uncles and aunts.   Rather anomalously, a gift in a will to either 'my grandchildren' or 'my nieces' included illegitimate persons who answered the description.

5.25   Nevertheless, there were still limits to the 1977 Order as it related to wills.   Most arose because the equality of treatment provisions were triggered by persons who were *capable of benefitting* so that the identification of persons for other purposes was outside their scope.   For instance, they did not cover a gift 'to my sister absolutely if she dies without leaving children', since the 'children' mentioned were not capable of benefitting.   If the sister in question had no legitimate children she would take absolutely, even though she had illegitimate children.

---

[34]And persons tracing their relationship through legitimate links.   See previous page.

5.26 The current legislation is the Children (NI) Order 1995, which applies to dispositions in wills made on or after 1 July 1995 and removes all but one of the limitations contained in the 1977 Order. The fundamental principle is that in dispositions by will references (express or implied) to any relationship between two persons shall be construed without regard to whether or not the father and mother of either of them or the father and mother of any person through whom the relationship is deduced, have or had been married to each other at the time.[35] This is subject to a contrary intention.[36] Unlike its predecessor, the 1995 Order therefore applies irrespective of whether the reference is to a person who is *capable of benefitting.*

5.27 A further change introduced by the 1995 Order is in relation to the word 'heir' and the creation of entails. The 1977 Order expressly exempted the word 'heir' or any expression used to create an entail from its ambit.[37] Property so subject therefore continued to pass down the legitimate line. However, the 1995 Order[38] provides that, *without more*, the use of the word "heir(s)" or any expression used to create an entail does not show the contrary intention needed to displace the fundamental principle that it is immaterial whether a person's parents were married to each other.

5.28 Only one of the statutory exceptions contained in the 1977 Order[39] has been preserved by the 1995 Order.[40] The common law position (ie legitimate persons or those claiming through a legitimate line only unless there is a contrary intention) still governs property which is limited to devolve with a dignity or title of honour.

5.29 The prospective nature of the above legislation has been noted; the 1977 Order applied to wills made on or after 1 January 1978 and the 1995 Order to those made on or after 1 July 1995. Furthermore for these purposes the confirmation of a will by a later codicil does not bring the will forward in time.[41] A will which was executed *before* commencement but is subsequently

---

[35]Children (NI) Order 1995, art 155 and para 2(1)(b) of Sch 6.

[36]Art 155(5).

[37]1977 Order, art 4(3).

[38]Para 2(2) of Sch 6.

[39]1977 Order, art 4(6).

[40]1995 Order, Sch 6 para 2(4).

[41]For confirmation in general see para 4.67 *supra.*

confirmed by a codicil which is executed *after* commencement, is *not* to be treated as made at the time of the codicil.[42]

Adopted children

5.30 Traditionally adoption was viewed as an artificial relationship and adopted persons were accordingly given very few property rights. The current policy, which is to integrate such persons fully into their adoptive families for all purposes, has been put on a statutory footing by article 40(1) of the Adoption (NI) Order 1987. This provides that an adopted child is treated as the legitimate child of the married couple who adopted him[43] and not as the child of any other person. Subject to a contrary intention, this principle applies to the construction of any will if a testator dies on or after 1 October 1989.[44]

5.31 Property which is limited to devolve with a peerage or dignity or title of honour has been expressly exempted from the scope of the 1987 Order,[45] so the onus is on a testator to make it clear that an adopted person is to benefit from such property.[46]

Words in a will which are defined by the 1994 Order

5.32 Article 26 interprets a number of words and expressions which commonly occur in wills. This provision, which operates unless a contrary intention appears from the will, is reproduced in full in Appendix F.

EXTRINSIC EVIDENCE

5.33 Although the court of construction is generally limited to ascertaining the testator's intention from the actual language which he employed in his will,[47] evidence outside the will is admissible to assist in understanding what the testator meant in limited circumstances. These circumstances have recently been extended by article 25 of the 1994 Order, but since this provision is not retrospective and applies only to wills of testators dying on or after 1 January

---

[42] 1977 Order, art 4(9); 1995 Order, para 2(7) of Sch 6.

[43] Or in any other case the legitimate child of his adopter (in practice this is adoption by an unmarried mother of her child).

[44] Art 42(1). Although note that a similar rule of construction applied under both the Adoption of Children Act (NI) 1950 (s 9(3)) and the Adoption Act (NI) 1967 (s 18(3)).

[45] Art 44(2).

[46] Art 44(3).

[47] Moreover the probate copy is conclusive evidence of the will's contents and the court cannot look at the original (*Oppenheim v Henry* (1853) 9 Hare 802) although it can look at the way in which the will was set out in the original - lay out, punctuation etc (*Houston v Burns* [1918] AC 337; *Morrall v Sutton* (1845) 1 Ph 533, 538).

1995,[48] it is also necessary to consider the common law rules which govern deaths before this date.

Deaths prior to 1 January 1995

5.34 At common law a distinction was made between direct and circumstantial evidence.[49]

5.35 *Direct* extrinsic evidence of a testator's intention was only admissible in cases of equivocation, or to rebut the equitable presumptions relating to satisfaction.[50] There is an equivocation (sometimes called a 'latent' ambiguity)[51] if the description used by the testator to describe beneficiaries or bequests fits two or more persons or things: for example, if a testator makes a gift of his "manor of Dale", but he owns two such manors, North Dale and South Dale;[52] or if she leaves property "to my nephew Arthur Murphy" but has three nephews of that name.[53]

5.36 *Circumstantial* evidence of a testator's intention was admissible under the so-called 'armchair principle' as an aid to interpretation in cases of uncertainty or ambiguity.[54] In such cases the court places itself in the testator's position (in his armchair, so to speak) at the time when he made his will and takes account of all of the facts which were known to him at that time.[55] There was, however, a limit to how far the court was prepared to allow circumstantial evidence to overcome the presumption that a person who completely satisfies the description in a will is entitled to benefit. For example, where a testator had given a legacy to "the National Society for the Prevention of Cruelty to Children" (the name of the English society) but he had always lived in Scotland, had benefitted other exclusively Scottish charities in his will, and there was evidence that the Scottish counterpart (the *Scottish* National Society for the Prevention of Cruelty to Children) had been brought to his attention before he

---

[48]Para 12 of Sch 1 to the 1994 Order.

[49]Instructions for the will or a written letter from the testator himself constitute direct evidence. Where the testator leaves his estate 'to my sweetheart' evidence that he habitually referred to his wife as such is circumstantial evidence.

[50]These equitable presumptions are discussed at para 7.72 *post*.

[51]Ie as opposed to a 'patent' ambiguity.

[52]*Miller* v *Travers* (1832) 8 Bing 244.

[53]*Re Jackson* [1933] Ch 237.

[54]See, eg *Kell* v *Charmer* (1856) 23 Beav 195; *Charter* v *Charter* (1874) LR 7 HL 364.

[55]*Boyes* v *Cook* (1880) 14 Ch D 53 at 56.

made his will, the House of Lords decided that the English society was entitled rather than the Scottish one.[56]

5.37   Extrinsic evidence was not available to complete total blanks in the will, for example, a gift to "Mrs ...".[57]

Deaths on or after 1 January 1995

5.38   Article 25 of the 1994 Order, which corresponds to section 21 of the Administration of Justice Act 1982,[58] has significantly extended the use of extrinsic evidence.   Extrinsic evidence, whether circumstantial or direct, can now be relied on as an aid to interpretation in three situations.

(a) Insofar as any part of a will is meaningless.

> An example of a will which is meaningless is one in which the testator has employed symbols or a code.[59]   As has been seen, prior to the enactment of the 1994 Order only *circumstantial* evidence was admissible in such a case.

> However, it would seem that the pre-1995 position whereby extrinsic evidence will not be admitted to explain complete blanks (eg £200 to Mrs ...) still remains.   There is nothing in such a case for a meaning to attach to, so it could not correctly be described as 'meaningless'.

(b) Insofar as the language used in any part of the will is ambiguous on the face of it (ie a patent ambiguity).

> As with category (a) above only *circumstantial* evidence was admissible under this heading prior to 1995.   Commonly encountered examples of patent ambiguities are the words "money", "belongings" and "effects".[60]

(c) Insofar as evidence, other than evidence of the testator's intention, shows that the language used in any part of the will is ambiguous in light of surrounding circumstances (ie a latent ambiguity).

---

[56]*National Society for the Prevention of Cruelty to Children* v *Scottish National Society for the Prevention of Cruelty to Children* [1915] AC 207; per Lord Loreburn "I do not think that in this case any ambiguity has been established".

[57]*Bayliss* v *Att-Gen* (1741) 2 Atk 239.

[58]Which implemented recommendations made by the Law Reform Committee on the Interpretation of Wills (Cmnd 5301,1973).

[59]*Kell* v *Charmer* (1856) 23 Beav 195 (symbols used in the course of his jeweller's business).

[60]*Perrin* v *Morgan* [1943] AC 399.

It should be noted that evidence of the testator's intention may not be admitted to *uncover* a latent ambiguity, but once such an ambiguity is found by other means the court may then admit evidence of his intention to show what that intention really was.

5.39 By way of conclusion, it must be emphasised that article 25 of the 1994 Order does not alter the caveat which introduced the comments on extrinsic evidence. Extrinsic evidence is admissible only as an aid to interpretation and it is of no assistance where the word or phrase in question is incapable of bearing the meaning indicated by the evidence. For example, to quote Nicholls J in *Re Williams*,[61] the leading English case on section 21 of the Administration of Estates Act 1982:

> "If ... the meaning is one which the word or phrase cannot bear, I do not see how, in carrying out a process of construction ... the court can declare that meaning to be the meaning of the word or phrase. Such a conclusion, varying or contradicting the language used, would amount to rewriting part of the will."

---

[61][1985] 1 WLR 905 at 912 - home-made will which merely listed 25 names in three groups; letter to solicitors indicating that different amounts of legacy to those in each group; letter was admissible but would be of no assistance unless court was to re-write the will; 25 named persons took equally.

CHAPTER SIX

ENTITLEMENT ON INTESTACY

GENERAL

6.01 This chapter examines distribution on intestacy, which is generally recognised as being the more common mode of succession.[1] Usually an intestacy results because no will has ever been executed, and although it is undoubtedly true that a small percentage of persons actively choose to die intestate,[2] the vast majority would seem to do so out of ignorance, idleness, procrastination or a simple reluctance to succumb to the formal step that acknowledges that death is the lot of all.[3] In addition, an intestacy will arise where a testator has executed a will which cannot be proved, or has executed a valid will which does not actually dispose of any property.[4] If there is a valid will which effectively disposes of only some of the testator's estate, a partial intestacy will arise.[5]

6.02 The enactment currently governing distribution on intestate deaths is the Administration of Estates Act (NI) 1955. This Act is effective for deaths occurring on or after 1 January 1956.

---

[1] In a recent survey carried out for the Law Commission in England only 33% of persons interviewed had made a will. Most likely to do so were those in socio-economic groups AB and elderly persons - *Distribution on Intestacy*, Law Commission Report No 187 (1989), paras 5 and 30.

[2] "... a deceased person may have deliberately chosen to be intestate, and the provisions provided by the legislature to cover the case where there is no will, or an incomplete will, may be as much the wishes of the deceased as those which he has expressed in a will." *Per* Goff LJ in *Re Coventry* [1979] 3 All ER 815, 822.

[3] See generally *Report of the Russell Committee* Cmnd 3051 (1966) para 31.

[4] Eg, the testator has executed a valid will which merely appoints executors - *Re Skeats* [1936] Ch 683 - in this case the only part of a pre-printed will form which the testator completed was that appointing executors. Or the gifts to the sole beneficiaries may have lapsed or failed, eg through non-observance of the requirement that a beneficiary cannot be a witness.

[5] Eg lapse only of a residuary gift. Partial intestacy is examined in more detail at para 6.83 *post*.

The basis of the law

6.03   The purported basis for the code of intestate succession in Northern Ireland, as it is in a number of jurisdictions, is *the presumed intention of the deceased*. The distribution laid down by law:

> "Should as nearly as possible provide for the distribution of the estate in the same manner as the deceased would probably have done had he made a will."[6]

Thus it is considered to be subjective in approach, rather than the more objective alternative, 'what would be a fair and reasonable distribution in the circumstances?' Yet in reality there can be only very limited subjectivity; the desire of the legislators was for a code which was fixed and certain, rather than one with an element of in-built discretion, which would be cumbersome and time-consuming to operate. The presumed intention is therefore that of the *average* potential testator and individual circumstances and idiosyncrasies are not taken into account. 'Hard cases' *may*, however, be redressed under the discretionary safety-net provided by the Inheritance (Provision for Family and Dependants) (NI) Order 1979.[7] This is generally perceived to be a mechanism for changing testamentary provision, and it is often overlooked that it is an equally important element to the overview of intestate succession.

6.04   The law regulating entitlement on intestate deaths was fundamentally overhauled in 1955 when the dichotomy between the succession to real and personal property and the preference of males and the male line were abolished.[8] In 1951 the then Minister of Home Affairs Brian Maginness set up the Committee on the Law of Intestate Succession in Northern Ireland, under the chairmanship of Judge Johnson and including in its membership representatives of both branches of the profession and the farming community in order to examine intestate distribution. England had departed from the former feudal-based inheritance laws for realty in 1925,[9] and by the early 1950s was also in the midst of a review of its intestacy law,[10] prompted by the

---

[6] *Johnson Committee* Cmd (NI) 308 (1952) para 13.

[7] See Chapter Eight. But note that the basis for a claim is the same as in testate succession - did the deceased fail to make reasonable financial provision for the applicant? In *Re Coventry* [1979] 3 All ER 815 Goff LJ refused to approve the argument of counsel that intestate cases should be treated differently to testate ones.

[8] The pre-1956 law is covered in more detail at para 6.08 *post*.

[9] Administration of Estates Act 1925.

[10] *Morton Committee on Intestates' Succession* Cmd 6310 (1951). The proposals were eventually adopted in the Intestates' Estates Act 1952.

Law Society, essentially because the provision made for a surviving spouse was considered to be inadequate. It was obviously desirable that the law in Northern Ireland should not be fundamentally different to that in England and in most key respects the recommendations of the Johnson Committee gave effect to the English 1925 Act, as amended in 1952. Certain peculiarities of this jurisdiction, however, precluded the Committee from recommending a mirror image of the English law. The Administration of Estates Act (NI) 1955 (hereafter the 1955 Act) was later enacted,[11] adopting the proposals of the Johnson Committee with some amendments.

6.05 It has been noted that the traditional basis for intestacy law is the presumed intention of the deceased. Since the early 1950s social, familial and economic conditions have undergone dramatic change, yet during the same period intestacy law has remained substantially unchanged, save for an occasional tinkering with the status quo.[12]

6.06 In England and Wales this piecemeal approach to reform has been continued by the Law Reform (Succession) Act 1995 which is effective for deaths on or after 1 January 1996. This Act, which does not extend to Northern Ireland, makes a number of minor changes to the former law[13] and implements recommendations made by the Law Commission in a recent report.[14] However, the most significant and far-reaching recommendation which was made in this Report, that the surviving spouse should always take the entire estate, has not been implemented.[15] Indeed, the 1995 Act represents the disappointing culmination of a process which promised much but achieved little. In July 1988 the Law Commission published a Working Paper which raised a number of topical issues for further discussion and commissioned a public opinion survey, the results of which demonstrated that the public are not happy with many aspects of the current intestacy code. Ultimately, however, the final report recommended that no change be made in the most controversial

---

[11] The delay was due to the need to wait for the enactment of the enabling Northern Ireland Act 1955.

[12] Most notably the Family Law Reform (NI) Order 1977 and the Children (NI) Order 1995 which have extended inheritance rights to illegitimate persons.

[13] Eg introduction of a 28 day survivorship condition before spouses inherit from each other; abolition of hotchpot; abolition of requirement for children to account for *inter vivos* advancements - see para 6.65 *post*. Similar provisions for Northern Ireland are contained in the Succession (NI) Order 1996 which should become effective around the start of 1997.

[14] *Distribution on Intestacy*, Law Commission Report, No 187 (1989).

[15] See Cretney, "Reform of Intestate Law, The Best We Can Do?" (1995) 111 LQR 77.

problem areas - mainly because to do otherwise would undermine the overriding desire for clarity and simplicity.[16]

6.07   Some years ago the Law Reform Advisory Committee for Northern Ireland gave notice of its intention to review intestate distribution as part of its programme of civil law reform. If the Committee does proceed, clearly the most controversial issue will be whether the peculiar social and cultural characteristics of a still predominantly rural jurisdiction have changed sufficiently since the mid-1950s to follow the lead of the English Law Commission in recommending that a spouse always takes everything. In any event, it is unlikely that it would recommend any significant departure from the English position and it now seems highly unlikely that there is going to be a fundamental overhaul of the Northern Ireland intestacy code until well into the twenty-first century.

DEATHS BEFORE 1956[17]

6.08   The Administration of Estates Act (NI) 1955 is only effective for deaths occurring on or after 1 January 1956. Prior to that date there were separate systems for the devolution on death of real and personal property. Realty was devisable according to the old inheritance laws which derived directly from the feudal system, whilst personalty was distributed in accordance with the rules laid down in the Statute of Distributions (Ir) 1695. From the passing of the Intestates' Estates Act 1890, however, there had been some measure of assimilation of the two types of property. This was the seminal legislation for what has become known as the 'spouse's statutory legacy'; the widow of an intestate who died after 1 September 1890, leaving *no* surviving issue, was entitled to the entire estate (both realty and personalty) if it did not exceed £500. If it did exceed this amount, the widow took a charge on £500 (with interest at 4 per cent) in addition to her share of the residue. This charge was payable out of realty and personalty *rateably.*

Real property

6.09   Subject to the above provisions of the Intestates' Estates Act 1890, realty passed to the heir-at-law subject to the widow's right of dower or the widower's right of curtesy.

---

[16] Reference is made to the Law Commission Report throughout this chapter.
[17] For a more detailed examination see Leitch, *A Handbook on the Administration of Estates Act (NI) 1955.*

6.10 Dower was the widow's life interest in one-third of her husband's freehold estate provided that issue capable of inheriting could have been born[18] and that dower had not previously been 'barred' by the husband.[19] Curtesy was a widower's life estate in the entire freehold estate to which his wife was seised at death, but it arose only if there had been issue capable of inheriting which had been born alive, even if they were no longer living at his wife's death.

6.11 Central to the inheritance laws for realty was the concept of 'primogeniture', which embraced the idea that the heir was generally a single person (unless two or more females were entitled in equal degree) rather than a class of next-of-kin. In establishing who was entitled as heir, the following principles were applied:

(a)   In the first instance the heir was traced by descent through the direct line of the issue of the 'last purchaser' *ad infinitum*.

(b)   Male relatives were preferred to female relatives in the same degree.

(c)   If two or more persons in the same degree were males, the eldest only inherited.

(d)   In the absence of males in any degree, females inherited equally as co-parcenors.

(e)   Lineal descendants inherited *ad infinitum* in place of their ancestor.

(f)   Initially a *fee* had not been capable of ascending, but this restriction was removed by the Inheritance Act 1833, and in the absence of descendants the heir was the nearest lineal ancestor, subject to the above rules and the rule that the father and his relatives were preferred to the mother and hers. Similarly, the father's or mother's paternal relatives were preferred to the father's or mother's maternal relatives.

---

[18] Eg if land had been given 'to Aloysis and the heirs of his body begotten upon Barbara', but Aloysis married Ciara then Ciara was not entitled to dower.

[19] After the enactment of the Dower Act 1833 dower could be barred if the husband alienated his estate either *inter vivos* or in his will, or had made a declaration in bar of dower.

6.12   Usually, of course, the heir was the deceased's eldest son.   The principle of representation applied to ensure that if this son predeceased his father, his issue were entitled (eldest son first, daughters equally in the absence of sons) before the father's second son.   A younger son therefore inherited only if his elder brother had predeceased his father and there was none of his issue surviving the father.   Daughters inherited (equally as co-parceners) only in the absence of sons and deceased sons' issue.

6.13   In the event of an intestate dying without an heir, his realty escheated to the Crown.

Personal property

6.14   The Local Registration of Title Act (Ir) 1891 expressly provided that registered land bought out under the Land Purchase Scheme was to be regarded as personalty and pass on death in accordance with the Statute of Distributions (Ir) 1695, notwithstanding its freehold status.   Thus after the passing of this Act the majority of rural land in Northern Ireland passed as *personalty*.

6.15   Under the Statute of Distributions (Ir) 1695 the following was the position:

(a)   Where the intestate left a widow and surviving issue, the widow took one-third and the child or children took the remaining two-thirds. Children who had pre-deceased the intestate were represented by their issue *per stirpes*.[20]

(b)   The widow's right to the first £500 if the intestate left *no* surviving issue has already been noted. In addition, the widow was entitled to one-half of the residue. The remaining one-half went to the intestate's "next-of-kin", no matter how remote.

(c)   Where the intestate was survived by issue, but not by a widow, his children took the estate absolutely in equal shares, with issue of deceased children taking *per stirpes*.[21]

---

[20] For the meaning of *per stirpes* see para 6.61 *post*.
[21] See para 6.63 *post*.

(d)   In the event of the intestate being survived by neither widow nor issue the estate went to the next-of-kin. If the intestate's father was still alive he was entitled to the exclusion of all others.   If he was dead, the intestate's mother, brothers, sisters and *children*[22] of deceased brothers and sisters were entitled equally and shared the estate. If children of deceased brothers and sisters were entitled by representation they generally took *per stirpes*, but in the event of there being no surviving mother and no surviving brothers and sisters, so that the next-of-kin were all nieces and nephews of the intestate, they took *per capita*. If the intestate left neither mother nor siblings or their children, the nearest blood relation took, with no limitations placed upon which degree of blood could qualify.

(e)   The widower of an intestate always took the entire personal estate, not under the Statute of Distributions, but by virtue of the common law marital right.

(f)   In the absence of next-of-kin, the personalty reverted to the Crown.

TABLE OF DISTRIBUTION FOR DEATHS ON OR AFTER JANUARY 1 1956

The following is a quick reference table illustrating distribution in the most common situations. Entitlement is dealt with in detail at paragraph 6.48 below.

SPOUSE SURVIVING

Relatives surviving in addition to spouse	*Entitlement*
Issue	The spouse gets the personal chattels, and the first £125,000[23] absolutely. If there is only one child the spouse takes one-half of the

---

[22]Not *issue* as is the situation in other cases of representation.

[23] The figures of £125,000 and £200,000 are effective for deaths on or after 1 January 1994. The relevant figures for deaths before this date are found at para 6.50 *post*. See also Appendix B.

	residue and the child the other half. If there are two or more children, the spouse takes one third of the residue, and the children divide the other two-thirds between themselves. Children who have pre-deceased the intestate leaving surviving issue of their own are represented by those issue. Parents and siblings receive nothing.
Parents (no issue)	The spouse is entitled to personal chattels and the first £200,000 absolutely. The spouse is also entitled to one-half of the residue. The remaining one-half residue is divided equally between the parents, if both alive, or given entirely to the sole parent.
Siblings	The situation is the same as that concerning the parents above, only the remaining half residue is divided between the siblings and if any siblings have pre-deceased the intestate leaving issue, then those issue take the share to which their parent would have been entitled.
No issue, no parent, no sibling (or issue)	In this case spouse takes everything absolutely.

NO SURVIVING SPOUSE

Relatives surviving	*Entitlement*
Issue	The issue take "*per stirpes*".
Parents	If two surviving, entitled to estate in equal shares, or if only one, the whole estate absolutely.
Siblings (whole or half-blood)	The whole estate in equal shares. Issue of a deceased brother or sister take their parents share by representation.

| Grandparents | If only one surviving, the whole estate absolutely. If more than one, the whole estate in equal shares. |
| Uncles and aunts | The whole estate in equal shares. Issue of a deceased uncle or aunt take their parents share by representation.[24] |

If there is more than one person of the same degree, the assets are distributed equally. In the case of siblings and uncles and aunts, the surviving issue of the siblings or uncles and aunts who have pre-deceased the intestate take *per stirpes*[25] the share that that sibling, uncle or aunt would have taken if he or she had survived the intestate. None of the later categories are represented by issue.

If the situation is not covered by any of the cases listed above, the 'pecking order' to determine the next-of-kin continues as follows:

great-grandparents;

grand-uncles and aunts;

great-great-grandparents;

great-grand-uncles and great-grand-aunts and children of grand-uncles and grand-aunts (these categories are both of the same degree);

great-great-great-grandparents;

second cousins (ie, children of the children of grand-uncles and grand-aunts or children of great-grand-uncles or great-grand-aunts);

other next-of-kin of the nearest degree.

In the absence of next-of-kin, the estate passes to the Crown as *bona vacantia*.

---

[24] In England and Wales "next-of-kin" are excluded beyond this point.
[25] For explanation of "*per stirpes*" see para 6.61 *et seq post*.

PERSONS ENTITLED

Persons entitled as the spouse

6.16   The entitlement is expressed in favour of a *surviving* spouse, and in order to inherit on intestacy as a spouse the person in question must have the status of a legally married husband or wife of the deceased at the date of death. The estate of a deceased spouse has no claim.[26] A *void* marriage, being void *ab initio*, is treated as if it had never taken place and a person who entered into such a marriage with an intestate during his lifetime is not a spouse for the purposes of intestacy law.   An *inter vivos* decree of nullity is merely declaratory in the case of a void marriage and it is thus irrelevant to the status of the parties whether or not one was obtained.[27]   By contrast, a voidable marriage[28] is treated as subsisting if it has not been annulled,[29] and until the marriage has been brought to an end by a decree of nullity the parties are entitled to inherit on each other's death as the surviving spouse.[30]

6.17   If the deceased was legally married at the date of death, no account is taken either of the length[31] or the state of the marriage.   For instance it is irrelevant that the surviving spouse was living apart from the deceased in adultery - provided that the parties were not judicially separated.

---

[26] When the draft Succession (NI) Order 1996 becomes effective (probably at the beginning of 1997) a spouse will only inherit if he survives the intestate by 28 days.

[27] In *Shaw v Shaw* [1954] 2 QB 429 a married man represented himself to be a widower and went through a ceremony of marriage. In the event, although the second 'wife' was unable to inherit under his intestacy, she was awarded damages (equal to the amount to which she would have been entitled as a surviving spouse) for breach of the promise to marry. This action has now been abolished by art 15 of the Family Law (Miscellaneous Provisions) (NI) Order 1984.   However, a person who *innocently* enters into a void marriage with an intestate can make a family provision claim. See para 8.26 *post*.

[28] For grounds on which marriage is voidable see Appendix D.

[29] Matrimonial Causes (NI) Order 1978, art 18.

[30] Eg see *Re Park* [1954] P 89.

[31] *Ibid* where the marriage lasted 17 days and *Re Davey* [1981] 1 WLR 164 in which a 92 year old patient married a 48 year old nurse who was working in the nursing home which she had recently entered, thus revoking her existing will.   She died shortly afterwards but the authorities had intervened to make a statutory will without the husband's knowledge. The issue for the court was essentially whether they had power to do so, but the case illustrates how a system which treats recent brides in the same way as those married for 50 years can be open to abuse.

Judicial separation

6.18   Although a decree of judicial separation does not alter the legal status of the parties as husband and wife, there has been statutory intervention for the purposes of intestate succession by article 20(2) of the Matrimonial Causes (NI) Order 1978. This provides that if either of the parties to a marriage dies while a decree of judicial separation is in force and is continuing, the property as respects which he or she died intestate shall devolve as if the other party to the marriage had then been dead. Article 20 (2) is effective for deaths on or after 18 April 1979.

6.19   In the case of deaths before this, the relevant legislation is section 15 of the Matrimonial Causes Act (NI) 1939. This had several shortcomings. First, it applied only as regards the property which a judicially separated husband would inherit on the death intestate of an estranged *wife*, but not vice versa. Secondly, it only applied to property which she acquired or inherited *after* the date of the decree. With one exception, all other property could still pass to the husband as if the parties were not subject to a decree of judicial separation; if the decree had been obtained *by the wife*, any property to which she was entitled for an estate in remainder or reversion *at the date of the decree* would pass on her intestacy as if her husband was already dead. These provisions, drawing arbitrary distinctions between husband and wife, the petitioner and the respondent, and before and after acquired property were clearly most unsatisfactory.

6.20   When the 1978 Order was originally enacted, article 20(3) expressly provided that non-cohabitation orders made under section 3(1)(a) of the Summary Jurisdiction (Separation and Maintenance) Act (NI) 1945 would not have the effect of a decree of judicial separation. This legislation has now been repealed and superseded by the Domestic Proceedings (NI) Order 1980 and the comparable orders to those under section 3(1)(a) are the personal protection and exclusion orders made under article 18 of the 1980 Order. No consequential amendments have been made, however, to article 20(3) of the 1978 Order. Nevertheless, it would seem a reasonable proposition that, by analogy, such orders are not to be considered as having the same effect as a decree of judicial separation.

Divorce and annulment

6.21   A person who was divorced from the deceased during his lifetime has no entitlement on his death intestate as a surviving spouse.[32] A divorce is not finalised until the decree absolute, and the spouse of an intestate who dies between the grant of the decree nisi and the decree absolute will still be entitled. The case of *Re Seaford*[33] illustrates this with unusually dramatic facts. A husband died after the decree nisi, but before the decree absolute: in fact he died in the early hours of the morning of the day on which the Notice of Application for the decree to be made absolute was filed in the District Registry (it had been posted by the wife's solicitor the previous evening). The Court of Appeal refused to apply the common law doctrine of 'relation back' from the earliest moment of the day, and the widow was held entitled to her share as surviving spouse:

> "Whom God had put asunder no man could join together, even
> for the purpose of putting them asunder again."[34]

6.22   The Law Commission[35] expressed concern that such a state of affairs, even with less extreme facts, does not reflect the presumed intention of the intestate and, in particular, is totally incongruous with the treatment of persons who are judicially separated at the date of death. Possible options suggested were to consider the cut-off point as the commencement of divorce proceedings, or, at least, the grant of the *decree nisi*. The Final Report, however, was not in favour of change.[36]

Cohabitants

6.23   Unmarried persons living together as husband and wife are afforded no rights of entitlement under the present intestacy regime. The desirability of extending succession rights between such couples was another issue discussed by the Law Commission, but although the public was generally in favour, it

---

[32] Although if he has not remarried, there is *locus standi* as a "former spouse" under the Inheritance (Provision for Family and Dependants) (NI) Order 1979, art 3(1)(b), see para 8.28 *post*. But see generally *Re Fullard* [1981] 2 All ER 796 for discussion of the difficulties facing former spouses who make such claims.

[33] [1968] P 53.

[34] *Ibid* per Russell LJ at p 73.

[35] In Working Paper No 108 (1988).

[36] The main reason for this reluctance to introduce the concept of the "unmeritorious spouse" was the disparity in individual circumstances; it was not felt unreasonable that a person who wished to exclude his spouse should get a judicial separation or make a will - see para 39 of the Final Report.

was decided that the priority of keeping the entitlement clear, simple, and fixed would be undermined if administrators were asked to determine complex questions of fact.[37] Instead it was recommended that cohabitants should be given automatic *locus standi* to make a family provision claim, without the need to show *dependence*. In England and Wales this recommendation has recently been implemented in the Law Reform (Succession) Act 1995.[38] Article 4 of the draft Succession (NI) Order 1996 which should become effective around the beginning of 1997 will introduce similar provision to Northern Ireland.[39]

Persons entitled as issue

6.24 The 1955 Act refers on different occasions to both "child(ren)" and "issue" of the deceased. At common law "children" referred only to the first generation of legitimate descendants by any marriage and "issue" to the legitimate descendants of every degree. Although both definitions have now been widened by the successive adoption enactments and, in relation to illegitimacy, by the Children (NI) Order 1995, intestacy law still adopts a relatively narrow definition of the word "child". In particular, other legislation in which a person may acquire some of the rights of a child if he is treated as such, has not been followed.[40]

A child en ventre sa mère

6.25 The 1955 Act requires that children (or issue if they are to take by representation) *survive* the intestate. Section 13 of the 1955 Act expressly provides that children and issue begotten in the lifetime of the deceased but

---

[37]The application of similar provisions in other fields, eg "persons living together as husband and wife" in art 24(3) of the Housing (NI) Order 1983 has not been without difficulty - the English counterpart has already generated considerable case law. Some Commonwealth jurisdictions have, however, given rights on intestacy to "de facto" spouses, eg the South Australian legislation recognises a "putative spouse" ie persons who have cohabited as husband and wife *de facto* for five years.

[38]Effective for deaths occurring after 1995.

[39]See para 8.38 *post*. Under the current law a cohabitant is afforded *locus standi* under art 3(1)(e) of the Inheritance (Provision for Family and Dependants) (NI) Order 1979, only if he can show that he was being maintained by the deceased immediately before death.

[40]Eg Inheritance (Provision for Family and Dependants) (NI) Order 1979, art 3(1)(d) grants *locus standi* to a person "treated as a child of the marriage". The Law Commission was against the extension of intestacy rights in this manner - again on the basis that it left administrators to resolve complex questions of fact (see para 49 of Law Commission Report).

born thereafter are to be treated as if they had been born in the lifetime of the intestate and had survived him.[41]

Adopted children

6.26   An adopted child is now fully transferred for inheritance purposes from his old family into his new and is treated for effectively all such purposes[42] as if he is the legitimate child of the adopter(s).   Article 40 of the Adoption (NI) Order 1987 provides that an adopted child is to be treated as if he had been born as a child of the marriage if the adopters are a married couple or, in any other case,[43] as if he had been born to the adopter in wedlock (but not as a child of any actual marriage of the adopter).[44]   All links with the former family are severed and inheritance from the natural parents, grandparents and siblings (and vice versa) is excluded by article 40(2) which provides that the child is not to be regarded as "the child of any other person".[45]   The 1987 Order applies to adoption orders made on or after 1 October 1989 in Northern Ireland, England, Wales, Scotland, the Isle of Man, the Channel Islands and also to various overseas adoptions which are recognised by the law of Northern Ireland.   The comparable inheritance provisions of its predecessor, the Adoption Act (NI) 1967,[46] which still remain relevant for deaths on or after 1 December 1969 but before 1 October 1989, extend only to children adopted in the United Kingdom, Channel Islands or Isle of Man.   The Adoption of Children Act (NI) 1950[47] is the governing legislation for deaths before 30 November 1969 and the

---

[41]This is more liberal than the interpretation by the House of Lords that a clause in a will benefitting "issue her surviving" excluded a child *en ventre sa mère*, *Elliot* v *Joicey* [1935] AC 209. For position of frozen embryos see para 6.39 *post*.

[42]Succession to certain peerages and dignatories of honour are excluded by art 43 of the Adoption (NI) Order 1987. The previous legislation, the Adoption Act (NI) 1967, also expressly excluded succession to fee tails but there is no equivalent provision in the 1987 Order.

[43]As joint adopters must be married, this generally refers to a mother or father adopting his or her own illegitimate child.

[44]The significance of this was that any adopted child could inherit from the grandparents, and siblings of the whole or half blood. Contrast the natural child of unmarried parents for deaths prior to 1 July 1995 - see para 6.30 *post*.

[45] Some Commonwealth jurisdictions retain the right of succession from natural relatives in limited circumstances, eg South Australian, Adoption of Children Act 1966-1976 s 30(3). Note that if an illegitimate child is adopted by his natural mother, the succession rights to his natural father's estate are removed.

[46] Ss 18 and 19.

[47] Ss 9 and 10 relate to intestacy.

inheritance provisions of this enactment only apply if the adoption was made in the United Kingdom.[48]

Stepchildren

6.27   Unadopted stepchildren, that is the children of the intestate's spouse by a third party, are not entitled.[49]

Illegitimate children

6.28   At common law any reference to "child", "children" or "issue" referred to legitimate persons only, that is, one whose parents were married to each other at the time of conception or birth, or both. Various piecemeal statutory reforms, culminating in the Children (NI) Order 1995 have now put illegitimate persons completely on a par with legitimate ones for the purposes of intestate succession. However, since this Order is not retrospective and only applies to intestate deaths on or after 1 July 1995, it is necessary to look at the earlier legislation.

Deaths prior to 1 January 1978

6.29   The strict common law position was first modified in limited respects by section 9 of the Legitimacy Act (NI) 1928.   This provided that an illegitimate child (or if he was dead, his issue) could inherit from his *mother's* estate the share to which he was entitled had he been born legitimate. The section only operated, however, in *the absence of surviving legitimate issue*. Similarly, the mother was entitled to succeed on the intestacy of her illegitimate child as if the child had been born legitimate and she was the sole surviving parent.

Deaths on or after 1 January 1978 but before 1 July 1995

6.30   The Family Law Reform (NI) Order 1977 (which corresponded to the English Family Law Reform Act 1969) put illegitimate children on an *equal* footing with legitimate ones for the purposes of intestate succession from both the mother *and* the father.[50] It did not, however, extend this equality of treatment to the succession to the estates of the wider family circle.   An

---

[48] For cases concerning foreign adoptions decided under the equivalent English provisions, see *Re Wilby* [1956] 1 All ER 27, and *Re Wilson* [1954] 1 All ER 997.

[49] But they may apply as a person "treated as a child of the family" under art 3(1)(d) of the Inheritance (Provision for Family and Dependants) (NI) Order 1979. For an example of a successful claim by an adult stepdaughter see *Re Leach* [1985] 2 All ER 754. See Chapter Eight.

[50] Art 3(1). Entailed interests are excluded - art 3(5).

illegitimate person could not inherit on the death intestate prior to July 1995 of his grandparents, his brothers and sisters or his aunts and uncles.

6.31   Consider A, a widow who died intestate in 1994. She had three children; B (legitimate) and C (illegitimate) who survive her, and D (legitimate) who predeceased her leaving issue - E who is legitimate and F who is illegitimate.

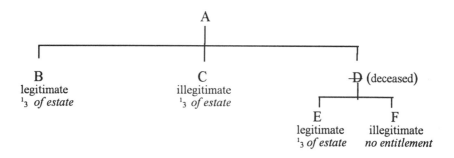

B and C are each entitled to one-third of A's estate,[51] but only E can take D's share by representation. F, being illegitimate, is not entitled. If *both* E and F had been illegitimate, the one-third share of the estate allocated to D's branch of the family would be shared between B and C.

6.32   Since 1 January 1978 all references to a child in a will have automatically included illegitimate persons[52] and this resulted in the somewhat anomalous position that a gift in a testator's will to a dead brother's children included illegitimate persons, yet on his death intestate only the legitimate children of the dead brother could take by representation.

Deaths on or after 1 July 1995
6.33   Articles 155 to 157 of and Schedule 6 to the Children (NI) Order 1995[53] have put illegitimate persons in exactly the same position as their

---

[51] Although C is illegitimate he is entitled to inherit from either *parent* equally with legitimate children under the Family Law Reform (NI) Order 1977. If A had died before 1 January 1978 C would not have been entitled because illegitimate children only took from their mother's estate in the absence of legitimate children.

[52] Family Law Reform (NI) Order 1977, art 4. See para 5.23 *supra*.

[53] Art 155 sets out the general principle that references to any relationship between two persons shall be construed without regard to whether or not the father or mother of either of

legitimate counterparts for the purposes of intestate succession to the estate of a deceased who died on or after 1 July 1995. Thus illegitimate persons can now inherit from the full family circle in the same manner as if they were legitimate. In the above example both E and F would now share D's part of her mother's estate.

Legitimated children

6.34 Children born illegitimate are legitimated by the subsequent marriage of their parents (to each other)[54] and the date of legitimation is the date of the marriage (or 1 July 1928 if the marriage was celebrated before this date). A legitimated person and his spouse, children and issue are entitled to take any interest in the estate of an intestate dying *after* the date of legitimation.[55] Initially there was one exception; a child who was conceived in adultery (ie, when at least one of his parents was married to a third party) could not be legitimated,[56] but this provision was later repealed by the Legitimacy Act (NI) 1961.[57] Such persons are treated as legitimate for the purpose of distribution of the estate of intestates dying on or after 1 September 1961.

Children of void or voidable marriages

6.35 While a voidable marriage is subsisting, a child of the parties is clearly legitimate (or legitimated). A decree of nullity which brings a voidable marriage to an end is now taken to have effect only from the date of the decree itself.[58] Thus any children born during the union remain legitimate after the decree. Formerly a decree of nullity acted retrospectively in a voidable marriage and the marriage was deemed never to have taken place. If this was taken to its logical conclusion, any children of the union would become illegitimate. Section 9(2) of the Matrimonial Causes Act (NI) 1939 expressly preserved the legitimate status of the children, in all cases except a marriage avoided on the grounds that the respondent was pregnant by a third party at the date of the celebration of marriage.[59] This section was later superseded by

---

them have or had been married to each other at any time. Art 157 and Sch 6 apply the principle to the determination of property rights on intestacy.

[54] Legitimacy Act (NI) 1928, s 1.

[55] *Ibid*, s 3.

[56] *Ibid*, s 1(2).

[57] S 1(1).

[58] Matrimonial Causes (NI) Order 1978, art 18.

[59] S 7(2) of the Matrimonial Causes Act 1937 which was the English equivalent excluded also marriages avoided because they were not consummated. Presumably this was because it was felt that the problem would not arise! But see *Dredge* v *Dredge* [1947] 1 All ER 29 in

section 3 of the Law Reform (Miscellaneous Provisions) Act (NI) 1951[60] which provided that where a decree of nullity was granted in respect of a voidable marriage, any child who would have been the legitimate child of the parties to the marriage if it had been dissolved rather than annulled on the date of the decree, would be deemed to be their legitimate child.

6.36   It has already been noted that a void marriage is void *ab initio*. Strictly, of course, any children of the union would be illegitimate, but again there has been statutory intervention to mitigate this harsh position. Section 2(1) of the Legitimacy Act (NI) 1961 provides that a child of a void marriage shall be treated as a legitimate child if the father was domiciled in Northern Ireland, and if at the time of the act of intercourse resulting in his birth (or at the time of the celebration of marriage, if later) both or either of the parties reasonably believed that the marriage was valid. The section applies equally to children born before or after the commencement of the Act,[61] but does not affect the entitlement on the intestacy of a person who died before commencement.

6.37   Children of a marriage which is dissolved by a decree absolute of divorce are (and always have been) legitimate.

Artificial insemination
6.38   Advances in modern medicine which have enabled children to be born as a result of artificial insemination of sperm and ova donation have created problems as to who in law should be regarded as the father or mother. At common law the natural father of a child born by artificial insemination of sperm is the donor of the sperm, rather than the husband or partner of the mother. Obviously in most cases the identity of the donor will be unknown, and whilst this would minimise the likelihood of a claim by the natural father on the child's intestacy, the possibility of such happening could not be completely ruled out. Secondly, the child would necessarily be illegitimate. The Human Fertilisation and Embryology Act 1990, which essentially gives effect to the recommendations of the Warnock Committee[62] and extends to Northern Ireland, provides that if a child is born to a married woman as the result of Artificial

---

which a 17 year old conceived before marriage was rendered illegitimate when the marriage was avoided due to wife's wilful failure to consummate union.

[60] Which is effective for marriages annulled on or after 13 February 1951.

[61] 1 September 1961.

[62] *Report of Committee of Enquiry into Human Fertilisation and Embryology* (The Warnock Committee), Cmnd 9314 (1984).

Insemination by Donor after the commencement of the 1990 Act[63] the child is presumed to be the child of that woman and her husband. The presumption is rebutted only by showing that the husband did not consent to the artificial insemination of his wife,[64] and even if this can be shown satisfactorily, the donor of the sperm is declared *not* to be the natural father. If the woman is not married, but she and a partner were treated *together* for infertility by a person with a licence, that partner is to be treated as the father of the child.[65] The 1990 Act also provides that the mother of the child is the woman carrying it, rather than the donor of the egg.[66]

6.39 It was noted earlier that all references to children under the 1955 Act include a child "en ventre sa mère". In the case of frozen embryos the Warnock Committee decided that it was undesirable that a child born sometime after his father's death should be able to pursue a claim against his estate. The 1990 Act gives effect to this recommendation by excluding embryos used after the death of a husband or partner.[67]

Persons entitled as parents

6.40 In the case of deaths on or after 1 January 1978 "parent" means the natural father or mother of the deceased, whether or not the deceased is legitimate or illegitimate.[68] In the case of the *father* of an illegitimate child, however, there is a presumption that the father predeceased the child, and the contrary has to be shown.[69] If an illegitimate intestate died before this date, the father has no entitlement, but by virtue of the Legitimacy Act (NI) 1928[70] the mother is entitled as if the child had been born legitimate and she had been the sole surviving parent.

---

[63] 1 August 1991.

[64] 1990 Act, s 28(2).

[65] S 28(3).

[66] S 27.

[67] S 28(6).

[68] Family Law Reform (NI) Order 1977, art 3 which has now been superseded by art 157 of and Sch 6 to the Children (NI) Order 1995, which was discussed at para 6.33 *supra*.

[69] Para 1(6) of Sch 6 to the Children (NI) Order 1995. This is to provide some measure of protection against fathers suddenly appearing to claim their inheritance. Once the father is shown to be alive, and the relationship confirmed, however, it is immaterial that he never actually knew (or maintained) his child.

[70] S 9.

6.41   If a child has been adopted, the inheritance rights of the natural parents are removed[71] and fully transferred to the adoptive parents.

6.42   Stepparents and parents-in-law have no entitlement.

Persons entitled as brothers and sisters

6.43   Both natural brothers and sisters, and adoptive brothers and sisters[72] are entitled. In England siblings of the whole-blood are preferred to those of the half-blood, but in Northern Ireland they inherit equally.[73]

6.44   The Children (NI) Order 1995 has removed all discrimination against illegitimate persons for the purposes of succession to the estates of persons who die intestate on or after 1 July 1995.[74] An illegitimate person can now inherit from the full family circle as if he was legitimate. However, it is presumed that an illegitimate person was not survived by any person related to him only through his father unless the contrary is shown.[75]

6.45   For deaths prior to 1 July 1995[76] an illegitimate person could not inherit on the death intestate either of his illegitimate brothers or sisters or of his legitimate brothers or sisters of the half-blood.[77] Similarly, a legitimate person could not inherit on the death intestate of illegitimate brothers or sisters of the half-blood.

6.46   As in the case of parents discussed above, relationships by affinity (stepbrothers, brothers-in-law) are excluded.

---

[71]Adoption Order (NI) 1987, art 40(2). See para 6.26 *supra*.

[72]*Ibid* art 40. If a child has been adopted the natural brothers and sisters are excluded.

[73]1955 Act, s 14. This principle extends to all relatives of the whole and half-blood in the same degree.

[74]In England this assimilation was achieved by the Family Law Reform Act 1987 which is effective for deaths on or after 4 April 1988.

[75]Para 1(2) of Sch 6 to the Children (NI) Order 1995.

[76]Although the Family Law Reform (NI) Order 1977, which applies to deaths on or after 1 January 1978, put illegitimate persons on a par with their legitimate counterparts for the purposes of intestate succession from parents, it did not extend this equality of treatment to the wider family circle.

[77]They could only be of the half-blood; if they were of the whole-blood the illegitimate child would have been legitimated.

THE EXTENT OF THE ENTITLEMENT

6.47   Distribution is in accordance with the rules set out in Part II of the Administration of Estates Act (NI) 1955. A quick reference table can be found at page 115.

Alteration of entitlement

6.48   The possibility of a testator executing a will which merely revokes all former wills and expresses his desire to die intestate has been noted.[78]   A will which states that he wishes to die intestate, but that certain next-of-kin are to be excluded will also be effective, provided that *all* next-of-kin are not excluded.[79] It might also be appropriate to note at this point that gifts under an intestacy can be disclaimed in the same way as testamentary benefits[80] and that if all the beneficiaries under an intestacy are *sui juris* they can agree to vary the original distribution.[81]

The entitlement of the spouse

General

(Note that when the Succession (NI) Order 1996 becomes effective (probably at the beginning of 1997) spouses will only be entitled if they survive the deceased by 28 days. A similar provision is already in force in England and Wales.[82])

6.49   On three occasions the surviving spouse will receive the entire estate:[83]

---

[78]See para 6.01 *supra*.

[79]*Re Wynn* [1983] 3 All ER 310.

[80]Originally it was assumed that the imperative nature of the intestacy code precluded disclaimer of benefits. Disclaimer was allowed in *Re Scott* [1975] 1 WLR 1260, and the better view would now seem to be that intestate benefits can be disclaimed, at least up until the interest has vested in the beneficiary, whether by way of assent or otherwise. This view is endorsed by the Inheritance Tax Act 1984, which in s 142 refers to benefits conferred by various dispositions being disclaimed, and includes dispositions "by will, under the law relating to intestacy or otherwise."

[81]*Saunders* v *Vautier* (1841) 10 LJ Ch 354. If this variation is executed in writing within two years of death, and notified to the Capital Taxes Office within six months of execution the variation will be the distribution taken for inheritance tax purposes, s 142 Inheritance Tax Act 1984.

[82]Law Reform (Succession) Act 1995.

[83]1955 Act, s 7.

(a)   if the deceased was also survived by issue and the estate, excluding personal chattels, does not exceed £125,000;

(b)   if the deceased, although not survived by issue, was survived by parents or siblings (or their issue) and the estate, excluding personal chattels, does not exceed £200,000;

(c)   if the deceased was not survived by issue, parents, siblings (or their issue) - whatever the size of the estate.

In other circumstances the entitlement of the spouse is as follows.

If the deceased is also survived *by issue and the estate is greater than £125,000* the spouse is entitled to:

(a)   the personal chattels;

(b)   the first £125,000;

(c)   and either -

(1)   one-half of the residue absolutely if there is only one child, or

(2)   one-third of the residue absolutely if there is more than one child.[84]

If the deceased is *not survived by issue, but is survived by parents, or siblings (or their issue)* the spouse is entitled to:

(a)   the personal chattels;

(b)   the first £200,000;

(c)   one-half of the residue absolutely, whether or not there is more than one parent surviving or more than one sibling.

---

[84]In England, in contrast, the number of surviving children does not affect the spouse's residuary entitlement - it is always to one-half. However, it is only to a *life interest* in that half, although there is an option to capitalise, Administration of Estates Act 1925, s 47A(1).

The fixed net sum

6.50 The fixed net sums of £ 125,000 and £ 200,000, which are generally referred to as the 'spouse's statutory legacy', are paid free of all duties, charges and costs,[85] and unlike other legacies, carry interest from the date of *death*. Strictly they are a charge on the intestate's estate, but in practice they take effect as an absolute gift. The figures are raised periodically by statutory instrument; the current ones are effective for deaths on or after 1 January 1994[86] and the relevant figures for deaths before this can be found in this table.

Deaths	*Issue surviving*	*No issue surviving*
1.1.56-1.3.70	£1,500	£5,000
2.3.70-2.8.73	£2,250	£7,500
3.8.73-31.12.77	£7,500	£20,000
1.1.78-31.5.81	£25,000	£55,000
1.6.81-30.11.87	£40,000	£85,000
1.12.87-31.12.93	£75,000	£125,000[87]

The interest payable is calculated at the following rates:

Deaths	*Interest per year*
1.1.56-31.4.80	4 per cent
1.5.80-28.2.85	7 per cent
1.3.85-present	6 per cent[88]

Personal chattels

6.51 "Personal chattels" is defined in section 45(1) of the 1955 Act as meaning:

> "Carriages, horses, stable furniture and effects, motor cars and accessories, garden effects, domestic animals, plate, plated articles, linen, china, glass, books, pictures, prints, furniture, jewellery, articles of household or personal use or ornament, musical and scientific instruments and apparatus, wines, liquors

---

[85]1955 Act, s 7(1)(b).
[86]NI SI 1993 426.
[87]NI SIs, 1973 No 199, 1977 No 283, 1981 No 124, 1987 No 378.
[88]NI SRs 1980 No 90; 1985 No 8.

and consumable stores, but does not include any chattels used at
the death of the intestate for business *or professional* purposes
nor money or security for money."

Apart from the addition of the words "or professional", this follows the English
definition contained in section 55 of the Administration of Estates Act 1925.
The quaint and anachronistic language obviously dates the section, but
criticisms that it is ill-equipped to cope with the mass of technical paraphernalia
and artefacts left by the intestate of the late twentieth century, have been offset
to a degree by the liberal and unrestrictive interpretation which the judiciary
have given the section.   The English courts have held the following to be
personal chattels: a large collection of watches and clocks;[89] stamp and coin
collections;[90]12 racehorses used for purely recreational purposes;[91] a motor
yacht used solely for pleasure[92] and cut, but unmounted, diamonds.[93]

6.52   It should be noted that the statutory definition embraces both specific
items and a more general description, namely "articles of household or personal
use or ornament". In the case of the former, the starting point has tended to be
the ordinary everyday meaning, and on occasions the Shorter Oxford
Dictionary has been consulted; for example, to confirm that the uncut gems
mentioned above could be described as "jewellery". Many of the fruits of
modern technology which are found in the typical suburban home will be
included within the terms "musical and scientific instruments and apparatus".

6.53   The scope of the more general "articles of personal use" was the
subject of some discussion in both *Re Reynolds*[94] and *Re Crispin*.[95]   In
Reynolds a stamp collection (valued at £1,850) which had been created and
maintained by a testator[96] as his only hobby was held to be an "article of
personal use", notwithstanding that its value was such that it might additionally

---

[89]*Re Crispin's Will Trusts* [1975] Ch 245.
[90]*Re Reynold's Will Trusts* [1966] 1 WLR 19; see also *Re Collin's Will Trusts* [1971] 1 WLR
    37. But note that money itself is expressly excluded.
[91]*Re Hutchinson* [1955] Ch 255.
[92]*Re Chaplin* [1950] Ch 507.
[93]*Re Whitby* [1944] Ch 210.
[94]*Supra* [1966] 1 WLR 19.
[95]*Supra* [1975] Ch 245.
[96]Many testators leave gifts of "my personal chattels as defined in s 45 of the Administration
    of Estates Act (NI) 1955". In *Crispin* one of the facts influencing the trial Judge was the
    intention of the testator. On appeal, it was held, *inter alia*, that such a clause was to be
    interpreted as on an intestacy. Much of the case law discussed in this section has actually
    arisen from provisions in wills.

be regarded as an investment; articles of personal use and investments are not mutually exclusive. The fact that the value of an item is irrelevant was confirmed by the Court of Appeal in *Re Crispin*, in which collections of watches and clocks making up £54,000 of an £83,000 estate were held to be personal chattels:

> "... the *only* question is whether an article comes within the ordinary meaning of the word used."[97]

6.54   The judge at first instance in *Crispin* had focussed only on "articles of personal use" and had allowed the watches (which were kept in a display cabinet and worn from time to time) but not the clocks (which were mainly kept in locked rooms in his house, and some of which had long ceased to function). On appeal it was not disputed that clocks, whether or not they were inoperative, were within the ordinary sense of the word "furniture", a fact which had seemed to go unnoticed in the lower court. It was also held to be irrelevant that many of them had been inherited, or that some had been borrowed by museums or stored in locked rooms. Watches, by their nature, were articles of personal use, a fact endorsed in this instance by the testator "cherishing by hand and eye". Also of interest was the Court of Appeal's disapproval of *dicta* in *Reynolds* which suggested that the stamp collection there would not have been an article of personal use if it had been *bought* by the testator. The Court of Appeal was of the opinion that the purpose or mode of acquisition should be irrelevant and the determination of whether or not particular items are "articles of personal use" should be restricted to the state of affairs existing at death.[98]   Little reliance can now be placed on these statements in *Reynolds*.

6.55   Motor cars, in the plural, and their assessories, are expressly mentioned. It is doubtful if the ordinary meaning of "assessories" includes caravans, trailers and trailer-tents, but these would be included in any event as "articles of personal use".[99] The most problematic issue with motor cars is the application of the business use exclusion. It will be remembered that section 45 of the 1955 Act excludes "any chattels used at the date of death of the intestate for business or professional purposes", but there is no elaboration as to whether

---

[97]*Per* Russell LJ at p 251, emphasis added.

[98]On this point see also Megarry (1966) 82 LQR 18 in which it is argued that the view that death is the relevant date is bolstered by the change in the exclusion from "acquired" for business purposes to "used at death" for business purposes which was made in England between the Law of Property Act 1922 and the 1925 Act.

[99]A motor car has been regarded as an "article of personal use"; *Re White* [1916] 1 Ch 172.

any degree of business use will activate the exclusion, or whether it only applies to chattels used mainly or exclusively for business purposes.[100] In the absence of words such as 'solely', 'substantially' or 'exclusively' it is arguable that any amount of business use could exclude the chattel. In the case of a motor car, presumably the intention of the legislature was not to exclude a vehicle if it is merely used for going to and from the place of work each day[101] and some business use over and above this would be required.

6.56   Little help can be gleaned from the case law, which to date has been scant. In *Re Ogilby*[102] a herd of shorthorn cattle, although farmed at a loss, was held to be a business chattel, reliance being placed upon the fact that it had been treated as such for the purposes of *tax* and rating.[103] This could suggest that if an intestate has been claiming the running of his car as an allowable expense deductible before tax, or has claimed capital allowances towards its acquisition,[104] the vehicle is not a personal chattel to which the spouse is automatically entitled.

The entitlement of issue

6.57   In Northern Ireland all issue who are entitled have an absolute interest, even if they are minors.[105]   By contrast, in England issue always take upon statutory trusts and only get a vested interest if they reach 18 years of age or marry before that age.[106]

---

[100]In New Zealand the comparable legislation refers to "any chattel used exclusively or principally at the death of the intestate for business purposes".

[101]Even this particular point is open to debate; whilst it is now considered axiomatic that such is "private" motoring for income tax purposes, see eg *Newson* v *Robertson* [1953] Ch 7, it has not been construed as "social, domestic or pleasure" purposes in insurance policies: *Seddon* v *Binions* [1978] 1 Lloyds' Reports 381.

[102][1942] Ch 288.

[103]If someone has been carrying on a business at a loss for successive years it is now open to the Inland Revenue to invoke the so-called "hobby-farming" rules found in ss 384 and 397 of the Income and Corporation Taxes Act 1988 to prevent them claiming continuous allowable losses. Presumably if this has been done the argument that it was not a business would carry substantial weight.

[104]Ie, practically anybody who is self-employed and has a car.

[105]Where a minor is entitled under an intestacy, s 38 of the 1955 Act empowers the personal representatives to appoint trustees to the infant's share and on the vesting of the property in such trustees, the personal representatives are discharged from further liability - see para 12.130 *post*.

[106]The entitlement of the spouse may therefore alter after the intestate's death; eg if initially two minor children survived but they both later died before they reached their majority.

6.58   It should be remembered that in all cases the *primary* entitlement is with the deceased's children; grandchildren or remoter issue can only take by representation of their parent's share, if that parent has predeceased the intestate. This is the case even if all the intestate's children are dead.

If there is a surviving spouse

6.59   If the intestate is survived by a spouse *and* issue, the issue have no entitlement if the estate, excluding personal chattels, does not exceed the sum of £125,000.[107] If the estate does exceed this sum then the entitlement is subject to the spouse's interest in the personal chattels, the fixed net sum and the residue, and the extent of the entitlement depends upon the total number of children who either survived the intestate or predeceased the intestate leaving issue surviving.[108]

6.60   If the deceased is survived by only one child (or the deceased is not *survived* by any children, but there is only one child who has predeceased the intestate leaving issue) that child (or the issue of the dead child) is entitled to one-half of the residue.

6.61   If the total of the children surviving the intestate and the children who have predeceased the intestate leaving issue surviving is more than one, then together they are entitled to two-thirds of the residue. This proportion is the same no matter how many persons are involved. Thus if A dies intestate leaving a widow and two children (both alive) and B dies intestate leaving a widow and five children (all still alive), then A's two children will each receive one-third of the residue whereas B's will each only receive two-fifteenths (ie a fifth of two-thirds).

6.62   Returning to the above example, if only three of the children had actually survived B, but the other two (C and D) had left issue surviving him, the two-thirds residue would be divided into five. The surviving children would each receive one of these shares (ie, two-fifteenths of the residue each, as before). Had the children who are now deceased still been alive, they too would each have been entitled to the same share. Because they are dead the issue who survive them are entitled in their place - but *only* to the share which the parent would have been entitled to if he was still living. Thus if C left four children,

---

[107]This is the relevant sum for deaths on or after 1 January 1994 and for deaths before this date see table at para 6.50 *supra*.
[108]1955 Act, s 8.

but D left only one, C's four would each be entitled to one quarter of two-fifteenths of the residue, but D's only child would be entitled to the full two-fifteenths.

6.63   Whilst the distribution in the above scenario is not generally thought too unreasonable, the same applies even if *all* the intestate's children have predeceased him. For instance, imagine that A's two children (E and F) had both predeceased him, and E was survived by his only child, but F was survived by four children. E's child would take the one-third residue to which his father would have been entitled had he still been alive, but F's four children would have to divide the one third residue to which F would have been entitled between them, thus receiving one-twelfth each.   This form of distribution, whereby the shares are attributed according to the branches of the family is known as *per stirpes* (by the stocks), as distinct from *per capita* (by the heads).[109] In the given example, the children of E and F are all grandchildren of the intestate A, and as such are of the same degree of relationship to A. There are no surviving children, yet the individual share to which each grandchild is entitled is dependent upon the number of siblings in that branch of the family. Although children of the same parent will always share equally, there is inequality of entitlement as between children from different branches of the family. For these reasons, it is widely thought that a *per stirpital* distribution amongst issue (at least when there are no surviving children) is contrary to the presumed intention of the intestate.   It is disappointing that the Law Commission recently decided that it would be preferable not to alter the status quo.[110]

If there is no surviving spouse

6.64   If an intestate is survived by issue, but there is no surviving spouse, the estate is divided amongst the surviving issue *per stirpes*.[111]   Stirpital distribution has been discussed at some length in the preceding section. This description is equally applicable if there is no surviving spouse; that is, distribution is by the stocks, primary entitlement is with the deceased's *children*, and issue have only a secondary right to take by representation the share to which their parent would have been entitled had that parent not predeceased the intestate. Thus surviving children always exclude their own

---

[109]Under a *per capita* distribution in the last example, the five grandchildren of the intestate would have taken the full two-thirds residue in equal shares, ie two-fifteenths each.

[110]The Final Report of the Law Commission (No 187) (1989), para 48.

[111]1955 Act, s 8.

children. The comments and criticisms made in the preceding paragraphs in relation to stirpital distribution are also relevant here.

Liability to account for advancements

6.65   The doctrine of *hotchpot* requires a person to bring certain lifetime gifts made to him by a deceased into account when the entitlement on that deceased's death is being computed.   Express hotchpot clauses are sometimes found in wills, while on an intestacy section 17 of the 1955 Act requires that *inter vivos* advancements made by an intestate to his child must be brought into account when the distribution as between that child and the intestate's other *children* is being calculated.   Consider an intestate A who is widowed but is survived by three children B, C and D and who leaves a net estate of £12,000. Without more, each of the children would obviously have been entitled to £4,000. If, however, B had been advanced £3,000 during A's lifetime this must be brought into account; the £3,000 is treated for this purpose alone as part of the estate and added to the £12,000. The total of £15,000 is then divided into the three shares to establish each child's total entitlement, that is, £5,000. Thus B is only entitled to a further £2,000 of the death benefits and the others receive £5,000 each.

6.66   The provisions *only* apply if the total share which the advanced child is to receive when the advancement has been accounted for is greater than the advancement itself.   Once the advancement is equal to or greater than the total share the child receives nothing of the *death* benefits, but there is no requirement to 'pay back' into the estate. If B above had already been advanced £9,000 instead of £3,000, his total share applying the same formula would work out as £7,000 (£21,000 divided by three) and he would actually owe money to the estate. In this case B retains the full £9,000, receives nothing on A's death, and C and D each receive £6,000 (£12,000 divided by two).

6.67   As noted, the requirement to account only extends *as between children*, although in the case of issue taking by representation from a child of the intestate those issue must account for any advances made by the intestate to their parent.[112] In addition, if the intestate actually stood *in loco parentis* to his or her grandchild, then section 17(6)[113] of the 1955 Act extends the duty to that *grandchild* to account for any advancements made to him. This is the only

---

[112]S 17 (6)(b).
[113]This particular provision has no counterpart in the English equivalent, s 47(1)(iii) of the Administration of Estates Act 1925.

extension of the obligation beyond the parent/child relationship and persons other than grandparents who stand in *loco parentis* are not affected. There is no requirement upon the intestate's children to bring advances into account in order to increase the share on death of a surviving spouse.

6.68 Litigation arising out of the hotchpot provisions has generally centred on which lifetime gifts are to be brought into account. The actual wording of section 17 of the 1955 Act refers to amounts "*advanced by the intestate by way of portion*"; and later (in relation to valuation) the term "advancement" is used. No statutory definition is given.[114] In this regard, section 17 is in exactly the same terms as its predecessor, the Statute of Distributions (Ir) 1695, which, in turn, mirrored its English counterpart, section 3 of the Statute of Distributions 1670, which was effective until its repeal by the Administration of Estates Act 1925. Indeed, the classic statements[115] on what constitutes an advancement emanate from two separate judgments of Sir George Jessel MR in the case of *Taylor* v *Taylor*,[116] which was decided under the 1670 Act in 1891:

> "..an advancement by way of portion is something given by the parent to establish the child for life, or to make what is called a provision for him - not a mere casual payment of this kind. You may make the provision by way of marriage portion on the marriage of the child. You may make it on putting him into a profession or business in a variety of ways: you may pay for a commission, you may buy him the goodwill of a business and give him stock-in-trade.....*if in the absence of evidence you find a father giving a large sum to a child in one payment, there is a presumption that that is intended to start him in life or make a provision for him*; but if a small sum is so given you may require evidence to show the purpose. .....It is not every payment made to a child which is to be regarded as an advancement, or an advancement by way of portion. In every case to which I have been referred there has either been a settlement itself, or the purpose for which the payment was made has been shewn to be that which everyone would recognise as being for establishing the child or making a provision for the child."[117]

> "... nothing could be more productive of misery in families than if he were to hold that every member of the family must account strictly for every sum received from a parent. ... *Prima facie, an advancement must be made in early life; but any sum given by*

---

[114]Contrast the Republic of Ireland's Succession Act 1965, s 63(6)

[115]"The nearest approach to a definition of what is an advancement that our case law has achieved" *per* Jenkins LJ in *Re Hayward* [1957] 2 All ER 474.

[116](1875) LR 20 Eq 155.

[117]*Ibid* at p157. Emphasis added.

> *way of making a permanent provision for the child would come within the term establishing for life.*"[118]

6.69 Applying these statements to the actual facts before it, the Court of Appeal held that the following constituted advancements by portion: payment of the admission fee to the relevant Inn of Court for a child destined for the Bar; the price of a commission and a uniform for a child entering the army and the price of plant and machinery for a child starting in business. In contrast, the following were held not to be advancements by portions: assisting a child in the clergy with house-keeping and other expenses; passage money to an officer and his wife who were going to India with his regiment and the discharge of debts incurred by the same officer while on the sub-continent. Similarly, in *Re Scott*[119] the sum of £5,000 given to a son to pay off his debts was held not to be an advancement but rather was regarded merely as temporary assistance.

6.70 When the English Statute of Distributions 1670 was replaced by the Administration of Estates Act 1925, the wording of what was now section 47(1)(iii) had altered significantly:

> "... any *money or property* which, by way of *advancement or on the marriage* of a child of the intestate, has been paid to such child [must be brought into account]."[120]

6.71 This obviously raises questions as to the persuasiveness in this jurisdiction of post-1925 decisions of the English courts. The English Court of Appeal had to address the relevance of *pre*-1925 cases to section 47(1)(iii) in *Re Hayward*.[121] Whilst conceding that the language of section 47(1)(iii) was now "radically different", and "if anything narrower than the Statute of Distributions", Jenkins LJ was of the opinion that decisions under the old Act were, "generally speaking", applicable to the new. The fact that the famous *Taylor* dicta formed the basis of the actual decision both in *Hayward* itself and the other leading modern case *Hardy* v *Shaw*[122] endorses this view. The learned Judge's qualification, however, suggested that he clearly envisaged some degree of divergence, and one example of such was made clear from the actual facts before him. The issue to be determined by the Court was whether two nominations made by a father in favour of his son (one of saving certificates,

---

[118]*Ibid* at p158. Emphasis added.
[119][1903] 1 Ch 1.
[120]Administration of Estates Act 1925, s 47(1)(iii).
[121][1957] 2 All ER 474, *per* Jenkins LJ at 477.
[122][1976] Ch 82.

the other of money in a Post Office account) had to be brought into account under section 47(1)(iii). At the time when the nominations were made the son was 43 years of age, married and in gainful employment. It was held that the nominations were not advancements within the meaning of the section, particular reliance being placed upon the second of Sir George Jessel MR's dicta in *Taylor*, and as the son in question was not in the first flush of youth, some element of permanent provision had to be established. Whilst the total sums nominated were not insignificant in relation to the rest of the estate (a fact upon which it was agreed *some* weight could properly be placed) they were not large amounts in themselves, and in the absence of further evidence as to circumstances or intention it was not possible to classify them as advances. What is of particular interest in this jurisdiction is the dictum in *Taylor* which suggests that a settlement is *per se* "an advancement by way of portion". In *Hayward* Jenkins LJ seemed prepared to concede that the nominations in question could be regarded as a revocable lifetime settlement, and if this description of them was accurate, the former provisions of the Statute of Distributions (which were the same as the existing provisions in Northern Ireland) would automatically have been invoked. The learned Judge was of the opinion, however, that one substantive change which accompanied the new wording was the fact that it was no longer sufficient merely to show the existence of a settlement. Considering that all three members of the Court of Appeal were in agreement that *Hayward* was a "border-line" case, it is questionable whether the same decision would have been reached under section 17 of the 1955 Act.[123]

6.72 In *Hardy v Shaw*[124] it was held that transfers of shares in the family business made by a mother to each of her two sons constituted an advancement; reliance being placed on both *Taylor* and *Hayward* as authority for the proposition that an advancement included "anything which may fairly be described as permanent provision". In this case, in contrast to *Hayward*, the amount of the advances, both relative to the total size of the estate, and in the abstract, was substantial.

6.73 In Northern Ireland section 17(2) of the 1955 Act expressly provides that the value of the advancement is to be reckoned as at the date it is made, although if the intestate himself has left a written valuation, this is to be taken.

---

[123]While statutory nominations of both savings certificates and Post Office accounts have been abolished, other statutory nominations do still exist, see para 10.08 *post*.
[124][1976] Ch 82.

In England the date of valuation is the death of the intestate.[125] Section 17(5) empowers the personal representatives to employ a "duly qualified valuer" for the purposes.

6.74 The onus of proving that such an advancement took place is on the person asserting it - unless it has been expressed in writing by the intestate.[126] A further distinction between this jurisdiction and England is the absence here of any provision enabling hotchpot to be excluded by a contrary intention.[127] Section 17 of the 1955 Act is therefore mandatory.[128]

Proposed repeal of section 17 of the Administration of Estates Act (NI) 1955

6.75 The obligation upon children to account for lifetime advances has been enshrined in the law since the enactment of the Statute of Distributions and derives from the equitable presumption against double portions. The objectives of hotchpot are simple and logical; to secure equality of treatment between the intestate's children insofar as this is possible. In general, however, it has been widely criticised as being complex and time-consuming:

> "For some reason, which is difficult to fathom, but presumably with an idea of producing fairness, the draftsmen of the Administration of Estates Act 1925 introduced hotchpot provisions into the sections of the Act dealing with intestacy. It seems to me that they made a great mistake in so doing, and that it would be better to have left the whole thing out".[129]

Hotchpot has recently been abolished in England and Wales by section 112 of the Law Reform (Succession) Act 1995[130] and similar provision is contained for this jurisdiction in the draft Succession (NI) Order 1996. Article 3(2) of this Order repeals section 17 of the 1955 Act.[131]

---

[125]Administration of Estates Act 1925, s 47(1)(iii). See *Farrand* (1961) 25 Conv 468 where it is argued that this can produce illogical results.

[126]S 17(3).

[127]S 47(1)(iii) of the 1925 Act. For a discussion of the type of factors which will prove a contrary intention, see *Hardy* v *Shaw* [1976] Ch 82.

[128]Nor do personal representatives have a discretion as to whether or not they apply the section.

[129]*Re Morton* [1956] Ch 644, *per* Danckwerts J at 647.

[130]Effective for deaths on or after 1 January 1996.

[131]It is expected that the Succession (NI) Order 1996 will be effective by the beginning of 1997.

Entitlement of other relatives

6.76   Parents have a residuary entitlement if the intestate was survived by a spouse but *not* issue, *and* the estate, excluding personal chattels, exceeds £200,000. They have an absolute entitlement only if the intestate was survived by *neither* spouse *nor* issue.[132] It will be noted that parents have no entitlement in any case where the intestate is survived by issue.

6.77   In the first case, where there is a surviving spouse, the extent of the entitlement of the parent(s) is one-half of the residue[133] and this proportion does not vary depending upon whether one or both parents survive. A sole surviving parent will be entitled to the full half himself and if both parents survive the intestate they will each be entitled to one-quarter of the residue. In the event of the parent(s) being entitled absolutely (because there is no surviving spouse or issue) the position is the same - a sole parent takes the entire estate absolutely and two surviving parents divide it between themselves equally.

6.78   The entitlement of siblings[134] of the intestate runs parallel to that of parents; they have only a residuary entitlement if the intestate was survived by a spouse but was survived by neither issue *nor* parents *and* the estate, excluding personal chattels, exceeds £200,000, and an absolute entitlement, whatever the size of the estate, if the intestate was survived by neither spouse nor issue nor parents.[135] Whether the entitlement is to one-half of the residue as in the first case or to the entire estate, it is divided in equal shares amongst the number of brothers and sisters who survived the intestate. If there are brothers and/or sisters who have predeceased the intestate leaving issue surviving him, those issue take by representation the share to which their deceased parent would have been entitled.[136]

6.79   Issue, parents and siblings (and the issue of siblings who have predeceased the intestate) are the only relatives of the intestate who can stop the surviving spouse from taking the entire estate.[137]

---

[132] 1955 Act, s 9.
[133] Ie, one-half of what remains after the spouse's statutory legacy of £200,000 and the personal chattels have been taken out.
[134] Those related to the intestate by whole-blood or half-blood take equally.
[135] 1955 Act, s 10(1).
[136] S 10(2).
[137] The distinction in England and Wales which is made between whole-blood and half-blood has already been pointed out. There, in the event of no surviving issue, parents or siblings of the whole-blood, siblings of the half-blood do not share the estate with the spouse.

6.80   Section 11(1) of the 1955 Act provides that if an intestate is not survived by spouse, issue, parent, brother or sister nor issue of any predeceased brother or sister, his estate shall be distributed in equal shares amongst his next-of-kin. By "next-of-kin" is meant the person or persons who at the date of the death of the intestate stand nearest in blood relationship to him.[138] Degrees of blood relationship are ascertained in the usual way: in the case of a direct lineal ancestor by counting up from the intestate, and in the case of any other relative by counting up from the intestate to the nearest ancestor common to the intestate and the relative, and then downwards from the ancestor to the relative.[139] It is expressly provided, however, that if a direct lineal ancestor is within the same degree of blood relationship to any other relative, then the relative is to be preferred. Thus, for example, aunts and uncles take in preference to great-grandparents even though both are one degree removed from the grandparent. The Table of Distribution at page 115 *supra* incorporates a list which ranks relatives in the order in which they constitute the next-of-kin and this will be sufficient for most circumstances. Little can usefully be added at this point to what has already been included there, and the only real difficulty surrounds the extent to which representation by issue of relatives who have predeceased the intestate is permitted.

6.81   It has already been noted that representation is permitted in the case of issue of brothers and sisters. The only other collaterals who are permitted to take by representation are the issue of an uncle or aunt.[140] The usual rule applies and these issue of a deceased uncle or aunt of the intestate take *per stirpes* the share that uncle or aunt would have taken as next-of-kin if he or she had survived the intestate.[141] This brings in first cousins. In the case of more remote collaterals, however, representation by issue is not available.[142]

Entitlement of the Crown - *bona vacantia*

6.82   When no surviving next-of-kin of an intestate can be ascertained the estate passes to the Crown as *bona vacantia*.[143] The Crown is generally prepared to make *ex gratia* payments, at least of part of the estate, on the application of someone such as a cohabitant who cannot inherit or a friend or

---

[138]1955 Act, s 12(1).
[139]S 12(2).
[140]1955 Act, s 11(3).
[141]1955 Act, s 11(2).
[142]The Johnson Committee recommended that the right of representation should extend to the issue of *all* collaterals, Cmd (NI) 308 (1952) para 30.
[143]1955 Act, s 16.

neighbour who can establish some sort of moral claim on the basis of services rendered. Such applications are made by way of supporting affidavit and further particulars can be sought from the Crown Solicitor's Office.

PARTIAL INTESTACY

6.83 It was noted earlier that intestacy can be either total or partial, and that the latter arises when the deceased leaves a will which does not effectively dispose of all his property. This may be because the will is a poorly drafted document without a residue clause, or it may be because the residuary gift has lapsed or failed. It is a common misconception that residue lapses into residue; if a will includes a residuary gift 'to my brothers Tom, Dick and Harry in equal shares' and Tom predeceases the testator a partial intestacy will arise as regards his share. It will *not* lapse into residue and benefit the other two brothers.[144]

6.84 Article 13 of the Wills and Administration Proceedings (NI) Order 1994 provides that where, after a testator has made a will, a decree of a court dissolves or annuls his marriage or declares it void, then, unless a contrary intention appears from the will, any gift to the spouse passes as if that spouse had died on the date of the termination of the marriage.[145] In order to reduce the number of partial intestacies which this provision was likely to generate, it is expressly provided that if the surviving spouse is to take merely a share of residue,[146] that share will be divided between the other residuary legatees.[147]

6.85 Section 18 of the 1955 Act provides that where the will of a testator effectively disposes of part only of his estate, then, unless it appears by the will that his personal representatives are intended to take the remainder of the estate beneficially, it is to be distributed by the personal representatives to the persons who would have been entitled if the testator had died intestate and left no other estate. Property subject to a partial intestacy is thus distributed in the same way as property subject to a total intestacy.

6.86 In England until recently issue of an intestate entitled under a partial intestacy were required to account for any testamentary benefits which they had

---

[144]Of course the problem can be avoided by drafting the clause 'to such of my brothers Tom, Dick and Harry as survive me in equal shares'.
[145]See para 7.51 *supra.*
[146]Lapse of which would normally create a partial intestacy as to that share.
[147]Art 13(3). See para 7.58 *post.*

received under the will.[148] In Northern Ireland, however, hotchpot has never applied to a partial intestacy.[149]

6.87   The requirement that children must bring *inter vivos* advancements into account in a total intestacy has already been discussed.[150] The wording of section 18 of the 1955 Act, which provides that the property subject to a partial intestacy is to be dealt with as if it were the sole estate, would seem to impose the requirements of section 17 as to *inter vivos* advancements on a *partial* intestacy. Thus while testamentary benefits need not be accounted for, lifetime benefits must. However, article 3(2) of the draft Succession (NI) 1996 which is expected to become effective at the beginning of 1997 repeals section 17 of the 1955 Act, thus abolishing the obligation to account.

---

[148]Administration of Estates Act 1925, s 49 - abolished for deaths on or after 1 January 1996 by the Law Reform (Succession) Act 1995.

[149]See *Re Roby* [1908] 1 Ch 71.

[150]See para 6.65 *supra*.

CHAPTER SEVEN

FAILURE OF GIFTS UNDER A WILL OR INTESTATE DISTRIBUTION

7.01 This chapter examines some of the reasons why the eventual distribution of a person's property after his death will differ from that laid down in his will or by the intestate code. Alteration of entitlement by an order of the court made under the Inheritance (Provision for Family and Dependants) (NI) Order 1979 is dealt with in Chapter Eight.

DISCLAIMER

Under a will

7.02 A beneficiary will not be forced to accept a gift under a will: "[t]he law is not so absurd as to force a man to take an estate against his will".[1] Common reasons for a beneficiary wishing to disclaim a gift under a will include the fact that tax advantages may result from doing so, or that he is ridding himself of an onerous obligation which contains little or no real benefit.

7.03 Disclaimer may be effected in writing, by deed or otherwise, or may be implied from conduct. It is generally retroactive to the date of death of the testator.[2]

Retraction of the decision to disclaim a benefit under a will

7.04 Case law has established that a beneficiary can retract his renunciation of benefits under a will at any time provided that no one has altered his position in reliance on the renunciation. Thus when the Committee of the Home of Rest for Horses, Cricklewood renounced the residuary gift left in a sympathiser's will, believing it to be onerous, it was held that this decision could be retracted when, over ten years later, the residue was sold for a considerable sum of money.[3]

---

[1]*Per* Abbot CJ in *Townson* v *Tickell* (1819) 3 B & Ald 31.

[2]*Parsons* v *Att-Gen* [1943] Ch 12.

[3]*Re Cranstoun's Will Trusts* [1949] Ch 523; following *Re Young* [1913] 1 Ch 272.

Disclaiming gifts which include onerous liabilities

7.05   One of the main reasons why a beneficiary may wish to disclaim is that any benefit which the gift might   provide for him is outweighed by its corresponding liabilities.   The classic example of such an 'onerous' gift is an unexpired lease of relatively short duration, but under which the beneficiary is responsible for considerable repairs.   The general rule is that it is unfair to accept the *benefits* which flow from a gift without taking the *liabilities* too, so it is not possible to accept one without the other.   Where, however, the benefits under a will to the same person are capable of being construed as two distinct legacies, and one is onerous but the other beneficial, *prima facie* the beneficiary is entitled to disclaim only the onerous one and take the other.   This presumption can be rebutted if a contrary intention on the part of the testator can be shown.[4]

7.06   Whether a benefit under a will is to be construed as a single gift or as two or more separate and distinct gifts is not always straightforward.   For instance, in *Re Joel*[5] a bequest of the "house at 74 Brook Street together with the contents" was construed as a single gift so that the legatee could not disclaim the house (a leasehold), but retain its contents.   By contrast, in *Re Lysons*[6] the gift of another leasehold property "together with all articles of [furniture belonging to me]" was construed as being a separate gift of the chattels, enabling the legatee to take them and disclaim the house.

7.07   A gift of *residue* is generally construed as a single gift.   Thus where part of an otherwise valuable residuary estate is a burdensome lease the residuary legatee must either accept all of the residue or none of it.[7]

7.08   It may be prudent for a beneficiary who is entitled to a gift in a will which has been made subject to onerous conditions to disclaim it, and then benefit under the residue, or resulting intestacy, *free from the conditions*.[8]

On intestacy

7.09   At one time there was a school of thought that *intestate* benefits, which were considered to be imperative in nature, could not be disclaimed in the same

---

[4]   *Guthrie* v *Walrond* (1883) 22 Ch 573 at 577.

[5]   *Re Joel* [1943] Ch 311.

[6]   *Re Lysons* (1912) 107 LT 146.

[7]   *Hawkins* v *Hawkins* (1880) 13 Ch 470.

[8]   If, however, the "condition" is a charge on the gift in favour of a third party it cannot be defeated in this way, and the residue or intestacy will also be charged with the relevant amount - *Wilson* v *Wilson* (1847) 1 De G & Sm 152.

way as testamentary gifts. However, disclaimer was allowed in *Re Scott*[9] and the better view would now seem to be that intestate benefits can be disclaimed, at least up until the interest has vested in the beneficiary, whether by way of assent or otherwise. This view is endorsed by the Inheritance Tax Act 1984, which in section 142[10] refers to benefits conferred by various dispositions being disclaimed, and includes dispositions "by will, *under the law relating to intestacy* or otherwise [emphasis added]".

Deeds of variation: post-mortem tax-planning

7.10 The efficacy of using a professionally drafted will as a tax saving instrument has been noted elsewhere and the counsel of perfection must be the periodic review of existing wills in the light of any annual changes to the capital taxation regime. Under the current inheritance tax regime a 'second bite at the cherry' may exist where this opportunity has not been availed of, or where the tax laws have outpaced the reviewing of wills.

7.11 By virtue of section 142 of the Inheritance Tax Act 1984, if all the beneficiaries under a will or intestacy, being *sui juris*,[11] agree to a variation of the entitlement and:

(a)   this is effected within two years of the date of death, and;

(b)   the Inland Revenue are notified within six months of the date of the instrument;

the variation will be treated for both inheritance tax and capital gains tax purposes as if the property had been left that way on death.

7.12 Moreover, although it was confirmed a few years ago in *Russell v IRC*[12] that a third bite of the cherry is not available - only one variation attracts the tax advantages and a subsequent one constitutes a variation of a *variation* which is not within the scope of section 142, the court may allow the deed to be

---

[9]   [1975] 1 WLR 1260.

[10] See para 7.10 *post*.

[11] Where infants or incapable persons are involved, the court may have power to give its consent on their behalf under s 57 of the Trustee Act (NI) 1958, provided that the variation is for their "benefit". Saving tax can constitute a benefit (although see *Re Weston* [1969] 1 Ch 223).

[12] [1988] 2 All ER 405.

rectified if the words mistakenly used do not give effect to the parties' intention. A beneficial application of this occurred recently in *Schneider* v *Mills*.[13]

7.13   These 'deeds of family arrangement' as they are popularly called, are employed frequently for post-death tax-planning and certainly can be very useful.   One caveat, however, should be borne in mind.   The 1989 Budget speech contained proposals which effectively sounded the death-knell for *tax-planning* for deeds of variation.   At the eleventh hour the Government backed down and the proposals were not enacted in the Finance Act.   Instead a full review into the use of such variations was promised.   Although nothing further has emerged, it must be emphasised that posthumous tax-planning can be a risky substitute for a properly drafted will.

KILLING THE TESTATOR OR THE INTESTATE

Unlawfully killing the testator or the intestate

7.14   Any person who unlawfully kills another is generally precluded from acquiring a benefit from that deceased's estate.   This common law rule, which is based on public policy, is referred to as the "forfeiture rule" in the Forfeiture (NI) Order 1982, the piece of legislation which alleviates its consequences in certain circumstances.[14]   It should be remembered that the rule itself remains part of the common law; the 1982 Order (which is in exactly the same terms as the English Forfeiture Act 1982) merely confirms its existence, but is not a statutory codification.

7.15   The first clear and explicit application of the rule is found in *Cleaver's Case*,[15] where Fry LJ declared:

> "The principle of public policy invoked is in my opinion rightly asserted.   It appears to me that no system of jurisprudence can with reason include amongst the rights which it enforces rights directly resulting to the person asserting them from the crime of that person."

7.16   Initially there had been some doubt as to whether the rule applied to *intestate* deaths, on the basis that it might have been inappropriate for a mere rule of public policy to over-ride the mandatory statutory distribution.   It has

---

[13][1993] 3 All ER 377; for a note on this case see *First Annual Review of Property Law* (1994) (SLS), p 150.

[14]See para 7.24 *post*.

[15]*Cleaver* v *Mutual Reserve Fund Life Association* [1892] 1 QB 147; it is surprising that this is as late as 1892 because the rule is generally regarded as 'long-standing'.

long since been confirmed, however, that the rule applies equally to testate *and* intestate deaths,[16] and the Forfeiture (NI) Order 1982 clearly recognises its application to *both* modes of succession.[17]

7.17   In addition, the rule extends beyond property which passes as part of the victim's estate, to that held under a joint tenancy with the killer. The victim's share in such property would otherwise pass to his killer by virtue of survivorship, but in such circumstances a severance in equity will be effected to prevent the killer benefitting from the deceased's share.[18]

Exceptions to the forfeiture rule

Insane killers
7.18   This rule of public policy postulates a *mens rea*, so insane killers are not within its scope and are not prevented from benefitting from the estates of their victims.[19] There is, however, a presumption of sanity.[20]

7.19   In England the forfeiture rule applies to those found guilty of unlawful killing by reason of diminished responsibility.[21] Presumably it therefore applies in Northern Ireland to those convicted of the equivalent offence, killing by reason of impaired mental responsibility.[22] This uncompromising line led to a number of very hard decisions, the most publicised of which, *Re Giles*,[23] probably precipitated the enactment of the forfeiture legislation referred to above.

Some forms of manslaughter?
7.20   While the forfeiture rule always applies to cases of murder by a sane person (whether or not there has been a conviction for the crime), there is still a small measure of doubt that some cases of manslaughter remain outside its ambit. However, the weight of authority suggests that it applies to every case of manslaughter.

---

[16]*Ibid.* See also *Re Pitts* [1931] 1 Ch 546; *Sigsworth, Bedford v Bedford* [1935] Ch 89.
[17]1982 Order, art 4(4)(a)(i).
[18]*Re K* [1985] Ch 85; [1985] 2 All ER 833 (CA).
[19]*Re Houghton* [1915] 2 Ch 173; *Re Pitts* [1931] 1 Ch 546.
[20]In *Re Pollock* [1941] Ch 219.
[21]Homicide Act 1957, s 2.
[22]Criminal Justice Act (NI) 1966, s 5.
[23][1972] Ch 544.

7.21   In *Re Giles*[24] the rule was applied to disentitle an unfortunate widow who had (surprisingly) killed her husband by a single blow with a domestic chamber pot.   At her trial for murder the widow had pleaded guilty to manslaughter by reason of diminished responsibility, and was sentenced to detention in Broadmoor.   On her behalf it was argued that as the sentence was remedial rather than punitive in nature, and thus implied no moral blameworthiness on her part, the rule of public policy should not apply.   In rejecting these submissions Pennycuick V-C stressed that moral culpability was *not* a necessary prerequisite to the application of the rule.

7.22   Contrary authority, supporting the view that there are some cases of manslaughter outside the scope of the rule, is generally found in cases dealing with entitlement under *insurance policies*.[25]   However, there is an *obiter dictum* by Vinelott J in *Re K*,[26] a case on the scope of the Forfeiture Act 1982, that the rule only extends to manslaughter cases where *violence* has been threatened.[27] An interesting question which has yet to be resolved by direct authority is whether causing the death of someone by reckless driving[28] invokes the forfeiture rule.[29]

Those claiming through the killer

7.23   The forfeiture rule not only precludes the killer from benefitting from his victim's estate, but excludes also those who claim either through or under him:

> "... the person who commits murder, *or any person claiming through him or her*, should not be allowed to benefit by his or her criminal act..."[30]

For example, in *Re Crippen*,[31] a husband murdered his wife and was subsequently executed for his crime.   His mistress, to whom he had left all his

---

[24]*Ibid.*

[25]*Gray v Barr* [1971] 2 QB 544; *R v Chief National Insurance Commissioner, ex p Connor* [1982] QB 758.

[26][1985] Ch 85, at p 98.

[27]In *Re K* itself the forfeiture rule was held to apply because the killer had deliberately threatened unlawful violence with a loaded gun.

[28]Contrary to the Road Traffic (NI) Order 1981, art 139(1).

[29]The weight of academic opinion, regarding the equivalent English offence, suggests that it does: (1974) 37 MLR 481 at 495; (1973) 89 LQR 235 at 239; (1972) 88 LQR 13; (1970) 35 MLR 426 at 427.

[30]*Per* Lord Esher MR in *Cleaver v Mutual Reserve Fund Life Association* [1892] 1 QB 147 at 152. See also *In the Estate of Crippen* [1911] P 108.   Ftnt [31] see overleaf.

property by his will, was not allowed to claim the sum which he would have inherited from his wife's intestacy.

The effect of the Forfeiture (NI) Order 1982

7.24   It has already been noted that the Forfeiture (NI) Order 1982 (hereafter the 1982 Order), which corresponds to the English Forfeiture Act 1982 and is in identical terms, gives the court power to modify the forfeiture rule in certain circumstances. This power is limited to cases of manslaughter and has no effect on the application of the forfeiture rule in the case of a person who stands convicted of murder.[32]

The basis for modification of the rule

7.25   A court can only exercise its powers under the 1982 Order to order modification of the forfeiture rule if it is satisfied that "the justice of the case" requires it to do so.[33] This must be assessed with regard to both the behaviour of the offender and of the deceased, and to such other circumstances as appear to the court to be material.[34]

7.26   *Re K*,[35] the first case in which the construction and scope of the identical English Forfeiture Act 1982 were considered judicially, provides a useful illustration of the exercise of the court's discretion. The applicant, whose marriage had been a catalogue of violent and threatening outbursts by her husband, had killed him when the shotgun which she had been aiming at him accidentally discharged. She would have taken a number of benefits under her husband's will and the matrimonial home under the right of survivorship. At her trial the applicant pleaded to a charge of manslaughter and, in light of the circumstances surrounding the killing, she avoided a custodial sentence, being merely placed on probation for two years. She applied successfully under the 1982 Act for modification of the forfeiture rule.

At first instance, Vinelott J primarily took into account the conduct of both the applicant and the deceased in the period before the fatal incident, concluding that the widow had been "a loyal wife who suffered grave violence at the hands of the deceased." Referring to the observation made by Lord Salmon in *DPP* v *Newbury*,[36] that cases of manslaughter necessarily vary infinitely in their

---

[31][1911] P 108.
[32]Art 7.
[33]Art 4(2).
[34]*Ibid*.
[35][1985] Ch 85.
[36][1977] AC 500 at 507.

gravity, the learned judge thought that the case in question was one "which weighs least heavily". In addition, Vinelott J considered the means of both the applicant and those who would have benefitted had the forfeiture rule been applied. The fact that, prior to discovering the considerable value of the deceased's estate (around £285,000), a number of members of the deceased's family had suggested in writing that they would have been willing to make *ex gratia* payments to the widow in an attempt to carry out the deceased's testamentary wishes, was also relied upon.

The deceased's nephew appealed to the Court of Appeal[37] on the ground, *inter alia*, that the trial judge had made an error in law in the exercise of his discretion. The appeal was dismissed; the Court of Appeal held that the discretion to modify the effect of the forfeiture rule conferred by the 1982 Act was in *wide* terms and that Vinelott J had exercised it correctly. The *Re Giles* type scenario discussed above[38] is clearly the sort of case which would now warrant modification of the forfeiture rule.

The power of the court under the Forfeiture (NI) Order 1982
7.27   The court can either completely relieve the offender from the consequences of the forfeiture rule, or decide instead to give only partial relief. The 1982 Order expressly provides two ways in which the latter can be achieved. In the case where more than one interest in property is affected by the rule, the court can modify the rule in respect of some, but not all, of those interests. Secondly, in relation to any given interest in property, the court can modify the rule only in respect of part of that interest.[39] Initially some doubts were expressed as to whether this wording actually prohibited the court from completely modifying the rule, but this ludicrous interpretation was totally rejected in *Re K*, where, it will be recalled, Vinelott J relieved the widow wholly from the effect of the rule in respect of all of the deceased's property.

Deaths before the commencement of the 1982 Order
7.28   The 1982 Order came into operation on 13 October 1982,[40] but a modification of the forfeiture rule can be ordered even if the unlawful killing in question took place before this date.[41] However, property which has already

---

[37] [1985] 2 All ER 833.

[38] See para 7.21 *supra*.

[39] Art 4(5)(a) and (b).

[40] Art 1(2).

[41] Art 1(3).

been distributed by the personal representatives to those entitled on the basis that the forfeiture rule would apply is protected.[42]

Time limit for modification of the forfeiture rule under the 1982 Order

7.29 Where the killer stands convicted, proceedings for modification of the forfeiture rule under the 1982 Order can only be brought within three months of the conviction.[43] There is no provision for extension of this time limit.

Inheritance (Provision for Family and Dependants)(NI) Order 1979

7.30 The right of a person with *locus standi* under the Inheritance (Provision for Family and Dependants) (NI) Order 1979 to apply for reasonable financial provision is expressly preserved notwithstanding that he is guilty of the unlawful killing of the deceased.[44] Of course, if the applicant was adequately provided for by either the deceased's will or his intestacy and the lack of provision resulted from the application of the forfeiture rule, the claim must necessarily fail.[45]

The effect of disentitlement if the forfeiture rule is applied

7.31 For many years there was no definite answer to the question of how an estate should be distributed after the forteiture rule has been applied. Is the property which would have gone to the killer to be distributed to those who would have benefitted in his absence? Or is the property in question to be regarded as *bona vacantia* and be taken by the Crown? It seems that the former is the correct approach. This was the solution adopted in *Re Callaway*,[46] where the point was considered directly for the first time. A daughter had murdered her mother, under whose will she was the sole legatee, and then committed suicide. The question to be resolved was whether the son (the only next-of-kin under the resulting intestacy) was entitled to the entire estate or whether the half-share which would have been the daughter's passed to the Crown. Vinelott J reluctantly held that the son, as the only qualified member of the class of next-of-kin, took the entire estate. He felt himself compelled to do so on the state of the authorities, although he did add that in

---

[42] Art 4(7). See the discussion of the equivalent English provision, s 7(2) in *Re K* [1985] Ch 85 in which it was held that this exception did not extend to property still held by the personal representatives pending administration.

[43] Art 4(3).

[44] Art 5(2)(b).

[45] *Re Royse* [1984] 3 All ER 339. This is discussed in more detail at para 8.14 *post*.

[46] [1956] Ch 559.

none of the earlier cases was the Crown properly represented and, in the event of the decision reaching a higher forum added his own personal preference that the Crown should benefit:

> "Seeing that her crime was against the Queen's peace, why should not the Crown, rather than the Plaintiff, get the benefit from it?"[47]

LAPSE

7.32   The ambulatory nature of a will has already been noted.[48] One of the consequences of this concept is that any gift in a will to a beneficiary who predeceases the testator ordinarily[49] fails or 'lapses'. The gift then falls into residue, or if it is residuary, there is a partial intestacy.

7.33   The doctrine of lapse does not apply to class gifts since those entitled to participate in such a gift are not ascertained until the date of the testator's death. Thus if a testator leaves the residue of his estate to be divided between "such of my brothers living at my death in equal shares", and one of his four brother dies before him, the remaining three brothers share the residue between them. If, however, the same testator tries to achieve a similar effect by providing that the residue be divided between 'my four brothers in equal shares' there is a quite different consequence. This is not a class gift and the dead brother's share lapses, effecting a partial intestacy.

7.34   Like class gifts, gifts to joint tenants are also outside the scope of the doctrine of lapse. If a testator makes a gift of his residue to "my four brothers jointly" there is no lapse unless all four brothers die before the testator. Should only three die, for example, the sole survivor takes the entire residue.

7.35   Although a declaration in a will that the doctrine of lapse is not to apply is ineffective,[50] its consequences can be prevented by providing substitutionary gifts in the will. It is best to do this by expressly naming the person who is to take the legacy if the event occasioning lapse occurs[51] and it is

---

[47]At p 563.

[48]See para 1.08 *supra*.

[49]For exceptions see below.

[50]*Re Ladd* [1932] 2 Ch 219: "to the intent that this my will shall take effect, whether I survive or predecease my husband."

[51]Although the courts have been prepared to interpret phrases such as "[if the original legatee dies in my lifetime] leaving issue and any of such issue shall be living at my death, the benefits hereinbefore given to him or her so dying shall not lapse but shall take effect as if

eminently sensible for practitioners to urge clients to give consideration to the possibility of persons not dying 'in the correct order'.

Commorientes
7.36   The order of death between a testator and a beneficiary will usually be easily determined and it will be obvious if lapse has occurred. Where the order of death is uncertain, the position in Northern Ireland is different to that in England. In England there is a statutory presumption, contained in section 184 of the Law of Property Act 1925, that where there is no evidence as to the order in which deaths have occurred then, for succession purposes, the younger is deemed to have survived the elder. Therefore a gift in the younger's will to the elder would lapse, but not vice versa.

7.37   No similar presumption applies in Northern Ireland, and when the order in which two persons died cannot be satisfactorily determined, neither is deemed to have survived the other, with the result that their estates cannot benefit from each other.   Unfortunately, the importance of determining the exact order of death may encourage certain relatives to pursue   distressing forensic examinations.   To avoid this it may be worth inserting an express survivorship condition (say, 28 days) where there is a likelihood that testator and beneficiary may die at the same time (for instance, husband and wife).

Exceptions to the doctrine of lapse
7.38   There are three exceptions to the doctrine of lapse; two statutory, the other non-statutory:

(a)   gifts to children or other issue of the testator;

(b)   entails;

(c)   gifts in satisfaction of a moral obligation.

Gifts to children who predecease the testator
7.39   A gift in a will to a child (or remoter descendant) of the testator who predeceases him will not lapse if that child leaves issue of his own who survive the testator. This statutory exception to the general rule is contained in article 22 of the Wills and Administration Proceedings (NI) Order 1994.   This replaces, with signifcant amendments, section 33 of the Wills Act 1837,[52] the

---

his or her death had happened immediately after mine" as preventing lapse - *Re Greenwood* [1912] 1 Ch 392.

[52]In England the original s 33 has been amended in the same way by s 19 of the Administration of Justice Act 1982.

effect of which was frequently misunderstood. Article 22 only applies to wills of testators who died on or after 1 January 1995, so section 33 will remain relevant for some years.

7.40   Under section 33 of the 1837 Act if a testator has made provision in his will for a child who predeceased him, and that child himself had issue, those issue saved the gift from lapsing. However, the issue merely *saved* the gift - they did not automatically inherit the saved gift themselves, as was commonly thought. Rather, the saved gift was considered part of the estate of the dead child and could be willed away from the issue who had saved it. The wording of section 33 therefore defeated the obvious intention of the provision, that is, to benefit the *issue* of a child who had predeceased his parent. This shortcoming has been rectified by article 22 of the 1994 Order, under which the issue who save the gift actually benefit from it: "the [lapsed] gift takes effect as a gift to the issue living at the testator's death".

7.41   Distribution to the issue who save the gift under article 22 is *stirpital*.[53]

7.42   "Issue" in article 22 of the 1994 Order expressly includes a person conceived before the testator's death and born living thereafter,[54] thus removing the earlier doubt under section 33, that the expression "*living* at the testator's death" excluded those *en ventre sa mère*.[55] It is also expressly provided that the illegitimacy of any person is to be disregarded.[56]

7.43   Although article 22 has removed a number of the shortcomings evident with section 33, it nevertheless remains preferable expressly to provide for the contingency of the testator's children predeceasing him rather than have to rely on the statutory exception.

7.44   Both section 33 of the 1837 Act and article 22 of the 1994 Order yield to a contrary intention, provided that such is evident from the will. In *Re Meredith*[57] a testator executed a codicil to his will after the death of his son, a beneficiary under the will. After reciting the fact of the son's death and that a gift to him of £100 and his share of the residue had consequently lapsed, the codicil made provision for the son's two children. Romer J held that, as regards

---

[53]Art 22(3).
[54]Art 22(4)(b).
[55]*Elliot* v *Joicey* [1935] AC 209.
[56]Art 22(4)(a).
[57][1924] 2 Ch 552.

the £100 and the share of residue, a contrary intention had been shown and section 33 did not apply. However, section 33 did still apply to a further gift of furniture in the will, which had not been mentioned in the codicil.

7.45   Section 33 of the 1837 Act applied only to gifts to the testator's child for an interest *not determinable at or before that child's death*. Thus section 33 had no application if the child took a life interest, or as a joint tenant, or if the gift was contingent upon him reaching a certain age, and he died before that date. Article 22 of the 1994 Order contains no similar restrictions. However, it is submitted that in all the illustrations given the provision would not apply because a contrary intention would be present from the will.

7.46   It has been noted that the doctrine of lapse does not apply to class gifts,[58] so it was unsurprising that section 33 did not extend to class gifts benefitting issue of the testator.[59] However, article 22(2) of the 1994 Order provides that where a will contains a gift to a class of persons consisting of children or remoter descendants of the testator and a member of the class dies before the testator, leaving issue who are living at the testator's death, the gift takes effect as if the class included those issue. Again, this yields to a contrary intention in the will. It is submitted that a gift in favour of "such of my children as *survive* me" would import such an intention.[60]

Entails
7.47   This exception is now contained in article 22(5) of the 1994 Order, which replaces and re-enacts section 32 of the 1837 Act. Land which is devised by a testator to his child or remoter descendants "in tail", that is, limited to the lineal descendants, will not lapse if that child predeceases the testator, provided that he himself had issue living at the testator's death who would be capable of inheriting under the entail.

This exception is also subject to no contrary intention appearing in the will.

Gifts in satisfaction of a moral obligation
7.48   This exception, the scope of which is open to question, derives from a number of early cases in which it was held that gifts in a will made with the intention of discharging a moral obligation did not lapse. For instance, a testator decides to benefit his creditor by the amount of his debt, although, in

---

[58]See para 7.33 *supra*.
[59]*Re Harvey* [1893] Ch 567.
[60]See the Canadian case *Re Horton* (1979) 88 DLR (3d) 264 (British Columbia).

fact, the said debt is now statute-barred, or the testator had been made bankrupt and the debt discharged. Ordinarily, there no longer being a *legal* obligation to pay the debt, the gift to the creditor is mere bounty and subject to the rules about lapse in the usual way, should the creditor predecease the testator. If, however, it is clear that the testator intended not to give a mere bounty to the creditor, but rather to discharge what he regarded as a *moral* obligation, and that obligation is still in existence at the testator's death, it seems that the doctrine of lapse does not apply.[61]

7.49   It has been suggested that personal representatives should apply this 'anomalous' doctrine only under the directions of the court, unless all concerned are of full capacity and authorise it.[62]

Charitable gifts

7.50   Although charitable gifts are not within the normal exceptions to the rule about lapse, they may be worth a passing reference at this juncture. If property is left to a charity which ceases to exist before the death of the testator it will be possible to apply the gift to another charity by the application of the doctrine of *cy-près*, provided that a *general charitable intent* can be found. Detailed discussion of this topic is beyond the scope of this work and should be sought from the standard works on charities.[63]

TERMINATION OF MARRIAGE

7.51   It has been noted elsewhere that the testator's marriage generally revokes any will which he made beforehand.[64] In contrast, termination of marriage after the execution of a will has no similar effect on the will and, under the Wills Act 1837, it did not even affect the actual gifts therein in favour of the former spouse. This position has been changed by article 13 of the 1994 Order, in relation to wills of testators who die on or after 1 January 1995. With the ever increasing number of divorces this is probably the change made by the 1994 Order which will have the greatest practical impact.

---

[61]*Stevens v King* [1904] 2 Ch 30 in which all the earlier authorities are cited; also *Re Leach* [1948] Ch 232. It is suggested that this later case extends the doctrine too far - see H A J Ford, "Lapse of Devises and Bequests " (1968) 78 LQR 88.

[62]Rossdale, *Probate and the Administration of Estates - A Practical Guide* (Sweet and Maxwell, 1991) at p 169.

[63]Cairns, *Charities: Law and Practice* (2nd ed, 1993).

[64]See para 4.05 *supra*.

Gifts in a will to a former spouse

7.52 Article 13(1)(b) of the 1994 Order provides that if a testator dies following a decree dissolving or annulling a marriage or declaring a marriage void, any property comprising or included in a gift to the former spouse passes as if the former spouse had died on the date on which the marriage was terminated. This provision applies only to the termination of marriage and does not extend to judicial separation.[65]

7.53 Article 13 implements the recommendations made by a recent report of the English Law Commission. The Law Reform (Succession) Act 1995 has recently[66] made corresponding provision for England and Wales, where legislation preventing a person from benefitting under his former spouse's will had first been enacted by section 18A of the Wills Act 1837.[67] The problem with this section was that it provided that the termination of the testator's marriage after he had made his will would cause any gift to the former spouse to "lapse". It did not, however, presume the former spouse's death and the difficulties that this could generate were soon exposed by the Court of Appeal in the case *Re Sinclair*.[68]

7.54 In *Sinclair* the testator left his entire estate to his wife, provided that she survive him for one month. In the event of her predeceasing him, or failing to survive the month, a cancer charity was to benefit. Four years after the will was executed the couple divorced and it was not disputed that, in consequence, Mrs Sinclair was precluded from taking any of the benefits under the will. The question for the Court of Appeal was who was entitled instead? Alternate interpretations of the word "lapse" in section 18A of the 1837 Act were suggested. Should it be interpreted as meaning "fail by reason of the death of the beneficiary in the lifetime of the testator" thus invoking the consequences which would happen if the wife had predeceased her husband - in this case benefitting the substitutionary legatee, the cancer charity? This was the view taken by Butler-Sloss J (as she then was) in *Re Cherrington*.[69] In the alternative, the word "lapse" could simply mean "fail" - no more, no less. It

---

[65] Judicial separation was included in the earlier draft legislation but was apparently jettisoned at a later stage in the interests of uniformity with England, where the corresponding legislation (since 1 January 1996 the Law Reform (Succession) Act 1995) applies only to divorce and annulment.

[66] S3 effective for deaths on or after 1 January 1996.

[67] Introduced by s 18(2) of the Administration of Justice Act 1982, which was effective for deaths on or after 1 January 1983.

[68] [1985] 2 WLR 795.

[69] [1984] 1 WLR 772.

was this latter interpretation which the Court of Appeal adopted, overturning the *Cherrington* decision, primarily on the ground that had the legislature intended that section 18A should both prevent the former spouse from benefitting, *and* designate the consequences thereafter, it would have done so expressly. Some regret was expressed at this decision, on the ground that had the testator given some thought to what had happened he would probably have wanted the charity to have his money, but the court felt unable to rewrite the will. As a result, because the exact event upon which the charity's gift over was contingent did not happen (Mrs Sinclair predeceasing her former husband, or failing to survive him by one month) the charity could not take and the estate passed to Mr Sinclair's brother under his intestacy. Under article 13 of the 1994 Order, of course, the cancer charity would have benefitted.

7.55   Article 13(1) of the 1994 Order is a significant improvement on the earlier English provision. However, the counsel of perfection is that an existing will should always be revoked on the termination of the testator's marriage and a new one executed, rather than rely on the legislature correctly reflecting the testator's intention.

Contrary intention

7.56   Article 13 is subject to a contrary intention appearing in the will.[70] Such an intention would be present, for example, if the will is said to be made in contemplation of the decree which terminates the marriage.

Family provision claims

7.57   The right of the former spouse to apply for financial provision under the Inheritance (Provision for Family and Dependants) (NI) Order 1979[71] is expressly preserved in article 13(4) of the 1994 Order.

Effect of lapse if spouse took a *share* of residue

7.58   When residue lapses a partial intestacy results. This is the case even when it is merely a share of residue, such as Tom's share where Tom has predeceased the testator who left his residue to "my brothers Tom, Dick and Harry in equal shares". Tom's share is not divided between Dick and Harry - unless, of course, they happen to take as next-of-kin when his third share of residue is distributed according to the intestacy laws. Partial intestacy can be cumbersome and difficult to operate, even in Northern Ireland, where the legal

---

[70] Art 13(3).

[71] See para 8.13 *post.*

profession has been excused the vagaries of hotchpot.[72] With the enactment of article 13 of the 1994 Order they are obviously going to arise more frequently. However, article 13(2) provides that where a gift which lapses under the article is one of a share of residue, the will takes effect as if the gift of the residue were to the other person or persons entitled thereto (and if more than one, in such shares as to preserve the ratio of their former shares) to the exclusion of the spouse. A partial intestacy is therefore prevented in a number of situations where they would otherwise arise.

Appointment of former spouse as executor or trustee

7.59   Article 13 not only affects the gifts to a former spouse in a will made before the termination of marriage - it also operates to prevent the appointment of the former spouse as an executor or as an executor and trustee of the will. Where the former spouse has been appointed as such, the appointment shall take effect as if the former spouse had died on the date on which the marriage was terminated.[73]

ADEMPTION

7.60   A consequence of the ambulatory nature of a will is that any *specific* gift made by the testator which is then disposed of before his death, cannot take effect. The gift is said to have 'adeemed'. Ademption in this sense should not be confused with the equitable doctrine of ademption of legacies by portions which is discussed below.[74]

7.61   The most straightforward example is a gift of, for instance, "my yacht to my brother Harry" in the will of a testator who, a few months before his death, sold the said yacht for £30,000. Unlucky Harry cannot demand the £30,000 sale proceeds in lieu. The doctrine of ademption only extends to *specific* gifts and not to general gifts or *demonstrative* gifts[75] - a pecuniary legacy of £2,000 must be satisfied by the personal representatives out of the deceased's general estate, even if there is insufficient cash to cover it. It is therefore of considerable practical significance whether a particular gift is specific or otherwise in nature and it would seem that the courts have shown a leniency of spirit in their attempts to classify gifts as general rather than

---

[72]See para 6.83 *supra*.

[73]Art 13(1)(a).

[74]See para 7.77 *post*.

[75] Eg "£500 out of my Advantage Account in the Bank of Ireland."

specific if at all possible and thus avoid ademption. A prime illustration of this approach is the decision in *Re Gage*.[76]

A testator bequeated to his niece "the sum of £1,150 Five Per Cent War Loan 1929-47 stock and to MG the sum of £500 New South Wales Five Per Cent stock now standing in my name". When he had made this will, the testator did have £1,150 worth of this War Loan stock, but by the time of his death he had disposed of it. Clauson J held that the two parts of the clause were disjunctive, so that the words "now standing in my name" only qualified the New South Wales gift, which was specific. This enabled the War Loan stock to be construed as a general gift, there was therefore no ademption and the personal representatives were ordered to purchase £1,150 worth of this particular stock for the beneficiary.

Changes in the nature of an asset

7.62   Once it has been determined that a gift is specific, whether or not it has adeemed is usually a relatively straightforward question. Difficulties can arise, however, when the asset involved has changed its nature. The recent case of *Re Dorman*[77] provided a useful review of the relevant authorities and principles.

The testatrix, a Mrs Audrey Dorman, had received income from a certain trust fund since the death of her husband and had paid the surplus of this income into a higher-rate deposit account with a particular High Street bank. By a clause in her will, made in 1987, she stipulated that the balance of this account, which consisted solely or substantially of income received from the trust fund, was to be added to the capital of the said trust fund. In 1989 the testatrix gave one of the defendants, who also happened to be the administrator of the trust fund, an enduring power of attorney over her affairs. Totally unaware of the terms of the will, and attracted solely by the better interest on offer, the defendant in question closed the original account and transferred the funds therein to a 'Capital Advantage' account in the same branch of the bank. Until the testatrix's death the income from the trust fund continued to be paid into this account and thereafter the question for determination was whether the monies in the 'new' account passed as a specific legacy to the trust fund under the clause in the will or whether the gift had adeemed, thus entitling the charities named as residuary legatees to the balance.

---

[76]*Re Gage* [1934] Ch 536.
[77][1994] 1 All ER 804.

7.63   Mr David Neuberger QC, sitting as a deputy High Court judge held, "after considerable hesitation" that the gift in question had not adeemed, but passed as a specific legacy under the clause in question.   His first point of reference was the well-established principle on ademption in cases where there has been a change in the nature of an asset.   The following passage from Williams, Mortimer and Sunnucks, *Executors, Administrators and Probate* was quoted:

> "The general rule is that, in order to complete the right of a specific legatee to receive his legacy, the thing bequeathed must, at the testator's death, remain in specie as described in the will: otherwise the legacy is adeemed. ... *unless it can be shown that the thing is changed in name or form only and remains substantially the same* [emphasis added]."

7.64   Was the change to a new bank account a change "in name and form only"?   Although there is a dearth of direct authority on bank accounts, the law reports abound with ademption cases concerning stocks and shares, generally involving a variation in the testator's shareholding following a reorganisation of the capital structure of the company.   Indeed, the classic test, cited with approval by Mr Neuberger emanated from Cozens-Hardy MR in one such case:

> "Where is the thing which is given?   If you cannot find it at the testator's death, it is no use trying to trace it unless you can trace it in this sense, that you find something which has been changed in name and form only, but *which is substantially the same thing* [emphasis added]."[78]

Applying this principle to the facts before him, the deputy judge noted the "striking similarity" between the two arrangements: the same debtor and creditor, indeed the same branch of the bank, and very similar terms, the only differences in the new account being the higher rates of interest and the need to give 30 days notice for withdrawal.

Relevance of intention

7.65   The testator's *intention* is generally irrelevant to the question of ademption[79] and the application of the doctrine may often defeat that intention.

---

[78]*Slater, Slater* v *Slater* [1907] 1 Ch 665 at 672.   In *Slater* itself, the testator made a specific bequest of shares in a particular water company.   The company was subsequently taken over and amalgamated with other companies to form a new Water Board, and stock in this new undertaking was issued to replace the original shares.   The Court of Appeal held that this was a change in substance so that the gift failed.   Compare this with the decision in *Re Clifford* [1912] 1 Ch 29, where the change was held to be in name and form only, so ademption did not occur.

[79]*Re Dorman* [1994] 1 All ER 804.

Moreover, it is immaterial that the ademption is caused by an act of the testator himself which he did not know or intend to have such effect.[80] However, the testator's intention may still be relevant in that the doctrine operates subject to a contrary intention. Therefore, for example, a testator who leaves "my dwelling house Blackacre, or such other home as I may own at the time of my death" has effectively excluded the operation of ademption on the specific gift of his house.

Republication

7.66 Republication or confirmation of a will does not generally prevent ademption. For example, in the earlier illustration of the yacht left to Harry (para 7.61), the confirmation of the will *after* the yacht had been sold would not have transferred Harry's interest to the sale proceeds. However, republication may effectively prevent ademption, by enabling the will to be construed at the date of the republication. Examples of this were given in Chapter Four.[81]

Ademption by a contract for sale

7.67 Consider a testator who has bequeathed Rosebud Cottage to Anna. He later enters into a specifically enforceable contract to sell Rosebud Cottage to Bertram, but dies before completion. As a consequence of the doctrine of conversion, the binding contract of sale adeems the specific gift to Anna and she is not therefore entitled to the sale proceeds from the cottage, which go instead to the residuary legatee.[82] However, Anna is entitled to occupy the cottage (or receive the rents and profits) from the testator's death until the actual completion.[83]

7.68 By contrast, if the testator did not make the above will until *after* he had entered into the binding contract of sale, Anna would take *all* of the testator's interest in Rosebud Cottage, and in the event of his death before completion is therefore generally entitled to the sale proceeds.[84] This is also the case if the will was made before the contract, but was later republished by a later codicil.[85]

Options to purchase - the abolition of *Lawes v Bennett*

7.69 Consider again that a testator has made a specific gift of Rosebud Cottage to Anna. After making the will he did not enter into a binding contract

---

[80]*Re Freer* (1882) 22 Ch D 622.

[81]See para 4.81 *supra*.

[82]*Farrar v Earl of Winterton* (1842) 5 Beav 1.

[83]*Watts v Watts* (1873) LR 17 Eq 217.

[84]*Re Calow* [1928] Ch 710.

[85]*Re Pyle* [1895] 1 Ch 724. For republication in general see para 4.79 *supra*.

for its sale, but granted Claude an *option* to purchase. What happens to Anna's gift if Claude does not exercise this option until *after* the testator's death? The logical conclusion would seem to be that the gift of Rosebud Cottage has not been adeemed - at the moment of death there was no binding contract of sale for which specific performance would be ordered. However, for the wills of testators who died before 1 January 1995, the anomalous rule in *Lawes* v *Bennett*[86] applied, effectively making the exercise of the option "relate back" to the date on which it was granted. The specific gift to Anna was therefore adeemed even if the option was not exercised until after the testator's death. This rather odd rule had its basis in the fact that as the testator in his own lifetime had granted to Claude and his assignee the unilateral power to decide at a future date whether the property in question should be converted from realty to personalty, he, and those claiming under his will, must take subject to this power and any exercise of it.

7.70 The rule in *Lawes* v *Bennett* has now been abolished by article 24 of the 1994 Order for wills of testators who die on or after 1 January 1995. The exercise of an option to buy land after the death of a testator therefore no longer adeems a specific gift of that land. In England and Wales there has been no corresponding statutory intervention and the common law position continues to apply.

WITNESS A BENEFICIARY UNDER THE WILL

7.71 The lapse of gifts to attesting witnesses and their spouses has already been dealt with in Chapter Three.

THE EQUITABLE DOCTRINES OF SATISFACTION AND ELECTION

Satisfaction

Satisfaction of a debt by a legacy
7.72 Where a testator is indebted to a creditor at the date of his death, and then leaves that creditor a benefit in his will, there are occasions when Equity will presume that this legacy was given by the testator *with the intention of discharging or satisfying his debt*. The creditor is thus precluded from claiming both the legacy and the debt, and is put to election which to take.

---

[86](1785) 1 Cox Eq 167.

7.73   At the outset the point must be made that this *equitable* presumption of satisfaction of a debt by a legacy should not be confused with the situation where a testator *expressly* gives a legacy in satisfaction of a debt. In the latter case the issue is one of construction of the document involved, and it is irrelevant whether or not the following prerequisites for the application of the equitable doctrine are present.

Prerequisites for the existence of the presumption.
7.74   The presumption only applies in the following circumstances:

(a) The legacy has to be equal in value to or greater than the debt.

> There is no presumption if the legacy is smaller than the debt - in such a case there is no satisfaction *pro tanto*.[87] Thus the presumption does not apply where the gift by will is one of *residue*, the actual value of which cannot be ascertained from the face of the will itself:
>
>> "It has been decided that in the case of a debt, a gift of the whole or part of the residue cannot be considered as satisfaction, because it is said that, the amount being uncertain, it may prove to be less than the debt."[88]
>
> This remains the case even if it is clear from the surrounding circumstances that the residue is more than sufficient to cover the debt.
>
> The presumption arises even though the legacy is *substantially* greater than the debt.

(b) The legacy has to be similar in nature to the debt.

> The presumption arises only where the legacy is similar in nature to the debt, and equally beneficial to the recipient. Thus a gift of land will not suffice to satisfy a debt of £15,000, even if the land is worth considerably more than £15,000.
>
> Problems may arise where payment of the legacy under the will is postponed. It is generally the case that legacies are not payable until after one year of death, the so-called executor's year,[89] and do not

---

[87]Although see *Hammond* v *Smith* (1864) 33 Beav 452 where the testator actually told the creditor that the legacy was to be taken in part satisfaction of the debt and the creditor had not objected.

[88]*Per* Lord Cottenham LC in *Thynne* v *Earl of Glengall* (1848) 2 HLC 131 at 154.

[89]See para 12.02 *post*.

attract interest until this year has expired. In *Re Horlock*[90] the debt owed by the testator (£300) was expressed to be payable within three months of death and Stirling J held that this was not satisfied by a legacy of £400 because no time for payment had been specified and this was not as advantageous. If correct, this view would greatly reduce the application of the doctrine. In *Re Rattenberry*,[91] however, Swinfen Eady J relied on the decision of Lord Hardwicke in *Clark* v *Sewell*[92] that interest on a legacy in satisfaction of a debt accrues from *death*, to hold that a legacy of £400 satisfied a debt of £150 with interest at five per cent.

(c) The debt must have existed at the date of the execution of the will.

This requirement stems from the basis of the doctrine, which presumes that the testator intended by a gift in his will to satisfy a debt which he owed.[93]

(d) The amount of the debt must be certain.

Like the preceding point, this requirement derives from the presumed intention of the testator to settle an existing debt. To do so, he clearly had to know the actual amount owing. Thus if the debt fluctuated *upwards* between the execution of the will and the date of death the presumption will not apply. It is different, however, if the testator had paid part of the debt during his lifetime, therefore *reducing* the debt between the date of the execution of the will and that of death.

(e) The operation of the presumption must not have been excluded by a contrary intention.

An express direction in the will to pay debts, for example, the commonly used "I direct that all my just debts and funeral expenses shall be paid as soon as conveniently may be after my decease"[94] will exclude the presumption. A contrary intention on the part of the testator may also be implied, for example, if there is a motive for making the gift, other than satisfaction of a debt.

---

[90]*Re Horlock* [1895] 1 Ch 516.
[91]*Re Rattenberry* [1906] 1 Ch 667.
[92](1744) 3 Atk 96.
[93]*Thomas* v *Bennett* (1725) 24 ER 757.
[94]*Re Manners* [1949] 2 All ER 201.

Satisfaction of a portion debt by a legacy and ademption of a legacy by a portion

7.75   The principle that "Equity leans against double portions" has been encountered earlier in this work in relation to intestate entitlement and the duty imposed upon children to account for *inter vivos* advancements.[95] The nature of a "portion" was also discussed at that juncture.[96] A "portion *debt*" is an obligation upon the testator (for instance, under a covenant) to give a portion.

Two separate principles are relevant, one the corollary of the other.

Satisfaction of a portion debt by a legacy

7.76   First there is satisfaction of a portion debt by a legacy. If a father, or someone else standing *in loco parentis*, enters into a binding obligation to provide a portion for his child, and then *subsequently* executes a will in which that child is left a further portion, there may be a presumption that the portion debt has been satisfied by the legacy. If the presumption applies the child cannot benefit from both the legacy and the debt, and is put to his election which to take. In many cases it will be more beneficial to take the debt, as the legacy may reduce under the rules of abatement.

Note that this presumption only applies if the portion *debt* is existing at the date of the will. If the debt has already been discharged before the execution of the will by the making of a portion in favour of the child, the testator is presumed to have intended the child to benefit twice. In addition there must be no substantial difference between the nature of the portion which was the subject of the obligation and that given under the will.

It will be remembered that in the ordinary case of satisfaction of a debt by a legacy, partial satisfaction is not presumed by a legacy smaller than the debt. In contrast, a portion debt can be satisfied *pro tanto* by a legacy smaller in amount than the debt.[97]

The rationale behind the principle against double portions is the preservation of equality between *children* of a testator. The fact that advances are only to be brought into account for the benefit of children amongst themselves was confirmed by *Meinertzagen* v *Walters*[98] where it was held that the rule is not to operate to benefit strangers.

---

[95]See para 6.65 *supra*.

[96]See para 6.68 *supra*.

[97] Warren v Warren (1783) 1 Bro CC 305.

[98] (1872) 7 Ch App 670.

As with the presumption of satisfaction of an ordinary debt by a legacy, the presumption relating to portion debts yields to a contrary intention evident from the face of the will.

Ademption of a legacy by a portion

7.77   The second situation involves the chronological reversal of events - this time the testator executes the will first, leaving a portion to his child, or someone else to whom he stands *in loco parentis*. Subsequent to this, he makes a portion in favour of that child. It may be the case that the legacy has been satisfied by this subsequent portion. The fundamental distinction between this and the satisfaction of a portion debt by a legacy discussed above is that in the latter case, as has been seen, the legatee is put to his election. In the former case there is no such option - the portion has extinguished or *adeemed*[99] the legacy. For this reason this part of the doctrine is generally referred to as "ademption of legacies by portions."

Like the related presumptions, equitable ademption only occurs where there is no substantial difference between the legacy and the portion.

Satisfaction of a legacy by another legacy

7.78   This presumption, which may also be referred to as "the presumption against repetition of legacies", has only limited similarities to the presumptions discussed above. It relates to testamentary documents which contain more than one legacy of a *similar kind* in favour of the same donee. Say a testator leaves Anna £10,000 in an early clause of his will, and then, in a later clause, leaves her a second £10,000. Are the legacies regarded as cumulative or is the second a substitute for the first? Or, say Anna is left £10,000 in a will, followed some months later by a further £10,000 in a codicil (which does not revoke the clause in the will). Is she entitled to the total £20,000, or merely to £10,000? Put simply, the rules are as follows.

(a)   If a legatee takes legacies of equal value under *the same instrument*, they will be presumed to be mere repetition, and, unless different motives are assigned for each gift, the legatee will take only one legacy. If the legacies are of unequal value, prima facie the legatee will take both.

---

[99]This election ademption should not be confused with the more common meaning of the word in succession contexts, discussed at para 7.60 *supra*.

(b)   If a legatee takes legacies of equal value under
          different instruments they will be presumed to be
          cumulative, unless the same reason is assigned for each
          gift.[100]

Note that in this context a will and its codicils constitute different
instruments.[101]

Election

7.79   On occasions a testator may purport to leave property which *he* does
not actually own. In fact, it takes little thought to produce illustrations which
demonstrate that such an occurrence is not as unusual as may appear at first
sight. Most typically, the testator will have been under a mistaken belief about
the extent of his interest in property - believing, for instance, that his interest
under a joint tenancy was alienable by will, or that he had a remainder rather
than a life interest. The equitable doctrine of election arises where the *true
owner* of the property which the testator is purporting to give away, also
happens to receive benefits under that will. In short, this legatee is not free
both to approbate[102] *and* reprobate[103] the instrument.[104] Rather, he must make a
choice:

(a)   First, he cannot be compelled to take the benefit given
          to him under the will - he can disclaim the legacy, and
          keep his own property which the testator attempted to
          give to another. Obviously this would be a prudent
          course of action if the legacy given to him by the
          testator was less in value than his own property given
          to the third party.

(b)   Alternatively, he can accept the legacy given to him by
          the testator, and either transfer to the third party the

---

[100]*Hurst* v *Beach* (1821) 5 Madd 351.

[101]Compare the doctrine of election, see para 7.79 *post*.

[102]Ie take the benefit given to him under the will.

[103]Ie deny the legacy where the testator has purported to give the legatee's property to a third
party.

[104]At least three different theoretical bases for the doctrine have been advanced - an implied
condition on the part of the testator; "natural equity" and unconscionability. These are
considered, together with the view that none of these now justify its application, in the
article by Neville Cargo in (1990) 106 LQR.

property he was to receive under the will or *compensate* him to its value.[105]

7.80   Election may be express or by implication, although for the latter it must be shown that the beneficiary was aware of all the material facts.[106] Once, however, it is shown that he was aware of them, acts dealing with the property given under the will may be enough to show that he has decided to take under the will.[107] In addition, the doctrine of election applies only if the following conditions are met.

The gifts must both be in the same instrument
7.81   If the purported gift of the legatee's property and the gift to the legatee are in different instruments the legatee is free to accept the gift to him and ignore the other. For this purpose a will and its codicils constitute a single instrument.[108]

The legatee's property must be freely alienable
7.82   If the legatee is unable to dispose of his property which the testator purported to leave, election does not arise.[109]

There must be an intention by the testator to dispose of an interest which he does not own
7.83   The presumption is that a testator only intends to give away what he himself owns. If a gift can be construed as either giving merely the lesser interest which the testator does own, or the greater interest which he does not, the former construction will be preferred.[110]

---

[105]The amount of compensation which has to be paid is ascertained according to the value of the asset at the date of the testator's death - *Re Hancock* [1905] 1 Ch 16.

[106]*Pusey* v *Desbouverie* (1734) 3 P Wms 315.

[107]*Re Shepherd* [1943] Ch 8.

[108]Compare the position with repetition of legacies, see para 7.78 *supra*.

[109]*Re Lord Chesham* (1886) 31 Ch D 466.

[110]*Per* Lord Eldon in *Lord Rancliffe* v *Lady Parkyns* (1818) 6 Dow 149 at 185.

CHAPTER EIGHT

FAMILY PROVISION[1]

GENERAL

8.01 It was observed in Chapter One that freedom of testation is no longer absolute. The Northern Ireland testator remains free to endow his bounty on the beneficiaries of his choosing, but this distribution may be wholly or partly altered by the court after his death in favour of his spouse or certain other relatives or dependants. The mechanism which empowers the court to do so is contained in the Inheritance (Provision for Family and Dependants) (NI) Order 1979. This legislation gives certain categories of person the right to apply for an award out of the deceased's estate if the deceased failed to make "reasonable financial provision" for them. However, this is all that it does - persons who fall within any of the categories are given a mere right *to apply* for financial provision. Whether or not an award is made in their favour is at the discretion of the court[2] and success is not automatic. This discretionary system is thus fundamentally different to the 'fixed legal right' system which guarantees certain relatives (usually spouses) a minimum share of the deceased's estate. Such systems are found in many American states, and, closer to home, in Scotland and the Republic of Ireland.[3]

8.02 The Inheritance (Provision for Family and Dependants) (NI) Order 1979 (hereafter in this chapter "the 1979 Order") is broadly similar to the corresponding English legislation, the Inheritance (Provision for Family and Dependants) Act 1975 (in this chapter "the 1975 Act"). Useful reference can therefore be made to the growing body of case law which has been decided under this Act.

---

[1] It should be remembered that in certain circumstances it is possible to achieve the same result by using the doctrine of proprietary estoppel - see eg *Re Basham* [1987] 1 All ER 405. This doctrine is beyond the scope of this work.

[2] Discretionary systems for the protection of the family were pioneered in Australasia - the first was the New Zealand Testator's Maintenance Act 1906.

[3] Part IX of the Succession Act 1965. The fixed legal right system extends only to spouses, although children may apply under a parallel discretionary system.

8.03   The 1979 Order is effective for deaths occurring on or after 1 September 1979.[4]

Historical background

8.04   The basic problem for every succession regime is to provide the means by which two conflicting policies can be reconciled. First, a person should be free to distribute his assets on death exactly how he chooses. Secondly, there may be a responsibility to provide for family and dependants which extends beyond the grave. In English jurisprudence each has in turn taken precedence to the *complete* exclusion of the other. For much of the feudal period realty was not devisable at all, but had to pass to the heir-at-law subject to the widow's right of dower.[5] Likewise no more than one-half of a deceased's personalty could pass by his will.[6] The pendulum then swung back, and following the enactment of the Dower Act 1833 which enabled a widow's right to dower to be barred,[7] there was a period of complete testamentary freedom. This ensued until the latter half of the present century, when it was reluctantly brought to an end by the Inheritance (Family Provision) Act (NI) 1960 (hereafter "the 1960 Act"), the predecessor to the 1979 Order.

8.05   In Northern Ireland the concept of restraining testamentary freedom received a welcome which could, at best, be described as lukewarm. In England and Wales family provision legislation had been enacted 22 years previously in 1938,[8] but at that time attempts to enact corresponding legislation for this jurisdiction had to be aborted. In 1937 the Wills (Family Provision) Bill failed to get a second reading in the Northern Ireland Parliament and the next year the similar Wills (Family Maintenance) Bill was counted out at an early stage of debate. Eventually, in 1953, the Family Provision Committee was established to examine the desirability of introducing restraints on testamentary freedom and empirical evidence of individual hardships was expressly requested. It is interesting to note, that with few exceptions, local practitioners

---

[4] Art 1(2).

[5] Realty became fully alienable by will after the enactment of the Tenures Abolition (Ir) Act 1662.

[6] Under the middle-age custom of *legitim*, if a deceased left a wife and children, the wife took one-third of the personalty, the children took another third and the remaining third (the "dead's part") could be willed as the deceased wished (although prior to the Reformation it was expected to be given to the Church for "pious purposes"). Where the deceased was survived by a wife but no issue her share was increased to one-half. *Legitim* was finally abolished by s 10 of the Statute of Distributions (Ir) 1695.

[7] For the nature of dower, see para 6.10 *supra*.

[8] The Inheritance (Family Provision) Act 1938.

saw no need for change.[9] In the end, although the arguments for and against were "finely balanced", legislation was recommended. It was finally enacted seven years later.

8.06   The repeal and replacement of this seminal legislation by the 1979 Order had the primary objective of accommodating changes in social attitudes by, for example, widening the range of potential applicants beyond the 'nuclear' family.   However, in key respects this new Order simply built on the foundations laid in 1960. A number of the cases decided under the earlier legislation[10] are thus still helpful.[11]

Basis of applications under the 1979 Order

8.07   The basis of *every* application under the 1979 Order is that the deceased by the disposition of his property effected by his will or the law relating to intestacy or the combination of his will and a partial intestacy, *did not make reasonable financial provision* for the applicant in question.[12]

8.08   However, where the applicant is the deceased's *spouse* a more generous standard within this basic test is applied. For applicants other than a spouse "reasonable financial provision" is defined as "such financial provision as it would be reasonable in all the circumstances of the case for the applicant to receive for his *maintenance* [emphasis added]".[13] A spouse alone is now[14] assessed against the more liberal standard that the financial provision be that which it would be reasonable *in all the circumstances of the case for a husband or wife to receive* and is not therefore restricted to "maintenance". The practical implications of this are discussed more fully below.

---

[9] *Report of the Family Provision Committee*, Cmd (NI) 330 (1953). The Incorporated Law Society of NI and all local solicitors' associations except Lurgan and Portadown were against introducing any restraints on testamentary freedom. This comment from a Cookstown solicitor is typical of those published: "I have been in practice here since 1917 and I cannot recollect a single instance where a testator's dependants were left without provision for their maintenance" (para 25).

[10] Which includes English cases decided under the Inheritance (Family Provision) Act 1938.

[11] See *Re Coventry* [1980] Ch 461 at 474 and 487. Although there is a limit to the reliance which can be placed on some such cases, eg surviving spouses under the earlier legislation were limited to a claim for maintenance.

[12] Art 4(1).

[13] Art 2(2).

[14] Under the 1960 Act spouses were not in a more privileged position to that of other applicants. The standard against which they are assessed was widened in 1979 in order to prevent the anomalous situation that a spouse could get better financial provision on divorce than on death - see para 8.43 *post*.

Intestate deaths

8.09   It should be remembered that persons have *locus standi* under the 1979 Order whether the alleged failure by the deceased to provide reasonable financial provision results from the distribution under his will or by his *intestacy*, or indeed, by the combination of his will and *a partial intestacy*. There is a tendency to view family provision solely as a mechanism for restraining testamentary freedom, with the consequence that its equally vital role of providing a discretionary 'safety-net' to the fixed and certain intestacy rules is often forgotten.

8.10   Exactly the same principles apply to testate and intestate deaths; the 1979 Order itself has not distinguished the two modes of succession and in *Re Coventry*[15] the English Court of Appeal confirmed that their treatment is to be identical. It is not therefore the case that the judiciary can be persuaded to intervene more readily on an intestate death, on the basis that in doing so they are not setting aside the *express* wishes of the deceased.[16]

Jurisdiction to apply

8.11   Applicants can apply under the 1979 Order only in cases where the deceased died domiciled in Northern Ireland.[17] The burden of proving this is on the applicant.[18] Where the deceased died domiciled in England or Wales an application can be made to the English courts under the equivalent 1975 Act.

Inheritance tax implications

8.12   For inheritance tax purposes the distribution of the deceased's property is that effected by a family provision order, if any, and not the original distribution which was laid down in his will or which resulted from the intestacy rules.[19]

Forfeiture (NI) Order 1982

8.13   The common law forfeiture rule which precludes a person from benefitting under the estate of someone whom he has unlawfully killed was dealt with in the previous chapter.[20] It will be recalled that the Forfeiture (NI)

---

[15] [1979] 3 All ER 815.

[16] See the comments of Goff LJ that, as some persons actively choose to die intestate, the intestate rules may be the express wishes of the deceased as much as a will. These were quoted at para 6.01 *supra*.

[17] Art 3(1).

[18] *Mastaka v Midland Bank Executor and Trustee Co Ltd* [1941] 1 All ER 236.

[19] Inheritance Tax Act 1984, ss 142 and 146.

[20] See para 7.14 *supra*.

Order 1982 gave the court discretion to modify the common law rule in cases other than murder where the "justice of the case" requires it. Article 5 of the 1982 Order expressly preserves the right of any person to whom the forfeiture rule applies to make an application for financial provision under the 1979 Order.

8.14 Note, however, that the lack of "reasonable financial provision" in such cases must still result from the disposition effected by either the deceased's will or intestacy. An application cannot succeed if the failure to provide for the applicant is simply a consequence of the forfeiture rule. This happened in *Re Royse*,[21] a family provision claim by a widow who had been convicted of the manslaughter of her husband. In fact, had the forfeiture rule not prevented the widow from benefitting, she would have been the sole beneficiary under her husband's will. Her application failed - it was the *forfeiture rule* which had denied her any financial provision and *not* the disposition effected by her husband's will.

Time limits

8.15 Applications under the 1979 Order must be made within six months of the date on which the grant of representation is first taken out, unless the leave of the court is obtained.[22] If a grant is initially taken out which does not relate to all of the property in the estate, time will not run for the purposes of the Order until the grant relating to the remainder is taken out.[23] "First taken out" means the first effective grant so that if a grant of probate is issued but later revoked, and a grant of letters of administration subsequently issued, time runs from the grant of the letters of administration.[24] However, if a grant of probate in common form is later followed by a grant in solemn form, time runs from the grant in common form.[25]

8.16 An application is made when the summons is issued.

---

[21] [1984] 3 All ER 339 - an application made six months before the English Forfeiture Act 1982 came into force.

[22] Art 6.

[23] Art 25.

[24] *Re Freeman* [1984] 3 All ER 906; see also *Re Bidie* [1948] 2 All ER 995. Obviously this is the only logical solution and to hold otherwise would put potential applicants in the impossible position of anticipating a claim when not dissatisfied with the distribution of the deceased's assets.

[25] *Re Miller* [1968] 3 All ER 844.

Permission for late applications

8.17   There is no statutory guidance on how the court will exercise its discretion to allow an out of time application.   Principles thus have to be gleaned from case law. The most comprehensive attempt by the judiciary at compiling a list of factors which the court should consider was that of Sir Robert Megarry in *Re Salmon*.[26] These non-exhaustive principles, which have been dubbed the 'Megarry guidelines' and which were commended by the Northern Ireland High Court in *Campbell* v *Campbell*[27] as "very useful", are as follows:

   (a)   The discretion   is   unfettered   by any statutory provisions, but must be exercised judicially, in accordance with what is good and proper;

   (b)   The time limit   is   a substantive   provision laid down by statute and not a mere procedural one which can be extended with the indulgence generally accorded to procedural time limits. The onus is on the applicant to show that there is a substantial case for the court to exercise its discretion to extend the time limit;

   (c)   Consideration must be given to how promptly after the time limit had expired that permission is being sought;

   (d)   It is relevant   whether or not   any   negotiations had been commenced within the time limit;

   (e)   It is relevant whether or not the estate had already been distributed;

   (f)   It is relevant whether, if permission to extend this time is not granted, the applicant would have any form of redress against anyone else.

8.18   These principles were approved in *Re Dennis*[28] in which a seventh was added, namely, has the applicant shown:

---

[26][1980] 3 All ER 532.
[27]*Per* Murray J (1982) 18 NIJB.
[28][1981] 2 All ER 140.

"...that he has an arguable case, a case fit to go to trial, and that in approaching that matter the court's approach is rather the same as it adopts when considering whether a defendant ought to have leave to defend in proceedings for summary judgment."[29]

8.19   It should be evident that extensions are not granted readily and it is imperative that practitioners ensure that applications are made in time. While each case must depend upon its own facts, *Re McNare*,[30] a case decided under the earlier English legislation, provides a useful illustration of the type of case in which leave to apply out of time will be granted. There the deceased had left nothing to his elderly blind and crippled widow. The widow did not find out about her husband's death until five months after the grant of probate had been issued to his son and she had no information about the size of his estate. The son had been obstructive when first contacted by the widow's sister for information and when negotiations were first commenced between the parties' solicitors there was complete deadlock. In allowing the widow to apply after the time limit the court was influenced by the lack of information which had been made available to her, the fact that negotiations had been proceeding, and that refusal to grant permission would cause hardship and operate unfairly against the applicant.[31]

8.20   By contrast, time was not extended where the applicant had an understanding of the nature and prospect of the success of a claim all along, decided not to pursue it in the interests of family harmony, but later had a change of heart due to the deterioration of her health.[32] Similarly, in *Campbell v Campbell*[33] it was made clear to a beneficiary who had considered a family provision claim but then decided not to proceed, that permission for a late application would not be treated sympathetically.[34]

8.21   There is no provision for extension of time when an order is sought under article 11 of the 1979 Order to include a deceased's share in a joint tenancy with the net estate.[35]

---

[29]*Per* Browne-Wilkinson J at p 145. This seventh requirement was based on the judgment of Denning J in *Re Stone* (1969) 114 SJ 36.

[30][1964] 3 All ER 373.

[31]See also *Re Trott* [1958] 2 All ER 296; *Re Ruttie* [1969] 3 All ER 1633.

[32]*Escritt* v *Escritt* [1982] 3 FLR 280.

[33](1982) 18 NIJB.

[34]See also *Re Longley* [1981] CLY 2885.

[35]See para 8.94 *post*.

LOCUS STANDI

8.22   Five categories of person have *locus standi* to apply under the 1979 Order. These are laid down in article 3(1) and are:

(a)   The wife or husband of the deceased;

(b)   The former wife or husband of the deceased who has not remarried;

(c)   A child of the deceased;

(d)   Any person (not being a child of the deceased) who   in the case   of any marriage to which the deceased   was at any time a party, was treated by the deceased as a child of the family in relation to that marriage;

(e)   Any person (not being included in categories (a) to (d) above)   who   immediately before the death of the deceased was being maintained either wholly or partly by the deceased.

8.23   Categories (a) and (b) were re-enacted from the 1960 Act while categories (d) and (e) were introduced for the first time in 1979. In addition, the 1979 Order extended the scope of category (c). Under the 1960 Act children of the deceased could only apply if they were minors or otherwise dependent (eg through disability or spinsterhood). The 1979 Order removed these restrictions and applications can now be made by all adult children.[36]

8.24   Article 3(1) requires that an applicant "survive" the deceased. A family provision claim is *personal* and an action started by an applicant cannot be continued by his personal representatives.[37] If, however, an order is already existing at the time of death it can be enforced by the personal representatives under section 14 of the Law Reform (Miscellaneous Provisions) Act (NI) 1937.[38]

---

[36]They may not succeed, of course.   The judicial approach to able-bodied adult children applicants is discussed at para 8.66 *post*.

[37]*Whyte* v *Ticehurst* [1986] 2 All ER 158; *Re R (dec'd)* (1986) 16 Fam Law 58; *Re Bramwell* [1988] 2 FLR 263; *Re O'Reilly* [1995] 6 BNIL 97.

[38]See para 12.32 *post*.

8.25 Each of the categories of applicant is now considered in turn. Note that the discussion at this juncture is confined to the issue of *locus standi*. The likely success or otherwise of claims is dealt with below.

Surviving spouses

8.26 This category includes a person who in good faith entered into a void marriage with the deceased, unless that marriage has been annulled or the person entered into a second marriage during the deceased's lifetime.[39] Polygamous marriages are recognised where these were valid in the country of marriage. The situation may therefore arise that a court is considering applications from two or more spouses.[40]

8.27 A spouse who was judicially separated from the deceased at the date of death[41] applies under this category, although such a person does not benefit from the wider interpretation of "reasonable financial provision" and is limited to a claim for maintenance.[42] This is subject to the separated spouse not having forfeited any future family provision claim as part of the separation agreement.[43]

Former spouses who have not remarried

8.28 A "former spouse" is defined in article 2(2) of the 1979 Order as a person whose marriage with the deceased was, during the deceased's lifetime, dissolved or annulled by a decree of divorce or of nullity of marriage granted under the Matrimonial Causes (NI) Order 1978 or the statutory provisions repealed by that Order. This precludes applications from a person whose marriage was dissolved or annulled in another jurisdiction, although if such a person was being maintained by the deceased he may have a successful claim under category (e) below.[44]

---

[39] Art 2(5). Such a person is not a spouse for the purposes of intestate entitlement - see para 6.16 *supra*.

[40] *Re Sehota* [1978] 3 All ER 385.

[41] And for whom the separation was still continuing at that date.

[42] Art 2(2).

[43] This facility to 'contract out' is discussed below in relation to former spouse applicants - see para 8.31 *post*.

[44] See para 8.38 *post*. Alternatively, if the deceased also had domicile in England or Wales an application could be made under the "former spouse" category of the 1975 Act (s 1(1)). Initially this was limited to marriages dissolved or annulled in England or Wales, but s 25 (2) of the Matrimonial and Family Proceedings Act 1984 has amended it to include cases in which the marriage was dissolved or annulled under the law of any part of the British Islands or in any country or territory outside the British Islands, provided that in this latter

8.29   A person who entered into a void marriage with the deceased for which an *inter vivos* decree of nullity has been granted can apply as a former spouse.[45]

8.30   It should be remembered that a former spouse automatically loses *locus standi* on remarriage. Furthermore, for these purposes a former spouse has "remarried" if the marriage in question is voidable or even *void*.[46]

Contracting out

8.31   The court cannot entertain applications from former spouses who have contracted out of a future family provision claim as part of their divorce settlement. The statutory basis for such an agreement is found in article 17(1) of the 1979 Order. By virtue of this provision the court, when granting a decree of judicial separation,[47] divorce or annulment, at that time,[48] or any time thereafter, if it considers it just to do so,[49] can order that neither of the parties shall be allowed to make a family provision claim on the death of the other party.

8.32   It is interesting to note that in *Re Fullard*[50] the English Court of Appeal advised practitioners actively to encourage the parties to divorce and judicial separations to take up the opportunity to contract out of future family provision claims. However, it seems that such an order will not be granted automatically, and the court must first be given some evidence of what the estate is likely to consist of at the time of death and of any persons who may have a prior claim. This was not done in *Whiting* v *Whiting*[51] and the court consequently refused to grant an order.

---

case, the divorce or annulment is entitled to be recognised as valid by the law of England and Wales.

[45] Art 2(2) of the 1979 Order.

[46] Art 2(6).

[47] The facility to "contract out" extends also to judicially separated persons - see para 8.27 *supra*. Note, however, that in this case the decree must be in force and the separation continuing at the date of death - art 17(4).

[48] An order may be made before the decree of divorce or annulment is made absolute, but it does not take effect unless and until it has been made absolute - art 17(2).

[49] Art 17(1) of the 1979 Order as amended by art 11(1) of the Matrimonial and Family Proceedings (NI) Order 1989. Art 17(1), as originally enacted, required both parties to be agreeable to such an order being made.

[50] [1981] 2 All ER 796.

[51] [1988] 2 FLR 189.

Child of the deceased

8.33 Included within this category are adopted and illegitimate children, and children *en ventre sa mère* at the date of the deceased's death.[52] A stepchild cannot apply under this category but may do so under the following one.

8.34 As has been noted already, a child of any age may apply. Indeed most applications within this category are now made by adults, although this is partly explained by the fact that no order can be made on the application of a minor child if the deceased is survived by both a spouse and children and he has made his spouse reasonable financial provision for both that spouse and the children.[53]

8.35 The relevant date on which an applicant must have *locus standi* is that of the application and not the death. In *Re Collins*[54] the deceased had died intestate while she and her husband were undergoing a divorce which had not been finalised, and he consequently took her entire estate. A family provision claim was made on behalf of the deceased's minor child, who had been taken into care after his mother's death and adopted shortly before the application was made. The claim failed. At the relevant date (that of the application) an adoption order was in force, and by virtue of the English counterpart of article 40(2) of the Adoption (NI) Order 1987, an adopted child is not to be treated in law as the child of any person(s) other than the adopter(s).

Persons treated as a child of the family

8.36 Any person who has been treated by the deceased as a child of the family in relation to any marriage to which the deceased was a party can apply under this category. This includes, for example, a child of the deceased's spouse by another person and a child of neither party provided that he has been treated as a child of the marriage. As with the previous category, adults may apply.[55]

8.37 It is sufficient that the *deceased* alone treated the child as part of the family. Moreover, the phrase "in relation" to the marriage is not to be read restrictively and means simply "stemming from" the marriage. This was confirmed in *Re Leach*,[56] a decision under the corresponding provision of the

---

[52] Art 2(2) of the 1979 Order.

[53] Art 4(5) of the 1979 Order.

[54] [1990] 2 All ER 47.

[55] *Re Callaghan* [1984] 3 All ER 790; *Re Leach* [1985] 2 All ER 754.

[56] *Ibid.*

1975 Act, in which the applicant was made an award out of the estate of her stepmother, who had died intestate.[57] The applicant had been 32 years of age when her father married the deceased and thereafter had never lived with them. On her father's death the applicant's relationship with the deceased became particularly close, but it was submitted by counsel for the next-of-kin that only the circumstances and treatment of the applicant when her father was alive and the marriage was subsisting were relevant. The judge held that the deceased's treatment of the applicant *after* her father's death was also a relevant matter.

Other persons being maintained by the deceased

8.38   This category is distinct from the others in that it is based on actual dependency rather than any particular legal relationship. Amongst the strange bedfellows who may fall within its ambit are cohabitants, less permanent paramours, relatives, platonic companions and housekeepers.

8.39   Article 3(1)(e) of the 1979 Order - a person "who immediately before the death of the deceased was being maintained, either wholly or partly, by the deceased" was certainly not drafted to inspire confidence. Not surprisingly, it has generated much litigation. Many of the difficulties have surrounded article 3(2), which provides that a person shall be treated as being maintained by the deceased if the deceased otherwise than for full valuable consideration was making a substantial contribution in money or money's worth towards the reasonable needs of that person. In *Jelley* v *Iliffe*[58] the English Court of Appeal held that this provision exhaustively defined "being maintained"; that is a person could *only* be treated as being maintained if the deceased was making a substantial contribution towards his reasonable needs.   This case also confirmed that "full valuable consideration" is not confined to consideration under a contract, and that "immediately" before death refers to the settled basis before death and not the actual fluctuating variation existing at the precise moment when the deceased died. Thus if the deceased spent his last few weeks in hospital, possibly being maintained *by the applicant*, it will not preclude a claim provided that the applicant had been maintained by the deceased in the status quo which existed before the hospitalisation.   However, if the maintenance of the applicant was abandoned by the deceased before death no claim can be entertained, no matter how quickly after the end of the arrangement death occurred.[59]

---

[57]Stepchildren are not entitled on their step-parent's intestacy - see para 6.27 *supra*.

[58][1981] 2 All ER 29.

[59]Eg in *Kourgky* v *Lusher* [1983] 4 FLR 65 the applicant had ceased to live with the deceased a few months before his death. See also *Layton* v *Martin* [1986] 2 FLR 277.

8.40   *Jelley* v *Iliffe* is instructive of the court's approach to determining whether the deceased has made "a substantial contribution ... otherwise than for full valuable consideration" and of the difficulties inherent therein.   The applicant, an elderly widower, had met the deceased at a scripture rally.   He moved in with her (purely platonic, it seems) and they had pooled their incomes. She was thus providing him with rent-free accommodation and, in addition, kept house.   For his part, he provided companionship, looked after the garden and attempted occasional DIY tasks.   To determine whether the deceased had been making a "substantial" contribution yet had not received proper consideration, the court had to balance these "imponderables".   If it appears that the deceased provided more to the applicant than he provided in return, or if there was a reasonable doubt that this may be the case, the applicant should be granted *locus standi*.   How then did accommodation, companionship and housework equate with companionship, gardening and DIY?   Their Lordships held that the provision of rent-free accommodation tipped the scales in favour of the applicant, and he was therefore granted *locus standi* to take a case on the merits.[60]

8.41   It should be remembered that *all* applicants under this category have to satisfy this often degrading 'dependency' hurdle.   In England and Wales the Law Reform (Succession) Act 1995, which applies to deaths on or after 1 January 1996, has granted cohabitants who have shared a household with the deceased for two years before his death automatic *locus standi* to apply under the 1975 Act.[61]   The requirement to show dependency has therefore been abolished.   The Succession (NI) Order 1996, which is expected to become effective around the beginning of 1997, proposes that similar provision be made for Northern Ireland.

REASONABLE FINANCIAL PROVISION

8.42   The court may only make an award under the 1979 Order if satisfied that the disposition of the deceased's estate effected by his will or the law relating to intestacy, or the combination of his will and a partial intestacy did not make reasonable financial provision for the applicant.   As has been seen there have been two standards of reasonable financial provision since 1979, which for convenience shall be called the 'spouse' standard and the 'ordinary' standard.

---

[60]Which apparently he won - the actual decision was not reported.

[61]This implements the recommendation made by the Law Commission Report, *Distribution on Intestacy* - Report No 187 (1989).

The two standards of reasonable financial provision

8.43   The ordinary standard, which applies to all applicants other than surviving spouses, means such financial provision as it would be reasonable in all the circumstances of the case for the applicant to receive for his maintenance.[62]   Under the 1960 Act this was also the standard for surviving spouses but the 1979 Order widened the scope of "reasonable financial provision" where the applicant is a surviving spouse. It is now "such financial provision as it would be reasonable in all circumstances of the case for a husband or wife to receive, whether or not that provision is required for his or her maintenance".[63]   This change, which was implemented in England by the 1975 Act, had been recommended by the Law Commission[64] primarily because restricting spouse applicants to a claim for maintenance could result in a widow or widower being less well off than if the marriage had terminated in divorce rather than death.[65]   The practical effect of this more generous standard is well illustrated by the *Besterman* case, which is discussed below.[66]

8.44   An applicant who was judicially separated from the deceased at the latter's death is limited to a claim for maintenance.   However, the court is empowered in limited circumstances to apply the more generous 'spouse' standard to both judicially separated and former spouse applicants.[67]   This concession is designed to prevent such applicants 'falling between two stools', as would happen where the marriage had already been terminated at the time of death, but no property settlement had yet been finalised. Such an applicant could be prejudiced significantly if limited to a claim for maintenance. However, this discretion, which is exercisable if the court "thinks it just to do so", is of very limited scope and only applies if the deceased died within 12 months of the separation, divorce or annulment.[68]

What is meant by maintenance

8.45   Maintenance has not been defined by statute. The following dictum of Goff LJ in *Re Coventry* is useful on the courts' approach to the concept:

---

[62]Art 2(2).

[63]*Ibid.*

[64]Law Commission Report No 61 (1974), paras 59-63.

[65]This was especially so after the increased property transfer powers which courts were afforded by the Matrimonial Causes Act 1973 (in NI the Matrimonial Causes (NI) Order 1978).

[66]See para 8.58 *post.*

[67]Art 16 of 1979 Order.

[68]Art 16(1).

"What is proper maintenance must in all cases depend on all the facts and circumstances of the particular case .... but I think it is clear .... that one must not put too limited a meaning on it; it does not mean just enough to enable a person to get by, on the other hand, it does not mean anything which may be regarded as reasonably desirable for his general benefit or welfare."[69]

8.46 The fact that maintenance is not just 'enough to get by' was confirmed by the Northern Ireland High Court in *Re McGarrell*[70] in which the judge rejected the argument that if the applicant is already surviving before the order, any award must then constitute more than mere maintenance. In the case in question it was accepted that the applicant was suffering 'financial hardship'.

8.47 The payment of a lump sum to enable an applicant to discharge his capital taxation debts and avoid bankruptcy has been construed as not being for his maintenance.[71]

The correct approach of the court

8.48 It cannot be emphasised too strongly that the role of the court is not to undertake a full-scale rewriting of the will. Nor is the court concerned with the subjective question of whether the testator acted *reasonably*. The only issue for the court is whether, considered *objectively*, reasonable financial provision was made for the applicant in question:

"The question is simply whether the will or the disposition has made reasonable provision, and not whether it was unreasonable on the part of the deceased to have made no provision, or no larger provision, for the dependant .... It is not whether the testator stands convicted of unreasonableness, but whether the provision in fact made is reasonable."[72]

"The court has no carte blanche to alter the deceased's dispositions or those which the state makes of his estate to accord with whatever the court itself might have thought would be sensible if it had been in the deceased's position."[73]

---

[69] *Re Coventry* [1979] 3 All ER 815 *per* Goff LJ at 819. Their Lordships rejected the earlier meaning given to maintenance in *Re Christie* [1979] 1 All ER 546 where it had been equated with general welfare or benefit.

[70] (1983) 8 NIJB.

[71] *Re Dennis* [1981] 2 All ER 140.

[72] *Per* Megarry J in *Re Goodwin* [1968] 3 All ER 12 at 15.

[73] *Per* Oliver J, in the Chancery Division, in *Re Coventry* [1980] Ch 461 at 475.

8.49   When assessing whether or not reasonable financial provision has been made for any particular applicant the court is required to consider a number of matters which are set down in article 5 of the 1979 Order. These are:

(a)   *General*   matters,   which   remain   constant   and must be considered in *all* applications; and,

(b)   *Specific*   matters   which   are   prescribed   for consideration   for   each   particular   category   of applicant.

8.50   The general matters are considered in the following paragraphs, while the specific matters are dealt with in the next section. In both cases it is the facts as known to the court *at the date of the hearing* which must be considered.[74] Account can therefore be taken of events which occurred after the deceased's death.

8.51   Finally, the proper approach of the court in assessing whether or not to make an order is two-tiered. First, it must consider whether reasonable financial provision has been made. Secondly, if the answer to the first question is in the negative, it must determine what order should be made. On *both* occasions the question should be answered by considering the various matters which are prescribed by article 5 of the 1979 Order.

General matters to be considered in all applications

8.52   The following matters must be considered irrespective of the class of applicant:[75]

(a)   The   financial   needs   and   resources   of   the applicant, including those likely in the foresee-able future;[76]

(b)   The   financial   needs   and   resources   of   any beneficiary under the estate;[77]

---

[74]Art 5(5).

[75]Art 5(1).

[76]In considering the financial resources of any person, the court must take into account his earning capacity and, in considering financial needs, it must take into account his financial obligations and responsibilities - art 5(6).

[77]This includes any financial benefits which accrue to the beneficiaries by reason of the death of the deceased but which do not form part of his estate, eg, sums received from a pension fund - *Jessop* v *Jessop* [1992] 1 FLR 591.

(c) The obligations and responsibilities which the deceased had towards the applicant;

(d) The size and nature of the net estate and the effect any order might have on a business undertaking;[78]

(e) Physical or mental disorders of any applicant or beneficiary;

(f) Any other matter (including conduct) which, in the circumstances, the court considers relevant.

Conduct

8.53 It will be observed that conduct is the only matter expressly mentioned within residual category (f) above. *Re Snoek*[79] confirmed that conduct in family provision cases involving spouses should be treated in the same way as in matrimonial breakdown cases. For the latter it has been held that conduct should only interfere with an award if it is both "obvious and gross".[80] In *Snoek* itself the behaviour of the applicant was certainly not trivial and included directing milk bottles, hot water and, most seriously, a car with a running ignition, towards her husband. The learned judge accepted that this behaviour was atrocious but he felt that it was not sufficient to cancel out the earlier, happier part of the marriage and made an award, albeit the relatively modest sum of £5,000. *Re Morrow*,[81] a recent decision of Campbell J in the Northern Ireland High Court, would seem to confirm that conduct is regarded as equally unimportant in this jurisdiction.

The deceased's reasons

8.54 Under the 1960 Act the court was expressly referred to the reasons, if any, which the deceased had for excluding the applicant.[82] These have diminished in importance in light of the more objective approach now adopted by the courts, but although there is no express mention of them in article 5 of the 1979 Order, they have sometimes been considered as relevant under the residual category:

---

[78]For an example of the Northern Ireland High Court considering the effect of an award on a business undertaking (ie the family farm) see *Re Morrow* [1995] 6 BNIL 98.

[79](1983) 13 Fam Law 18.

[80]*Watchel* v *Watchel* [1973] 1 All ER 113.

[81][1995] 6 BNIL 98.

[82]1960 Act, s 2(2).

"Indeed, I think any view expressed by a deceased person that he wishes a particular person to benefit will generally be of little significance because the question is not subjective but objective. An express reason for rejecting the applicant is a different matter and may be very relevant to the problem."[83]

For example, in *Re Leach*[84] evidence that the deceased had intended to benefit the applicant under her will was held to be of considerable weight, and in *Re Collins*[85] an unexecuted will of the deceased was taken into account. Moreover, article 23 of the 1979 Order makes express provision for the admission in evidence of a statement of the deceased (whether documentary or oral) as to his reasons for excluding persons under his will. Obviously, therefore, it is intended that these may be relevant in certain circumstances.[86]

APPROACH TO PARTICULAR APPLICANTS

8.55   Each category of applicant is now considered in turn. The specific matters[87] which the court must take into account are examined along with a few 'pointers' on how the court may exercise its discretion in each type of case. The issue of *locus standi* has already been discussed above.

Surviving spouses

Specific matters
8.56   Where the applicant is a surviving spouse the court must consider:

(a)   the age of the applicant and the duration of the marriage;

---

[83]*Per* Goff LJ in *Re Coventry* [1979] 3 All ER 815, at 822.

[84][1985] 2 All ER 754.

[85][1990] 2 All ER 47.

[86]Such a statement will only be admissible as evidence of any fact stated therein of which direct oral evidence by the deceased, if he could have been called as a witness, would have been admissible. Evidence of oral statements will be admitted only if it is direct oral evidence by a person who heard or otherwise perceived the statement being made, unless the statements were made during prior legal proceedings in which case it may be proved by any manner authorised by the court (art 23(2)). A statement in a document can be proved by production of the original or an authenticated copy, even if the original is still in existence (art 23(3)).

[87]These are in addition to the general matters which must be considered in every application. These were considered at para 8.52 *supra*. It is expressly stated in art 5 (2), (3) and (4) that all specific matters are without prejudice to the generality of the "any other matter" which is to be considered in every case.

(b)   the contribution made by the applicant to the welfare of the family of the deceased, including any contribution made by looking after the home or caring for the family;

(c)   the provision which the applicant might reasonably have expected to receive if, on the day the deceased died, the marriage had been terminated by divorce instead.[88]

Decided cases

8.57 Although the legislation itself draws no distinction between the three factors listed above, the judiciary have tended to give priority to the final one - the expected award had the applicant and the deceased divorced on the date of death. This particular approach was succinctly summarised by the English Court of Appeal in *Re Moody*,[89] a successful claim by a widower who had been bypassed completely when his wife left everything by will to her stepdaughter from her first marriage. To quote from Waite J:

> "The objective is that the minimum posthumous provision for a surviving spouse should correspond as closely as possible to the inchoate rights enjoyed by that spouse in the deceased's lifetime by virtue of his or her prospective entitlement under matrimonial law....
>
> When stripped to its barest terms [the 1975 Act] amounts to a direction to the judge to ask himself in surviving spouse cases: What would a family judge have ordered for this couple if divorce instead of death had divided them; what is the effect of any other section 3 [in Northern Ireland article 5] factors of which I have not taken account already in answering that question, and what in the light of those two enquiries, am I to make of the reasonableness (when viewed objectively) of the dispositions made by the will and/or intestacy."[90]

8.58 A similar approach had been adopted by the Court of Appeal in 1984 when one Mrs Besterman[91] successfully appealed against the level of a family provision award. Mrs Besterman, the widow of an eccentric Oxford millionaire (one of whose foibles was that he believed himself to be the reincarnation of Voltaire), was only left personal chattels and a life interest in war stock (which

---

[88] Art 5(2). Point (c) is not relevant in the case of a judicially separated spouse.

[89] [1992] 2 All ER 524 at 533.

[90] *Ibid* p 534. This approach has recently been endorsed by Campbell J in the Northern Ireland High Court in *Re Morrow* [1995] 6 BNIL 98.

[91] [1984] 2 All ER 656.

produced an annual income of £3,500) by her late husband's will. The bulk of his large estate was given to the Taylor Institute at Oxford University for the continuation of his life's work, the translation of the Voltaire manuscripts. Apparently there was nothing malicious in the behaviour of Dr Besterman, who genuinely believed that he had provided well for his wife, but not uncommonly amongst his gender was in the habit of grossly underestimating the amount required to keep a wife in the style to which she had become accustomed. When awarded £259,000 at first instance Mrs Besterman appealed to the Court of Appeal on the ground that the judge had erred in law in not taking proper account of the sum which she would have received on divorce. Her award, on this basis, was increased to £378,000.

8.59   However, two recent English cases may provide some evidence of a less generous attitude towards surviving spouse applicants. In *Davis* v *Davis*[92] the deceased had been married to the applicant, his second wife, for seven years before his death and although he had given her a capital sum of £15,000 the year before he died, his will provided her with only a *life* interest in his residuary estate of £117,000. The other main beneficiary under the trusts in this will was his only child, a 16 year old son from his first marriage. At first instance the applicant's claim of failure to make reasonable financial provision, based on the absence of any capital provision on death, was dismissed as "startling" by Thorpe J. Indeed, the learned judge was of the opinion that the husband "could not have done more". The applicant appealed to the Court of the Appeal on the ground that the trial judge had not taken proper account of the imaginary divorce guideline and, more specifically the fact that prior to the marriage the applicant had the security of owning her home, albeit at the very bottom rung of the property ladder. In short, it was argued that the High Court had erred in law in not transferring the freehold of the testator's house to the widow. However, the Court of Appeal was unanimous that the applicant had "manifestly failed to cross the threshold" which would have enabled substitution of the original decision on appeal.

8.60   In *Davis* v *Davis* the English Court of Appeal has certainly moved away from the more rigid formula which it postulated in *Re Moody* and it remains to be seen whether this will develop into an ongoing trend. From the practitioner's view, the "surviving spouse" category has been the one in which "reasonable financial provision" was most easily quantified, precisely because of the heavy reliance on the hypothetical divorce factor. Any retreat from this

---

[92][1993] 1 FLR 54. The second case which is broadly similar is *Re Clarke* [1991] Fam Law 364.

position clearly removes much of the previous certainty. However, the *Moody* formula has since been expressly approved in the Northern Ireland High Court.[93]

Former spouses

Specific matters

8.61 In the case of an application from a former spouse the court must have regard to the following:[94]

    (a)   the age of the applicant and the duration of the marriage, and;

    (b)   the contribution made by the applicant to the welfare of the family of the deceased, including any contribution made by looking after the home or caring for the family.

Decided cases

8.62 It is evident from the decided cases that it is exceptionally difficult to show that a deceased failed to make reasonable financial provision for a former spouse. This is because the mechanism for property adjustment on divorce will have, in the normal course of events,[95] provided a full and final settlement. In 'clean break' situations, in particular, it is highly unlikely that a former spouse applicant will succeed.

8.63 The leading decision in respect of this category, which illustrates these opening remarks very well, is that of the English Court of Appeal in *Re Fullard*.[96] The applicant and the deceased divorced a couple of years before the latter's death. Neither was wealthy, and when the deceased died he left his entire estate of just over £7,000 to the female friend who had taken him in during his final years. The divorce settlement had required the deceased to transfer the matrimonial home to the applicant for the sum of £4,500, meaning that the bulk of his estate consisted of this money which he had received from the applicant. The applicant's claim for financial provision failed; there was nothing in her favour to discharge the heavy burden that it was unreasonable

---

[93]*Re Morrow* [1995] 6 BNIL 98.

[94]Art 5(2) of the 1979 Order.

[95]For situations where the deceased died within 12 months of the termination and there has not yet been a full and final property adjustment, see para 8.44 *supra*.

[96][1981] 2 All ER 796.

not to provide for her on death. Furthermore, their Lordships were of the view that in order for a former spouse applicant to succeed there must be "exceptional circumstances" - and the mere accretion of wealth by the deceased after the dissolution of the marriage is not, in itself, sufficient to warrant the making of an award.[97] Extreme situations which the court suggested *obiter* might justify an order being made in favour of a surviving spouse are where periodical payments which have been in force for a *long* period of time have ceased on death,[98] or if a substantial lump sum has been unlocked by death (such as one from an insurance policy).

8.64   The few reported cases in which former spouses have been successful have generally involved a deceased who has failed during his lifetime to pay his estranged spouse the maintenance which he had been ordered.[99]

Child of the deceased

Specific matters
8.65   The following matter must be considered where the applicant is a child of the deceased:

> The manner in which the applicant was being, or in which he might expect to be, educated or trained.

Decided cases
8.66   If the deceased has not provided for a minor child, it is not difficult to establish that he failed to make reasonable financial provision.[100]   To quote from Carswell J in *Re Patton*:[101]

> "A child's financial needs should rank very highly in the order of priorities ... they should normally rank well above the needs of other beneficiaries."

---

[97]This departed from an earlier dictum by Lane LJ in *Re Eyre* [1968] 1 All ER 968 that accretion of wealth after the termination of a marriage would be enough.

[98]However, it is surely questionable why the *length* of time for which a former spouse has been in receipt of periodical payments is relevant to the dependence upon them.

[99]*Re Crawford* [1983] 4 FLR 273; *Re Farrow* [1987] 17 Fam Law 14.

[100]As has been noted earlier (para 8.34 *supra*) the 1979 Order operates on the basis that the best method of providing for non-adult children is to provide for the surviving parent. Thus no order can be made on the application of a minor child, if the deceased is survived by both a spouse and children, and he has made that spouse reasonable financial provision for both that spouse and the child - art 4(10).

[101](1986) 3 NIJB 35.

In the case in question two illegitimate minor children of the deceased were each awarded lump sums of £10,000 out of a £46,000 estate. It is likewise if the applicant is a disabled or otherwise dependent adult child.[102] Much more controversial is the extent to which an award is appropriate for an able-bodied and self-sufficient child of full age.[103]

8.67 *Re Coventry*,[104] the leading English case on the matter, established that adult persons should only succeed in "exceptional circumstances". The applicant, the deceased's only child, returned home to live with both his parents at the age of 26. Shortly afterwards his mother left and continued to live apart from the deceased until his death 20 years later, during which period the applicant looked after both the deceased and his home. On the deceased's intestate death his entire estate passed to his estranged wife. Notwithstanding that the applicant's salary as a chauffeur was only sufficient to fund the necessities of life and that he had no savings, nor alternative accommodation, his claim for family provision was rejected by Oliver J:

> "[Awards in favour of] able-bodied and comparatively young men[105] in employment and able to maintain themselves must be relatively rare and need to be approached .... with a degree of circumspection."[106]

This decision was affirmed by the Court of Appeal; there was no "special circumstance" (eg a moral obligation upon the deceased to provide for his son) which made the failure to provide financial provision unreasonable.[107]

8.68 That something more is needed for success under the 1975 Act than an adult son or daughter in necessitous circumstances was later confirmed in *Re Dennis*:

> "A person who is physically capable of earning his own living faces a difficult task in getting provision made for him, because the court is inclined to ask 'why should anybody else make provision for you if you are capable of maintaining yourself?'"[108]

---

[102]*Re Debenham* [1986] Fam Law 101.

[103]For a useful review of a number of cases involving adult children, see Miller, "Inheritance Claims by Adult Children" [1995] Conv 22.

[104][1979] 3 All ER 815.

[105]Or a young woman in a similar position - *Re Rowlands* [1984] 5 FLR 813.

[106][1980] Ch 461 at 465.

[107]This approach has since been confirmed by the same court in *Re Jennings* [1994] 3 All ER 27.

[108][1981] 2 All ER 140, *per* Browne Wilkinson J at 145.

However, in Northern Ireland the judiciary has tended to adopt a more generous approach to adult children applicants, on occasions making awards to self-sufficient persons who could in no way be described as dependent upon the deceased. The cases *Re McGarrell*[109] and *Re Creeney*[110] are illustrative.

8.69   *Re McGarrell* was a successful claim by an adult daughter who had been excluded completely when her father left his property by will between a charity and the husbands of his two nieces. The applicant, who was maintained by her husband and not the deceased, based her claim on the 'meals on wheels' and 'home-help' type services which she had provided for the deceased. In awarding her a one-quarter share of her father's estate, Hutton J held that her actions had established a moral claim on the estate. However, while this behaviour was highly commendable, it does not detract from the fact that the deceased had no obligation, legal or moral, to maintain the applicant while she was alive and that she had been independent for many years.

8.70   *Re Creeny* involved an application by an adult son of a deceased who had left everything by will to his daughter. The applicant had lived in England since a family disagreement a number of years before and he had little spare cash. In contrast, his sister had the fortune to marry well (a Belfast dentist) and enjoyed a very comfortable standard of living which included an annual cruise. The applicant's case relied heavily on work which he had done in the family shoe shop while still in his teens and in particular on the fact that he had been given assurances by the deceased that this business would eventually be his. Carswell J awarded him two-fifths of the estate. However, there was no dispute that for the best part of his adult life the son had been independent from his father.

8.71   The above cases come perilously close to sanctioning exactly what the courts claim that they have no authority to do, that is rewrite the deceased's will. It is respectfully submitted that they result from the incorrect question being asked, that is, "did the deceased act unreasonably?", rather than "is the *provision* unreasonable?" It should be remembered that it was not the objective of the 1979 Order to interfere with the freedom which every testator enjoys to exclude an adult, able-bodied child from his will, any more than it was to prescribe fairness and equality between offspring.

---

[109](1983) 8 NIJB.
[110][1985] NI 397.

Person treated as a child of the deceased

Specific matters

8.72   Where the applicant was treated as a child of the deceased's family the following matters must be considered:[111]

<blockquote>

(a)   The manner in which the applicant was being, or in which he might expect to be, educated or trained;

(b)   *Whether* the deceased has assumed any responsibility for the applicant's maintenance *and if so*, the extent to which the deceased assumed that responsibility and the length of time for which the deceased discharged it [emphasis added];

(c)   Whether, in discharging that responsibility, the deceased knew that the applicant was not his own child;

(d)   The liability of any other person to maintain the applicant.

</blockquote>

Decided cases

8.73   This category clearly has much in common with the previous one. In particular, many of the comments made then about *adult* applicants are equally relevant here.

The facts of *Re Leach*, a successful claim by an adult stepchild, have already been discussed.[112]   The factors which influenced the court's decision included the facts that the deceased had intended to leave the applicant considerable sums in her will had procrastination not got the better of her, and that much of the deceased's money had originated from the applicant's natural father. Again, however, the correctness of this approach can be questioned, in that at no time could the applicant be described as *dependent* upon her stepmother. Reference has already been made to the views expressed by the English Court of Appeal in *Re Coventry*[113] that intestate deaths are to be treated in the same manner as testate ones. The *Leach* decision suggests that this approach is not entirely

---

[111]Art 5(3) of the 1979 Order.

[112]See para 8.37 *supra*. See also *Re Callaghan* [1984] 3 All ER 790.

[113]See para 8.10 *supra*.

uniform and that the courts may be more amenable to relieving the 'hard cases' of the intestacy code than to changing the distribution under a will.

8.74 Attention need hardly be drawn to the fact that this category is especially significant as a supplement to the intestacy rules which, as has been seen, adopt a very narrow interpretation of the word "child" and do not, for example, afford any rights to a stepchild.[114]

Persons being maintained by the deceased

Specific matters
8.75 For applicants who apply under category (e) of the 1979 Order on the basis that they were being maintained by the deceased the court must have regard to the following:[115]

(a) The extent to which and the basis upon which the deceased assumed responsibility for the maintenance of the applicant;[116]

(b) The length of time for which the deceased discharged that responsibility.

Decided cases
8.76 Reference has already been made to the wide variety of potential applicants under this category.[117] Initially christened 'the mistress's charter', many applications have actually arisen out of platonic relationships (eg *Jelley* v *Iliffe* above).[118] The problems inherent in the requirement to show *dependence* have already been highlighted and the amendment to the law in England to give automatic *locus standi* to *cohabitants* of two years standing by the Law

---

[114]See para 6.27 *supra*.

[115]Art 5(4).

[116]Compare this to the similar provision in the category immediately before it. The omission of the words "whether" and "and, if so" were considered by the English Court of Appeal in *Jelley* v *Iliffe* [1981] 2 All ER 29, to make the assumption of responsibility a *sine qua non* of an application under category (e): ie, in order to make a claim under this category the deceased must have assumed responsibility for the applicant's maintenance. However, their Lordships were in agreement that such an assumption of responsibility could be inferred simply by the deceased *actually* maintaining the applicant.

[117]The following selection of cases demonstrate this variety: *Re Wilkinson* [1978] Fam 22 (sister); Re Haig [1979] 129 NLJ 420 (cohabitant); *Harrington* v *Gill* [1983] 4 FLR 265; *Re Viner* [1978] CLY 3091 (brother); *Bishop* v *Plumley* [1991] 1 WLR 582.

[118]See para 8.40 *supra*.

Reform (Succession) Act 1995 is to be welcomed. Article 4 of the draft Succession (NI) Order 1996 proposes that similar provision be made for Northern Ireland.[119] However, the change is of no benefit to non-cohabitants, who still have to pass the dependency hurdle. The most notorious of the early cases under this category was *Malone v Harrison*,[120] which is instructive of the type of dependency which may found a successful claim.

8.77 Mavis Malone, the applicant, could most accurately be described as the 'part-time' mistress of the deceased, a very wealthy businessman. In addition to Mavis, he kept a common-law spouse, Christina (passed off to Mavis as a jealous housekeeper); a number of more temporary lovers, and a wife from whom he had been separated for years. The deceased had met Mavis when she was 23 years of age and he was 59. They never lived together but she accompanied him on many business trips and over the years he provided her with a flat, furs, cars and other gifts. At his request she had given up her work to enable her to be free for his sporadic visits: in short, he had "monopolised her for 12 years of her life", and when he died she received no benefits under his will, of which Christina was the main beneficiary. At 35 years of age, Mavis was left with little money and, in view of her employment history, prospects of only menial, poorly paid work. She was awarded a lump sum of £19,000.

8.78 Again this category is particularly useful as a plug for some of the more obvious gaps in the intestacy code. Its effectiveness as such will obviously increase if the dependency requirement is removed for long-standing cohabitants.

POWERS AVAILABLE TO THE COURT

8.79 The Inheritance (Family Provision) Act (NI) 1960 Act generally restricted the court to making periodical payments.[121] The broadening of the definition of "reasonable financial provision" in 1979 to take account of more than just maintenance where the applicant is a surviving spouse necessitated a corresponding widening of the court's powers. Article 4 of the 1979 Order empowers the court to order any of the following.

---

[119] In order to apply an applicant must have lived in the same household as the deceased as his or her husband or wife during the whole period of two years ending immediately before the date when the deceased died. As with all applicants other than a surviving spouse, they are limited to a claim for maintenance.

[120] [1979] 1 WLR 1353.

[121] 1960 Act, s 1(4).

(a) Periodical payments for a specified period.[122]

> The court can specify the actual amount of each payment, or it may order that part of the estate be set aside, the income of which will constitute the payments. Equally, it is free to determine the amount of the payments in any other way it thinks fit.[123] Note, however, that where an amount is to be set aside to meet periodical payments, only that amount which will meet those payments *at the date of the order* can be set aside. No account is taken of inflation.[124]

(b) Payment of a lump sum.[125]

> Decided cases would suggest that this is the preferred award with every category of applicant, notwithstanding that in all cases other than surviving spouses the sole responsibility of the court is to provide *maintenance*. In such cases, of course, income has been 'capitalised' into a lump sum.[126]

> One practice which has received considerable criticism is that of providing for infant children by a lump sum, the income from which maintains them during minority while on majority they receive the capital. In *Re Patton*[127] the Northern Ireland High Court agreed with the view first expressed by Goff LJ in Re *Coventry*[128] that this practice goes beyond the confines of mere maintenance.

(c) Transfer any property of the estate to the applicant.[129]

(d) Settle any property of the estate for the applicant's benefit.[130]

(e) Acquire specified property out of the estate funds (eg a house) which is then transferred to the applicant or settled for his benefit.[131]

---

[122] Art 4(1)(a).

[123] Art 4(2).

[124] Art 4(3). Compare the practice in Commonwealth countries where periodical payments are often index-linked - see eg *White* v *Barron* (1980) 30 ALR 51.

[125] Art 4(1)(b).

[126] The court can also order the lump sum to be used to purchase an annuity or be paid in instalments - art 9(1).

[127] (1986) 3 NIJB.

[128] [1979] 3 All ER 815.

[129] Art 4(1)(c).

[130] Art 4(1)(d).

[131] Art 4(1)(e).

(f) Vary any marriage settlement to which the deceased was a party.[132]

8.80 In addition the court may make such consequential and supplemental provisions as it thinks necessary or expedient. For example, in *Campbell* v *Campbell*[133] the Northern Ireland High Court granted a rent-free licence to a son who spent his life working the family farm and who would otherwise have been left homeless, with only £6,000 in his pocket, following his father's intestate death.[134]

8.81 The *Campbell* case raised another point of some interest about the scope of the court's residual powers. It was argued on behalf of the most needy of the children of the deceased (other than the applicant), that these residual powers, taken in conjunction with article 5 of the 1979 Order (which requires the court to consider the needs and obligations of the other beneficiaries), enabled an order to be made increasing the share of persons other than the actual applicant. This was rejected on the ground that it would be giving the courts a carte blanche to undertake mass re-writing of wills. In this sort of case the court is therefore limited to the negative step of not providing the applicant's award out of the needy beneficiary's share. In deciding from which share of the estate the award is to be made, the court has complete discretion.[135]

Interim orders

8.82 The court also has power to grant interim orders in cases of urgency. Article 7 of the 1979 Order provides that this can be exercised where:

> (a) It appears to the court that the applicant is in immediate need of financial assistance, but it is not yet possible to determine what order should be made, and;

---

[132] Art 4(1)(f). Note that this can only be done if the variation is for the benefit of the surviving party to the marriage, a child of the marriage or any person who was treated by the deceased as a child of the marriage. It cannot therefore benefit an applicant under category (e).

[133] (1982) 18 NIJB.

[134] See also *Re Moody* [1992] 2 All ER 524 where the English Court of Appeal directed that a widower be granted a right of residence in property for his lifetime. Generally, of course, the provision of accommodation *for life* would be more in keeping with the requirement of *maintenance* than an absolute interest. In the recent Northern Ireland decision *Re Morrow* [1995] 6 BNIL 98, part of a farm was transferred to the applicant, but her son (from whom it had been taken) was given an option to purchase at market value.

[135] See, eg *Malone* v *Harrison* [1979] 1 WLR 1353 where the court refused to make an award out of the share of the deceased's common law spouse.

(b)   part of the net estate can   be made available to
        meet the interim order.[136]

8.83   When making an interim order the court has to consider the same matters as it would when making any order under article 4 of the 1979 Order, insofar as this is possible in view of the inherent urgency of the situation.[137] Its powers include the right to order such *sum* or sums as it thinks reasonable, so it is open to the court to grant a lump sum.[138]

8.84   Any sums paid out under an interim order are taken into account when the court makes the full award.[139]

Variation of periodical payments

8.85   An order for the making of periodical payments (but not any other order made under article 4)[140] can be varied, discharged or temporarily suspended[141] on the application of any of the following persons:[142]

(a)   Any person who has applied under the order;

(b)   Any   person who could have applied under the order but for the time limit;

(c)   The personal representatives of the deceased;

(d)   The trustees of any property comprised   in   the net estate of the deceased;

(e)   Any beneficiary of the deceased's estate.

8.86   Category (b) above allows an application for variation to be made by a person who had *locus standi* to apply under the 1979 Order but who did not do so and is now time-barred.   It is interesting to note that article 8(2) permits the

---

[136]Art 7(1)(b).

[137]Art 7(3).

[138]See, eg, *Re Besterman* [1984] 2 All ER 656.

[139]Art 7(4).

[140]Although if a lump sum was ordered to be paid in instalments an application can be made under art 9(2) to have the amount or number of the instalments varied.   The lump sum itself cannot be altered.   In *Re Besterman* [1984] 2 All ER 656 the English Court of Appeal considered that this warranted taking more account of inflation when making a lump sum award.

[141]Art 8.

[142]Art 8(5).

variation to be made in *favour* of such a person. It is therefore possible to circumvent the strict six-month time limit[143] provided that an order has already been made in favour of someone else.

8.87   Before varying an order the court has to consider any changes in the matters which it had to take account of when making the original order.[144]

8.88   A variation can take the form of periodical payments of a different amount or duration, the payment of a lump sum or the transfer of property.[145] However, any such periodical payments, lump sums or property must be capable of being taken from the capital set aside for the purposes of meeting the original periodical payments, which is termed the "relevant property".[146]   It is not possible to use any other property from the estate.[147]

8.89   Orders are commonly framed so that periodical payments are to cease on the expiration of a particular period of time, or on the happening of a certain event.   In these cases applications for a variation to enable the payments to continue, notwithstanding that the time has expired or the event has happened, can still be made under article 8 of the 1979 Order.[148]   One exception is where periodical payments are to cease on the remarriage of a *former* spouse.   This cessation is automatic and cannot be varied.[149]

8.90   When the court makes a variation it can make whatever consequential directions it thinks necessary.[150]   For example, the alteration of periodical payments might result in a surplus capital sum.

The court has power to make second and subsequent variation orders, so a further variation may be sought.

---

[143]See para 8.15 *supra*.

[144]Art 8(7).

[145]Art 8(2).

[146]Art 8(6).

[147]See, eg *Fricker* v *Fricker* [1982] FLR 228.

[148]Art 8(10). However, in such cases the application for the variation must be made before six months have elapsed from the date of the event or the expiry of the period of time - art 8(3).

[149]However, there is nothing which precludes an application for a variation by a *surviving* spouse who has remarried and whose periodical payments were expressly stated to stop on remarriage. Of course, if payments to a surviving spouse are not expressly stated to stop on remarriage, they will continue thereafter.

[150]Art 8(8).

PROPERTY AVAILABLE FOR FINANCIAL PROVISION

8.91 The property which is available to meet any family provision award is the "net estate" of the deceased,[151] a concept which has been given an artificially wide definition by the 1979 Order and, for example, can include property held by the deceased as a joint tenant and which would otherwise pass automatically to the surviving joint tenants. In addition, the 1979 Order introduced a number of anti-avoidance provisions which empower the court to open up certain *inter vivos* transactions. These are discussed more fully below.

8.92 Naturally all property within the usual meaning of "net estate" (any property of which the deceased had power to dispose by will less the amount of any funeral, testamentary and administration expenses, debts and liabilities)[152] is available for a family provision award. This includes property in respect of which the deceased held a general power of appointment, whether or not he exercised it during his lifetime. However, property exercisable by a special power is expressly excluded.[153]

8.93 In addition, various property which is not normally regarded as being part of the "net estate" is *automatically* included for family provision purposes by the 1979 Order. Property which the deceased nominated under a statutory provision before his death[154] and any property which was received as a *donatio mortis causa*[155] made by the deceased fall within this category.

Severing a joint tenancy

8.94 Article 11 of the 1979 Order[156] empowers the court, at its discretion,[157] to include within the "net estate" such of the deceased's share in a joint tenancy immediately before his death as appears just in all the circumstances of the case for the purposes of facilitating the making of a family provision award. However, such an order can only be made within six months of the date of the

---

[151] Art 2(2).

[152] *Ibid.* This includes any inheritance tax payable out of the estate on death.

[153] *Ibid.*

[154] Art 10(1). Statutory nominations are dealt with at para 10.08 *post*. Note that only *statutory* nominations fall within art 10, and not "cold, contractual arrangements" - *Re Cairnes* [1983] FLR 225. See also *Jessop v Jessop* [1992] 1 FLR 591.

[155] Art 10(2).

[156] In England, s 9 of the 1975 Act.

[157] In contrast to art 10 this provision does not operate automatically.

grant of representation, or within 18 months from death, whichever is sooner.[158] These time limits are absolute so that even if leave is granted for a late application under article 4,[159] joint property will not be affected.

8.95 Although there has only been a handful of reported cases,[160] some guidance has emerged about how the courts will exercise their discretion. First, the time at which the court should decide to exercise the discretion is at the initial hurdle of deciding *whether* to make an order, and not when deciding *which* order is appropriate.[161] Secondly, once such an order has been made the property subject to it should be treated no differently to any other property in the estate.[162]

Anti-avoidance measures

8.96 Circumventing the provisions of the 1960 Act was not difficult and could be achieved if the deceased simply gave away as much of his estate as possible *inter vivos* or contracted to dispose of it by will.[163] The 1979 Order strengthened the effectiveness of the family provision regime in a number of ways. Article 12[164] enables property which has been disposed of within six years of death, with a view to defeating a family provision claim, to be clawed back into the estate, while article 13 gives the court broadly similar powers where a contract to leave property by will has been made with the intention of defeating a potential claim.

Property disposed of within six years of death

8.97 An order can only be made under article 12 of the 1979 Order if the court is satisfied of the following:[165]

    (a)   that the deceased made a disposition less than
           six years before death;

---

[158]Art 11(1). The corresponding English legislation does not contain the alternative 18 months from death formula.

[159]See para 8.15 *supra*.

[160]The most recent decision of the Court of Appeal, *Jessop v Jessop* [1992] 1 FLR 591, is worth reading for its dramatic facts alone.

[161]*Kourgky v Lusher* (1983) 4 FLR 65, which was approved by the Northern Ireland High Court in *Re Patton* (1986) 3 NIJB.

[162]*Re Crawford* [1983] 4 FLR 273; *Jessop v Jessop* [1992] 1 FLR 591.

[163]See, eg *Schaefer v Schuhmann* [1972] AC 572.

[164]Which corresponds to s 10 of the 1975 Act.

[165]Art 12(2).

(b)   that full valuable consideration was not given;

(c)   that the disposition was made with the *intention* of defeating an application for financial provision; and

(d)   that exercising such powers would facilitate the making of financial provision for the applicant under the order.

8.98   Condition (c) is satisfied if, on the balance of probabilities, the intention of the deceased (although not necessarily the *sole* intention) in making the disposition was either to prevent a claim for financial provision being made or to reduce the amount which might otherwise be granted.[166]

8.99   In exercising its powers under article 12 of the 1979 Order the court is directed to have regard to: the circumstances in which the disposition was made; if any valuable consideration was given; the relationship between the deceased and the donee; the conduct and financial resources of the donee and all other circumstances of the case.[167]   A surviving spouse applicant successfully invoked article 12 of the 1979 Order in *Re Morrow*[168] when her late husband had transferred his farm (his only significant asset) to his son about a year before he died.

8.100   The powers of the court do not cease because the donee has already disposed of the property in question and in such circumstances the court may order him to provide the estate with a specified sum or specified property. However, the amount is limited to the value which the property transferred to him had at the date of death.[169]   Where the donee has died the powers under article 12 of the 1979 Order may be exercised against his personal representatives.   However, in this case if the property has already been distributed the personal representatives are no longer liable.

8.101   The court can only exercise its powers under article 12 if a special application requesting it to do so has been made.   Once such an application has been made in relation to a particular disposition it is open to the court to look into any other disposition and, if satisfied that the necessary criteria exist, make the same sort of order in relation to it.

---

[166]Art 14(1).

[167]Art 12(6).

[168][1995] 6 BNIL 98.

[169]Less any inheritance tax payable by the donee.

Contracts to leave property by will

8.102   As has been noted article 13 of the 1979 Order empowers the court to intervene where the deceased has entered into a contract to leave property by will with the intention of defeating a potential family provision claim.   In this case, however, no time limit is prescribed so contracts made more than six years before death are within its scope.[170]   Where property has already been transferred under the contract the court can order the donee to transfer specified sums or property into the estate.   Where the property has not yet been transferred it can direct the personal representatives not to proceed.

8.103   An order can only be made under article 13 if the court is satisfied that:[171]

(a)   the deceased made a contract by which he agreed either to leave a sum of money or property to a person by his will or that a sum of money or property would be paid or transferred to a person out of his estate;

(b)   the contract was made with the intention of defeating an application for financial provision;

(c)   full valuable consideration was not given or promised; and

(d)   by exercising its powers the court would facilitate the making of financial provision for the applicant.

8.104   The court need only be satisfied on the balance of probabilities that the deceased's intention (albeit not necessarily his sole intention) was to defeat a potential claim.[172]   Furthermore, where absolutely *no* valuable consideration[173] was given or promised, the court must presume that the contract was made with the intention of defeating an application, although this presumption can be rebutted.[174]

8.105   Before exercising its powers under article 13 the court must have regard to the following: the circumstances surrounding the making of the

---

[170]Although it does not apply to contracts made before 1 September 1979.

[171]Art 13(2).

[172]Art 14(1).

[173]Marriage is not valuable consideration for these purposes.

[174]Art 14(2).

contract; the relationship between the deceased and the donee; the conduct and financial resources of the donee, and all the other circumstances of the case.[175]

PROTECTION FOR PERSONAL REPRESENTATIVES

8.106 The 1979 Order affords a number of protections to personal representatives. Most significantly, the personal representatives are not personally liable for distributing the estate after six months have elapsed from the date of the grant of representation, on the ground that they should have borne in mind the possibility of an out-of-time application.[176] It follows on from this that a personal representative who has any reason to suspect that a family provision claim will be made should not distribute[177] the estate for at least six months after the grant has been issued. It should be remembered that this protection only benefits the personal representatives and does not prejudice the right of claimants to recover property from the beneficiaries of the estate.

8.107 Article 22(2) provides that personal representatives shall not be liable for making payments under an interim order if it later transpires that the net estate was insufficient to make such payments. However, this protection does not extend to personal representatives who at the time of making the payment had reasonable cause to believe that the estate would not be sufficient.

8.108 Personal representatives are authorised to postpone payment[178] under any contract to leave property by will if they have reason to believe that the anti-avoidance measures discussed above will be invoked.[179]

---

[175]Art 13(4).

[176]Art 22(1).

[177]He can, of course, pay the debts and funeral, testamentary and administration expenses during this time.

[178]Until six months after the grant of representation, or, if proceedings have already been commenced, their determination.

[179]Art 22(3).

CHAPTER NINE

EXECUTORS AND ADMINISTRATORS

9.01 This chapter examines the law relating to the appointment of executors and administrators. Since this subject is inextricably linked to the nature of the *grant of representation* which will be extracted, it is necessary to start with a number of definitions.

Personal representatives

9.02 These are the persons entrusted with the administration of the estate of a deceased person[1] and it is they who are responsible for the payment of the funeral, testamentary and administration expenses; for the discharge of the deceased's debts and other liabilities; and for the distribution of the estate among those entitled under the deceased's will, or on his intestacy, as the case may be. The authority for the personal representatives to act as such is generally established from a *grant of representation*.

Executor

9.03 A personal representative appointed by the deceased's will is known as an executor and the grant in this case will be a *grant of probate*.

Administrator

9.04 Anyone other than an executor to whom representation is granted is an administrator. Where the deceased left a valid will it will be a *grant of letters of administration with the will annexed*; otherwise it will be a straight *grant of letters of administration* (sometimes referred to as a grant of letters of administration *simpliciter*).

9.05 The grants of probate and of administration, with and without the will annexed, are the three basic types of grant. In addition, a number of 'special' grants exist,[2] although these may all be regarded as refinements on one of the basic grants.

---

[1] The adjective 'personal' dates from the separate vesting of real and personal property on death (see para 6.08 *supra*). Although this is now an anachronism the term "personal representative" remains a statutory definition.

[2] These are considered in detail at para 11.53 *post*.

Grant in common form

9.06   The vast majority of grants are in 'common form', that is, issued by the Probate Office following a quasi-administrative process governed by the Non-Contentious Probate Rules (NCPR).[3]   A grant in common form can be subsequently revoked or amended by the court.[4]

Grant in solemn form

9.07   A grant in solemn form is a grant made after a probate action.   It differs from a grant in common form in that it can only be revoked or set aside if obtained by fraud.

EXECUTORS

The appointment of executors

9.08   There are three ways in which executors can be appointed:

> (a)   by the testator in his will, either expressly or by implication, and in either case the appointment may be absolute or qualified;

> (b)   under a power conferred by the testator in his will;

> (c)   by the court, under its statutory power to appoint executors in certain circumstances.

Express appointment by testator in his will

9.09   The most common mode of appointment is by an express clause in the testator's will or codicil, for example: "I appoint [name] of [address] (and [name] of [address]) to be executor(s) of my will". If there is no possibility of trusts arising under the will, the testator need appoint only an executor or executors. Otherwise, he should also appoint trustees. It is common practice to appoint the same persons in both capacities, but separate appointments can be made. On a purely practical note, it is always prudent to obtain the consent of any person whom the testator wishes to appoint as executor.[5]

9.10   Care should be taken to identify the executor(s) as clearly as possible. For instance, the executor(s) should actually be named in the will and not simply referred to by description, and it is preferable that the address(es) be

---

[3] RSC 0 97.

[4] See para 11.102 *post*.

[5] Even though the giving of such agreement does not stop the executor so appointed from renouncing his office, see para 9.44 *post*.

included to facilitate identification. Where an executor is appointed by reference to his office, probate will be granted to the holder of that office at the date of *death*, and not the date of the will, unless there is evidence to the contrary.[6]

9.11 The appointment of an executor is subject to the usual rules about certainty, and if the identity of the person is not clear, for example, "any two of my sons",[7] the appointment will be void for uncertainty. However, where the identity of a person expressly appointed as an executor is unclear, extrinsic evidence of the testator's intention will be admitted to identify the executor where there is an ambiguity either on the face of the will, or when the will is considered in the context of the surrounding circumstances.[8]

9.12 For wills made before 1 July 1995, executors designated by a relationship have to answer it through a *legitimate* relationship.[9] Thus an appointment of 'my eldest son' would exclude an illegitimate son. This restriction has been removed by the Children (NI) Order 1995 for appointments in wills made on or after this date.[10]

9.13 Difficulties may arise when a firm of solicitors is appointed as executor. This is considered below.

Implied appointment
9.14 A person may be appointed by a will or codicil to act as executor by implication rather than expressly - he is said to be an executor 'according to the tenor'. In such a case it must be clear that the testator intended the particular person to carry out the functions of an executor; that is, to collect the assets, pay the debts and funeral expenses and discharge the legacies contained in the will.[11] Ultimately it is a question of construction. For example, a simple direction to pay debts may be enough to constitute the person as an executor according to the tenor.[12] In contrast, where the debts are to be paid out of a

---

[6] *Re Jones Estate* (1927) 43 TLR 324.

[7] *In the Goods of Bayliss* (1862) 2 Sw & Tr 613.

[8] Wills and Administration Proceedings (NI) Order 1994, art 25; see para 5.38 *supra*.

[9] Family Law Reform (NI) Order 1977, art 4(2)(a).

[10] Art 155 of and Sch 6 to 1995 Order. In England, ss 1 and 19(1) of the Family Law Reform Act 1987.

[11] *Re Adamson* (1875) L R 3 P & D 253.

[12] *In the Goods of Pamela Cook* [1902] P 114; *Re Fawcett* [1941] P 85.

particular fund which has been given to the putative executor, it is more likely to be construed as a mere legacy subject to the payment of debts.[13]

9.15   Where the testator has appointed certain named persons as 'trustees' and goes on either to demonstrate that he regards them as responsible for payment of debts,[14] or to introduce the term 'executor' later in the course of the document without naming any such persons,[15] the trustees will generally also be executors according to the tenor.   Other examples of implied appointments which have been upheld by the courts include the direction to X "to hold and administer in trust all my estate well known to the said X"[16] and "to carry out this will ... for the due execution of this my will".[17]

9.16   The fact that a person is the sole beneficiary of the entire estate is not enough in itself to entitle him to probate as an executor according to the tenor.[18]

9.17   Once probate is granted to an executor according to the tenor he is in the same position as an executor expressly named in the will, so that if a testator has both expressly appointed an executor and appointed another by implication, probate will be granted to both.[19]

Conditional or qualified appointments

9.18   The appointment of executors (express or implied) may be absolute or conditional.   In the latter case the appointment may be made subject to a condition *precedent*, for example, upon a person reaching a certain age or the refusal of another to act, or a condition *subsequent*, such as an executor going to live abroad or the testator's widow remarrying,[20] in which case the appointment lapses and the executor will generally be substituted by another named person.

9.19   Whenever a substitute executor is included, for instance, "I appoint A to be my executor, but in the event of him predeceasing me or renouncing

---

[13]*Re Davis* (1843) 3 Curt 748; *Re Fraser* (1870) LR 2 P&D 40.

[14]*In the Goods of Rufus Kirby* [1902] P 188.

[15]*In the Goods of the Earl of Leven and Melville* (1889) 15 PD 22; *In the Goods of Lush* (1887) 13 PD 20.

[16]*In the Goods of Nicholas Way* [1901] P 345.

[17]*In the Goods of Russell* [1892] P 380.

[18]*In the Goods of Pryse* [1904] P 301; *In the Goods of Oliphant* (1860) 1 Sw & Tr 525.

[19]*Re Brown's Goods* (1877) 2 PD 110.

[20]*Re Lane's Goods* (1864) 33 LJPM & A 185; *Re Langford's Goods* (1867) LR 1 P & D 458.

probate, I appoint B" it should be made clear *exactly* when the substitute becomes effective.[21]

Article 30 of the 1994 Order provides a convenient solution to a problem which may arise with substitute executors. Where a will contains a provision for a substitute executor which is operative if an executor designated in the will either dies before or contemporaneously with the testator, and this designated executor dies in circumstances rendering it uncertain which of them survived the other, then, for the purposes of probate the case for which the will provides is deemed to have occurred.

9.20   Although it is usual for an executor to act in respect of the whole of the deceased's estate, it may be appropriate to limit the appointment to a particular type of property. A typical circumstance when this might happen is when the deceased has left valuable unpublished literary works and a special literary executor who possesses the necessary editorial skills is appointed.

Person nominated to appoint executor(s)

9.21   Instead of appointing named executors the testator may in his will appoint a person or persons to be entrusted with the task of *nominating* executors; for example, "it is left to the legatees mutually to appoint two intelligent and trustworthy persons to execute this deed...."[22] Such nominations are relatively uncommon.

9.22   It is open to the person so appointed to nominate himself, provided that the terms of the will do not preclude this.[23]

Appointment by the court

9.23   Under article 5 of the Administration of Estates (NI) Order 1979[24] the High Court has the power to pass over an executor and appoint some other person as administrator if, by reason of the circumstances, it appears "necessary or expedient" to do so. In England, the corresponding provision,

---

[21] *In the Goods of Foster* (1871) LR 2 P&D 304 (testator's wife was appointed executrix and died, having taken out probate, but before the estate had been fully administered - held that an appointment which was to take effect in *default* of the wife, took effect on her death); *In the Goods of Betts* (1861) 30 LJPM&A 167; *In the Goods of the Reverend Sir John Lighton* (1828) 1 Hag Ecc 235.

[22] *In the Goods of William Cringan* (1828) 1 Hag Ecc 548.

[23] *In the Goods of Anne Hill Ryder* (1861) 2 Sw & Tr 127.

[24] Replacing s 21 of the 1955 Act, which in turn repealed, and widened, s 78 of the Probates and Letters of Administration Act (Ir) 1857.

currently section 116 of the Supreme Court Act 1981, has been invoked to enable an executrix who was serving a life sentence for the manslaughter of the testator to be passed over,[25] and to pass over an elderly and infirm married couple who had continually refused to extract probate and who, if forced to do so, were highly likely to cause the estate further expense and delay.[26] However, in *Re Edwards-Taylor*[27] the court refused to exercise its discretion to pass over the residuary legatee for a grant of administration with the will annexed on the ground of her immaturity. Willmer J held that this question went beyond administration and that it would set a bad precedent to use the discretion for an ulterior motive, namely protecting the beneficiary from herself.[28]

9.24   Administration granted under article 5 may be limited as the High Court thinks fit.[29]

Chain of executorship

9.25   It has been noted that executorship is an office of personal trust and, as such, it cannot usually be assigned.[30] There is one exception to this general principle - the automatic transmission of the office on death through proving executors. Consider A, the sole and last remaining executor of a testator T, who obtains probate of T's will but then dies testate, before completing the administration of the estate. In such a situation a 'chain of executorship' may arise. If A's executor obtains probate of A's will, he is not only the executor of A's will, but also *the executor by representation of T* and this pattern may be continued so long as the executors continue to take out probate of the wills.[31]

9.26   A chain can only arise where A was the sole and last remaining executor of T. Consider T who appoints two executors, A and B. A dies shortly after T (testate, appointing an executor who proceeds to prove his will). B also dies (intestate) before the administration of T's estate is complete. No chain arises since on A's death the executorship to T's estate vests in B automatically by survivorship.

---

[25]*In the Estate of S* [1968] P 302.

[26]*In the Estate of Biggs* [1966] P 118.

[27][1951] P 24.

[28] See also *In the Goods of Kaufman* [1952] P 325.

[29]Art 5(2)(b).

[30]*Re Skinner* [1958] 1 WLR 1043.

[31]The chain of executorship is a creation of the common law, which was confirmed by statute in Northern Ireland relatively recently by art 32 of the Administration of Estates (NI) Order 1979. In England, the corresponding codification was achieved by s 7 of the Administration of Estates Act 1925.

9.27   Automatic transmission of office through proving executors has the advantage of continuity, and thus reduces potential delays in the administration of the remaining estate, since otherwise a *de bonis non* grant[32] relating to the unadministered property would have to be extracted by a new administrator. It is, however, not without problems. First, it makes a mockery of the essentially personal nature of executorship in that a total stranger may be in control of a deceased's estate relatively soon after his death. The justification that because the testator had confidence in the person whom he appointed as executor, he must also have confidence in *his* choice of executor is hardly logical.   In addition, the subsequent executor is left with the burden of administering two or more estates, at least one of which may be totally unfamiliar to him. Indeed, it is for this reason that a potential chain of representation is one of the classic situations where it may be prudent for the executor to renounce probate. The attractiveness of this course of action is increased by the fact that it is not possible to accept office as executor of the latest will yet renounce the executorship(s) by representation.[33] It was these reasons which persuaded the legislature in the Republic of Ireland to abolish the chain of representation.[34]

9.28   An executor by representation has the same rights in respect of a testator's estate as the original executor would have had if still living[35] and is, to the extent which the estate of that testator has come to his hands, answerable as if he were an original executor.[36]

Termination of the chain
9.29   A chain of executorship is broken on the happening of any of the following events:[37]

(a) An intestacy.

(b) A testator who dies testate, but who omits to appoint executors.

(c) Failure to prove the first executor's will.

---

[32]See para 11.72 *post*.

[33]*In the Goods of Perry* (1840) 2 Curt 655. Although it is possible to renounce probate and then take out representation with the will annexed - if entitled to.

[34]Succession Act 1965, s19(1). This section applies whether the testator died before or after the commencement of this Act.

[35]Art 32 (4)(a) of the 1979 Order.

[36]Art 32 (4)(b).

[37]Art 32(3).

(d) The issue of a discretionary grant under article 5 of the Administration of Estates (NI) Order 1979. It is expressly provided in article 5(3) that once the High Court exercises its discretion and grants administration under the article no person shall be or become entitled to administer the estate by virtue of the chain of representation.

A difficulty which can arise in practice is where an executor has acted and died, appointing an executor who has not yet proved his testator's will and constantly ignores requests to do so. When this problem arose in *Re Gilkinson*,[38] Andrews LCJ held that the court had power to make a full grant (and not merely an *ad colligenda bona* one) to the unadministered estate of the original testator to the person next entitled, but limited in time until the recalcitrant executor obtained probate of the new will. At the time, however, the statutory power to pass over those otherwise entitled was contained in section 78 of the Probates and Letters of Administration Act (Ir) 1857, a provision which was much narrower in ambit than the current article 5 of the Administration of Estates (NI) Order 1979. It is submitted that a similar situation today would result in the court making a discretionary grant under article 5. As has been seen, this brings the chain to an end and is the practice which is followed in England in these circumstances.

(e) Where the first testator had appointed a second executor who, at the time that probate was granted to the first executor, had reserved his right to act but who then subsequently obtains a grant of *double probate*.[39]

(f) The chain also fails if the original appointment was to the estate as a whole, but the succeeding executor's appointment is limited to only part of the estate.[40] In contrast, if the first executor has been granted limited probate, the chain will be continued by a subsequent executor who is granted probate to the whole estate.[41]

9.30 A grant of probate made in England or Wales is effective to carry on a chain of representation in Northern Ireland,[42] but a Scottish confirmation will not be effective and will thus break the chain.[43] Similarly, a grant made in Northern Ireland will carry on a chain in England or Wales.[44]

---

[38][1948] NI 42.

[39]Art 32(1)(b). See para 11.76 *supra*.

[40]*In the Goods of Rachel Bayne* (1858) 1 Sw & Tr 132.

[41]*In the Goods of Rebecca Beer* (1851) 2 Robb Ecc 349.

[42]Administration of Estates Act 1971, s 2(1).

[43]*Ibid* s 2(4).

[44]*Ibid* s 1(4).

Executor de son tort

9.31 An executor *de son tort* is a person who has not actually been appointed as an executor, expressly or impliedly, but who acts as if he had been, for example, by intermeddling in the estate of the deceased.

Who should be appointed as an executor?

Personal qualities

9.32 It is to be expected that persons will be appointed as executors for qualities such as trustworthiness, business acumen and familiarity with the deceased's family situation. In the case of large and/or complex estates, for example, where the testator is a sole trader (or a last surviving partner), it may be prudent to appoint professional executors, but in the majority of cases there is no reason why suitable relatives and friends of the family cannot act.

Professional executors

9.33 Since the office of executor is a fiduciary position, professional executors can only charge if an express charging clause is inserted in the will. It is sometimes overlooked that such clauses are construed as legacies, and as such will fail if the executor also acts as a witness to the will.[45]

Number

9.34 In Northern Ireland there is no limit placed on the *number* of persons who can act as executor at the same time. This is in contrast to England where, although any number of persons can be appointed, probate can only be granted to *four* executors in respect of the same property.[46] If several executors have been appointed, however, it may be prudent for some of them either to renounce probate or have it reserved.

9.35 Where there is more than one executor, any one of them may apply for a grant without the need to consult the others. Furthermore there is no requirement to notify the others of an application for a grant.[47] Probate will then be granted to the applicant, with power reserved to the others to prove subsequently. Unless and until the others do prove, the one who has probate has full authority.[48]

---

[45] See para 3.43 *supra*.

[46] Supreme Court Act 1981, s 114(1).

[47] This is in contrast to the position in England where other executors have to be formally notified about any application.

[48] Administration of Estates (NI) Order 1979, art 31(1).

9.36   There is no minimum number and probate will be granted to a sole executor. In the interests of prudence and convenience, however, it is better to avoid appointing a single executor and if a sole executor is to be appointed, it is at least sensible to include a substitute, in case the first choice predeceases the testator or refuses to act. It will be recalled that where land is settled by will but there are no trustees of the settlement, the executors are deemed to be the trustees for the purposes of the Settled Land Acts. However, a *sole* executor will not be deemed to be such until at least one other trustee has been appointed.[49]

Restrictions on executorship

9.37   A testator is free to appoint any person of his choice as executor, but certain categories of person are prohibited from acting as such.   Before examining the categories of person who cannot act as executors, it may be worth noting that a beneficiary under the will can (and very often will) be an executor.

Minors

9.38   Although a minor can be appointed as an executor, he is unable to act until he reaches his majority. In certain circumstances, however, it may be appropriate to appoint a minor nearing majority, such as a 17 year old son, as one of at least *two* executors in the reasonable expectation that he will be capable of acting by the time the need has arisen.[50]

Persons suffering from mental or physical incapacity

9.39   A person who is incapable of managing his own affairs, by reason of either mental or physical incapacity, cannot act as an executor.[51]

Former spouses

9.40   Article 13(1)(a) of the Wills and Administration Proceedings (NI) Order 1994 provides that if a testator dies following a decree dissolving or annulling his marriage or declaring that marriage void, any appointment to the former spouse as executor or trustee will take effect as if the former spouse had died on the date that the marriage was terminated. This provision, which applies to deaths on or after 1 January 1995, is subject to a contrary intention appearing from the will.[52]

---

[49]Administration of Estates Act (NI) 1955, s 40(5).

[50]For grants of administration for the use and benefit of a minor, see para 11.62 *post*.

[51]NCPR, r 29; see para 11.67 *post*.

[52]Art 13(3).

Executors other than individuals

Corporation sole

9.41 A corporation sole may be appointed as an executor and take probate in his personal name.[53]

Trust corporations

9.42 A trust corporation may be appointed as executor, either alone or jointly with another person, and probate will be granted to the corporation either solely or jointly with another person, as the case requires.[54] "Trust corporation" is defined in article 9(4) of the 1979 Order.[55]

Unincorporated bodies - the problems with firms of solicitors

9.43 An unincorporated body, that is, one which lacks any legal identity, obviously cannot be granted probate in its own right, and any attempt to appoint such a body as an executor will be construed as an appointment of the individual members.[56] In practice, the issue arises most frequently in connection with firms of solicitors, where the main problem is finding a form of wording which provides for a number of contingencies (eg changes of personnel, a change of name or an amalgamation of the firm). In *Re Horgan*[57] the following wording was approved by Latey J:[58]

> "I appoint the partners at the date of my death in the firm of
> [   ] of [   ] or the firm which at that date has succeeded to
> and carries on its practice to be executors and trustees of this my
> will (and I express the wish that two and only two of them shall
> prove my will and act initially in the trusts)."[59]

Acceptance and renunciation of office as an executor

9.44 No one can be forced to take upon himself the onerous office of executorship. A person appointed by a testator as an executor is not obliged to accept the office, even if the testator asked him to do so before his death and agreement had been forthcoming:

---

[53]*Re Haynes Goods* (1842) 3 Curt 75.

[54]Administration of Estates (NI) Order 1979, art 9(1)(a).

[55]See Appendix F.

[56]*Re Fernie* (1849) 6 NC 657.

[57][1971] P 50.

[58]*Ibid* at 61.

[59]Note that the words in brackets are precatory only.

> "No man has a right to make another an executor without his
> consent; and even if in the lifetime of the testator he has agreed
> to accept office, it is still in his power to recede."[60]

This right to renounce the executorship continues until the executor has *accepted* office or is *deemed* to have accepted office.

Citation to accept or refuse

9.45 Although an executor cannot be compelled to accept probate, he can be compelled to decide whether he will accept office, and the court has power to issue a "citation" summoning a person who has been named as executor to either prove, or renounce probate of, the will. Citations are dealt with more fully at paragraph 11.86 below.

Acceptance

9.46 The most usual way of accepting an executorship is by applying for probate; the grant of probate fixes an executor with "duties and liabilities which he cannot afterwards shake off".[61] In addition, doing acts commensurate with the office of executor which show an intention to take up the executorship can also constitute acceptance. Actions which have sufficed have included collecting assets and paying debts; inducing an insurance company to pay the policy money to the mortgagees on account of their debt[62] and inserting advertisements calling upon persons to send in their accounts.[63] Ultimately, however, whether or not acts constitute acceptance in any particular case depends on the circumstances.

9.47 Merely swearing the executor's oath without further intermeddling in the estate does not constitute acceptance.[64] The same is true of trivial acts or "works of mercy or necessity", such as arranging for the remains to be buried[65] or feeding the deceased's livestock.[66]

---

[60]*Per* Lord Redesdale in *Doyle* v *Blake* (1804) 2 Sch & Lef 231, 239; *Hargreaves* v *Wood* (1862) 2 Sw & Tr 602.

[61]*In the Goods of Veiga* (1862) 32 LJPM & A 9,10.

[62]*Re Stevens* [1897] 1 Ch 422.

[63]*Long and Feaver* v *Symes and Hannan* (1832) 3 Hag Ecc 771.

[64]*McDonnell* v *Prendergast* (1830) 3 Hag Ecc 212.

[65]*Harrison* v *Rowley* (1798) 4 Ves 212.

[66]*Long and Feaver* v *Symes and Hannan* (1832) 3 Hag Ecc 771.

Renunciation

9.48 As has been seen, an executor is free to renounce probate up until the time he has accepted the office. A renunciation must be in writing and there is English authority that it does not become effective until it is filed and recorded in the probate registry.[67]

9.49 Following the executor's renunciation his rights in respect of the executorship "wholly cease, and the representation to the testator and the administration of his estate shall devolve and be committed in like manner as if that person had not been appointed executor."[68] Where the executor has, in addition, been appointed as a trustee, his rights in this regard shall also wholly cease.[69] This is in contrast to the English position, where a renunciation of the office of executor does not affect any other appointment which he is given in the will, so that a person who is appointed both an executor and a trustee and later renounces probate is still entitled to act as a trustee.[70]

9.50 An executor must generally renounce the office as a whole. He is not free to renounce part and accept the remainder[71] and, as has been seen, where there is a chain of representation, he cannot accept one executorship and renounce the others which devolve under the chain.[72]

9.51 Renunciation of probate does not operate as a renunciation of any other right which that person may have to administration in some other capacity, unless that right is also expressly renounced.[73] Therefore it is possible for an executor who has an interest in the residuary estate to renounce probate because there is a chain of representation, yet later apply for a grant of administration with the will annexed. In contrast, a person who has renounced *administration* in one capacity may only obtain a grant to the same estate in another capacity with the leave of the Master.[74]

---

[67] *In the Goods of Robert Morant* (1874) LR 3 P & D 151.

[68] Administration of Estates (NI) Order 1979, art 29(1)(c).

[69] The trusteeship shall then devolve or be determined as if the person in question had not been appointed as trustee. This provision is without prejudice to his subsequent appointment as trustee.

[70] *Re Gordon* (1877) 6 Ch 531.

[71] *Brooke v Haymes* (1868) 6 Eq 25.

[72] See para 9.27 *supra*.

[73] NCPR, r 36(1).

[74] NCPR, r 36(3).

Why renounce?

9.52   Apart from an individual's personal circumstances there may be sound legal reasons why a renunciation would be prudent. Moreover, it is especially important that these are considered at the outset because renunciation is precluded once an executor has accepted.

(a)   Arguably the most persuasive reason for renouncing probate is to avoid becoming an executor by representation under a chain. This was considered in more detail at paragraph 9.25 above.

(b)   A second broad category of case in which renunciation may be the best course is where there is a potential conflict between interest and duty. For example, if the person entitled to the grant of probate accepts office, he may be in the position of having to deal with the estate in his personal capacity, say because he had been in contractual relations with the deceased or because there is a subsisting claim in tort.

(c)   Finally, the estate may be unduly complex (eg where the deceased was a sole trader or a sole surviving partner) , and its administration might be best relinquished to a professional trust corporation.

Retraction of a renunciation

9.53   Once a renunciation becomes effective,[75] it can only be withdrawn with the permission of the court.[76] The Non-Contentious Probate Rules allow the Master to order that a renunciation of probate be retracted at any time, although it is expressly provided that leave will be given to an executor to retract a renunciation of probate after a grant has been made to some other person entitled in a lower class only in "exceptional circumstances".[77] The question in every case is whether the retraction is in the best interests of the estate as a whole.[78]

9.54   Where permission has been granted to withdraw a renunciation and prove the will, the probate shall take effect and be deemed always to have taken

---

[75]See para 9.48 *supra*.

[76]Administration of Estates (NI) Order 1979, art 30(1).

[77]R 36(3).

[78]*In the Goods of Gill* (1873) LR 3 P & D 113.

effect without prejudice to the previous acts and dealings of and notices to any other person who had previously proved the will and to whom administration had been granted.[79] Any trusteeship which automatically ceased along with the executorship is also revived, unless the court directs otherwise.[80]

ADMINISTRATORS

9.55 It has already been noted that a personal representative who is not an executor is an administrator and that his authority to act as such is by way of a grant of letters of administration. A grant of letters of administration with the will annexed will issue in cases where there is a will to be proved, but either there are no executors appointed or the executor has renounced his rights, died or otherwise failed to prove the will. If the deceased died wholly intestate a simple grant of letters of administration will issue.

9.56 It is the Non-Contentious Probate Rules which regulate the classes of person entitled to a grant of letters of administration, either with or without the will annexed and the order of priority between them. As between themselves, all the persons within the same class have an equal right to a grant, and *all* must be 'cleared off' before a member of a lower class can take a grant, although where several persons are equally entitled, one or more can apply without notice to the others. In all cases the court has power to 'pass over' the person who would have been entitled under the normal order of priority but who is unsuitable.[81]

Persons entitled to the grants

Grant with will annexed
9.57 Entitlement to a grant of administration with the will annexed generally follows the right to property. The order of priority, set down in rule 18 of the Non-Contentious Probate Rules, which applies where the deceased died on or after 1 January 1956 domiciled in Northern Ireland, is as follows:

(a) any residuary legatee holding in trust for any other person;

(b) any residuary legatee for life;

---

[79] Administration of Estates (NI) Order 1979, art 30(2)(a). A memorandum of this subsequent probate will be endorsed on the original grant (art 30(2)(b)).

[80] *Ibid*, art 30(2)(c).

[81] See para 9.70 *post*.

(c)   the ultimate residuary legatee or, if the residue is not entirely disposed of by will, any person entitled in the event of a total intestacy, if such a person has an interest;

(d)   any specific legatee or any creditor, or the personal representative of such a person, or, if the estate has not been completely disposed of by will, any person who, notwithstanding he had no interest under the estate immediately, may be entitled in the event of an accretion thereto;

(e)   any legatee, residuary or specific, entitled on the happening of any contingency or any person, not having an interest in the will, who would have been entitled to a grant if the deceased died wholly intestate.

9.58   Where a share of residue has lapsed, for example where the residue was given to 'A, B and C in equal shares' and C has predeceased the testator, therefore effecting a partial intestacy of the share which C would have taken if still alive, the person entitled to the share on intestacy can apply in the same class as those entitled to the residue under the will.

9.59   Any person who is precluded from taking the benefit given to him under a will, because he is a witness or the spouse of a witness to the will, does not have a right to a grant as a *beneficiary*, although any right to a grant in another capacity is preserved.[82]

9.60   Where there is a dispute between persons entitled in the same degree as to whom is entitled to letters of administration, the court in its discretion will select the person(s) who will best administer the estate in the interests of the beneficiaries and creditors.[83]   In the absence of specific objections against individuals, the court is guided by the rule of thumb that the grant will be given to the applicant with the largest interest.[84]

Simple grant of administration

9.61   Rule 20 of the Non-Contentious Probate Rules stipulates the order of priority under which the persons having a *beneficial* interest in the estate of a deceased, who died wholly intestate on or after 1 January 1956 and domiciled

---

[82]NCPR, r 19.

[83]*Warwick* v *Greville (*1809) 1 Phill 123.

[84]*Dampier* v *Colson* (1812) 2 Phill 54.

in Northern Ireland, shall be entitled to a grant of administration. It is as follows:

(a)   The surviving spouse;

(b)   The children of the deceased (including any persons entitled by virtue of any enactment to be treated as if they were children of the deceased born in lawful wedlock); or the issue (taking *per stirpes*) of any child who has died during the lifetime of the deceased;

(c)   The father or mother of the deceased or, in the case of an illegitimate person who died before 1 January 1978 without having been legitimated, the mother;

(d)   Brothers and sisters of the deceased (whether of the whole or half-blood); or the issue (taking *per stirpes*) of any deceased brother or sister (whether of the whole or half-blood) who has died during the lifetime of the deceased.[85]

9.62   Where the deceased died and no person within the above classes survived him, the following persons will be entitled to the grant in the following order of priority, namely:-

(a)   Grandparents;

(b)   Uncles and aunts (whether of the whole or half-blood); or the issue (taking *per stirpes*) of any uncle or aunt (whether of the whole or half-blood) who has died during the lifetime of the deceased;

(c)   Great-grandparents;

(d)   Grand-uncles and grand-aunts (whether of the whole or half-blood);

(e)   Great-great-grandparents;

(f)   Great-grand-uncles and great-grand-aunts (whether of the whole or half-blood); or children of grand-uncles and of grand-aunts (whether of the whole or half-

---

[85]Illegitimate persons have only been entitled in this capacity for deaths on or after 1 July 1995 - see para 6.45 *supra*.

blood); or children of grand-uncles and of grand-aunts (whether of the whole or half-blood);

(g)   Great-great-great-grandparents;

(h)   Children of the children of grand-uncles and grand-aunts (whether of the whole or half-blood); or children of great-grand-uncles and of great-grand-aunts (whether of the whole or half-blood);

(i)   Other next-of-kin of nearest degree (whether of whole or half-blood).

9.63   In default of any person having a beneficial interest in the estate of the deceased, the nominee of Her Majesty shall be entitled to the grant.[86]

9.64   This order follows interest. More detailed reference on *who* is actually entitled as, for example, a spouse or child, is contained in Chapter Six, which deals with entitlement on intestacy.[87]

9.65   Personal representatives of any of the persons mentioned in the various classes are entitled to the same grants as the persons whom they represent.[88] However, administration shall be granted to a living person in preference to the personal representative of a member of such a class who has died after the deceased, unless the Master directs otherwise.[89]

9.66   Where there is a dispute between members of a class entitled to a grant, those nearer in kin to the deceased shall be preferred to the more remote, unless the Master directs otherwise. For example, if the class entitled consists of a sister of the deceased together with the children of the deceased's brother (who predeceased him) and the parties cannot reach agreement, representation would generally be granted to the sister.

9.67   Once *all* the persons entitled to a grant have been 'cleared off', a grant may be made to a creditor of the deceased, or the personal representative of a creditor.[90] A grant may also be made, on the direction of the Master, to a

---

[86]R 20(4); see art 10 of 1979 Order.

[87]See para 6.16 *supra*.

[88]R 20(3).

[89]R 22(3).

[90]R 22(6).

person who does not have an immediate beneficial interest in the estate but who may have a beneficial interest in the event of an accretion to it.[91]

Grants to assignees

9.68   Where all the persons entitled to the deceased's estate under his will or intestacy have assigned their whole interest in the estate, the assignees replace their respective assignors and have the same priority to apply for a grant as that possessed by the assignor prior to the assignment.[92]   Where there are two or more assignees, administration may be granted with the consent of the others to any one or more (not exceeding four) of them.[93]

9.69   In all cases where administration is sought by an assignee, a copy of the instrument of assignment must be lodged in the Probate Office.[94]

Passing over a person entitled to administration

9.70   The power to pass over an executor contained in article 5 of the Administration of Estates (NI) Order 1979 has already been considered.[95]   This power extends also to the passing over of the persons who would otherwise have been entitled to a grant of administration, with or without the will annexed.   For example, in *Re Ardern*[96] a husband who was entitled to the administration of his wife's estate was mismanaging a public-house which was part of the estate, and was passed over under the corresponding English provision.[97]

9.71   In addition to the statutory discretion contained in article 5, the court always has an inherent jurisdiction to make a grant to anyone it wishes.[98]   It is highly unlikely, however, that this would now be invoked, in view of the wide ambit of the statutory power.

---

[91] *Ibid.*
[92] NCPR, r 21(1).
[93] R 21(2).
[94] R 21(3).
[95] See para 9.23 *supra.*
[96] [1898] P 147.
[97] For some further illustrations of the type of situation which will lead to a passing over, see para 9.23 *supra.*
[98] *Re Schwerdtfeger's Goods* (1876) 1 PD 424.

No transmission of the office on death

9.72   There is no automatic transmission of the office on the death of the sole, or last surviving, administrator, as no equivalent exists to the chain of executorship. It is necessary in this situation to extract a new grant, a *de bonis non*, relating to any unadministered property.[99]

The nature of administrators

Number

9.73   The maximum number of administrators is generally four. Rule 34 of the Non-Contentious Probate Rules provides that administration shall not be granted to more than four persons in respect of the same part of the deceased's estate, unless the Master directs otherwise.

9.74   No minimum number is prescribed. In particular, there is no Northern Ireland equivalent to section 114(2) of the Supreme Court Act 1981. This provides that where under a will or an intestacy any beneficiary is a minor, or a life interest arises, administration must be granted either to a trust corporation or to not less than two individuals, unless it appears to the court to be expedient in all the circumstances to appoint an individual as sole administrator.

Capacity

9.75   The points already made regarding the incapacity of minors or persons suffering from disability to act as executors[100] apply also to administrators. Neither a minor nor a person who is incapable of managing his own affairs by reason of mental or physical incapacity can take a grant of administration.[101]

Acceptance and renunciation of administration

Acceptance

9.76   Any person entitled to take out administration can either accept or renounce the office - as in the case of a person who has been appointed as an executor, office cannot be forced upon him.[102] Moreover, in contrast with an

---

[99]See para 11.72 *post.*

[100]See para 9.38 *supra.*

[101]For the type of grants which will be extracted where such a person is involved, see paras 11.62 and 11.67 *post.*

[102]It should be remembered that renunciation of office as an administrator does not effect a disclaimer of interest and the person who has renounced is still entitled to benefit under the estate.

executorship, acceptance of office will not be deemed by intermeddling,[103] but must be demonstrated by the actual taking of a grant of administration.

Renunciation

9.77 The renunciation essentially takes the same form as that of a renouncing executor - in writing and filed in the probate office.[104] As has been seen, however, it is not necessary for the renunciant to declare that he has not intermeddled.[105]

Retraction

9.78 A renunciation of administration can only be retracted with the leave of the Master.[106] The same principle applies as when it is the renunciation of an executorship which is to be retracted - that is, in order to do so it must be in the best interests of the estate as a whole.[107]

---

[103] *In the Goods of David Davis* (1860) 4 Sw & Tr 213.

[104] See para 9.48 *supra*.

[105] *In the Goods of William Walker Fell* (1861) 2 Sw & Tr 126.

[106] NCPR, r 36(3).

[107] See para 9.54 *supra*. See, eg *In the Goods of Thacker* [1900] P 15.

CHAPTER TEN

ADMINISTRATION WITHOUT A GRANT

10.01 This chapter covers two very different situations where an estate is being administered yet there is no grant of representation.   First, the circumstances where no grant is required and secondly, those where although a grant will eventually be extracted, the personal representatives have started to administer the estate before this has been done.

SITUATIONS WHERE NO GRANT IS REQUIRED

10.02 Generally, it is not possible for personal representatives to administer an estate without a grant. Exceptionally, however, there has been statutory authorisation of the payment of relatively small sums to the person entitled, without the need for a grant. In addition, some property can operate effectively on death without being subject to a grant. This is because it passes on death directly to those entitled and not through the hands of the personal representatives who do not therefore need to make title to it.

Statutory power to make payment on death without proof of title

10.03 By virtue of section 1 of the Administration of Estates (Small Payments) Act (NI) 1967 (hereafter "the 1967 Act"), a number of institutions and paying authorities are *empowered* (but not obliged) to make "small payments" which are due to the deceased's estate *without* the need for a grant. Proof of death, generally by way of a death certificate, is all that is required.

10.04 The financial threshold up to which a sum constitutes a "small payment" within the terms of the 1967 Act is raised periodically. The current limit of £5,000, was set by the Administration of Estates (Small Payments) (Increase of Limits) (NI) Order 1985[1] and is effective for deaths occurring after 31 March 1985. The previous financial limits are as follows:

Deaths before 22.4.1967	£100
Deaths after 21.4.1967	£500[2]
Deaths after 1.4.76	£1,500[3]

---

[1] NI SI 1985 No 9.

[2] 1967 Act.   Ftnt [3] overleaf.

The limit applies in respect of each item and if the sum exceeds the limit, a grant is required to establish title to the entire sum and not just the excess.

10.05   Schedule 1 to the 1967 Act lists the enactments which authorise the disposal of various sums without a grant.   Monies which are covered fall into two broad categories; sums invested in various forms of saving scheme and the pay and pensions of certain public employees.   The following are included:

> Mainstream banks, for example, the Northern Bank,
> Bank of Ireland, Ulster Bank, First Trust Bank;
>
> National Savings Bank;[4]
>
> TSB;[5]
>
> Savings Certificates;[6]
>
> Premium Bonds;
>
> Building Society Accounts;[7]
>
> Judicial Pensions;
>
> Arrears/salaries to civil servants

10.06   It should be noted that the legislation is merely *permissive*, and if the institution in question refuses to exercise its discretion a grant of representation must be extracted.   Where the power has been exercised, payment can be made to either the person appearing to be entitled to a grant, or to the beneficiary entitled to the asset concerned.

10.07   The detailed rules governing each type of payment should be sought from the relevant statutory provisions.   Generally, however, protection is afforded to any payers who avail of their right to pay out without a grant but, in some cases, the next-of-kin or personal representative of the deceased is given a remedy to recover any money paid against the person who has received it.[8]

---

[3]   NI SI 1976 No 6.

[4]   National Savings Bank Act 1971, s 9.

[5]   Trustee Savings Bank Act 1981, s 27(4).

[6]   Savings Certificates Regs 1972, SI No 641.

[7]   Building Societies Act 1962, s 46.

[8]   Eg Friendly Societies Act 1974, s 68.

Statutory nominations

10.08 There are a small number of statutory provisions which enable a person to make a *nomination* of property in certain specified investments which will take effect on his death. Where such a nomination has been made correctly, in accordance with the required formalities, payment of the nominated sum must be made on the investor's death to the person nominated by him. Such property therefore effectively passes outside the will or the operation of the intestacy rules. It is still, however, part of the estate for inheritance tax purposes.

10.09 Statutory nominations are now of very limited scope. Currently, it is only possible to nominate monies deposited in Friendly Societies[9] and in Industrial and Provident Societies.[10] In both cases, it is up to a limit of £5,000. Where the nomination is above this amount, it is valid to the extent of the limit.[11]

10.10 Previously, it was also possible to nominate funds in Trustee Savings Banks (until 30 April 1979),[12] the National Savings Bank (until 30 April 1981)[13] and in respect of National Savings Certificates (until 30 April 1981).[14] Nominations made before these dates remain effective, unless they have been revoked.

10.11 A nomination can be made once a person attains the age of 16, so minors who are unable to make a will can avail of this power. To be effective, the nomination must be in the particular form prescribed by the relevant regulations; for example, in writing and delivered to the registered office of the society.[15]

10.12 Nominations are revoked by marriage, by a later nomination, or by the death of the nominee prior to the nominator,[16] but not by will.[17] The last point raises a potential danger; the relative ease and lack of formality with which a

---

[9] Friendly Societies Act 1974; ss 66 and 67.

[10] Industrial and Provident Societies Act 1965, ss 23 and 24.

[11] *Bennett* v *Slater* [1899] 1 QB 45.

[12] Trustee Savings Bank Regs 1972, SI 1972, No 583; amended by SI 1979 No 259.

[13] National Savings Bank Regs 1972, SI 1972, No 764; amended by SI 1981 No 484.

[14] Savings Certificates Regs 1972, SI 1972, No 641; amended by SI 1981 No 486.

[15] Friendly Societies Act 1974, s 66.

[16] *Re Barnes* [1940] Ch 267. The statutory exemption to lapse contained in art 22 of the Wills and Administration Proceedings (NI) Order 1994 would not apply.

[17] *Bennett* v *Slater* [1899] 1 QB 45.

nomination may be made could lead to improper pressure being exerted on investors to make one. Thereafter, its existence may be forgotten, yet any attempt to will the same property will be ineffective. It is submitted that this disadvantage far outweighs the original reason for the creation of such statutory nominations, the saving on the expense of will-making and extracting representation in small estates, and the restriction of their extent in recent times is to be welcomed.

10.13 It should be remembered that nominated property is still automatically part of the net estate for the purposes of the Inheritance (Provision for Family and Dependants) (NI) Order 1979.[18]

Trust policies and pension scheme benefits
10.14 The statutory nominations discussed above must not be confused with pension scheme benefits or insurance trust policies, many of which also refer to nominations. For example, it is common for pension schemes to confer on their members a power to 'nominate' those persons to benefit after their death. However, in such cases the nomination is theoretically *non*-binding, and the trustees retain complete discretion whether or not to make an award, and, if so, to whom. The deceased has no beneficial interest in the sum, so it therefore does not form part of his estate. Indeed because it does not even form part of his estate for inheritance tax purposes, it is a useful vehicle for the payment of such tax.

10.15 In the same way, where a policy of life assurance is written 'in trust' for a third party, the deceased has no interest in it. The policy monies are payable directly to the beneficiary, simply on production of a death certificate as proof of death. It should be remembered, however, that many life insurance policies are not 'trust' policies and will devolve on death in the usual way, to the personal representatives as part of the estate passing under the will or the intestacy rules.

Joint tenancy
10.16 Co-owned property, held by the deceased as a joint tenant, rather than as a tenant in common, passes automatically to the surviving joint tenant(s) by virtue of the right of survivorship.

10.17 Joint property is most commonly encountered in the case of the matrimonial home or bank accounts of a married couple. A death certificate is

---

[18] Art 10 of the 1979 Order.

all that is required, as proof of death, in the case of a bank account or to make good title to unregistered land. Where land is registered, however, the death certificate must be supplemented by an affidavit from the survivor or his solicitor.

10.18 The deceased's share of a joint tenancy still forms part of his estate for inheritance tax purposes. In addition, the court has discretion to include the deceased's severable share of the joint tenancy as part of the 'net estate' for the purposes of a family provision claim, if it thinks that the interests of justice require it.[19]

Donationes mortis causa
10.19 *Donationes mortis causa* were discussed in Chapter One.

ACTIONS BEFORE THE GRANT OF REPRESENTATION

10.20 The fundamental distinction between executors and administrators has already been mentioned; an executor derives his authority from the will itself,[20] while an administrator derives his from the grant of administration (whether with or without the will annexed). One consequence of this is that the deceased's property vests in an executor from the date of *death*, whereas it vests in an administrator only from the date of the *grant*. There cannot be a vacuum in ownership, however, so between death and the grant of administration the entire estate vests in the Probate Judge.[21]

Executors
10.21 Although an executor derives his authority from the will, and the grant of probate merely confirms his rights, he can prove his right only by taking out a grant of probate. An executor of full age can therefore act *before* the grant; and can do almost all the acts appertaining to his office: in short, he can do anything that does not require him to show the grant. For example, he may pay and release debts,[22] receive payments, sell chattels, pay legacies[23] and even start legal proceedings.[24] Equally, however, he may be sued by a creditor of the

---

[19]Inheritance (Provision for Family and Dependants) (NI) Order 1979, art 11.

[20]*Chetty* v *Chetty* [1916] 1 AC 603, 608.

[21]Administration of Estates Act (NI) 1955, s 3. "Probate Judge" is defined in s 42(3) of the Interpretation Act (NI) 1954.

[22]*Re Stevens* [1897] 1 Ch 422.

[23]*Woolley* v *Clark* (1822) 5 B & Ald 744.

[24]*Easton* v *Carter* (1850) 5 Exch 8, 14; *Re Crowhurst Park* [1974] 1 WLR 583.

testator,[25] provided that he has actually accepted office.[26] On the other hand, he does require a grant in order to:

(a) sue to judgment, and;

(b) make *title*, if this is necessary.

Although, therefore, proceedings may be commenced before the grant, probate must be obtained before the hearing of the action. In some cases, however, proceedings may be stayed until the plaintiff has obtained his grant.[27]

10.22 Assets of the deceased can be sold or transferred to a purchaser by the executor before he obtains the grant of probate and a conveyance of the testator's unregistered land in these circumstances will vest the legal title of the property in the purchaser. However, the purchaser can only establish the authority of the executor to sell by way of the grant of probate,[28] so in practice he will insist on the production of the grant before completion. A transfer of registered land cannot be completed before the grant is taken out.

Executor who has accepted office dies before grant
10.23 If an executor does any acts relating to his office, but then dies *before* the grant of probate has been issued (so that there can be no chain of executorship),[29] the executorship ceases on the death,[30] but the acts done remain valid.[31]

Administrators
10.24 An administrator, with or without the will annexed, has no authority before the grant is issued and therefore has no power to do anything as administrator before this time. In contrast to an executor, he cannot commence any action in his representative capacity before the grant, a point which is well illustrated by the following case. In *Ingall* v *Moran*[32] a father issued proceedings as his son's 'administrator', following the son's death in a wartime

---

[25]*Mohamidu Mohideen Hadjiar* v *Pitchey* [1894] AC 437.

[26]See para 9.47 *supra*.

[27]*Webb* v *Adkins* (1854) 14 CB 401.

[28]Or, if the executor dies before obtaining probate, by a grant of administration with the will annexed.

[29]See para 9.25 *supra*.

[30]Administration of Estates (NI) Order 1979, art 29(1)(a).

[31]*Re Stevens* (1704) 1 Salk 299.

[32][1944] KB 160.

motor accident which was caused by the defendant's negligence. At the time a limitation period of one year which ran from the date of death applied and the father duly issued the writ with just two days to spare. Unfortunately, however, he did not actually extract the grant of administration until a further two months had passed. The Court of Appeal held that the action had to fail because the father had no title to sue when he issued proceedings.[33] Moreover, it was now too late to issue new proceedings. Of course, it would have been very different if the son had happened to make a will, appointing his father as *executor*, in which case the fact that no grant of probate had yet been obtained would have been no bar to the issue of proceedings.

The doctrine of "relation back"

10.25 On occasions an administrator may feel he should take action *before* the grant, as a matter of urgency and necessity, in order to preserve the deceased's estate for those beneficially entitled. For this reason the doctrine of *relation back* was developed for the limited purpose of protecting the deceased's estate from wrongful injury in the interval between his death and the grant of administration to his estate. The effect of this fiction is to relate the subsequent grant of administration back in time to the date of death, therefore enabling an administrator to sue in respect of any wrongdoing to an asset of the deceased's estate during the time between death and the grant.

10.26 However, the doctrine is limited by the parameters for which it was created, that is, the protection of the deceased's estate from wrongdoing. It cannot, as one judge has put it: "breathe new life into a corpse".[34] For instance, relation back cannot give reality to a statement of claim which was not preceded by a duly issued writ and so cannot rectify the *Ingall* v *Moran* scenario discussed earlier. Similarly, where the asset the title to which it is sought to relate back has been extinguished or destroyed in the interval between death and the grant, relation back cannot apply. It cannot resurrect a tenancy which has been lawfully determined by a notice to quit served on the landlord before the grant was issued; the title must exist at the date of the grant of administration.[35]

---

[33] See also *Finnegan* v *Cremation Co Ltd* [1953] 1 QB 688 and *Burns* v *Campbell* [1952] 1 KB 15, a case arising when Northern Ireland grants had to be resealed in England.

[34] *Per* Asquith LJ in *Fred Long & Sons Ltd* v *Burgess* [1950] 1 KB 115, at p 121.

[35] *Ibid*, where a lease had been extinguished in the interval. The proper application of the doctrine to leasehold property in an estate would be where such property had been reduced in value in the interval through breaches of covenant.

10.27   Relation back only applies to validate acts before grant done for the benefit of the estate. It does not validate acts which prejudice the estate. This was confirmed relatively recently in *Mills* v *Anderson*.[36] Mr B A Hytner QC, sitting as a deputy High Court judge, refused to apply the doctrine in order to bind an administrator who, before he had taken out a grant, had settled the fatal accident claim which he was pursuing on behalf of his son.   After this settlement had been negotiated, the judgment in *Gammell* v *Wilson*[37] was published, indicating that a much higher level of damages was appropriate, so that the administrator, having now obtained the grant, was free to renegotiate the settlement. The rather unfair consequence is that an executor who makes an unwise settlement on behalf of the estate before the grant of probate is bound by it, but an administrator in the same circumstances is not.

---

[36][1984] QB 704.
[37][1982] AC 27.

CHAPTER ELEVEN

THE GRANT OF REPRESENTATION

JURISDICTION TO MAKE GRANTS

11.01 The three basic grants of representation, together with the circumstances appropriate for each, were discussed in Chapter Nine. In this chapter the procedures for obtaining and revoking such grants are examined. In addition, the situations in which the more unusual grants will issue are discussed.[1]

11.02 A grant of representation is an order under seal of the Family Division of the High Court of Justice, which has exclusive jurisdiction to issue grants in Northern Ireland. The overwhelming majority of probate[2] business is "non-contentious"[3] (sometimes called "common form"). Contentious (or "solemn form") business is also conducted in the Family Division, although the County Court has a concurrent jurisdiction in cases where the net estate does not exceed £15,000.[4]

Probate Office and branch office

11.03 An application for a grant of representation to the estate of a deceased who resided anywhere in Northern Ireland may be made through a solicitor or in person at the Probate and Matrimonial Office of the Family Division ("the Probate Office").[5] In addition, where the deceased resided in Counties Londonderry, Fermanagh or Tyrone, the application can be made via the "branch office" in Londonderry.[6]

---

[1] See para 11.52 *post*.

[2] In this sense used to refer to both grants of probate and grants of administration with or without the will annexed.

[3] Defined in art 2(2) of the Administration of Estates (NI) Order 1979 as "the business of obtaining grants where there is no contention as to the right thereto, the obtaining of grants in contested cases where the contest has been terminated, the entry of caveats under article 14 and all business of a non-contentious nature in matters of testacy or intestacy not being proceedings in an action."

[4] Administration of Estates (NI) Order 1979, art 12.

[5] Situated at the Royal Courts of Justice, Chichester Street, Belfast.

[6] Situated at 13 Bishop Street, Londonderry.

Nil estate grants

11.04 The High Court is empowered by virtue of article 4(4) of the Administration of Estates (NI) Order 1979 to make a grant in respect of a deceased notwithstanding that he left no estate in Northern Ireland.[7] However, there must be a reason before this discretion can be exercised;[8] for example, a parent may wish to obtain a grant to sue in respect of the death of his minor child who had no assets.[9] If the discretion is exercised the grant is made to the person who would have been entitled had the deceased left nominal assets in Northern Ireland.[10]

11.05 In addition, the High Court has power to make a *de bonis non* grant in respect of unadministered estate, notwithstanding that there is no unadministered estate in Northern Ireland.[11]

OBTAINING THE GRANT OF REPRESENTATION

11.06 Every application for a grant of representation must be supported by an oath and such other papers as the Master may require.[12] These documents are lodged, personally or through a solicitor[13] at the Probate Office, where they will be scrutinised by the staff. A grant of representation will issue if everything is in order.

11.07 There follows a brief checklist of the papers which are required to be lodged before any of the three basic types of grant can be issued. The more important of these documents are then considered in some detail. It is imperative that the greatest care is taken when preparing these papers; the

---

[7] Prior to the enactment of s 2(2) of the Probates and Letters of Administration Act (NI) 1933 the High Court was unable to make a grant where there was no property in the jurisdiction.

[8] *Aldrich* v *Att-Gen* [1968] P 281, 295.

[9] Some foreign jurisdictions require a grant from the country of domicile before they will issue a grant. This therefore aids persons dying with Northern Ireland domicile but with all their property in a foreign jurisdiction.

[10] R 33(b).

[11] 1979 Order, art 4(3)(b). This provision, which was absent from the Probates and Letters of Administration Act (NI) 1933, was first introduced by s 28(1) of the Administration of Estates (NI) 1955 Act, primarily to cover the situation where the deceased left estate in Northern Ireland which has been completely administered, but other property in a foreign jurisdiction, which has not. The 1933 Act only applied where the deceased "*left* no estate or effects", and the Court did not have jurisdiction to make a *de bonis non* grant as there were no unadministered assets in the jurisdiction.

[12] NCPR, r 5(1).

[13] 1979 Order, art 18(2).

issuing of a grant is frequently delayed as a consequence of needless mistakes and oversights which could easily have been avoided.

11.08 In order to obtain a grant of probate, the following documents are required:

(a)   Notice of Application (see Appendix E);

(b)   The original will[14] and any codicils;

(c)   Oath for Executor;[15]

(d)   Any necessary affidavits of due execution;[16]

(e)   Probate Engrossment[17] if necessary;

(f)   Renunciation, if appropriate;

(g)   Inland Revenue account, if necessary.[18]

11.09 To obtain a grant of letters of administration with the will annexed the following should be lodged:

(a)   Notice of Application;

(b)   Original will and any codicils;

(c)   Oath for Administrator with will annexed;[19]

(d)   Any necessary affidavits of due execution;[20]

---

[14] If for whatever reason it is not possible to lodge the original will, see para 11.12 *post*.

[15] See para 11.16 *post*.

[16] See para 11.41 *post*.

[17] Ie, the will in typed form suitable for photocopying. R 8 of the NCPR empowers the Master to ask for such if the will in its original form is not suitable for photographic reproduction. In practice, an engrossment will be required where the will is handwritten, or of an unusual size. In addition, where alterations have been made on the will but they are inadmissible, an engrossment of the will without the alterations must be lodged - r 8(2). Engrossments must follow the punctuation, spacing and paragraphing of the will -r 8(3).

[18] See para 11.47 *post*.

[19] See para 11.16 *post*.

[20] See para 11.41 *post*.

(e)   Guarantee in certain cases;[21]

(f)   Engrossment of will, if necessary;

(g)   Renunciation, if appropriate;

(h)   Inland Revenue account, if necessary;

(i)   Consents of   any persons entitled in priority, if
        appropriate.

11.10   To obtain a simple grant of letters of administration the following
should be lodged:

(a)   Notice of Application;

(b)   Oath for Administrator;

(c)   Guarantee, if required;

(d)   Renunciation, where appropriate;

(e)   Inland Revenue account, if necessary;

(f)   Consents of any person entitled in priority.

The original will and other testamentary documents
11.11   The will and any other testamentary documents must be 'marked', that
is, signed or initialled, both by the applicants for the grant and the
commissioner before whom the oath is taken.[22]   If any part of the will has been
written in *pencil* a copy of that part must also be lodged with the portion which
was written in pencil underlined in red ink.[23]

Original will not available
11.12   Where an original will or codicil is not available, say because it has
been lost or accidentally destroyed without the intention of revoking it, an
application can be made to the Master for an order admitting the will to probate
as contained in a copy or a draft or a reconstructed copy. In such a case the
applicant needs to prove:

---

[21] See para 11.42 *post*.
[22] NCPR, r 7.
[23] R 8 (4).

(a)   That the original will was duly executed. Most typically this will be through affidavit evidence from one or more attesting witnesses.[24]   A satisfactory explanation (by affidavit) of the disappearance of the will must also be provided.

(b)   The contents of the will. This may be done orally,[25] or by comparing a copy[26] and adducing evidence of its accuracy.

In addition, if the will can be traced into the testator's possession and it was not found at death, its absence raises the presumption that the testator duly revoked it by destruction[27] and this presumption has to be rebutted.

11.13   The burden of proof required to obtain probate of a lost will is the usual civil standard, the balance of probabilities. This was confirmed by Oliver J in *Re Yelland*[28] who rejected the earlier view expressed by Lord Herschell[29] that it should be equated to that resting on the prosecution in a criminal trial. If the only evidence is that of a beneficiary, the court must be sure that there were no suspicious circumstances,[30] but it is not precluded from proving the will; in both *Sugden*[31] and *Yelland*[32] the only evidence came from a beneficiary.

11.14   When a grant is made in respect of a 'missing' will it will generally be limited until the original is found.[33] If the lost will does subsequently appear, it should be lodged with the grant in the Probate Office and a *de bonis non* grant applied for.

11.15   It should be remembered that the above powers only extend to circumstances where there is satisfactory evidence of the will's non-existence. If the will is not available for lodging because it is in the possession of someone

---

[24]Although this is not always necessary if there is evidence of an effective attestation clause - *In the Estate of Phibbs* [1917] P 93. Also *Harris* v *Knight* (1890) 15 PD 170.

[25]*Sugden* v *Lord St Leonards* (1876) 1 PD 154; *Re Yelland* (1975) 119 Sol Jo 562. See also *Re Gilliland* [1940] NI 125 - contents proved by letter written by testatrix.

[26]Eg *Sterling* v *Bruce* [1973] NI 255.

[27]*Allan* v *Morrison* [1900] AC 604; *Re Webb* [1964] 1 WLR 509.

[28](1975) 119 Sol Jo 562.

[29]In *Woodward* v *Goulstone* (1886) 11 App Cas 469.

[30]See generally para 2.33 *supra*.

[31](1876) 1 PD 154.

[32](1975) 119 SJ 562.

[33]*In the Goods of Lemme* [1892] P 89; *In the Goods of Von Linden* [1896] P 148.

who refuses to lodge it, the High Court has power by virtue of article 15 of the Administration of Estates (NI) Order 1979 (exercisable whether or not legal proceedings are pending) to require him to do so.[34]

The executor's or administrator's oath

11.16   The grant of representation is based on the oath which all applicants must swear.[35]   This essentially sets out the relevant facts and contains an undertaking by the personal representative(s) that the estate will be duly and faithfully administered. In non-contentious business the oath is taken as proof of the facts deposed therein, although the Master does have a discretion to require proof of identity beyond that contained in the oath of either the deceased or the applicant for the grant.[36]

11.17   The oath must be in an affidavit sworn by the applicant[37] before a commissioner of oaths or an independent solicitor authorised to take oaths. Law Stationers produce pre-printed forms which will generally form their foundation and thereafter the actual format will depend upon the circumstances of the case; the facts required to be deposed to when a grant of probate is sought will obviously differ from those where an administrator is seeking a simple grant of administration. The following paragraphs are designed to provide some guidance on the content of an oath - both matters which are common to all oaths and those which relate specifically to oaths for a particular type of grant.

Matters common to an executor's and an administrator's oath

The full name and last address of the deceased
11.18   The true full name[38] of the deceased should be inserted after the pre-printed words "In the Estate of ...." which appear at the top of the oath form.

---

[34]This power extends to "any paper or writing, being or purported to be testamentary" which has been shown to be in his possession or under his control. The Master may make a subpoena on application supported by an affidavit which sets out the grounds of the application (NCPR,r 49(1)(a)). If the person then denies that the will is in his possession he may file an affidavit to that effect (r 49(3)).

[35]Note that it is not actually necessary to *swear* the oath and the option exists to *affirm*. Where the applicant prefers to affirm the words "make oath and say" are replaced by "do solemnly and sincerely affirm" and in the jurist the word "sworn" is substituted with "affirmed".

[36]R 4(2).

[37]R 5(1).

[38]Ie, the one on the birth certificate, or if a married woman who was known by her husband's name, her husband's surname.

Usually this will not present many difficulties, although sometimes an 'alias' name will have to be included in an executor's oath, as any discrepancies with the will must be accounted for. This arises most commonly where a testator did not make his will in his full name: for example, if a testatrix whose full name is Charlotte Suzanne Dougal signed her will "Suzy Dougal" she should be described in the oath as "Charlotte Suzanne Dougal otherwise known as Suzy Dougal".

11.19 The deceased's last residential address must be recited. Where the address given in the will is different, the most recent address is recited, followed by the words "formerly of ... [the address in the will]". Intervening changes of address can be ignored.

The personal details of the applicants

11.20 The first paragraph of the oath identifies those who are applying for the grant. The true full names of each applicant should be given and, as with the deceased, any discrepancy must be accounted for; for example, "Bernadette Kelly (in the will called Binny Kelly)"; "Alastair Jones (in the will called Alistair Jones)" or "Charlotte Dougal married woman (formerly and in the will called Charlotte Smith spinster)".[39] Where a testator has merely used a form of description without actually naming executors, for example, "my husband", further proof of the applicant's identity will be required. It is usually sufficient to swear in the oath that the applicant was the lawful husband of the deceased at the date of the will and that the marriage was not dissolved or annulled before her death.

11.21 In an oath for executor the order in which the applicants are listed must be the same as in the will. If it is desired to amend this order, all the executors must consent to the change and this consent must be lodged with the papers.

11.22 The full postal address should be given for each applicant. Former addresses need only be given if they are relevant in establishing an executor's identity or if the address in the will appears to be an error (eg if the will states '16 Allen *Drive*' when the oath states '16 Allen *Park*'). Solicitors and others acting in a professional capacity may give their business addresses but other applicants must give the address where they reside and not, for example, an address care of a bank.

---

[39] In this case details of the marriage must be recited.

11.23 The occupation or status of each applicant whether male or female should also be given. It should be noted that *unemployed* person or *retired* person is not acceptable. The words unemployed or retired should be followed by a former occupation. In addition, any relationship of an executor to the testator (eg nephew) should be recited.

Making out the applicant's title for the grant

11.24 The essence of the oath is to establish the "capacity" in which the proving personal representatives claim to be entitled to the grant. The requirements for the different types of grant are considered below.

Undertaking to carry out the duties of a personal representative

11.25 The duties of a personal representative are described as follows in article 35(1) of the Administration of Estates (NI) Order 1979:

> "(a) to collect and get in the estate of the deceased and administer it according to law;
>
> (b) when required to do so by the High Court, to exhibit on oath in that court a full inventory of the estate and when so required render an account of the administration of the estate to that court;
>
> (c) when required to do so by the High Court, to deliver up the grant of representation to that court."

In the oath the applicant undertakes that he will faithfully administer the estate. In practice, this part of the oath is pre-printed and needs no alteration.

The death of the deceased

11.26 The applicant is expected to swear to the death of the deceased, stating the place and the date of death, if this is known. A death certificate does not have to be produced. The exact date need not be ascertained when the fact of death is certain[40] and the oath should simply state that the deceased "was last known to be alive on ... and whose dead body was found on ... at ... "

11.27 In circumstances where it is not possible for the applicant to swear to the death of the deceased, but there is evidence from which his death may be presumed (eg he was on board a ship involved in a maritime collision) an application may be made to the Master for leave to swear to the death.[41] This,

---

[40]*Re Long-Sutton* [1912] P 97; body found in river - exact date of death uncertain.

[41]R 52. The application is by way of affidavit setting out the grounds and shall contain particulars of any policies of insurance effected on the life of the presumed deceased. The

however, is simply *permission to depose to* the death and does not, in itself, prove anything. It should not be confused with a declaration presuming someone's death.

The domicile of the deceased

11.28 The oath shall state the place of the deceased's domicile, unless the Master directs otherwise.[42]

Value of the estate

11.29 The oath recites both the gross value[43] *and* the net value of the deceased's estate in the United Kingdom. Property which does not pass to the personal representatives (eg the share in a joint tenancy; nominated property; *donationes mortis causa*) is not relevant for these purposes and is not included.

11.30 Where the deceased died domiciled outside Northern Ireland, the value of the estate *in Northern Ireland* only is included.

Matters relevant to an oath for an executor only

Establishing title

11.31 It has already been noted that an executor derives his title from the will itself and the grant of probate is merely evidence of that title.[44] He must therefore swear in the oath as to the identity of the documents which are being put forward as admissible to probate. This is done by the applicants and the person before whom the oath is sworn marking the will and any other testamentary documents by signing their names or initials on each document. The oath then recites the executor's relationship to the deceased and that he is the executor of the will. The wording will obviously depend upon the circumstances. For example, where the will only appointed one person, "the sole executor/executrix" is used. Where there is more than one, and they are either all male or of mixed gender, it is "the executors", while if they are all female "the executrices". In the event of an implied appointment the description "the executor according to the tenor" is used.

11.32 When not all the executors are able or willing to accept probate, the others must be accounted for. Therefore the fact that one or more of the

---

oath should recite that the deceased died "on or since" the date of the order and details of the order should be given.

[42] R 5(3).

[43] Ie, before deduction of debts and liabilities.

[44] See para 10.21 *supra*.

executors have died, or have renounced probate, or have reserved their right to act, must be recited in the oath. For example, where one or more of the appointed executors have died, the applicant(s) should be described as "the surviving executor(s), [   ] having died in the lifetime of the testator/having survived the testator but since died." Similarly, where some have renounced probate the executor(s) accepting should be described as "one [or two] of the executors". In this latter case the renunciation must be referred to, marked as an exhibit by both the applicants and the commissioner, and be filed with the papers which lead to the grant. Renouncing executors should not mark the will as an exhibit.

Solicitors and trust corporations appointed as executors

11.33 Where a firm of solicitors has been appointed as an executor[45] the oath must state that the applicants were partners in the firm at the date of the death. The other partners must be accounted for by death, renunciation or by reserving their rights.

11.34 Where a trust corporation has been appointed as an executor, the grant will issue to the corporation in its corporate name. However, an officer of the corporation is appointed by special resolution to swear the oath on behalf of the corporation. It is necessary to state that it is a trust corporation within article 9 of the Administration of Estates (NI) Order 1979 and has power to accept grants.

Matters relevant to an oath for administration with the will annexed only

Establishing title

11.35 The oath must state the precise capacity in which the applicant claims to be entitled to a grant. Before this, however, the oath must always 'clear off' (in effect, 'account for') all those who have a 'better' title to a grant under rule 18 of the Non-Contentious Probate Rules. All oaths for administrators with the will annexed must therefore account for the fact that there is no *executor* applying for probate; for example, by reciting that no executors were appointed, or that they are all dead, or have renounced.[46] The extent of additional clearing beyond this will obviously depend upon the capacity in which the applicant seeks a grant and how far down the 'list' he comes.[47] It

---

[45] See para 9.43 *supra*.

[46] The renunciation must be referred to, marked as an exhibit by the applicant and the commissioner, and filed with the papers.

[47] For order of priority, see para 9.57 *supra*.

should be remembered that all persons in each class have an equal right to a grant and *all* must be cleared off before any member of a lower class can take a grant.[48] If there is no person in a particular class (eg no residuary legatee was appointed) he does not have to be cleared off.

11.36 The capacity in which the applicant is applying must be stated clearly. For example:

> "the residuary legatee and devisee under the said will";

> "the lawful sons and next-of-kin of the deceased";

> "one of the specific legatees and devisees named in the said will".

Matters relevant to an oath for simple administration only

Establishing title

11.37 As has been seen, title follows interest[49] and the entitlement to a grant essentially depends upon the applicant's relationship to the deceased. Again it is necessary to account for those with a better right to the grant under rule 20 of Non-Contentious Probate Rules than the applicant. The statement in the oath that the deceased died intestate should be followed by:

(a) A description of the deceased's marital status:

> - "a bachelor/spinster"

> - "a married man/woman"

> - "a widow/widower"

> - "a single man/woman" (if divorced).[50]

> If the deceased was judicially separated at the date of death, the appropriate description is 'married man/woman' but the details of the decree and a statement that the separation was continuing until the date

---

[48] Although a grant may be made to one or more members of a class without notice being given to other members of that class. See para 9.56 *supra*.

[49] Note that where, eg an intestate's brother or sister survives the intestate but dies thereafter, his or her issue are not entitled to the grant as they have no beneficial entitlement.

[50] Where the deceased was divorced the details of the divorce (date of decree etc) must be recited and it must be sworn that he or she had not remarried.

of death should be included. Where the deceased's marriage had been annulled, the deceased should be described as having the status which he had immediately before that 'marriage'.

(b) Any of those with a prior entitlement under rule 20, although it is not necessary to clear off those entitled in the *same* category as the applicant(s). This is essentially a matter of showing that the deceased was not survived by any relative(s) in the classes above the applicant(s), or that any such surviving relatives have since died or renounced, or have failed to appear to a citation.

The following table is useful for the relatively straightforward case where there are no *surviving* relatives with a better right to the grant:

Person who must be cleared	Swear that the deceased
Spouse	a bachelor, spinster, single man/woman, widow/widower
Issue	without issue
Parents	(or) parent
Siblings or their issue	(or) brother or sister or issue thereof
Grandparents	(or) grandparent
Uncles/aunts or their issue	(or) uncle or aunt or issue thereof

So, for example, if the intestate's sister is the nearest surviving relative and is seeking a grant the oath would take the following form: "that the deceased died intestate *a bachelor without issue or parent* him surviving..."

11.38   The oath must then recite the capacity in which the applicant(s) seeks the grant; for example, the lawful husband; the lawful son/daughter; the lawfully adopted son/daughter;[51] the brother/sister.

---

[51]The oath should also contain details of the adoption order and that it is still subsisting.

11.39 Any renunciations must be lodged with the papers and referred to in the oath and marked by the deponent and the commissioner.

Oath for Administrators de bonis non
11.40 The oath leading to a *de bonis non* grant must give details of the issue of the original grant. In addition, the reason for the need for the *de bonis grant* must be recited (eg, the death of the original grantee). If the original grant was a grant of *probate*, the oath must recite the fact that the chain of representation has been broken.

Affidavits of due execution of the will
11.41 There are occasions when the Probate Office will require affidavits of due execution of the will to be lodged with the application for the grant of probate. The exact circumstances when these will be required have already been dealt with in the chapters dealing with the formal validity of wills,[52] and the alteration[53] of wills.

Guarantees
11.42 The old requirement that an administrator enter into a bond[54] was abolished by the Administration of Estates Act (NI) 1971, which merely required that *guarantees* be given in limited cases only. The current position is governed by the Administration of Estates (NI) Order 1979, article 17 of which empowers the High Court to make the granting of letters of administration conditional upon one or more persons acting as sureties to a guarantee. The sureties guarantee that they will make good any loss[55] which a person interested in the administration of the estate may suffer in consequence of a breach of duty by the personal representative.

11.43 The situations in which a guarantee will be required are listed in rule 38(1) of the Non-Contentious Probate Rules. They are, where it is proposed to grant administration:

    (a)   to a creditor of the deceased, or to a personal representative of a creditor, or to a person who has no immediate beneficial interest in the estate but who may

---

[52]See para 3.59 *supra*.

[53]See para 4.55 *supra*.

[54] Governed by the Probates and Letters of Administration (Ir) Act 1857.

[55]The limit of their liability is the gross amount of the estate sworn on the application for the grant - r 38 (6)(d).

have such an interest because there has been an
accretion to the estate;

(b)   to a person having a *spes successionis*;

(c)   to the attorney of a person entitled to a grant;

(d)   for the use and benefit of a minor;

(e)   for the use and benefit of a person who is incapable of
managing his own affairs;

(f)   to a person who appears to the Master to be resident
outside the United Kingdom.

In addition, the Master has a discretion to require a guarantee in any other case
where he considers that there are "special circumstances" making it desirable to
do so.[56]   However, a guarantee cannot be required where the administrator
entitled to the grant is the Treasury Solicitor, or the Crown Solicitor for
Northern Ireland or a consular officer of a foreign state.[57]   Furthermore, a
guarantee will not be required if the applicant is a trust corporation,[58] or a
solicitor holding a current practising certificate,[59] or a servant of the Crown
acting in his official capacity,[60] unless there are "special circumstances".[61] This
is the position even if the case falls within one of the above headings.

11.44   If a guarantee is required two sureties are needed unless the gross value
of the estate does not exceed £500, when one will suffice.[62]   Sureties should be
resident in the United Kingdom[63] and the solicitor representing the applicant for

---

[56]Although in such a case where the Master considers there to be "special circumstances" he
must give the applicant or his solicitor the opportunity of being heard (r 38(3)).

[57]Art 17(5)(a).

[58]R 38(2)(a).

[59]R 38(2)(b).

[60]R 38(2)(c).

[61]R 38(2). In addition, the applicant must be given the opportunity to be heard before he does
so - r 38(3).

[62]R 38(6)(a).

[63]Unless the Master directs otherwise.

the grant may not act as surety.[64] A corporation shall only be accepted as a surety with the approval of the Court.[65]

11.45 A guarantee must be in Form 1 in Appendix C of the NCPR[66] and unless the surety is a corporation, the signatures of the sureties must be attested by an authorised officer, a commissioner for oaths or other person authorised to do so.[67]

11.46 No action shall be brought on a guarantee without the leave of the High Court.[68]

Inland Revenue accounts

11.47 No grant of representation will be issued until any inheritance tax due on the estate has been paid. Inheritance Tax is due six months after the end of the month in which death occurred,[69] and thereafter interest accrues.

11.48 Unless the estate is an "excepted estate" it will not normally be possible for the personal representatives to obtain the grant until they have submitted the relevant Inland Revenue account.

Excepted estates

11.49 Where the estate is an "excepted estate" no account need be presented. An "excepted estate" is one where *all* of the following conditions are met:[70]

> (a) the total gross value of the estate before any debts are deducted for tax purposes does not exceed £145,000;

> (b) the estate consists only of property which has passed under the deceased's will or intestacy, or by nomination or beneficially by survivorship;[71]

---

[64]Nor his clerk, nor his apprentice. However, this rule can be departed from with the leave of the Master - r 38(6).

[65]R 38(6)(f).

[66]R 38(4).

[67]R 38(5).

[68]Art 17(3) of the 1979 Order.

[69]Although personal representatives are under a duty to deliver an account within 12 months from the end of the month of death.

[70]These conditions apply from 1 July 1995 to the estate of any person who died on or after 6 April 1995. The previous limit (which applied to someone dying on or after 1 April 1991) was £125,000.

[71] See overleaf.

(c)   not more than £15,000 is property situated outside the United Kingdom;

(d)   the deceased died domiciled in the United Kingdom and had not made lifetime gifts chargeable to inheritance tax.

Thus an estate is not an "excepted estate" if it includes trust property, or if there is property passing under a *donatio mortis causa*.

11.50   There is a random audit of estates which are claimed to be "excepted", whereby the Capital Taxes Office will give notice in writing within 35 days of the issue of the grant that a form is to be completed. If it is subsequently discovered that the estate is not an excepted estate an account must be filed within six months of the discovery.

TIME LIMITS

11.51   The general rule is that neither a grant of probate nor a grant of letters of administration with the will annexed can be issued until seven days from the date of death. A grant of simple administration cannot be issued until 14 days from the date of the death.[72] The leave of the Master must be obtained if these time limits are to be waived.[73] This will only be granted in exceptional circumstances. At the other end of the spectrum, there is no limit on the time after death when a grant may be obtained. In addition, the draft Succession (NI) Order 1996, which is passing through Parliament at the time of writing, proposes that a surviving spouse should only inherit if he or she survived the deceased by a period of 28 days. Since administration can generally only be granted to a person who has a beneficial interest in the estate, once this provision becomes effective a grant of administration will only be granted to a surviving spouse when 28 days have passed from the date of death.

At the other end of the spectrum, there is no limit on the time after death when a grant may be obtained.

---

[71]Where any of the value of an estate relates to joint property passing by survivorship, it is the value of the deceased's beneficial interest in that property which counts for the purposes of the £145,000 limit.

[72]In England the practice is to construe the word "issue" as meaning that the papers can be lodged before the expiry of the time limit. It seems that the Northern Ireland Probate Office give it a different interpretation and may not accept papers before expiry of the time limits.

[73]R 4(3).

SPECIAL GRANTS

11.52 So far we have concentrated on the procedure for obtaining straightforward grants of probate or administration which are unlimited in relation to both property and time. In addition, 'special' types of grant which are limited in a particular way will be issued in appropriate circumstances.

Grants for a particular purpose

Grant of representation ad colligenda bona defuncti

11.53 The *ad colligenda* grant, as it is more commonly termed, is essentially a preservation grant - an emergency measure issued in cases where estates are in need of immediate protection and it is not possible to wait until the person entitled applies for the grant of representation in the usual manner.[74] For example, it might be prudent to obtain such a grant if an estate includes a house which is liable to trespass and the removal of valuable goods.

11.54 An application for an *ad colligenda* grant must be made to the Master supported by an affidavit which sets out the grounds for the application.[75] The grant, which is a grant of administration, is usually limited for the purposes of collecting, getting in and receiving the estate. When this has been done it ceases and an ordinary grant of representation can be obtained. Where there is a will it is not proved until the application for this further grant has been made.

Grant pendente lite

11.55 A grant *pendente lite* means a grant of administration pending suit. In short, it is a grant limited to the continuance of a probate action in order that the estate is properly managed and preserved for the benefit of those who are found to be entitled.

11.56 Article 6(1) of the Administration of Estates (NI) Order 1979 empowers the High Court to make a grant *pendente lite* where there are any legal proceedings pending "touching the validity of the will of a deceased person, or for obtaining or revoking any grant". Legal proceedings must actually have been commenced; for instance, it is not enough that a caveat or a citation has been issued.

---

[74] Eg *IRC* v *Stype Investments (Jersey) Ltd* [1982] 3 All ER 419.
[75] NCPR, r 51(b).

11.57   An application for administration *pendente lite* is made by summons to the Master, supported by an affidavit setting out the grounds for the application.   An appointment will only be made if it is necessary for the preservation of the estate[76] and is generally only made in favour of an independent person such as a solicitor who has no interest in the estate.   Once appointed the administrator *pendente lite* is subject to the immediate control of the High Court and acts under its direction.[77]

11.58   An administrator *pendente lite* has the same rights and powers as a general administrator except that he cannot distribute the estate.[78]   In contrast to the general position,[79] the court may grant him reasonable remuneration.[80]

11.59 When the legal proceedings have been determined the grant ceases and the person then entitled can apply for a full grant of representation.

Grants limited in time

Grant of administration durante absentia
11.60   Where the personal representative to whom a grant has been made is residing outside Northern Ireland after 12 months have elapsed from the date of the deceased's death, the High Court may grant administration *durante absentia* to either a creditor or a person interested in the estate.[81]   The application for an order for such a grant must be made to the court on motion.[82]   After the order has been obtained the application for the grant is made in the usual manner, save that the official copy of the order for the grant must be exhibited, together with a copy of the original grant.

11.61   A grant *durante absentia* may be in such form as the court thinks fit[83] but is usually limited until the original representative returns to the jurisdiction.

Administration during a minority
11.62   It will be recalled that a minor cannot take out a grant of representation.[84]   Where at least one of several executors appointed in a will is

---

[76]*Horrell* v *Witts and Plumley* (1866) LR 1 P & D 103.
[77]Art 6(2).
[78]Administration of Estates (NI) Order 1979, art 6(1).
[79]See para 12.135 post.
[80]Art 6(3).
[81]Administration of Estates (NI) Order 1979, art 8(1).
[82]NCPR, r 54.
[83]1979 Order, art 8(1).   Ftnt [84] see overleaf.

of full age, probate will be granted to those of full age, with the rights of those who are minors reserved until they attain the age of 18 and apply for a grant of probate (ie a "double" grant).[85]

11.63 Where a minor is appointed as the sole executor of a will,[86] administration with the will annexed is granted for his use and benefit until he reaches his majority and obtains a grant of probate.[87]

11.64 Grants of administration for the use and benefit of a minor will be granted to the following persons in this order of priority:

(a) Where the minor has been appointed as an executor but has no interest in the residuary estate, it will be granted to the residuary legatee.[88]

(b) If the minor is an executor but has an interest in the residuary estate or if he is entitled to a grant of administration, then his guardian is entitled. In the first instance this is his testamentary guardian or any guardian appointed by a court of competent jurisdiction under the provisions of the Guardianship of Infants Act 1886.[89] If there is no such guardian and the minor is at least 16 years of age he can nominate his next-of-kin (or if a married woman she can nominate her husband provided that he is at least 18 years of age).[90]

(c) In addition the Master has an overriding discretion to assign a guardian. An application for such is made by filing an affidavit sworn by the applicant which sets out the grounds of the application, the ages of the minors and the size of the estate.[91] Usually an affidavit of fitness sworn by a responsible person is also required.[92]

---

[84]See paras 9.38 and 9.75 *supra*.

[85]See para 11.76 *post*.

[86]Or if there is more than one minor, administration is granted for their use and benefit until one of them attains 18 years of age and applies for and obtains a grant - NCPR, r 27(6).

[87]Administration of Estates (NI) Order 1979, art 7(1).

[88]R 27(4).

[89]R 27(1)(a), or when the Children (NI) Order 1995 becomes effective, a guardian appointed under PT XV of that legislation.

[90]R 27(1)(b). Moreover, such a person can represent any other minors within the class who are under 16 years of age (r 27(2)).

[91]R 27(3).

[92]*Ibid*.

11.65 It should be remembered that only a person assigned as a guardian by the Master under the procedure in (c) above can actually renounce administration on a minor's behalf.[93]

11.66 An administrator for the use and benefit of a minor has all the powers of an ordinary administrator[94] although obviously these powers are to be exercised on behalf of the minor. A chain of representation is not broken by a grant of administration for the use and benefit of a minor, provided that probate is subsequently granted.[95]

Administration during mental or physical incapacity

11.67 A distinction must be made between the case where the person entitled to extract the grant is suffering from a mental or physical incapacity and that in which a grant is already in existence and a grantee becomes incapable. Incapacity *after* the grant has been made is considered below in the context of the revocation of grants.[96] At this juncture we are concerned solely with incapacity before the grant is extracted.

11.68 Where the person entitled to take out a grant is incapable of managing his affairs by reason of either mental or physical incapacity, a grant of administration (either simple or with the will annexed as appropriate) will be issued for his use and benefit.[97] This will normally be limited to the duration of his incapacity, but may be limited in such other manner as the Master directs.[98] However, a grant of administration for the use and benefit of an incapable person will not generally[99] be made unless all of the persons who are entitled in the same class have been cleared off.[100]

11.69 The persons entitled to a grant of administration for the use and benefit of a person who is incapable of managing his affairs are, in order of priority:[101]

In the case of mental incapacity:

---

[93] R 27(5).
[94] *Re Cope* (1880) 16 Ch D 49.
[95] Administration of Estates (NI) Order 1979, art 32(2).
[96] See para 11.105 *post*.
[97] See generally, r 29 of the NCPR.
[98] *Ibid* r 29(1).
[99] Ie, unless the Master so directs - r 29(1).
[100] R 29(2).
[101] R 29(1).

(a)   The person authorised by an order of the Master of the Office of Care and Protection to apply for a grant;

(b)   Where the incapable person is entitled as an executor, the person entitled as residuary legatee. Where the incapable person is entitled as an executor and has an interest in the residue or where he is entitled as an administrator, the person who would be entitled to a grant in respect of his own estate should he die intestate;

(c)   Any other person as the Master may by order direct.

In the case of physical incapacity the order is the same, save that (a) does not apply.

11.70   Before such a grant is issued the Master must be satisfied that the person in question is incapable of managing his affairs. The oath must contain a statement to this effect, together with the date of any order made by the Office of Care and Protection. Moreover, in any case in which a grant is being made for the use and benefit of a person who is suffering from mental incapacity, notice must first be given to the Office of Care and Protection, unless that person is an executor and has no beneficial interest in the estate.[102] In cases of physical incapacity notice must be given to the person himself, unless the Master directs otherwise.[103]

11.71   Where there are at least two executors entitled to a grant of probate and only one is suffering from mental or physical incapacity, the grant will be made to the capable persons with power reserved to the others to be joined when the disability ceases.

Grants limited to particular property

Grant de bonis non administratis
11.72   Where all the persons to whom a grant of probate or administration has been made have died but the estate is still not fully administered, it will generally be necessary for a new grant, a *de bonis non* grant, to be issued to a new representative in order that the estate can be duly administered. The one exception, where it is not necessary to obtain a second grant, is if the original

---

[102]R 29(3).
[103]R 29(4).

grant was a grant of probate and a 'chain of representation' has been constituted.[104]

11.73   The person entitled to a *de bonis non* grant is the person next entitled under the usual rules for priority.[105]

11.74   The procedure for obtaining a *de bonis non* grant is the same as the full procedure for obtaining any grant of representation. In particular, it should be remembered that an Inland Revenue account relating to the unadministered part must be submitted.

Miscellaneous grants

Grant to attorneys
11.75   In certain circumstances the person entitled to a grant of probate or administration may appoint an attorney to take out a grant on his behalf. Such a grant will be limited to his use and benefit until either he shall obtain a grant himself, or in any other way the Master directs.[106]

This power can be exercised in the following circumstances:

(a)   when the person entitled resides outside Northern Ireland;[107]

(b)   where the person entitled is residing in Northern Ireland but the Master is satisfied by affidavit that it is desirable for a grant to be made to his attorney.[108]

Grant of double probate
11.76   If probate has been granted to one or more executors named in a will, but one or more executors have reserved their power to act, those whose power has been reserved can apply for a grant of double probate at any time in the future. This grant runs concurrently with the first grant.

---

[104]See para 9.25 *post*. It should be remembered that it is only necessary to extract a *de bonis non* grant where none of the original representatives remains. If there is a surviving representative he completes the administration himself.

[105]NCPR, r 35.

[106]NCPR, r 26.

[107]Although note that where he is an executor, administration will not be granted to his attorney without notice first being given to the others executors, if any. The Master has power to dispense with this requirement - r 26(1).

[108] NCPR, r 26(2).

CAVEATS AND CITATIONS

Caveats

11.77   There are circumstances when it may be desirable to prevent a grant of representation being issued before notice is given to an interested party. That party may wish to object to the grant, say because he disputes the validity of a will which is about to be proved, or he might simply want time to make further enquiries to determine whether there are indeed grounds for opposing the grant, or he may be a potential family provision claimant and does not want to be outside the strict six-month time limit for applications. To this end any person having an interest in a deceased's estate[109] may enter a *caveat*,[110] which operates to ensure that no grant will be sealed[111] to the estate in question without notice first being given to the *caveator* (ie the person entering the caveat). Once a grant has been sealed, however, a subsequent caveat will have no effect.

11.78   A caveat does not itself institute proceedings, although it is essentially a hostile act which often terminates in a probate action. In Northern Ireland a caveator may be ordered to give security for the costs arising from the caveat.[112] This is in contrast to the position in England where the courts have held that a caveator cannot be asked to provide such security.[113]

Procedure for entry

11.79   A caveat may be entered at the Probate Office or the branch office in Londonderry, if appropriate, by the caveator personally or by his solicitor.[114] It must be in the form prescribed in Appendix C[115] of the Non-Contentious Probate Rules[116] and, in the case of a caveat entered by a solicitor on the caveator's behalf, the full name of the caveator must be stated. In addition, the form contains the name and address of the deceased; the date and place of death; the address for service and the date of entry.

Two or more persons wishing to enter caveats must enter separate caveats.

---

[109]It is not actually necessary to have a legal interest - anybody can enter a caveat.

[110]For the rules governing caveats in general, see NCPR, r 43.

[111]Or if relating to a grant made outside Northern Ireland, it will not be resealed (r 43 (16)).

[112]*Dobler* v *Walsh* [1950] NI 150.

[113]*Re Emery* [1923] P 184; *Rose* v *Epstein* [1974] 1 WLR 1565.

[114]R 43(1).

[115]Form 4.

[116]R 43(2).

Duration of caveat

11.80 A caveat generally remains in force for six months, beginning with the date on which it is entered.[117] Thereafter it ceases to have effect, without prejudice to the entry of a further caveat. It may, however, be renewed; the six-month period will be extended for a further period of six months on a written application from the caveator (or his solicitor) lodged in the Probate Office (or the Londonderry office if the caveat was entered there) at any time during the final month.[118] This procedure can be repeated without limit in the last month of successive six-month periods.

11.81 A caveat will cease to be effective before the expiration of the six-month period if the caveator withdraws it (which he can do at any time) or if it has been 'cleared off'. A caveat will be cleared off by the non-appearance of the caveator after he has been 'warned'.

Warning of caveats

11.82 An applicant seeking a grant to an estate for which a caveat is in force may only proceed if he has the caveat removed. This is done by *warning* it. Any person who has had his application for a grant stopped, or any person claiming an interest in the estate may issue such a warning to the caveat[119] at the Probate Office, by completing Form 5 in Appendix C of the Non-Contentious Probate Rules. This requires him to state his interest (including the date of any will under which he is claiming) and requires the caveator to give particulars of any contrary interest. The warning or a copy thereof is then served on the caveator or his solicitor.

11.83 The warning requires the caveator to enter an appearance within eight days of service of the warning[120] upon him. An appearance to a warning is lodged in the Probate Office using Form 6 in Appendix C of the Non-Contentious Probate Rules. A copy will be served on the person who warned the caveat. The caveat will then remain in force until the probate action[121] has been concluded.

---

[117] R 43(3); note, however, that a caveat shall not affect any grant sealed on the day on which the caveat has been lodged (r 43(7)).

[118] R 43(4).

[119] R 43(8).

[120] Inclusive of the day of such service upon him - r 43(10).

[121] When a probate action is commenced, the Master gives notice to any caveator other than the plaintiff.

11.84 A caveator may withdraw his caveat at any time before he has entered an appearance to a warning, although if the caveat has been warned, the caveator must give notice of withdrawal of the caveat to the person who warned the caveat.

11.85 If no appearance is entered within the requisite time limit, the caveat ceases to have effect and the person warning the caveat may then obtain a certificate of the non-appearance of the caveator.

Citations

General
11.86 A common difficulty is that the persons entitled to the grant appear unwilling to extract it, yet do not renounce their rights to enable the person next entitled to take out the grant. The issue of a *citation* may provide an effective remedy for this sort of delay. A citation is an instrument which is issued from the Probate Office under the seal of the court, requiring the person cited (ie "the citee") to enter an appearance and take the necessary steps described therein.[122] Note, however, that a citation is only effective for delay *before* a grant of representation has been made. Furthermore no citation to take a grant shall issue while proceedings as to the validity of the will are pending.[123]

There are three types of citation:

    (a)   a citation to accept or to refuse a grant of representation;

    (b)   a citation to propound a will;

    (c)   a citation to take probate.

Citation to accept or to refuse a grant of representation
11.87 A citation to accept or to refuse to take a grant may be issued at the instance of any person who would himself be entitled to a grant in the event of the citee renouncing his right thereto.[124] For example, the residuary legatee of a will could cite the executor of the will to either accept or to renounce probate.

---

[122]For citations in general, see NCPR, r 44.
[123]R 45(3).
[124]R 45(1).

11.88   Where power has been reserved to an executor, he may be cited to accept or to refuse probate by the proving executors or by the executor of the sole or last survivor of them.[125]   This may be important if it is desired to establish a chain of representation.

Citation to propound a will

11.89   One possible reason for delay in issuing a grant of representation is that there has been a claim that there is a will (or a later will), but no further steps have been taken to justify it.   In these circumstances a citation to propound a will is frequently all that is needed to confirm that the claim is without proper foundation.   If, however, it is probable that the asserted claim will be taken further, the citation merely adds an extra procedural step to the inevitable probate action and it may be more sensible to proceed directly and issue a writ impugning the disputed will.

11.90   A citation to propound a will can be issued by anyone who has a contrary interest to the executors or beneficiaries under that will. It must be issued to *all* the persons interested under the will in question.[126]

11.91   An executor under a will to which there is a doubtful codicil is not permitted to issue a citation to propound the *codicil*.[127]

11.92   It has been noted above that citations are only available before a grant of representation has been extracted.   This includes a grant of probate in common form; once such a grant has been obtained, a probate action must be commenced to determine any dispute which arises about the validity of a will.

Citation to take probate

11.93   By a citation to take probate anyone interested under an estate can require an executor *de son tort* who has intermeddled in the estate to show cause why he should not be compelled to extract a grant.[128]   Such a citation cannot be issued until six months after the death of the deceased.[129]

---

[125]R 45(2).

[126]R 46(1).

[127]*Re Muirhead* [1971] P 263.   The duty of such an executor, unless he has renounced, is to execute the true last wishes of the testator as expressed in the will *and* codicil.   The proper way to proceed in such a case is for the executor to apply for a grant in solemn form and adduce satisfactory evidence that the codicil was invalid.

[128]R 45(3).

[129]*Ibid.*

11.94 The citation to take probate is a little used remedy - not least because it inevitably leads to the undesirable result that the will is being administered by a person who is hostile to the citor (ie the person taking out the citation). It is possible, however, for the citor then to ask the court to pass over the executor[130] and to make a discretionary grant to someone else.[131]

Procedure common to all citations

11.95 The draft citation should first be settled by the Master.[132] Every averment which it contains, together with any other information which the Master should require, must be verified by affidavit sworn by the person extracting the citation[133] and any will referred to in a citation is generally required to be lodged before the citation can be issued.[134] In addition, any person taking out a citation must also first enter a caveat[135] to the estate.[136]

11.96 The citation must then be served on the citee (and in the case of a citation to propound a will, on all the persons interested under the will). Personal service is required, and although the Master has a discretion exercisable "on cause shown by affidavit" to direct another mode of service (eg notice by advertisement), he will only do so in very exceptional circumstances.[137]

11.97 The procedure subsequent to the above steps will depend upon the *type* of citation and the action taken in response by the citee.

Citation to accept or to refuse a grant

(a) If the citee is willing to do what is requested, he should enter an appearance[138] and seek a grant in his favour by applying *ex parte* to the Master for an order for a grant.[139]

---

[130]By virtue of art 5 of the 1979 Order - paras 9.23 and 9.70 *post.*

[131]*In the Estate of Biggs* [1966] P 118.

[132]R 44(1).

[133]R 44(2). If there are two or more citors the affidavit may be sworn by any one of them. The Master is empowered to accept an affidavit from the *solicitor* acting for the citor "in special circumstances".

[134]R 44(5). Note, however, that the Master may dispense with this requirement where the will is not in the citor's possession and he is satisfied that it would be 'impracticable' to insist upon it being lodged.

[135]See para 11.77 *supra.*

[136]R 44(3).

[137]R 44(4).

[138]See para 11.98 *post.*

[139]R 45(4).

(b) If no appearance has been entered, then an application may be made to the Master for an order for a grant in favour of the citor,[140] or, if the citee is an executor who had reserved his right to act, an order that a note be made on the grant that no appearance has been made and that all rights to the executorship wholly cease.[141] The application must be supported by an affidavit showing that the citation was duly served and that no appearance has been entered.[142]

(c) If the citee renounces, the citor can obtain a grant without an order.

(d) If the citee has entered an appearance but does nothing further within a "reasonable time", the citor may also apply for an order for a grant.[143]

Citation to propound a will
(a) The person cited may seek to propound the alleged will, and a probate action should be commenced against the citor.

(b) If no appearance has been entered (or an appearance has been entered but no further steps have been taken within a reasonable time)[144] the citor may apply to the Master by summons[145] for an order requiring such person to take a grant within a specified time or for a grant to himself or some other person specified in the summons.[146]

Citation to take probate
(a) The citee may enter an appearance and seek a grant in his favour.

(b) If the citee does not enter an appearance, (or enters an appearance but does nothing further within a reasonable time) the citor may apply for an order requiring the citee to take a grant within a specified time, or he will be passed over and the grant issued to the citor or some other named person.

Entering an appearance
11.98 A citee can enter an appearance (which is done using Form 5 in Appendix C of the Non-Contentious Probate Rules) any time within eight days inclusive of the day of service. In addition an appearance can be entered even

---

[140]R 45(5).
[141]R 45(5)(b).
[142]R 45(6).
[143]R 45(7).
[144]*Ibid.*
[145]Which must be served on the person cited.
[146]R 45(5)(c).

after the expiry of this time limit, provided that the citor has not yet made any further application to the Master in relation to the citation.[147]

RECOGNITION AND RESEALING OF GRANTS

11.99 The grant of representation should generally be taken out in the country of the deceased's domicile. Therefore if the deceased was domiciled in Northern Ireland, the grant should be extracted in Northern Ireland; if the deceased died domiciled in England, it should be extracted there. Prior to 1972 grants made in one part of the United Kingdom had to be resealed before they were effective for another part. This requirement, which could cause considerable inconvenience and delay, was removed by the Administration of Estates Act (NI) 1971,[148] which provides for the direct reciprocal recognition of grants throughout the United Kingdom without the need for resealing. A pre-requisite for its application is that the grant in question was extracted in the jurisdiction in which the deceased died domiciled. Thus a grant of representation made in Northern Ireland in respect of any person dying domiciled in Northern Ireland is automatically effective for the rest of the United Kingdom, without the need for resealing.[149] The converse is also true; for example, a Scottish confirmation[150] extracted in respect of a deceased domiciled in Scotland will be effective for any property which he owned in Northern Ireland.[151]

11.100 The reciprocal arrangements of the 1971 Act do not extend to property in the Isle of Man or the Channel Islands and if the deceased had property in either it will be necessary to extract an additional grant relating to that jurisdiction - usually by instructing a firm of solicitors there. This is also the position if a deceased with Northern Ireland domicile owned property in the Republic of Ireland.[152]

11.101 The High Court has a discretion to reseal a grant of representation which was obtained in a country to which the Colonial Probates Acts 1892 and 1927 apply (in practice, most Commonwealth countries),[153] whereupon it has the same effect as if it had been granted in this jurisdiction. The procedure for

---

[147]R 44(6).

[148]Which extends to grants made before commencement - s 1(6).

[149]S 1(4).

[150]The equivalent to a grant of probate.

[151]S 2(2).

[152]Eg *Finnegan* v *Cementation Co Ltd* [1953] 1 QB 688.

[153]S 2 of the 1892 Act.

the resealing of such grants is contained in rule 39 of the Non-Contentious Probate Rules.

REVOCATION OF GRANTS

The grounds for revocation

11.102 Article 11(1) of the Administration of Estates (NI) Order 1979 confers on the High Court the power to revoke[154] any grant of representation. The circumstances in which it would be appropriate to exercise this power generally fall within two broad categories:

(a)   The grant has been made to the person(s) not truly entitled;[155]

(b)   At the time when the grant was made it was made to the person who was entitled, but events subsequent to its granting have been such that it should be revoked in the interests of those beneficially entitled to the estate.

11.103 It should be noted that a person is not barred from seeking revocation of a grant by his acquiesence in its making[156] nor by his accepting a legacy under the will which hc is challenging.[157]

Grant to person not entitled

11.104 Probably the most common situation in which a grant will be revoked is where a later will is found after a grant of probate of an earlier will has issued - either a grant of administration has been extracted and a will is then found, or a grant of probate has been taken out and a later will turns up. Other examples include a 'deceased' who is later discovered to be still alive and well;[158] a grant made to a particular person as being related to the deceased in a certain manner which then transpires not to be the case;[159] or a grant made to

---

[154]In addition, the seal can be removed from foreign grants which have merely been resealed in this jurisdiction.

[155]See also art 11(2) of the 1979 Order which provides "without prejudice" to the generality of the preceding subsection that a grant should be revoked when "it appears to the High Court that ... [it] either ought not to be made or contains an error ..."

[156]*Re Jolley* [1964] P 262.

[157]*Bell* v *Armstrong* (1822) 1 Add 365.

[158]*Re Napier's Goods* (1809) 1 Phillim 83.

[159]*Re Moore* (1845) 3 NC 601; grant made to deceased's "widow" who later turned out to be merely his "common law" wife. It is irrelevant that the "deception" happened through fraud or simple ignorance.

someone who is discovered to be still a minor. In addition, a grant may have been issued to the wrong person because of an official error; for example, a grant issued inadvertently while a caveat was in force, without notice to the caveator.[160]

Changes of circumstance since the grant was made

11.105 The classic cases which fall within this second category concern a personal representative who has become incapable of acting since the grant was extracted, or who has permanently left the jurisdiction or otherwise cannot be found.[161]

11.106 Where one of several personal representatives becomes incapable of acting through mental or physical incapacity, the grant is revoked and a further grant issued to the other(s).[162] In the case of an executor, power is reserved to him until he regains his capacity.[163] Where a sole representative becomes incapable, however, the grant will usually be impounded during the period of incapacity but not revoked.[164] Instead a grant of administration *de bonis non* and for the use and benefit of the incapable grantee, limited during his incapacity, is made.

11.107 The authorities are not entirely clear as to whether it is appropriate to revoke a grant simply because the grantee has committed a breach of duty. Although there is an *obiter dictum* in *Re Loveday*[165] which is sufficiently wide to include revocation for breach of duty, the court in *Re Cope*[166] refused to revoke a grant in this situation because the beneficiaries could be protected by another means (on this occasion section 25 of the Administration of Estates Act 1925[167] which provides that personal representatives can be compelled to account by inventory). It is submitted that *Cope* does not detract from the principle that there may be cases where revocation of the grant is the best means of securing the proper administration of the estate.

---

[160]*Timblestown* v *Timblestown* (1830) 3 Hag Ecc 243.

[161]Eg *Re Loveday* [1900] P 154 - widow obtained administration and then could not be found. Grant revoked and a *de bonis non* grant made in favour of one of her children.

[162]Eg *In the Goods of Newton* (1843) 3 Curt 428.

[163]*In the Estate of Shaw* [1905] P 92.

[164]*Re Cooke's Goods* [1895] P 68.

[165][1900] P154.

[166][1954] 1 All ER 698.

[167]The Northern Ireland equivalent is found in art 35 of the Administration of Estates (NI) Order 1979.

Procedure for revocation

11.108 Rule 41 of the Non-Contentious Probate Rules envisages that applications for revocation of a grant will, in most cases, be made by or with the consent of the person to whom the grant was made and provides that a grant can only be revoked on the application of some other party if there are 'special circumstances'. In practice, however, it is not difficult to establish 'special circumstances' and any of the illustrations outlined above would clearly constitute such.

11.109 An uncontested application for the revocation of a grant is made by affidavit setting out the facts, accompanied by any other relevant evidence[168] and the grant to be revoked. The latter is retained by the Probate Office after revocation. Where a grant cannot be submitted[169] (eg because it has been lost or cannot be traced) the High Court has power to revoke the grant without it being called in.[170]

11.110 A new grant cannot generally[171] be made until the old grant has been revoked.[172]

Consequences of revocation

11.111 The actions of the personal representatives carricd out while the grant was in force remain valid even though the grant is later revoked.[173] It follows from this that a grant must actually be revoked - even if it has been made incorrectly. Once, however, a personal representative has notice of a potential claim against his grant he can no longer safely distribute under it;[174] this is a rule which can generate considerable problems, especially when the 'claim' is

---

[168]Eg if the application is based on the incapacity of the personal representative, medical evidence of this is required.

[169]Although note that a personal representative is under an obligation to deliver up his grant when called upon to do so by the court (s 9 of the Administration of Estates Act (NI) 1971; the English position is governed by s 25(c) of the Administration of Estates Act 1925 which was substituted by s 9 of the Administration of Estates Act 1971).

[170]Art 11(3) of the 1979 Order.

[171]A rare exception occurs where *more than one* executor has become incapable. In this case a *combined* application may be made by the capable grantees for revocation of the grant *and* the issue of a new one. The procedure is considerably streamlined - the affidavit setting out the facts leading to the revocation can be used in place of the oath and it is not necessary to remark the will.

[172]*Re Hornbuckle's Goods* (1890) 15 PD 149.

[173]*Hewson* v *Shelley* [1914] 2 Ch 13; *McParland* v *Conlon* [1930] NI 138.

[174]*Guardian Trust & Executors Company of New Zealand Ltd* v *Public Trustee of New Zealand* [1942] AC 115.

something like a letter which is uncorroborated by further evidence. In such a case a personal representative is not expected to bring a probate action himself, but should apply to the court for directions.

Protection of personal representatives

11.112 Article 38(1) of the Administration of Estates (NI) Order 1979[175] provides that "every person making or permitting to be made any payment or disposition in good faith shall be indemnified and protected in so doing, notwithstanding any defect or circumstance whatsoever affecting the validity of the grant". The English equivalent is found in section 27(1) of the Administration of Estates Act 1925. A former personal representative is therefore protected as regards any payment or disposition (eg, discharging the deceased's debts or distributing the estate to the beneficiaries entitled under the grant in question) made in good faith[176] before the grant was revoked.

11.113 Article 38 does not affect the principle already referred to, which emanates from the decision of the Privy Council in *Guardian Trust & Executors Company of New Zealand Ltd* v *Public Trustee of New Zealand,*[177] that a personal representative who has notice of a potential claim casting doubt on his grant, but who proceeds to distribute under that grant in disregard of the claim, will be liable to the deceased's estate if his grant is later revoked.

11.114 When a grant has been revoked the former personal representative is entitled to be reimbursed the expenses which he incurred while he acted as such.[178]

Protection of persons making payments to personal representatives

11.115 Article 38(2) of the 1979 Order provides that any payments made in good faith *to* the personal representatives before the grant was revoked are a valid discharge to the person making them.

---

[175] Only effective in relation to the estates of persons dying on or after 1 January 1972 - art 38(3).

[176] An example of a personal representative who did not act in good faith and who was consequently denied an indemnity under the corresponding English provision is found in *Re Bloch, The Times*, 2 July 1959 - the misdemeanour in question was the earlier withholding of material evidence when an application was made for leave to swear death (the reason for the revocation of the grant being the 'deceased's' reappearance).

[177] [1942] AC 115.

[178] 1979 Order, art 38(2).

Protection of purchasers from personal representatives

11.116 In *Hewson* v *Shelley*[179] the English Court of Appeal held that a conveyance by personal representatives in good faith and for value remains valid notwithstanding that the grant under which they hold is subsequently revoked. This decision was followed by the Northern Ireland Court of Appeal in *McParland* v *Conlon*.[180] It has been suggested that this principle has been given statutory recognition by section 33(1) of the Administration of Estates Act (NI) 1955.[181] However this provision, which protects *bona fide* purchasers in their dealings with personal representatives, does not expressly refer to grants which are subsequently revoked and it is submitted that it is not sufficiently wide to include these.[182] Purchasers should therefore continue to base any such case on the judicial authorities rather than section 33(1).

Amendment of grants

11.117 Rule 41 of the Non-Contentious Probate Rules gives the Master power to *amend* a grant of representation. However, it will only be exercised where a non-substantial error (eg small mistakes in names or addresses, or in the place or date of the deceased's death) has been made in the grant. More significant mistakes will require the grant to be revoked and a new one issued.

11.118 An application for amendment is by way of affidavit sworn by the grantee, explaining the nature of the error and the alteration required. In addition, if the error is the date of the deceased's death, a death certificate should be lodged.

---

[179] [1914] 2 Ch 13.

[180] [1930] NI 138.

[181] Eg Leitch, *The Administration of Estates Act (NI) 1955* at p 93.

[182] In contrast, the English equivalent, s 37(1) of the Administration of Estates Act 1925, includes the wording "notwithstanding any subsequent revocation or variation".

CHAPTER TWELVE

ADMINISTRATION OF ASSETS

GENERAL

12.01 A personal representative has a statutory duty "to collect and get in the estate of the deceased and administer it according to law".[1] In essence, this process of administration involves the personal representatives collecting and, if necessary, preserving the assets; paying the funeral expenses and discharging other debts and liabilities; and finally distributing the net estate according to the terms of the will or intestacy rules.

Time allowed for administration

12.02 There is no absolute time limit within which an estate must be administered, but section 41 of the Administration of Estates Act (NI) 1955 requires the personal representatives to *distribute*[2] the deceased's estate "*as soon after his death as is reasonably practicable* having regard to all other relevant circumstances "[Emphasis added]. Historically the expiry of the first year after death (known as the "executor's year") has been seen as a significant cut-off point, by which time, in the normal course of events, the estate should have been wound up. This view has been given a certain statutory approval by section 41, which further provides that proceedings against the personal representatives in respect of their failure to distribute can only be brought within the first year after death if the leave of the court has been obtained.[3] However, it must be stressed that the one-year time limit is only a rule of thumb and in some situations it will not be unreasonable that the estate is unadministered for a longer period.

---

[1] Administration of Estates (NI) Order 1979, art 35(1)(a).

[2] Obviously the estate can only be distributed when the other aspects of the administration have been completed.

[3] See also s 34(3) of the Administration of Estates Act (NI) 1955 Act which empowers persons in whose favour the personal representatives have failed to assent after a year of death to require the court to intervene - para 12.126 *post*. Furthermore, interest on general legacies does not run until one year after death, unless the will expressly provides to the contrary (*Re Pollock* [1943] Ch 338) or the testator stands *in loco parentis* to an infant legatee who is to be maintained out of the interest (*Re Moody* [1895] 1 Ch 101). After the executor's year interest is payable at 6% (RSC O 44 r 10).

12.03   At the other end of the spectrum, personal representatives must now be careful not to distribute the estate too hastily. It has already been noted how applications for a family provision award under the Inheritance (Provision for Family and Dependants) (NI) Order 1979, or for the rectification of a will under article 29 of the Wills and Administration Proceedings (NI) Order 1994 must be made within six months of the date of the grant of representation (*not* the death), unless the leave of the court has been obtained. In both cases personal representatives are expressly protected against any potential liability when they distribute the estate *after* the six months have expired.   By implication they may be liable if they distribute it beforehand.   Personal representatives who have any reason to suspect that there will be a family provision claim or an application for rectification of a will should not therefore distribute the estate until at least six months have elapsed from the date of the issue of the grant.

Nature of beneficiaries' rights during the administration

12.04   Until the extent of the residue has been ascertained a beneficiary does not have any beneficial proprietary interest in the deceased's unadministered estate.[4]   On a person's death his assets are said to vest in his personal representatives "in full ownership without distinction between legal and equitable interests".[5] What the beneficiaries do have, even before the residue has been calculated, is an equitable chose in action to ensure due administration of the deceased's estate[6] and this right can be enforced by administration proceedings.

Inventory and account

12.05   Beneficiaries and other persons interested in the estate[7] can apply to the High Court to obtain information about the property comprised in it and the manner in which it is being administered.   Article 35(1)(b) of the Administration of Estates (NI) Order 1979 imposes a duty upon personal

---

[4] This position derives from the basic concept of Equity that the fetters of a trust can be imposed only where there is specific property which is capable of being identifiable as the trust fund. One possible exception is a specific gift - see Parry and Clark, *The Law of Succession*, (10th ed), p 479.

[5] *Commissioner of Stamp Duties (Queensland)* v *Livingston* [1965] AC 694 at p 707. See also *Kavanagh* v *Best* [1971] NI 89.   This position is certainly not without theoretical difficulties. Exactly where *is* the equitable interest? It can hardly be with the executor, so is it *in vacuo*? See eg Mellows, *The Law of Succession*, (5th ed) 411-414 and Thomas and Cooper, "The Nature of the Beneficiary's Interest in the Administration and Distribution of An Estate", [1995] Liverpool Law Review at 69.

[6] *Commissioner of Stamp Duties (Queensland)* v *Livingston, ibid* at 717.

[7] Eg someone with a probable or contingent interest - *Burgess* v *Marriott* (1843) 3 Curt 424.

representatives[8] to exhibit on oath a full inventory of the estate and/or an account of its administration[9] when the court requires them to do so.

The nature of personal representatives' powers

12.06 Considerable powers are conferred upon the personal representatives to enable them to collect, to manage and to distribute the deceased's assets. Some of these powers derive from common law; others from statute (mainly Part IV of the Administration of Estates Act (NI) 1955 and sections 12-26 of the Trustee Act (NI) 1958). In addition, an executor is commonly given a number of *express* powers by the will.

The more important of these powers are described in the course of this chapter but at this point some comments of general application might not be inappropriate.

12.07 First, it should be remembered that the personal representatives hold their powers in a fiduciary position; they are conferred upon them for the administration of the estate and should not be used for any other purpose. Moreover, they must be exercised in the interests of the estate as a whole.[10]

12.08 Personal representatives can act both jointly *and severally*[11] in exercising most of their powers. *Trustees*, by contrast, must act jointly.[12] However, there are a number of important statutory exceptions to the general rule. In the following situations all (or both) of the personal representatives are required to act together.[13]

    (a)   When exercising the power of sale under section 32 of the 1955 Act;[14]

    (b)   When exercising the power to grant leases under section 40(1) of the 1955 Act;[15]

---

[8] This includes an executor *de son tort* (art 35(2)) and a former personal representative whose grant has since been revoked (*In the Estate of Thomas* [1956] 1 WLR 1516).

[9] Personal representatives are under a duty to keep clear and accurate accounts of the administration - *Ottley* v *Gilbey* (1845) 8 Beav 602.

[10] *Re Hayes* [1971] 1 WLR 758, at 764.

[11] Ie , the act of one binds the others.

[12] Eg *Attenborough* v *Solomon* [1913] AC 76, where the distinction was crucial.

[13] Non-proving executors, including those who have merely reserved their right to act, are not personal representatives - 1955 Act, ss 32(2) and 34 (6).

[14] See para 12.40 *post*.

[15] See para 12.44 *post*.

(c)   When exercising the power to raise money by mortgage under section 40(4) of the 1955 Act;[16]

(d)   When assenting in respect of land under section 34 of the 1955 Act.[17]

(e)   In addition, the transfer of shares in a company regulated by the Companies legislation is uaually required to be executed by all of the personal representatives.[18]

12.09   Where there is a *sole* personal representative acting as such,[19] he has exactly the same powers as two or more personal representatives would have. Note, in particular, that there is no corresponding provision to the rule that a sole *trustee* (other than a trust corporation) cannot give a valid receipt for land.[20]

DEVOLUTION OF ASSETS ON DEATH

12.10   As has been noted elsewhere,[21] the term "personal representative" derives from the era when only the *personal* estate devolved automatically on the executor(s) or administrator(s), while realty devolved directly on the beneficiary named in the will or the heir upon intestacy. Gradual changes were made to this position by the Land Transfer Act 1897 and the Law Reform (Miscellaneous Provisions) Act (NI) 1937[22] but full assimilation of the rules governing the devolution of real and personal property was not achieved until the enactment of the Administration of Estates Act (NI) 1955. The general principle is laid down in section 1(1):

> "Real estate[23] to which a deceased person was entitled for an estate or interest *not ceasing on his death* shall on his death,

---

[16] See para 12.48 *post.*

[17] S 34(6). See para 12.119 *post.*

[18] Companies (NI) Order 1986, arts 192 and 193; Table A, arts 29-31.

[19] In addition, s 45(2) of the 1955 Act confirms that where one of two or more proving executors has died the survivor(s) can exercise any of the powers conferred on personal representatives.

[20] Settled Land Act 1882, s 39(1); Trustee Act (NI) 1958, s 14(1).

[21] See para 9.02 *supra.*

[22] S 1(1).

[23] Defined in s 44(a) of the 1955 Act as including "chattels real and land in possession, remainder, or reversion, and every estate or interest in or over land (including real estate on trust or by way of mortgage or security, but not money to arise under a trust for sale of land, nor money secured or charged on land) to which a deceased person was entitled at the time of his death".

notwithstanding any testamentary disposition, devolve upon and become vested in his personal representatives *from time to time* as if it were personal estate vesting in them ....[Emphasis added]."[24]

The words "from time to time" in the above provision ensure that where the original personal representatives are replaced by others (eg because a grant is revoked) the estate automatically vests in the new representatives.

Property which does not devolve on the personal representatives

12.11 Property which ceases on the deceased's death does not devolve upon the personal representatives. Examples include a life estate for the deceased's own life,[25] or property which the deceased held as one of two or more joint tenants.[26] Other property which does not devolve on the personal representatives includes the subject-matter of a *donatio mortis causa*;[27] property which is disposed of by a statutory nomination;[28] and property passing by way of a life insurance policy written in trust for a third party.[29] These were all considered in more detail in previous chapters.

In addition, the following property does not devolve on the personal representatives.

Fee tails

12.12 Where the deceased is tenant-in-tail of an unbarred entail his interest is deemed to cease on death.[30]

---

[24]This is subject to the rule discussed earlier (para 10.20 *supra*) that where the deceased dies intestate the estate vests in the Probate Judge until the grant of administration has been extracted - 1955 Act, s 3.

[25]A life estate *pur autre vie* devolves on the personal representatives of the holder in the usual way should the holder predecease the person for whose life he holds - s 1(3) of the 1955 Act (this provision abolished the old occupancy rules, on which see Wylie, *Irish Land Law* (1986,2nd ed) p 240).

[26]The right of survivorship (the *jus accrescendi*) vests the entire title in the other joint tenant(s). This well-established principle was given statutory confirmation in s 44(d) of the 1955 Act - "the estate or interest of a deceased person under a joint tenancy where any tenant survives the deceased person shall be deemed to be an interest ceasing on his death". Joint tenants were considered more fully at para 10.16 *supra*.

[27]See para 1.28 *supra*.

[28]See para 10.08 *supra*.

[29]See para 10.14 *supra*.

[30]1955 Act, s 44(c). The old inheritance laws for realty, discussed at para 6.08 *supra,* still govern the descent of an entailed interest. Fee tails are now extremely rare.

Property vested in a corporation sole

12.13   On the death of a corporation sole (ie a single person who occupies a particular office, such as the Bishop of Connor) any interest which he has in the corporation's property ceases.[31]

Residential tenancies[32]

12.14   It has been seen that leaseholds devolve on the personal representatives in the usual way.[33] However, the security of tenure ("the status of irremovability") which legislation has conferred on many residential tenants, in both the public and private sectors, may be automatically transmitted on the tenant's death to certain members of his family. The rules governing such successions are statutory and cannot be overridden by will.

12.15   Within the private-rented sector Schedule 1 to the Rent (NI) Order 1978 provides for up to two transmissions on the death of a protected or statutory tenant. In the first instance, the tenancy passes to the spouse of the tenant, provided that he or she was residing with the tenant at his death. Where there is no such spouse it passes to a member of the deceased tenant's family who was living with him at the time of death.[34]

12.16   In the public-rented sector there is only a single statutory transmission[35] on the death of a secure tenant. Article 26(1) of the Housing (NI) Order 1983 provides that on the death of a secure tenant the tenancy vests in the person qualified to succeed him, if there is one. To qualify, the person in question had to:

(a)   occupy the dwelling-house as his only or principal home at the time of the tenant's death;

(b)   and either,

(i) be the tenant's spouse, or;

---

[31] 1955 Act, s 44(e).

[32] See further, Hadden and Trimble, *Housing Law in Northern Ireland* (SLS,1985).

[33] 1955 Act, s 1(1). Thus a notice to quit must be served on the personal representatives (or the Probate Judge in the case of an intestate death prior to the grant) before possession can be recovered from the landlord.

[34] See also art 4 of the 1978 Order.

[35] Although it appears that the Northern Ireland Housing Executive will, by concession, permit a second transmission.

(ii) another member of the tenant's family[36] who has resided with the tenant throughout the 12 months prior to his death

Property warranting further consideration

Powers of appointment

12.17 *Realty* over which the deceased exercised by will a *general* power of appointment devolves upon the personal representatives.[37] In contrast, personal property subject to such an appointment does not;[38] nor does any property (real or personal) over which the deceased exercised a *special* power of appointment by will.[39]

Partnership interests[40]

12.18 On the death of a partner any assets of the partnership which were vested in the deceased devolve on his personal representatives. Further, any assets held by the deceased and his partners as *joint tenants* are considered in *Equity* to be held as tenants in common,[41] so that the surviving partner(s) hold such property *upon trust* for the personal representatives. However, notwithstanding this position the deceased's property in the business does remain "partnership assets" in the sense that it is the surviving partners who will deal with it for the purposes of the partnership[42] - usually in accordance with express provisions of the partnership deed. The involvement of the personal representatives in the matter is thus very minimal:

> "Unless all the partners have agreed to the contrary, when one of them dies, his executors have no right to become partners with the surviving partners; nor to interfere with the partnership

---

[36]If there is more than one such person the spouse is preferred - art 26(3).

[37]1955 Act, s 1(6).

[38]S 1(6) of the 1955 Act extends only to real property and in the absence of any statutory authority personal property must still be governed by *O'Grady* v *Wilmot* [1916] 2 AC 231. Note, however, that both real *and* personal property of which a deceased disposed by will in pursuance of a general power of appointment are assets for payment of his debts (1955 Act, s 29(1) - see para 12.58 *post*).

[39]And does not constitute assets for the payment of debts unless the power has been exercised in the deceased's own favour; *Re Penrose* [1933] Ch 793.

[40]See generally *Lindley and Banks on Partnership*, Sweet and Maxwell, (16th ed) especially ch 26.

[41]Partnerships are one of the limited number of cases where "Equity leans against a joint tenancy" on the basis that the co-owners would not have intended the *jus accrescendi* to apply - see Wylie, *Irish Land Law*, (2nd ed), p 394.

[42]Partnership Act 1890, s 38.

business; but the executors of the deceased represent him for all
purposes of account ..."[43]

12.19   In the absence of an express clause to the contrary in the partnership
agreement, the consequences of the death of a partner are governed by the
Partnership Act 1890. Section 33(1) of this Act provides that the partnership is
dissolved on the death of one of the partners; the partnership assets must be
sold[44] and after payment of the liabilities all the former partners (including the
estate of the deceased partner) are paid what is due to them.[45]   In practice,
however, the partnership deed should contain express provisions which override
the statutory rules. A partnership deed should always be made available to the
draftsman of the will to enable proper account to be taken of its terms.

COLLECTION AND PRESERVATION OF THE ESTATE

12.20   The statutory duty on the personal representatives "to collect and get
in" the assets has already been noted. This they must do with due diligence,[46]
taking all reasonable steps to maintain the value of the estate. However, they
are not liable for any fall in value of the security if they act honestly and
prudently and in the belief that they had taken the best course of action for all
parties interested in the trust estate:

> "An executor or administrator is in the position of a gratuitous
> bailee who cannot be charged with the loss of his testator's
> assets without wilful default."[47]

12.21   The first concern of the personal representatives will be to acquaint
themselves with the nature of the estate and to "assume control" over it,
ensuring that all title deeds, share certificates, passbooks and other
documentation relating to the estate are securely under their control as soon as
possible. Some assets may by their nature require immediate attention; for
example, animals or perishable goods.

---

[43]*Per* Lord Lindley, cited in *Lindley and Banks on Partnership* at p 648.
[44]Partnership Act, s 39.
[45]In the proportion in which the profits were divided unless otherwise agreed - Partnership
   Act, s 44. Lord Lindley described the interest of a deceased partner which is available for
   distribution as that partner's "proportionate interest in the partnership assets after they have
   all been realised and converted into money, and all the partnership debts and liabilities have
   been paid and discharged".
[46]Eg *Re Tankard* [1942] Ch 69.
[47]*Per* Jessel MR in *Job* v *Job* (1877) 6 Ch D 562.

Debts owing to the deceased

12.22 Prompt payment should be sought of any unsecured debts owing to the deceased and if necessary proceedings brought to recover them.[48] There is greater latitude where a loan is an investment which has been authorised by the will and in *Re Chapman*[49] the English Court of Appeal refused to uphold the submission that personal representatives are under an absolute duty, without exercising their own judgment, to call in all securities (including those which are not required for the payment of funeral expenses, debts or legacies) within 12 months of death.[50]

Power to compromise

12.23 Both section 40(9) of the Administration of Estates Act (NI) 1955 and section 15(1)(e) of the Trustee Act (NI) 1958[51] confer wide powers on personal representatives to compromise and settle claims on behalf of the estate. The rationale of these provisions was to give the personal representatives the same scope to deal with the estate as a prudent and reasonable person would have with his own property. For example, a personal representative is given the power to allow any time for payment of any debt and to compromise, compound, abandon, submit to arbitration or otherwise settle any debt, account, claim or other matter relating to the estate of the deceased.[52]

12.24 It must be emphasised that personal representatives are not absolved from exercising their own judgment and *Re Greenwood*[53] confirmed that the statutory protection[54] only applies when a personal representative has actively considered whether or not to forego the debt.

---

[48]In *Caney* v *Bond* (1843) 6 Beav 486 an executor who failed to recover money owing to the deceased on the basis that it was "as safe as in the Bank of England" was held personally liable to make good the loss occasioned when the debtor died insolvent two years later. See also *Hayward* v *Kinsey* (1701) 12 Mod Rep 568 (debt statute barred); although it is different if the personal representative had reasonable grounds for believing that the debt could not be recovered even if he did sue - *Clack* v *Holland* (1854) 19 Beav 262.

[49][1896] 2 Ch 763 - loans made on mortgages of farmland.

[50]Ie, a period of time commensurate with the "executor's year" - see para 12.02 *supra*.

[51]The duplication arose because the 1955 Act was designed to give personal representatives the same powers as had been given to personal representatives and trustees in England by s 15 of the Trustee Act 1925 (which replaced the narrower s 21 of the Trustee Act 1893). When the Trustee Act (NI) 1958 was duly enacted (with s 15 again in similar terms to its English counterpart), s 40(9) of the 1955 Act was expressly preserved (1958 Act, s 15(2)).

[52] 1955 Act, s 40(9)(e); 1958 Act, s 15(1)(f).

[53](1911) 105 LT 509.

[54]In *Greenwood* the provision under discussion was the predecessor of s 15 of the 1925 Act, ie s 21 of the Trustee Act 1893.

Rent

12.25   Section 40(7) and (8) of the 1955 Act enabled personal representatives to distrain upon land for arrears of rent due or accruing to the deceased person in the same manner as the deceased could have done if still alive. This right of distress was abolished by section 122 of the Judgments (Enforcement) Act (NI) 1969 (itself since superseded by the Judgments Enforcements (NI) Order 1981). The personal representatives must now obtain a judgment for the rent due and, if necessary, have this enforced through the Enforcement of Judgments Office.

Power to insure

12.26   Section 19 of the Trustee Act (NI) 1958 empowers personal representatives to insure any building or other insurable property against various hazards up to the full value.[55] In addition they may pay the premiums out of the income from either the insured property or any other property which is "subject to the same trusts",[56]without obtaining the consent of the persons otherwise entitled to it.[57]

Oddly this is a mere *power* to insure - not a duty.[58] It is therefore often prudent to include an express obligation to insure in the will.

Deposit of documents

12.27   Any bearer securities[59] which personal representatives[60] retain or invest in *must* be deposited for safe custody and collection of income with a bank.[61] In addition, personal representatives are empowered by section 22 of the Trustee Act (NI) 1958 to deposit any other documents relating to the estate with a bank for safekeeping and pay any consequential expenses out of the income of the estate.

---

[55]This differs from the corresponding English provision, s 19 of the Trustee Act 1925, which only empowers insurance up to three quarters of the value of the property, a restriction which has been criticised by the Law Reform Committee - Twenty Third Report, *The Powers and Duties of Trustees*, Cmnd 8733 (1982) para 4.31.

[56]See *Re Earl of Egmont's Trusts* [1908] 1 Ch 821.

[57]See also *Re Kinahan's Trusts* [1921] 1 IR 210, where the court authorised premiums to be paid out of capital because they were unusually high (to cover damage arising out of riots).

[58]*Re McEacharn* (1911) 103 LT 900.

[59]A "bearer security" is a security which does not bear the owner's name but is payable to the bearer ie they pass by mere delivery and thus present a significant security risk.

[60]Although if the personal representative is a trust corporation he is exempt from this requirement - Trustee Act (NI) 1958, s 7(1).

[61]*Ibid.*

Authorised investments

12.28 A will may contain an express clause empowering the executors to invest in particular securities. In the absence of such express provision personal representatives investing estate property are confined to the relatively limited scheme of investment which is authorised by the Trustee Investment Act 1961.[62]

12.29 The 1961 Act divides authorised investments into two broad categories: "narrower range"[63] (safe but low return, such as gilts) and "wider range" (more risk but higher potential yield - generally shares quoted on the London Stock Exchange). Property can always be invested in the narrower range investments, but before estate property can be invested within the wider range the entire property to be invested must be divided into two parts of equal value. One half *must* be invested within the narrower range; the other half in either the wider or narrower range, in whatever proportions the personal representatives decide. The 1961 Act also contains detailed provisions governing transfers, accruals and withdrawals and these should be consulted if necessary.

12.30 It is widely accepted that the Trustee Investment Act 1961 has failed to keep pace with modern investment conditions.[64] Many testators thus choose to confer wider powers on their personal representatives and trustees, such as an unfettered discretion to decide upon investments. It should be remembered, however, that it is not enough to ensure that investments are authorised under the 1961 Act, or even by the will. In all cases personal representatives are under a statutory duty[65] to consider the need for diversification of investments and the suitability of the particular investments contemplated.

12.31 A final point to bear in mind is that while statute confers the same investment powers on personal representatives as on trustees, the fundamentally different functions of the two offices may mean that a prudent course of action for trustees is different from that for personal representatives. The latter are essentially under an obligation to wind up an estate as expeditiously as possible; the former are required to hold on trust, often for long periods of time. Investment for a personal representative is therefore generally within a much

---

[62] Made applicable to Northern Ireland by the Trustee (Amendment) Act (NI) 1962. The following account is extremely brief. More detailed commentary on this Act can be found in all the standard works on trusts.

[63] Which is further sub-divided into those which require expert advice and those which do not.

[64] Eg shares in private companies are not authorised under either range. See, eg the Law Reform Committee, 23rd Report on *The Powers and Duties of Trustees*, Cmnd 8733 (1982) para 3.20 and Moffatt, *Trusts Law, Text and Materials* (2nd ed) (Butterworths) p 370.

[65] Trustee Investment Act 1961, s 6.

narrower context than for a trustee and personal representatives should think carefully before placing estate property in any security which cannot readily be realised, and which may thus impede the distribution.[66]

Causes of action vested in the deceased at the time of death

12.32 Section 14 of the Law Reform (Miscellaneous Provisions) Act (NI) 1937[67] provides that any cause of action vested in the deceased at his death survives for the benefit of the estate. Similarly, any cause of action subsisting *against* the deceased survives against the estate.

12.33 Personal representatives are therefore entitled to enforce a contract which the deceased had made with another before his death, but equally they are liable to that other for any breach, whether it was committed before or after the deceased's death.[68] One exception is a contract for *personal* services,[69] which contains an implied term that the contract is terminated on death.[70] However, a personal representative still remains liable for any breach of a personal contract which occurred *before* death. For example, a servant can sue his master's personal representative for arrears of wages due before death.[71]

12.34 Causes of action relating to any tort, with the exception of defamation, similarly survive for or against the estate.[72]

Fatal accidents

12.35 The above causes of action must not be confused with a claim under the Fatal Accidents (NI) Order 1977. Under this Order the personal representatives can recover damages on behalf of various *dependants* of the deceased where his death was caused by a wrongful act in respect of which the deceased could have sued if he had not died. Damages awarded under the Fatal

---

[66] *Re Walker* (1890) 62 LT (NS) 449 at 451.

[67] Which corresponds to s 1(1) of the English Law Reform (Miscellaneous Provisions) Act 1934.

[68] As regards *contractual* liability the 1937 Act merely codifies the common law - eg *Hambly* v *Trott* (1775) 1 Cowp 371; *Wentworth* v *Cock* (1839) 10 Ad & El 42; *Marshall* v *Broadhurst* (1831) 1 Cr & J 403. This is not to be confused with the personal representative's own liability for contracts which he himself made after the deceased's death in the course of the administration. This is dealt with at paras 12.40 and 12.143 *post*.

[69] Eg a contract between master and servant or a contract with an artist to commission a painting, or with an author to write a book - *Robinson* v *Davison* (1871) L R 6 Ex 269.

[70] Eg *Farrow* v *Wilson* (1869) L R 4 CP 744; *Graves* v *Cohen* (1929) 46 TLR 121.

[71] *Stubbs* v *Hollywell Railway Co* (1867) L R 2 Ex 311.

[72] In this respect the 1937 Act effected a change to the common law, which was governed by the principle *actio personalis moritur cum persona*, so that a personal representative could not be sued for any tort committed by the deceased.

Accidents Order are designed to compensate dependants for loss of the breadwinner; they therefore belong to the dependants in question and are *not part of the deceased's estate*.

Carrying on the deceased's business

12.36 It has been noted elsewhere that a personal representative will generally have no power to carry on the deceased's business if that business was carried on either in partnership[73] or through a limited company.[74] At this juncture we are concerned with the personal representatives' powers to carry on the deceased's business where the deceased was a *sole trader*.

12.37 First, it should be remembered that the business assets of a sole trader vest on his death in his personal representatives in the usual manner. The general rule is that, in the absence of express authority, the representatives have no power *to carry on* the business. Often, however, it will not be possible to sell the business immediately and it may be in the interests of the beneficiaries for it to be continued pending a sale. Thus, as an exception to the above rule, personal representatives have authority to carry on the deceased's business for a reasonable time with a view to the "proper realisation of the estate".[75] What constitutes a "reasonable time" depends on the circumstances.[76] However, it will not ordinarily be more than the executor's year,[77] so it may be appropriate to give personal representatives the express power to carry on the business for so long as they think necessary.[78]

12.38 Unless there is an express provision in the will to the contrary, the personal representatives who are carrying on the deceased's business may utilise only the assets used in the business at the date of the deceased's death. They may not use any other part of the estate.

12.39 Personal representatives are personally liable for debts incurred in running the deceased's business after his death. Where they are acting properly they are entitled to an indemnity out of the estate to the extent of the assets

---

[73] See para 12.18 *supra*.

[74] See para 12.128 *post*.

[75] *Dowse* v *Gorton* [1891] AC 190.

[76] Eg in *Re Smith* [1896] 1 Ch 71, two years was held to be reasonable.

[77] See para 12.02 *supra*.

[78] Note that even an express clause does not give the personal representatives power to carry on the administration indefinitely. Note also that where business property is subject to a trust for sale and conversion and there is also a power to postpone this sale, there appears to be an implied power to carry on this business during the postponement - *Re Crowther* [1895] Ch 56.

available for use in the business. If they are carrying on the business under the implied power, (ie for its proper realisation) this right of indemnity takes priority over both creditors and beneficiaries.[79] If, however, it is in exercise of an express power conferred by the will, the right of indemnity has priority over the beneficiaries but not the creditors.[80]

Power of sale

12.40   A personal representative had power both at common law and in Equity to dispose of the *personal* estate (including leaseholds) of the deceased for the purposes of administering his estate[81] and neither beneficiaries nor creditors could follow the property in the hands of the purchaser.[82] Section 32 of the 1955 Act has given this power statutory effect and extended it to the deceased's real estate.[83] Subsection (1) provides that:

> "The personal representatives may sell the whole or any part of the estate[84] of a deceased person for the purpose not only of paying debts, but also (whether there are or are not debts) of distributing the estate among the persons beneficially entitled thereto ..."[85]

There are two provisos to this extensive power.

(a)   Notwithstanding the express power to sell assets for the purpose of "distributing the estate", assets which have been specifically bequeathed can only be sold if to do so is necessary for the payment of debts.[86]

(b)   Before proceeding to sell the personal representatives are under a statutory obligation to take into account the wishes of the beneficiaries - "so far as is

---

[79]*Dowse* v *Gorton* [1891] AC 190.

[80]*Ibid*. The distinction arises because the beneficiaries are considered to be bound by the terms of the will.

[81]*Attenborough* v *Solomon* [1913] AC 76.

[82]*Haynes* v *Forshaw* (1853) 11 Hare 93; *Whale* v *Booth* (1785) 4 TR 625n.

[83]See also, 1955 Act s 2(1)(c).

[84]"Estate" is defined sufficiently widely in s 44(a) of the 1955 Act to include easements and other rights over land.

[85]See also para 12.45 *post* - the power to dispose of land by fee farm grant with nominal reversion where this is appropriate.

[86]*Re Weiner* [1956] 2 All ER 482; *Re Cohen* [1960] Ch 179.

practicable".[87] It is not necessary, however, for the beneficiaries to agree to the sale.[88]

12.41 A sale may be effected by public auction or by private contract and may be subject to such conditions as the personal representative thinks fit.[89] It should be remembered that the power of sale must be exercised by *all* the personal representatives, unless the leave of the court has been obtained.[90]

Protection of purchasers

12.42 It has already been noted in the preceding paragraphs that even at common law a person purchasing from the personal representatives in good faith was protected against both creditors and beneficiaries. This principle was put on a statutory footing by section 33(1) of the 1955 Act; a purchaser in good faith and for value from the personal representatives is entitled to hold the property freed from the debts and liabilities of the deceased person and from the claims of the beneficiaries.[91] Such claims and liabilities are, of course, transferred to the purchase proceeds in the hands of the personal representatives.[92]

12.43 One caveat must be made to this apparently unequivocal protection. There is old authority predating the statutory protection to the effect that where considerable time has elapsed the purchaser is not justified in presuming that the sale is being made in the due course of the administration. For example, in *Re Molyneaux and White*[93] the Irish Court of Appeal held that an executor could not give good title to a purchaser unless there was proof that the debts had been paid where 37 years had elapsed from the testator's death.[94] It seems that a purchaser cannot safely rely on the enactment of section 33 of the 1955 Act having altered this position and if a lengthy period has elapsed (eg 20 years

---

[87]S32 (1) of the 1955 Act.
[88]*Ibid.* Note also that a purchaser does not have to enquire as to whether the beneficiaries' wishes were considered - s 32(1)(a) of the 1955 Act.
[89]Trustee Act (NI) 1958, s 12(1).
[90]S 32(2) of the 1955 Act - see para 12.08 *supra*.
[91]See also s 32(2) which deals with a purchaser from a *beneficiary*. Such a purchaser in good faith and for value shall be entitled to hold the property free from the claims of creditors of the deceased except claims of which the purchaser had actual or constructive notice at the time of the purchase.
[92]For the rights of the creditors to follow property see s 39 of the 1955 Act, discussed at para 12.91 *post*.
[93](1874) 15 LR Ir 383.
[94]See also *Venn and Furze's Contract* [1894] 2 Ch 101.

or more) a purchaser should inquire whether there are still debts remaining unpaid.[95]

Power to lease

12.44   At common law a personal representative could only grant leases if they were for the due administration of the estate.[96] This principle has now been given statutory approval, and extended, by section 40(1) of the 1955 Act. Under this provision the personal representatives are empowered to grant leases of the deceased's land if:

> (a)   It is reasonably necessary for the due administration of the estate (this merely restates the common law);[97] or

> (b)   The consent of the beneficiaries or the approval of the court has been obtained. In this case the lease may be for such term and on such conditions as the personal representatives think proper.

12.45   In addition, section 40(1)(c) empowers the personal representatives to dispose of land by way of sub-fee farm grant or sub-lease, with a nominal reversion, if they are satisfied that this is the most appropriate method of disposing of the land in the course of the administration. Where the personal representatives have exercised their power under this sub-section, the grantee/lessee is entitled to assume that they have done so properly.

12.46   The statutory power to lease must be exercised by all the personal representatives together, unless the court directs otherwise.[98]

12.47   It should be remembered that in England the statutory power to grant leases is much wider, since section 39(1) of the Administration of Estates Act 1925 confers upon personal representatives all the powers to manage the land which are given to the tenant for life by the Settled Land Act 1925. Furthermore, the circumstances in which personal representatives can invoke these powers are also of much wider scope, since they can be exercised during

---

[95]See in particular the Irish case *Crowley* v *Flynn* [1983] ILRM 513 where Barron J states of the Republic's equivalent to s 33, s 51 of the Succession Act 1965: "if more than twenty years had elapsed since the death of the testator there is nothing in the section to negative the rule in *Molyneaux* v *White* ..."

[96]*Evans* v *Jackson* (1836) 8 Sim 217; *Oceanic Steam* v *Sutherberry* (1881) 16 Ch D 236.

[97]Where a lease is made under this subsection (though not (b) or (c)) the restrictions of the Business Tenancies Act (NI) 1964 do not apply - s 40(2).

[98]1955 Act, s 32(2) - see para 12.08 *supra*.

the minority of any beneficiary or the subsistence of any life interest or until the period of distribution arrives.[99]

Power to mortgage

12.48 Section 40(4) of the 1955 Act empowers personal representatives to raise money by way of mortgage for the payment of debts or inheritance tax.[100] In addition, provided that they have the consent of all of the beneficiaries being *sui juris* or the court (but not otherwise) they can raise money by way of mortgage for the erection, repair, improvement or completion of buildings, or the improvement of lands forming part of the estate of the deceased.

This power can only be exercised by all the personal representatives acting together, unless the approval of the court is obtained.[101]

Equitable apportionment - the duty to convert

12.49 Personal representatives have a duty to act impartially, balancing the interests of *all* of the beneficiaries. In particular they must hold an even hand between life tenants and remaindermen. This general obligation has been supplemented by two more specific equitable rules which have developed to achieve greater fairness between those entitled to the income and to the capital in certain circumstances. First there is the rule in *Howe* v *Lord Dartmouth*.[102] Secondly, there is the rule in the *Earl of Chesterfield's Trusts*,[103] which essentially derives directly from the former. Space precludes a detailed discussion here and these rules, which may require the personal representatives to convert certain assets into authorised investments, are mentioned simply to remind readers of their continued existence. In particular, it should be remembered that where the qualifying conditions are satisfied these rules apply automatically, yet they are widely regarded as anachronistic, achieving little other than complicating the accounting and increasing the expense of the administration. For these reasons it is usually prudent to exclude their operation[104] from any will to which they might apply.

---

[99] Administration of Estates Act 1925, s 39(1)(iii).

[100] At common law the personal representatives had power to raise money required for purposes of administration by mortgaging any of the deceased's estate - *Mead* v *Orrery* (1745) 3 Atk 235; *Earl Vane* v *Rigden* (1870) LR 5 Ch App 663.

[101] 1955 Act, s 32(2) - see para 12.08 *supra*.

[102] (1802) 7 Ves 137.

[103] (1883) 24 Ch D 643.

[104] This is best achieved by a clause which simply states that the rules in question will not apply. Alternatively they can be excluded by an indication to do so, eg, an intention that the residuary property is to be enjoyed *in specie* or by a clause directing that none of the property is to be sold. Eg *Brown* v *Gellatly* (1867) 2 Ch App 751; *Re Pitcairn* [1896] 2 Ch 199; *Re Wilson* [1907] 1 Ch 394.

The rule in Howe v Lord Dartmouth

12.50 This rule operates to benefit the remainderman and only applies where *residuary personalty* (not specific gifts or realty) is enjoyed by persons *in succession*. It requires the personal representatives to realise any part of the estate of a hazardous or wasting nature or which is an unauthorised investment,[105] (eg copyrights or leases with less than 60 years to run) and invest the proceeds in an authorised security.

The rule in the Earl of Chesterfield's Trusts

12.51 This rule is complementary to that in *Howe v Lord Dartmouth*, this time working in favour of the life tenant. If a reversion or other interest which is not producing income falls into possession or is sold, an apportionment has to be made. In short, a part of the amount actually received is treated as arrears of income and the remainder regarded as capital. The precise figures are worked out in accordance with the following formula:

> The amount treated as capital is the sum which, if invested at four per cent compound interest at the date of the testator's death with yearly rests, would, after allowing for the deductions of income tax at basic rate for the time being in force, have produced the sum actually received. The remainder is regarded as income.

PAYMENT OF DEBTS

12.52 The personal representatives are under a duty to pay the deceased's debts with due diligence having regard to the assets in their hands which are properly applicable to that purpose and to all the circumstances of the case.[106] This duty is owed to both creditors *and* beneficiaries, since the ultimate object of the administration, that is, to put the beneficiaries in possession of their interest, cannot be achieved until the debts have been paid. The personal representatives will thus be liable in *devastavit*[107] for any loss to the estate which results from their failure to pay the debts with due diligence; for example, because a creditor has involved the estate in avoidable expense.[108]

12.53 In order to satisfy the "due diligence" standard the personal representatives will ordinarily have to pay the debts before one year has elapsed from the deceased's death. As with administration in the wider sense, this rule is not absolute and the circumstances may be such as to warrant a lengthier

---

[105]Ie, neither authorised by general law (see para 12.28 *supra*) nor by the will.
[106]*Re Tankard* [1942] Ch 69.
[107]Literally, the wasting of the estate. See para 12.147 *post*.
[108]*Seaman v Dee* (1672) 2 Lev 40.

period for discharging the deceased's liabilities. However, where the payment of debts has not been completed within a year of death it seems that the onus is placed on the executors to justify the delay.[109]

12.54 The general rule is that the personal representatives should only pay the debts which they are under a *legal* obligation to discharge. Thus they should not pay a debt which is unenforceable, say because of non-compliance with the Statute of Frauds.[110] Similarly, it seems that they should not pay a debt which is statute-barred[111] although they have a discretion to do so on occasions.[112]

Ascertaining creditors

12.55 The personal representatives cannot reasonably be expected to know of all the claims existing against the deceased. In order to protect themselves against liability for distributing the estate when there are creditors remaining unpaid they should advertise in accordance with section 28 of the Trustee Act (NI) 1958. The precise requirements of this provision are discussed below.[113]

Property available for the payment of debts

12.56 The nature and extent of the property which devolves upon the personal representatives has already been considered.[114] Here the separate question of which property of the deceased is available for the payment of his debts is examined. Not all property which vests in the personal representatives is available for the payment of his debts, while liabilities can be discharged out of some property which does not devolve.

12.57 The starting point is the non-exhaustive definition contained in section 29(1) of the Administration of Estates Act (NI) 1955:

> "The real and personal estate, whether legal or equitable, of a deceased person, to the extent of his beneficial interest therein, and the real and personal estate of which a deceased person in pursuance of any general power disposes by his will, are assets for payment of his debts ..."

Note that the deceased's property is only available to the extent of his *beneficial* interest. While therefore property which was vested in the deceased as a sole

---

[109]*Re Tankard* [1942] Ch 69 at 73.
[110]*Re Rownson* (1885) 29 Ch D 358.
[111]*Midgley* v *Midgley* [1893] 3 Ch 282.
[112]*Norton* v *Frecker* (1737) 1 Atk 524 at 526. Although there is no such discretion if the debt has actually been declared statute-barred or if the estate is insolvent.
[113]See para 12.97 *post*.
[114]See para 12.10 *supra*.

surviving trustee[115] devolves on his death upon his personal representatives, it is not available for the payment of his personal debts.

12.58 It has already been noted that while real property over which the deceased had a general power of appointment by will devolves on his personal representatives, personalty so subject does not. Both, however, are assets out of which debts can be paid.[116] Property which is appointable under a *special* power does not constitute assets unless the deceased has made a valid appointment to himself.[117]

In addition, the following property constitutes "assets" for the purposes of paying debts.

Property arising after death[118]
12.59 Property available for the payment of debts may include property which never vested in the deceased during his lifetime. Examples include income arising after death and assets by remainder or by natural increase. The classic illustration of the last category are lambs borne by the deceased's sheep.[119]

Donatio mortis causa
12.60 Property which is the subject-matter of a *donatio mortis causa* is available for the payment of debts if all the other assets have been exhausted. This was considered more fully in Chapter One.[120]

Order for payment of debts
12.61 One of the greatest difficulties facing personal representatives is to determine how the burden of the debts, funeral and testamentary expenses is to be borne as between the various assets of the estate. How the personal representatives are to proceed to apply the assets towards the payment of the various liabilities depends upon whether the estate is solvent or not. By a

---

[115]Where property is vested in two or more trustees and one dies, it passes to the other(s) by the right of survivorship.

[116]S 29(1) of the 1955 Act. In addition, it seems that property appointed under a general power by a *deed* which is in favour of a volunteer and which only took effect at the deceased's death is available as the last resort - *O'Grady* v *Wilmot* [1916] 2 AC 231. Where the deceased failed to exercise his power of appointment, the property subject to it is only available if the deceased himself was entitled in default - *Homes* v *Coghill* (1802) 7 Ves 499; (1806) 12 Ves 206.

[117]*Re Penrose* [1933] Ch 793.

[118]*Re Tong* [1931] 1 Ch 202.

[119]*Re Tong* [1930] 2 Ch 400, 404.

[120]See para 1.28 *supra*.

'solvent' estate is meant one in which the assets are sufficient to pay all the funeral, testamentary and administration expenses, debts and liabilities.[121]

12.62 Obviously if the estate is *insolvent* the beneficiaries will have absolutely no entitlement and the only issue for the personal representatives is how the shortfall is to be borne by the creditors. In a solvent estate the creditors will all get paid in full and the concern for the personal representatives will be how the liabilities are to be distributed between the various classes of beneficiaries. Often in such an estate the creditors will be paid out of the first assets coming into the hands of the personal representatives[122] and if necessary the personal representatives can 'marshall' the assets, (ie the name given to the procedure whereby adjustments are made *between beneficiaries*).[123]

12.63 An insolvent estate is administered in accordance with the rules set out in Part I of the First Schedule to the Administration of Estates Act (NI) 1955,[124] while the order for payment of debts in a solvent estate is contained in Part II of the First Schedule.[125] In the latter, but not the former, this statutory order can be changed by the direction of the testator.

Insolvent estates[126]

Methods of administration
12.64 Where an estate is insolvent there are three different ways in which it can be administered.

(a) First, it can simply be administered by the personal representatives in the usual way, without any court intervention. This is the most common method but the disadvantage is that the personal representatives are

---

[121]*Re Leng* [1895] 1 Ch 652.
[122]*Re Tong* [1931] 1 Ch 202 at 212.
[123]See further Snell, *Principles of Equity*,(27th ed) p 321.
[124]1955 Act, s 30(1).
[125]1955 Act, s 30(3). Where it is not entirely clear whether the estate is solvent, it is prudent to follow the order for insolvent estates - *Re Milan Tramways Co* (1884) 25 Ch D 587. Although note the protection given by art 37 of the Administration of Estates (NI) Order 1979.
[126]In this book attention is directed solely at an insolvency arising *after* death. Where a debtor against whom a bankruptcy petition has already been presented dies, then, unless the court directs otherwise, the proceedings continue as if he were still alive, subject to some modifications contained in the Administration of Insolvent Estates of Deceased Persons Order (NI) 1991. For more detail on this, and all aspects of insolvent estates, see Hunter, *Northern Ireland Personal Insolvency* (SLS).

afforded no special protection and may be personally liable if they do not pay the debts in the correct order.[127]

(b) Secondly, either the personal representative or a creditor can apply to the court under the Insolvency (NI) Order 1989 to have the estate administered "in bankruptcy", following an *insolvency administration order*. Where such an order is granted the estate vests in the Official Receiver and thereafter the trustee in bankruptcy. The advantage for the personal representatives is that they are absolved from any liability.[128]

(c) Finally, the estate can be administered under the direction of the court following an order for administration in the Chancery Division of the High Court.[129]

Whichever way the estate is being administered, the order of priority for the payment of debts remains the same.

Order for payment of debts in an insolvent estate

12.65 Part I of Schedule 1 to the 1955 Act provides that the funeral, testamentary and administration expenses are to have priority. Thereafter the same rules are to prevail and be observed as may be in force for the time being under the law of bankruptcy with respect to the assets of persons adjudged bankrupt. This is currently the Insolvency (NI) Order 1989, as modified and supplemented for deceased insolvents by the Administration of Insolvent Estates of Deceased Persons Order (NI) 1991.[130] The basic scheme of the Insolvency Order is to classify unsecured debts into four broad categories, which are, in order of priority: preferential debts; ordinary debts; interest on debts, and deferred debts.[131] All are examined in more detail below, after some consideration is given to funeral expenses and secured creditors.

Funeral expenses

12.66 "Reasonable" funeral expenses have priority over other debts and liabilities.[132] Moreover, it seems that for this purpose "funeral" expenses are

---

[127]Although note that art 37(2) of the Administration of Estates (NI) Order 1979 provides that a personal representative who in good faith and at a time when he has no reason to believe that the deceased's estate is insolvent, pays any creditor (including himself) shall not be liable to account to other creditors of the same degree if it subsequently appears that the estate is insolvent.

[128]*Re Bradley* [1956] Ch 615, 622.

[129]The procedure is governed by RSC O 85.

[130]NI SR 1991/365.

[131]Insolvency Order, art 300.

[132]*R* v *Wade* (1818) 5 Price 621.

distinct from the "testamentary and administration" expenses, and are to be paid before them.

12.67 The funeral expenses which are allowed if the estate is insolvent are less than those permitted if the estate is solvent. In short, the funeral expenses in an insolvent estate must be "reasonably necessary", a concept which was held to include the following by Lord Holt more than 300 years ago: "the coffin, ringing the bell, parson, clerk, bearers' fees, but not a pall for ornaments!"[133] However, as in a solvent estate, much depends upon the circumstances of the case, and material considerations have been held to include the station and occupation of the deceased,[134] his religious beliefs,[135] and any wishes which he expressed about his funeral. The fact that it is hard to draw concrete principles from the decided cases is well-illustrated by those dealing with the cost of a tombstone, which has been allowed in some cases but not in others.[136]

12.68 The judiciary have not been oblivious to the fact that the personal representatives often have to bury the deceased before they have a full appreciation of the health of the estate finances, and have demonstrated a certain leniency of spirit where the estate looked solvent (eg it contained a number of large legacies) but later transpired not to be.[137]

Testamentary and administration expenses
12.69 The phrase "testamentary and administration expenses", used in the 1955 Act in connection with both insolvent and solvent estates, is not defined by statute. In essence, it covers those expenses properly incurred by the personal representatives as incidental to the performance of their duties in administering the estate. Included, for example, is the expense of obtaining the grant of representation,[138] the cost of any legal advice relating to the

---

[133]*Shelly's Case* (1693) 1 Salk 296.
[134]*Offley* v *Offley* (1691) Prec Ch 26 (£600 allowed in 1691 because deceased was very famous); *Stag* v *Punter* (1744) 3 Atk 119; *Re Walter* [1929] 1 Ch 647, 655.
[135]*Gammel* v *Wilson* [1982] AC 27, at 43.
[136]*Goldstein* v *Salvation Army Assurance Society* [1917] 2 KB 291, see especially Rowlatt J at 295 "while I do not say that in every case a tombstone must be part of the funeral expenses, I do not say as a matter of law it is not"; *Re McIntyre* (1930) 64 ILTR 179; *Hart* v *Griffith-Jones* [1948] 2 All ER 729. Note that the cost of a tombstone and the engraving thereof is an allowable deduction for inheritance tax purposes. (SP 7/87).
[137]*Stag* v *Punter* (1744) 3 Atr 119.
[138]*Re Clemow* [1900] 2 Ch 182.

administration,[139] the costs of collecting or preserving the assets of the estate,[140] the costs of advertising for claimants, and any inheritance tax payable.[141]

Statutory order for other debts

12.70   After the funeral, testamentary and administration expenses have been paid the other debts are paid in the order below. If the assets are insufficient to pay all of the unsecured debts within a particular category, they are to be paid *pari passu*. The shortfall is thus borne rateably.

(a) Secured creditors

> A creditor whose debt is secured (eg by a mortgage or charge) over the deceased's property is in a more favourable position than an unsecured creditor, in that he is entitled to realise his security and retain sufficient to discharge the debt, regardless of which of the following categories the debt falls into. If the security is equal to or greater than the value of the debt the creditor will therefore suffer no loss. Where the security is less than the amount owed, the creditor should realise his security and prove for the balance of the debt.[142]

(b) Preferential debts

> These are listed in Schedule 4 to the Insolvency (NI) Order1989.[143] They include the following: debts due to the Inland Revenue in respect of income tax deducted by the deceased under PAYE from the emoluments of his employees during the 12 months before death; debts due to Customs and Excise in respect of VAT referable to the six months preceding the date of death; arrears of Class 1 and Class 2 National Insurance Contributions due within 12 months before the deceased's death; arrears of state and occupational pension scheme contributions and arrears of wages of employees for the period of four months before death.[144]

---

[139]*Sharp* v *Lush* (1879) 10 Ch D 468.

[140]*Ibid.*

[141]Inheritance Tax Act 1984, s 211.

[142]In theory he has the option of surrendering the security and proving for the whole debt - *Ex p Robinson* (1886) 15 LR Ir 496, but it is difficult to conceive of a fact situation where this course of action would be attractive.

[143]Arts 346-347.

[144]This is subject to a limit of £800 per employee.

(c) Ordinary debts

> Ordinary debts are any other debts of unsecured creditors which do not fall within the other categories.

(d) Interest on debts

> If any surplus remains it is next used to pay interest arising on preferential and ordinary debts from the date of death. No difference is made for these purposes between preferential and ordinary debts.

(e) Postponed or deferred debts

> This category consists essentially of debts in respect of credit provided by the deceased's spouse.

Retainer and preference

12.71 In the past personal representatives enjoyed the special rights of retainer and preference. The right of retainer[145] empowered a personal representative who was also a creditor of the estate to pay any debt which was due to himself in priority to any debt which ranked equally, thus compensating him for the fact that he could not sue himself and get priority by obtaining judgment. The right of preference was the right of a personal representative to prefer one creditor to another in respect of debts which ranked equally.[146]

Both retainer and preference were abolished by the Administration of Estates Act (NI) 1971.[147]

Solvent estates

12.72 The administration of a solvent estate obviously raises very different issues. Competition between the different types of creditor is no longer the problem since they will all get paid in full, with the doctrine of marshalling being invoked, if required, to make any necessary adjustments between the beneficiaries. The focus has now shifted to consideration of two parallel, yet separate issues. First, what is the incidence of the *debts and liabilities* between the various beneficiaries? Secondly, what is the incidence of the different types of *legacies* between them?

---

[145] The common law rule was widened by s 30(2) of the 1955 Act, which extended to all the deceased's assets and not just legal interests in non-freehold estates.
[146] This was also codified in s 30(2) of the 1955 Act.
[147] S 3(1).

12.73   It was noted earlier that the order for application of assets towards the payment of unsecured debts if the estate is solvent is set out in Part II of the First Schedule to the 1955 Act. Before this order is examined there are some preliminary matters which should be addressed.

12.74   The first is a caveat. Unfortunately the statutory order contained in the First Schedule to the 1955 Act consists of a number of tortuous and notoriously complex provisions, with the result that the answers to many of the questions posed in the following paragraphs are not as clear as they should be. The area is characterised by ambiguity and conflicting judicial authorities and to suggest that a complete statutory overhaul is long overdue is something of an understatement.

12.75   Secondly, special rules apply to debts which are *charged* on the deceased's property and these are considered separately.[148]

12.76   Finally, a refresher on some basic definitions of types of gift might be useful.   Legacies are generally classified into three broad types: specific, general and demonstrative legacies. The distinction is important not only for present purposes but also because of the doctrine of ademption.[149] A *general* legacy is not a gift of any particular thing, but is one to be provided out of a testator's general estate at death. For example, "I leave Claude £1,000". A *pecuniary* legacy is strictly a gift of *money*, although as will be seen it bears a much broader meaning for the purposes of the statutory order below. A *specific* legacy is a gift of specified property, which is to pass to the legatee *in specie*: "I leave Marilyn my ruby engagement ring". A *demonstrative* legacy is by nature a general legacy, but is specified to be satisfied out of a particular fund or part of the testator's property: "I leave Joe £1,000 to be taken out of my building society deposit account". If the fund is insufficient to satisfy the legacy it will not fail but becomes a general legacy.

12.77   The *residue* of the estate is that part which is left when property which has been specifically devised or bequeathed has been taken out. Whether a gift is residuary or not is a question of construction and is not always easily determined; for example, "all moneys of which I die possessed shall be shared by my nephews and nieces now living" (residuary personalty).[150] Moreover, if a specific asset is named it does not necessarily mean that the disposition is specific, for example, if there is a gift of "the residue of my estate including my

---

[148]See para 12.86 *post*.
[149]See para 7.60 *supra*.
[150]*Perrin* v *Morgan* [1943] AC 399.

bank account" the balance in the bank account forms part of the residue and is not a specific gift.[151]

Statutory order for the payment of debts

12.78 When applying the statutory order laid down in Part II of the First Schedule to the 1955 Act the following points should be borne in mind.

(a) The order can be varied by a contrary intention in the deceased's will. This is discussed below.[152]

(b) All the assets in a particular category must be exhausted before resort can be had to those in the category below.

(c) If any property of the deceased is capable of belonging to two separate categories it falls within the higher one.[153]

(d) Where not all of the property within a particular class is needed for the payment of debts, it seems that the debts are always borne rateably between all of the assets in that class. This is expressly provided for Classes VI and VII, but it is submitted that the better view is that this principle applies universally, with the pre-1955 distinction whereby personalty had to be exhausted before realty no longer applicable.[154]   There is some English authority that the corresponding Administration of Estates Act 1925 does not affect the incidence of debts within a class and that the distinction between realty and personalty remains.[155]   However, this view is against the entire tenor of the 1955 Act, one of the objectives of which was the assimilation of the laws relating to real and personal property, and more specifically is contrary to section 29(1) which provides that "the real and personal estate ... are assets for the payment of his debts".   Moreover, the process of assimilation appears to have been more complete in Northern Ireland than in England and in view of the following general provisions in section 2 of the 1955 Act there can be no justification for continuing to administer real property in a different manner from personalty.

> "2(1) All ... rules of law relating to ... (e) all ... matters with respect to the administration of personal estate *shall*, so far as the same are applicable, extend and apply to real estate as if it were personal estate; and subsequent provisions of this section shall not prejudice the generality of this sub-section.

---

[151]*Macdonald* v *Irvine* (1878) 8 Ch D 101.
[152]See para 12.80 *post.*
[153]*Re Kempthorne* [1930] 1 Ch 268.
[154]For the former law see *Caughey* v *Copeland* [1925] NI 206.
[155]See eg *Re Anstead* [1943] Ch 161.

(5) In the administration of the assets of a deceased person, his real estate shall be administered, subject to and in accordance with the provisions of Part IV, in the same manner and with the same incidents as if it were personal estate."

The statutory order laid down in Schedule 1, Part II is as follows:[156]

I. Property of the deceased person undisposed of by will, subject to the retention thereout of a fund to meet any pecuniary legacies.

This category includes not only those assets which the testator did not atttempt to dispose of by his will,[157] but also those which in fact he did not dispose of;[158] for example, a share of residue which lapses or fails.

II. Property of the deceased person not specifically devised or bequeathed but included (either by a specific or general description) in a residuary gift, subject to the retention out of such property of a fund sufficient to meet any pecuniary legacies, so far as not provided for as aforesaid.

The problems which may arise in ascertaining whether or not a gift is residuary have already been discussed.[159] Prior to the enactment of the 1955 Act all gifts of freehold land were treated as specific - even though residuary in form[160] but gifts of residuary realty now fall within Class II and not Class VI.

III. Property of the deceased person specifically appropriated or devised or bequeathed (either by a specific or general description) for the payment of debts; and

IV. Property of the deceased person charged with, or devised or bequeathed (either by a specific or general description) subject to a charge for, the payment of debts.

---

[156]Compare the order prior to the enactment of the 1955 Act. Debts were first discharged out of the residuary personal estate and thereafter, in the following order: real estate devised in trust for payment of debts; real estate as to which the testator died intestate; real estate devised, charged with the payment of debts and specifically bequeathed subject to such charges, rateably *inter se*; pecuniary legacies; specific gifts not charged with debts; property appointed under a general power of appointment. For further details see Leitch, *The Administration of Estates Act (NI) 1955*, p 142.

[157]Eg where a will does not contain a residue clause.

[158]*Re Lamb* [1929] 1 Ch 722; *Re Worthington* [1933] Ch 771.

[159]See para 12.77 *supra*.

[160]*Hensman v Fryer* (1867) 3 Ch App 420.

Property is "appropriated" for the payment of debts if the deceased has expressly set it aside for such and does not leave it to anybody whereas property is "charged" with the payment of debts if it is left to certain beneficiaries but subject to them paying either some or all of the testator's debts. It is appropriate to consider these two Classes together.

These Classes have generated a disproportionate number of the difficulties which have arisen out of the statutory order, with the main problem being how these provisions are to be reconciled with that empowering the testator to vary the order by will. As Leitch has put it: "To the layman it may well seem strange that property deliberately set aside for this purpose should not be used first".[161] This is discussed below.

It should be remembered that *residuary* property which is appropriated for or charged with the payment of debts falls into Class II above and not into Classes III or IV.

V The fund, if any, retained to meet pecuniary legacies.

"Pecuniary legacy" is defined widely in section 45(1) of the 1955 Act as including:

> "An annuity, a general legacy, a demonstrative legacy so far as
> it is not discharged out of the designated property, and any other
> general direction by a testator for the payment of money ..."

It will be recalled that a demonstrative legacy is a legacy which is to be satisfied out of a specified fund or part of the testator's property[162] and that if the fund is insufficient to satisfy the legacy it will not fail but becomes a general legacy. If this happens that part which cannot be satisfied out of the specified fund is regarded as a pecuniary legacy and falls within Class V. The part which can be discharged out of the designated fund is a specific legacy (Class VI).

Where there are insufficient assets to meet the pecuniary legacies in full, they abate rateably.[163]

VI. Property specifically devised or bequeathed, rateably according to value.

---

[161] Leitch, *Handbook on the Administration of Estates Act (NI) 1955,* p 144.
[162] Eg "The sum of £1,000 sterling as her sole and absolute property to be paid out of the estate and effects inherited by me from my mother in terms of her last will" (*Walford* v *Walford* [1912] AC 658).
[163] *Boyd* v *Boyd* [1928] NI 14.

As was noted above, a demonstrative legacy falls within this category to the extent that it is satisfied out of the designated fund.

VII. Property appointed by will under a general power, rateably according to value.

> This category would appear to include only property which has been *expressly* appointed by the testator, and property which passes by virtue of article 20 of the Wills and Administration Proceedings (NI) Order 1994 comes within Class II above. Article 20, which re-enacts section 27 of the Wills Act 1837, provides that where a testator fails to exercise a general power of appointment, the property which is subject to the appointment passes under a residuary gift, unless a contrary intention appears from the will.[164]

Property not within the classes

12.79 The classes of property enumerated in Schedule I to the 1955 Act are not comprehensive and other assets are also available for the payment of debts and liabilities after all seven categories have been exhausted. These are:

(a)   Property subject to a *donatio mortis causa*;

(b)   Property subject to a general power of appointment exercised by deed;[165]

(c)   Property in the deceased's will which is subject to an option to purchase.

In *Re Eve*[166] Roxburgh J held that the option to buy shares at an undervalue which the testator had given in his will, was neither a specific gift of the shares themselves nor of the benefit to the purchaser (ie the difference between market value and the price actually paid). Rather, the option did not fall anywhere within the statutory order and was therefore the last property available for the payment of debts.

There is, as yet, no authority on how these three categories of asset are to rate *inter se*.

---

[164]It is discussed at para 5.19 *supra*.

[165](a) and (b) have been considered elsewhere. See para 1.29 *supra*.

[166][1956] Ch 479.

Excluding the statutory order

12.80 The answer to the apparently straightforward question "what is a sufficient provision in a will to exclude or vary the statutory order?" is far from clear. As was noted above, most of the difficulties have stemmed from the existence of Classes III and IV. If property which the testator has specifically appropriated for or charged with the debts is only taken after property which is not disposed of by will and the residue, what *is* actually required in order to vary the statutory order?

12.81 While it cannot be denied that the judiciary have drawn a number of artificial distinctions, the principle which does seem to emerge from the case law is that a mere appropriation or charging of property does *not* displace the statutory order. For example, in *Re Gordon*[167] a £50 legacy was charged with payment of debts, funeral and testamentary expenses. The statutory order was held to apply, so that the debts were actually paid out of a part of the residue which had lapsed. What is needed to displace the statutory order is, in addition, an *intention to exonerate other property*. In some cases, however, this intention to exonerate seems to have been taken automatically, as for example, in *Re James*[168] where the testator directed the debts from a particular fund and this was held to exonerate the residue.[169]

12.82 A second broad type of case has concerned lapsed shares of residue (Class I property) where there is a direction along the lines that debts are to be paid out of "the residue as a whole". On some occasions this has been held to vary the statutory order, so that the property not disposed of by will (ie the part that lapsed) is not primarily liable but that the debts are to be borne out of the residue as a whole and not just the lapsed share.[170]

12.83 It is well-established that the statutory order is not excluded by the standard direction to pay debts, without specifying out of which assets.[171]

Application of statutory order to payment of legacies

12.84 One issue which is shrouded in uncertainty is whether the order laid down in the 1955 Act for the payment of debts extends to *legacies*. If the answer is no, the incidence of legacies would still be governed by the same rules

---

[167][1940] Ch 769.

[168][1947] Ch 256.

[169]See also *Re Meldrum* [1952] Ch 208.

[170]See eg, *Re Harland-Peck* [1941] Ch 182; also *Re Petty* [1929] 1 Ch 726 and *Re Kempthorne* [1930] 1 Ch 268.

[171]*Re Lamb* [1929] 1 Ch 722; *Re Tong* [1931] 1 Ch 202.

as prior to the enactment of the 1955 Act. For instance, consider that Tom leaves Barbara £5,000 charged with a legacy to Keith of £500, and the residue to Paul. If the statutory order in Part II of Schedule 1 does apply, the £500 legacy is paid out of Paul's residue (which being in Class II is the first to be taken in the absence of Class I property). If the 1955 Act has not affected the position it will be taken out of Barbara's £5,000.

12.85 In England, where the same problem has arisen out of the Administration of Estates Act 1925 there is judicial authority in support of both views.[172] For example, Clauson J in *Re Thompson* was of the opinion that the new provisions did not apply to legacies:

> "Section 34(3) of the Administration of Estates Act 1925 [the equivalent of section 30(3) of the 1955 Act] is concerned with the way in which funeral, testamentary and administration expenses, debts and liabilities are to be met. There is no indication that there is any intention of altering the law in respect of the rights of the legatees."

With respect it is submitted that the phrase "debts and *liabilities*" in section 30 in the 1955 Act which governs Schedule 1 can be read so as to include legacies and that this is the more logical way of proceeding.

Debts charged on the deceased's property
12.86 It was noted earlier that secured debts are not part of the statutory order but are dealt with separately.[173]

12.87 At common law a charge or mortgage on devised land was discharged primarily out of the residual personal estate. This position was reversed by the Real Estate Charges Acts 1854, 1867 and 1877 (commonly known as "Locke King's Acts") which provided that the burden of discharging mortgages on real property generally descended with the property in question. The position is now governed by section 31 of the 1955 Act which repealed and replaced Locke King's Acts. Unlike its predecessors, this provision extends to all property - personalty as well as realty.

12.88 Section 31[174] provides that where a person dies possessed of, or entitled to, or under a general power of appointment by his will disposes of, an interest

---

[172]Eg *Re Worthington* [1933] Ch 771 and *Re Lamb* [1929] 1 Ch 722 in which it was held that the statutory order does apply to legacies; and *Re Thompson* [1936] Ch 676 in which it was held that it does not. Thus the law remains unclear.

[173]See para 12.75 *supra*.

[174]Which corresponds exactly to s 35 of the Administration of Estates Act 1925.

in property, which at the time of his death[175] is charged with the payment of money, whether by way of legal or equitable mortgage or charge or otherwise then,[176] subject to a contrary intention, the interest so charged shall, as between the different persons claiming through the deceased person, be primarily liable for the payment of the charge. It is further provided that every part of the interest bears, according to its value, a proportionate part of the charge on the whole.

12.89 The deceased's contrary intention to modify or exclude the operation of section 31 of the 1955 Act can be shown by will, deed or other document. However, section 31(2) provides that a general direction by a testator for the payment of his debts (even if it is *"all* of his debts") out of his general personal estate or his residuary real or personal estate, or his residuary real estate is not sufficient. In addition, there must be some words which expressly or by necessary implication refer to all or some part of the charge. For example, if a testator's estate includes Rosebud Farm, which is subject to a mortgage, a direction by the testator in his will that all his debts be paid out of the residue is not sufficient to exclude section 31. To do so he would expressly need to mention the mortgage in question - "all my debts, including the mortgage on Rosebud Farm". Alternatively, by stating "all my debts except the mortgage on Big Acre Farm" he excludes section 31 by necessary implication.[177]

12.90 It should be remembered that section 31 of the 1955 Act merely regulates the incidence of a charge as between the various *beneficiaries*. It does not affect the rights of the person entitled to the charge and section 31(3) expressly preserves the rights of the chargee to obtain payment from the other assets of the deceased. Where this right has been exercised any injustice between the beneficiaries will be addressed by marshalling.

Right of creditors to follow property
12.91 A creditor has the right to follow property into the hands of either:

(a)   a beneficiary, or;

---

[175]For an example of a charge not created at the time of death, see *Re Birmingham* [1959] Ch 523.

[176]S 31 is not confined to charges created by the parties but extends to those created by statute - eg a charge in favour of the Inland Revenue created under s 237 of the Inheritance Tax Act 1984.

[177]For an example of a contrary intention, see *Re Valpy* [1906] 1 Ch 531.

(b)   any person (other than a *bona fide* purchaser for value) who is claiming under that beneficiary.[178]

12.92 It will be remembered that a purchaser in good faith and for value is protected under section 33(2) of the 1955 Act.[179] However, the beneficiary who has sold or mortgaged the property, even if done in good faith, remains personally liable up to, but not beyond, the value of the debts to which the property was liable when it vested in the personal representative.

12.93 The extent of the powers available to the court were considered in the Irish case *Welwood* v *Grady*.[180] In England, by contrast, specific powers have been enumerated by statute.[181]

The rule in *Allhusen* v *Whittell*[182]

12.94 We have already encountered two of the equitable apportionment rules which seek to strike a balance between those entitled to income and capital.[183] The rule in *Allhusen* v *Whittell* aims to strike a fair balance between life tenant and remainderman *in the payment of debts* and is "founded on the broad equitable principle that where residue was limited to persons in succession, their successive enjoyment should be an enjoyment of the same fund."[184]

12.95 The rule applies when the residuary estate has been limited to persons in succession, and essentially provides that any funeral expenses, debts, liabilities or legacies be paid out of both *income and capital*. It is most simply illustrated by example. Consider a testator who leaves his entire estate of £100,000 to A for life remainder to B. Debts amount to £5,000. If interest is at three per cent and the debts are not paid until a year after death, the estate would have increased in value to £103,000. After deduction of debts from this figure the net estate is worth £98,000, which represents capital plus interest thereon at three per cent. This fund must now be apportioned. To do so it is necessary to ascertain X, where:

---

[178]S 39 of the 1955 Act, codifying the common law - see *National Assurance* v *Scott* [1909] 1 IR 325.
[179]See para 12.40 *supra*.
[180][1904] 1 IR 388.
[181]S 38(2) of 1925 Act.
[182](1867) LR 4 Eq 295.
[183]See para 12.49 *supra*.
[184]Per Sargeant J in *Re McEwen* [1913] 2 Ch 704, 713.

$$X \text{ plus } 3\% \text{ of } X \;=\; £98,000$$

$$\text{then } X \;=\; £95,146$$

Thus £95,146 represents capital, and £2,854 (£98,000 - £95,146) represents income (which goes to the tenant for life). The benefit which has accrued to the estate because the debts were not paid for a year is enjoyed by both the remainderman and the life tenant.

12.96   In view of the complicated accounting and administrative expense it is probably prudent expressly to exclude the operation of the rule. It should be remembered that simply excluding the rule in *Howe* v *Lord Dartmouth*[185] does not exclude the rule in *Allhusen* v *Whittell*.[186]

DISTRIBUTION OF THE ESTATE

Difficulties tracing beneficiaries

Advertising for claimants

12.97   It is a fundamental duty of personal representatives that they distribute the deceased's estate to the persons properly entitled under his will or the intestacy laws. It is therefore important that they protect themselves against liability in case they fail to do so;[187] for example, if they distribute in ignorance of a particular beneficiary. Under section 28 of the Trustee Act (NI) 1958[188] the personal representatives may give notice of their intention to distribute the estate and require any interested person to send particulars of his claim within a stated time, not being less than two months from the date of the notice. On the expiry of this period the personal representatives may distribute to the persons entitled having regard only to the claims of which they have notice, and they will not be liable to any person whose claim they did not have notice of at the time of the distribution. The section only affords protection to the personal representatives; the right of a disappointed beneficiary or creditor to follow the

---

[185]See para 12.50 *supra*.

[186]*Re Ullswater* [1952] Ch 105.

[187]This is particularly important following the recent significant change in the position regarding the liability of personal representatives when distributing property to which illegitimate persons may be entitled. By virtue of art 6 of the Family Law Reform (NI) Order 1977, special protection was given to personal representatives, empowering them to convey or distribute an estate to the beneficiaries without having ascertained the existence of any illegitimate children. This protection has now been abolished by the Children (NI) Order 1995 (Sch 6, para 3).

[188]In England, s 27 of the Trustee Act 1925.

estate into the hands of the person to whom it was distributed is expressly preserved.[189]

12.98 Notice must be by published advertisement - once in the Belfast Gazette and twice in each of any two daily newspapers printed and published in Northern Ireland, or if the property includes land, in any two newspapers circulating in the district in which the land is situated.[190] The two-month time limit runs from the publication of the last notice. These requirements must be followed precisely or the protection will be lost.[191]

12.99 The substance of the advertisement should be such as to "indicate to normal people that it is not merely the claims of creditors which are required to be sent in, but also those of beneficiaries".[192] In addition, the advertisements should be published as soon as possible after death.[193]

12.100 It must be stressed that section 28 of the Trustee Act (NI) 1958 does not operate mechanically and placing the advertisements does not absolve personal representatives in respect of claims of which they were aware[194] (even though the claimant did not respond to the notice). The section cannot be excluded by a contrary provision in the will.[195]

Benjamin order

12.101 A *Benjamin* order[196] is an order of the court authorising the personal representatives to distribute the estate on the basis of a particular assumption (eg as in *Re Benjamin* itself, that a beneficiary is dead).[197] Appropriate inquiries must be made before the court will grant an order; it is usual practice to advertise under section 28 of the Trustee Act (NI) 1958 first and on occasions the court may direct more extensive searches or advertisements.[198]

12.102 Personal representatives distributing on the basis of a *Benjamin* order are protected from any liability should the assumption transpire to be

---

[189]Trustee Act (NI) 1958, s 28(2)(a).
[190]S 28(1).
[191]*Stuart* v *Babington* (1891) 27 LR Ir 551 - notice twice in only one local paper.
[192]*Per* Danckwerts J in *Re Aldhous* [1955] 2 All ER 80 at 82.
[193]*Re Kay* [1897] 2 Ch 518, 522.
[194]*Re Beatty* (1892) 29 LR Ir 290.
[195]S 28(3).
[196]Which takes its name from the case *Re Benjamin* [1902] 1 Ch 723.
[197]For other assumptions see *Re Gess* [1942] Ch 37; *Hansell* v *Spink* [1943] Ch 396.
[198]Although there is no need to advertise where the evidence is irresistible - *Re Green's Will Trusts* [1985] 3 All ER 455.

inaccurate. However, a beneficiary who did not receive what he was entitled to can recover from any 'overpaid' recipients of the deceased's estate.

Power to appropriate

12.103 It is recognised that a beneficiary who, for example, has been given a pecuniary legacy may wish instead to take particular items of the same value from the deceased's estate. Thus section 37 of the 1955 Act[199] confers on personal representatives (both executors and administrators)[200] wide powers to appropriate any part[201] of the estate in the actual condition or state of investment thereof in or towards satisfaction of any legacy or interest or share in the estate.[202] Apart from one significant difference[203] this section corresponds broadly to section 41 of the English Administration of Estates Act 1925.

12.104 Section 37(6) of the 1955 Act allows a testator to extend this statutory power of appropriation by express provisions in his will. Sometimes, for example, a will may empower the personal representatives to appropriate property without obtaining the necessary consents or serving the requisite notices. In addition, the common law power of appropriation has been expressly preserved.[204] However, since this is so much narrower than that authorised by section 37, it is effectively redundant.[205]

Consequences of an appropriation

12.105 Where the personal representatives have properly exercised their power to appropriate, the beneficiary's interest is thereafter confined to the appropriated assets. The "property appropriated is taken by the legatee for better or worse",[206] so that the beneficiary gains from any subsequent accretion, but bears any subsequent loss.[207] All other assets of the estate are therefore freed for distribution to the remaining beneficiaries.

---

[199]Which applies whenever the deceased died - s 37(9).

[200]It was not entirely clear whether s 4 of the Law Reform (Miscellaneous Provisions) Act (NI) 1937, the predecessor of s 37, extended to *intestate* deaths. S 37(9) of the 1955 has confirmed that the section applies "whether the deceased died intestate or not".

[201]Although note the position with property which has been specifically bequeathed - see para 12.109 *post*.

[202]The wording is clearly wide enough to permit a personal representative to appropriate in satisfaction of his own share. Obviously in such a case caution should be exercised.

[203]See para 12.112 *post*.

[204]S 37(6).

[205]For the common law power see *Re Lepine* [1892] 1 Ch 210.

[206]Withers, *Reversions* (2nd ed) at p 26.

[207]*Ballard* v *Marsden* (1880) 14 Ch D 374; *Re Richardson* [1896] 1 Ch 512.

12.106 Once an appropriation is made it is binding on all persons interested in the estate[208] including those whose consent was not required.

12.107 There would be little point in appropriating property which the recipient would then have to realise, so any property duly appropriated under section 37 of the 1955 Act is thereafter deemed to be an authorised investment.[209] This, however, does not detract from the statutory duty which the personal representatives are under to have regard to the interests of everyone involved and by appropriating property of a hazardous nature they may be in breach of this duty.

Valuation of appropriated property
12.108 Property which is appropriated is valued at the time of the appropriation, not the time of the death.[210] In order to value any part of the estate with a view to appropriation, section 37(3) empowers the personal representatives to employ a duly qualified valuer, where necessary. Although this provision is merely permissive, it is submitted that the opinion of a qualified valuer should always be obtained; the personal representatives may end up committing a breach of their duty if they fail to do so.[211]

Property specifically bequeathed
12.109 Section 37(1)(a)(i) of the 1955 Act provides that no appropriation shall be made so as to affect prejudicially any specific bequest or devise. The consent of the specific legatee must therefore be obtained before property which has been specifically bequeathed can be appropriated.

Consents required
12.110 In most cases it will be necessary to obtain the consent of the beneficiary (or others on his behalf) before an appropriation can be made in his favour. The principles are as follows:

(a) Where the person in whose favour the appropriation is to be made is *sui juris* his consent alone is required.[212] Consider Abigail who leaves Beatrice a pecuniary legacy of £10,000 and the rest of her estate to Camilla. The estate includes an oil painting valued at £8,000. Provided that Beatrice consents, the painting can be appropriated to her in part satisfaction of her legacy and the balance (£2,000) paid in cash. Where the person in whose

---

[208]S 37(4).
[209]S 37(2).
[210]*Re Charteris* [1917] 2 Ch 379; *Re Collins* [1975] 1 WLR 309.
[211]See, eg *Re Brookes* [1914] 1 Ch 558.
[212]S 37(1)(b)(i).

favour the appropriation is to be made is an infant, the consent of his parent or guardian[213] is required and where he is of unsound mind, consent must be given by his controller.[214]

(b) Where an appropriation is being made in respect of any settled legacy, share or interest,[215] consent must first be obtained from either the trustee of the settlement (provided that he is not also the personal representative) or the person entitled to the income (provided, of course, that he is *sui juris*).[216]

It is not necessary to obtain the consent of any person who may come into existence after the time of the appropriation, or who cannot be found or ascertained at that time.[217]

Requirement to give notice to residuary legatees

12.111 In Northern Ireland notice of an intended appropriation must be served on all parties interested in the residuary estate.[218] For instance, in the above example notice of the appropriation of the oil painting would have to be served on Camilla. Note that it is merely *notice* which must be given; there is no requirement to actually obtain *consent*. Within six weeks of receiving such notice any person may apply to the court requesting a prohibition of the proposed appropriation.

12.112 In England there is no requirement under section 41 of the Administration of Estates Act 1925 to give notice to interested parties.

Matters influencing the exercise of the powers

12.113 The statutory power is exercisable in such manner as to the personal representatives seems "just and reasonable" according to the respective rights of the persons interested in the deceased's property.[219] In addition the personal

---

[213]In the absence of both, the court may grant consent on the application of his next friend - *ibid.*

[214]Although if no such controller has been appointed consent does not have to be obtained provided that the property to be appropriated is an investment authorised either by the general law or the will - s 37(1)(d).

[215]Defined in s 37(8) to include "any legacy, share or interest to which a person is not absolutely entitled in possession at the date of the appropriation, also an annuity."

[216]If, however, there is no trustee apart from the personal representative and the tenant for life is not *sui juris*, consent does not have to be obtained provided that the property to be appropriated is an investment authorised either by general law or by the will - s 37(1)(e).

[217]S 37(1). Although the personal representatives are under a duty to have regard to the rights of such persons when making an appropriation - s 37(5), see para 12.113 *post*.

[218]Except those who may come into existence after the time of the appropriation or who cannot be found or ascertained at that time.

[219]S 37(1).

representatives are required by virtue of section 37(5) of the 1955 Act, to have regard to the rights of persons not yet in existence or who cannot be found or ascertained or whose consent is not required.

Protection of purchasers

12.114 A purchaser who buys property from a beneficiary to whom it has been appropriated is protected by section 37(7) of the 1955 Act, provided that it was bought in good faith and for value. This provision deems the appropriation to have been made in accordance with the statutory requirements and consents.

Tax consequences

12.115 Personal representatives should always pay attention to the taxation implications of any proposed appropriation.[220]

Assents

12.116 It has already been noted that a beneficiary has no legal or equitable proprietary interest in the estate, at least until the residue has been ascertained. Technically an *assent* is merely an acknowledgment by the personal representatives that they do not require a particular asset for the payment of debts, and that it is therefore available for distribution to the persons entitled. An assent is thus sometimes described as "activating" the gift of property under the will or the share of the estate on an intestacy.[221] Following an assent the beneficiary's rights change; for example, once an executor has assented to a specific legacy the legatee may bring an action to recover possession of it.[222]

12.117 At common law there were no formal requirements for an assent of pure *personalty*,[223] a position which has not been altered by the Administration of Estates Act (NI) 1955. An assent of personalty may be in writing, but it can also be oral or simply inferred from conduct, such as the delivery of the property to the person entitled to it,[224] or the completion of the administration.[225]

---

[220]*Re Collard* [1961] Ch 293 at 302.

[221]Eg - "the will becomes operative so far as its dispositions ... are concerned only if and when the executor assents to those dispositions" (*Attenborough v Solomon* [1913] AC 76 at 82).

[222]*Stevenson* v *Mayor of Liverpool* (1874) LR 10 QB 81; *Re West* [1909] 2 Ch 180; *Re Culverhouse* [1896] 2 Ch 251.

[223]Ie personalty other than leaseholds. Although note that certain types of personal property, such as company shares, are not transferred by assent but require greater formality. This is considered at para 12.128 *post*. If there has been an assent of shares, without more, the personal representative holds the legal title as trustee for the beneficiary until it is properly transferred - see *Re Grosvenor* [1916] 2 Ch 375.

[224]*Quinton* v *Frith* (1868) Ir 2 Eq 494.

[225]*Attenborough* v *Solomon* [1913] AC 76.

In each case the question of whether there has been an assent is one of fact on the particular circumstances.[226] However, disputes may arise and notwithstanding the absence of formal requirements it is prudent that all assents be documented in some manner.

12.118 In contrast, an assent of *land* must be *in writing*, a requirement introduced by the 1955 Act. It is this written instrument relating to transfers of land by the personal representatives which is generally meant by the term "assent".

Assent in respect of land
12.119 The statutory power of executors and administrators to transfer an estate or interest in land by means of an assent is contained in section 34(2) of the 1955 Act.[227]

> "Without prejudice to any other power conferred by this Act on personal representatives[228] with respect to any land[229] of a testator or intestate, the personal representatives may execute an assent vesting any estate or interest in such land in *the person entitled* thereto ...[Emphasis added]."

It is further provided by section 34(4) that "an assent not in writing shall not be effectual to pass *any* estate or interest in land [emphasis added]". The writing requirement therefore extends to both legal *and equitable* interests in land. In this respect it is wider than the corresponding English provision which applies to *legal* interests only.[230]

The phrase "the person entitled" includes:

    (a)   Persons entitled beneficially to an interest in the the deceased's estate "whether by devise, bequest,

---

[226]*IRC* v *Smith* [1930] 1 KB 713.

[227]In England, s 36(1) of the Administration of Estates Act 1925.

[228]Note that the power is limited to personal representatives and does not extend to trustees.

[229]This includes land to which the testator or intestate was entitled or over which the testator exercised a general power of appointment by will. Compare the English provision, s 36(1) of the 1925 Act which contains the additional words "... and which devolved upon the personal representatives". Does the Northern Ireland provision thus extend to land which is conveyed to the personal representatives after the deceased's death? See *Re Stirrup's Contract* [1961] 1 WLR 449.

[230]S 36 of the Administration of Estates Act 1925.

devolution,[231] appropriation *or otherwise* [Emphasis added]".

(b)   A personal representative who is himself entitled beneficially.

(c)   The trustees or the personal representative of any other person. Thus a vesting assent can be made in favour of the personal representative(s) of a beneficiary who was entitled under the deceased's will or intestacy but who died before distribution.

The scope of the word "otherwise" in (a) above has been the subject of some debate. It would appear to authorise an assent *in favour of a purchaser* and the case *GHR Co Ltd v IRC*[232] has confirmed that an assent can be used to make title where the testator had sold his property but died before he executed a conveyance. However, there has as yet been no authority that an assent can be effective in favour of a purchaser from a beneficiary and it is suggested that an assent should not be used in such circumstances.

12.120 A written assent is necessary even when land is being transferred to the personal representatives in a different capacity, as for example, where the personal representative is entitled as a beneficiary. This remains the case even if this new capacity is still to hold the bare legal title (eg personal representatives becoming *trustees* of the land).[233]

12.121 It was noted earlier that where there are two or more personal representatives they must all[234] exercise the power to assent in respect of land, unless the leave of the court has been obtained.[235]

---

[231]The word "devolution" covers a beneficiary entitled under the intestacy code. The previous legislation, s 3 of the Law Reform (Miscellaneous Provisions) Act (NI) 1937 authorised personal representatives to assent only where there was a devise by will. S 34 of the 1955 Act leaves the position in no doubt - and, as has been seen, refers throughout to the "testator *or the intestate*".

[232][1943] KB 303.

[233]*Re King's Will Trusts* [1964] Ch 542. Prior to this decision "it was fairly generally thought by conveyancers that, where the legal estate in land had become vested in a person beneficially entitled to that land but had become so vested in some capacity ... other than the capacity of beneficial owner, no assent in writing was necessary to clothe that person with the legal estate in his capacity as beneficial owner." (*Per* Buckley LJ in *Re Edwards' Will Trusts* [1982] Ch 30 at 33). For criticisms of the position after *Re King*, see Garner (1964) Conv 28 and Walker (1964) 80 LQR 328.

[234]This does not include non-proving executors who have reserved the right to act - s 34(6)(a) of the 1955 Act.

[235]1955 Act, s 34(6).

12.122 Assents may be made subject to a charge for the payment of any money which the personal representatives are liable to pay, in which case the personal representatives cease thereafter to be liable in respect of the land.[236] Where a personal representative is assenting under section 34 of the 1955 Act he gives the same covenants as if he were executing a conveyance "as personal representative", unless the assent provides otherwise.[237]

12.123 The actual form of a written assent in respect of land depends upon whether the land is registered or not. Section 35 of the 1955 Act provides that an assent in respect of *unregistered* land must be signed by the personal representatives[238] but otherwise no particular form is prescribed.[239] It does not have to be by *deed*. However, it is deemed for the purposes of registration in the Registry of Deeds to be a conveyance from the personal representatives to the beneficiary[240] and is thus registrable. Moreover, the beneficiaries are entitled to require the personal representatives to register the assent, although the costs must be borne by the beneficiaries themselves.[241] Obviously beneficiaries would be well advised to seek registration and thus establish their priority.[242]

12.124 An assent in respect of *registered* land[243] must be in the form prescribed by the Land Registration Rules.[244] This is now Form 17 in all cases.[245]

---

[236]If an assent is made subject to such a charge all liabilities of the personal representatives in respect of the land shall cease, except as regards acts done before the assent.

[237]These are contained in s 7(1) of the Conveyancing Act 1881 and include a covenant that there are no incumbrances. See further Wylie, *Irish Conveyancing Law* (1978) p 823.

[238]S 35(1)(b).

[239]In England s 36 of the 1925 Act requires the person in whose favour the assent is made to be named. No corresponding provision exists in Northern Ireland but obviously if this is unclear the assent will be void for uncertainty.

[240]S 35(1)(c).

[241]S 35(2).

[242]Note that an assent of unregistered land is deemed, unless there is a contrary intention, to relate back to the death of the deceased for the purposes of establishing the title of a beneficiary to intervening rents and profits - s 35(1)(e).

[243]On the death of a registered owner of land his personal representatives alone are recognised by the Registrar as having any right to deal with the registered land (Land Registration Act (NI) 1970, Sch 4, para 1). Production of an assent or transfer in the prescribed form from them authorises the Registrar to register the person named in the assent or transfer as owner (Sch 4, para 4).

[244]NI SR 1994 No 424, r 42.

[245]R 55 of the earlier rules (NI SR 1977/154) provided different forms for testate and intestate transmissions.

Form 17 which includes a certificate of identity should be accompanied by a certified copy of the grant of representation.

It should be remembered that since Land Registry staff are no longer required to check that the terms of an assent are correct, the personal representative and his solicitor should take the utmost care to ensure that the estate is being administered correctly.

Protection of a purchaser
12.125 Section 35(3) of the 1955 Act expressly provides that an assent of unregistered land by the personal representative(s) is, in favour of a purchaser, "*sufficient*" evidence that the person in whose favour it is given is the person entitled. The practical utility of this provision is questionable. The first observation which must be made is that it is something of a misfit. It mirrors the English provision[246] which was designed to complement the scheme of the 1925 legislation in keeping the trust of a will off the title - which, of course, is not applicable to this jurisdiction. Secondly "sufficient" does *not* mean "conclusive",[247] but rather sufficient evidence until, on a proper investigation by the purchaser of the vendor's title, the contrary is shown. While a purchaser is not expected to examine every aspect of an administration to ensure that it is in order[248] he would be advised to investigate the title without relying too heavily on section 35(3).

Personal representatives reluctant to assent
12.126 If, after one year from the deceased's death, the personal representatives have failed on request to execute an assent in favour of the person entitled, that person may apply to the court under section 34(3) of the 1955 Act. The court may, if it thinks fit and following notice to the personal representatives, order the transfer to be made. Thereafter if the personal representatives have still not assented the court can make an order vesting the land in the person entitled.[249] In addition, the court always has an inherent

---

[246]1925 Act, s 36(7).

[247]*Re Duce and Boots' Cash Chemists (Southern) Ltd's Contract* [1937] Ch 642 - a purchaser who was in possession of information indicating that the assent or conveyance was given or made to the wrong person is not protected.

[248]And note also the protection in s 33(2) - see para 12.40 *supra*.

[249]In certain circumstances this procedure can be short-circuited for registered land - Sch 4, para 5 to the Land Registration Act (NI) 1970 empowers the court to dispense with the requirement to give notice to the personal representatives provided that it is satisfied that at least six years have elapsed since the death of the deceased registered owner and that the personal representatives are dead or out of the jurisdiction.

jursidiction to compel personal representatives to transfer property where they are unreasonably withholding assent.[250]

Other modes of transfer

12.127 We have seen that the transmission of land must be by assent or transfer in writing. The formalities which must be observed when transferring other commodities depends upon the nature of the asset involved; for example, accounts in building societies are usually transferred by completion of the prescribed transfer forms.

Company shares[251]

12.128 Shares in a United Kingdom company are not transferable by assent but by the completion by the personal representatives of the appropriate stock transfer form. This form is then lodged, together with the share certificates and the grant of representation, with the company's registrar for registration of the change of ownership and for the issue of the new share certificate(s).

12.129 The company's memorandum and articles of association must be consulted[252] since any restrictions therein are binding on the personal representatives.[253] For example, the articles of a family company will frequently limit the persons who may become shareholders. By contrast, shares in a publicly-quoted company are usually[254] transferable in writing without restriction.[255]

Some difficulties where there are infant beneficiaries

12.130 Infant beneficiaries may potentially present difficulties. Prior to the enactment of the 1955 Act these were particularly acute and often personal representatives had no alternative but to pay the infant's share into court or wait until he reached majority.[256] Section 38 of this Act attempts to circumvent these problems by empowering the personal representatives to appoint trustees for property to which an infant is *absolutely* entitled[257] under a will or an

---

[250]*Martin* v *Wilson* [1913] 1 IR 470.

[251]Shares in companies which are registered outside the UK are governed by the law of the jurisdiction in which the company is registered and are beyond the scope of this book.

[252]This should also have been done when the will was being drafted!

[253]*Roberts* v *Letter "T" Estates* [1961] AC 795.

[254]But not always, eg Rolls Royce and P & O.

[255]Companies (NI) Order 1986, art 193.

[256]See, eg *McCreight* v *McCreight* (1849) 13 Ir Eq R 314; *Crawford* v *Carlin* [1904] 4 NIJR 150.

[257]Eg it does not extend to cases where the entitlement is merely contingent.

intestacy.[258] Once such property has been vested in the trustees the personal representatives are discharged from all further liability.[259] It should be noted that there must be at least *two* trustees - even when one is a trust corporation.[260] The personal representatives are not precluded from appointing themselves.[261]

12.131 The personal representatives or trustees appointed by them under section 38 are deemed to be trustees for the purposes of sections 42 and 43 of the Conveyancing Act 1881, as amended by section 32 of Trustee Act (NI) 1958.[262] These provisions confer wide powers of management on the trustees during an infant's minority, including the power to apply income for maintenance, education or benefit. In addition, and without prejudice to these powers, it is expressly provided that the personal representatives or the trustees appointed by them, may apply up to half of the capital of any infant's share for his advancement or benefit in such manner as they in their absolute discretion think fit.[263]

12.132 The sale by an infant of land in which he has an interest in possession is governed by sections 59 and 60 of the Settled Land Act 1882. It will be recalled that these provisions operate by deeming the land to be "settled land" within the terms of the 1882 Act and the infant the tenant for life. The trustees can exercise on behalf of the infant all the powers[264] which would otherwise be vested in the tenant for life. These provisions also apply when an infant is selling land which he *inherited* - whether by will or following an intestacy.[265] The personal representatives[266] or, where they have exercised their powers under section 38 of the 1955 Act, the trustees appointed by them, are deemed to be the "trustees of the settlement".

---

[258]S 38(1). This is of much wider application than the corresponding English provision, s 42 of the 1925 Act, because in England infants do not generally take an absolute interest on intestacy.

[259]S 38(2).

[260]In England a trust corporation can act alone - 1925 Act, s 42(1).

[261]*Re Sampson* [1906] 1 Ch 435; *Re Power* [1951] 1 All ER 932.

[262]Ss 69 and 70(2).

[263]S 38(5) as extended by s 33 of the Trustee Act (NI) 1958.

[264]Most importantly, of course, to sell the land to a purchaser free from encumbrances (which then attach to the sale proceeds).

[265]S 2 of the Settled Land Act 1882 referred to an interest arising "under an instrument", raising doubts that it did not extend to intestacy. S 38(3) of the 1955 Act has since confirmed that it does.

[266]Provided that there is more than one - under the Settled Land Act there must be at least two trustees to give a valid receipt.

Operation of the Apportionment Act 1870

12.133 Income which arises from a specific gift in a will (eg dividends from shares, rents from land) entirely in respect of a period *after* the testator's death accrues to the recipient of that gift. For example, if Tom leaves his shares to Maud and the residue of his estate to Mildred and a dividend which relates to the period after death is declared, Maud is entitled to it. If, however, the dividend relates entirely to the period before Tom's death (even though it is not declared until afterwards) it forms part of Tom's residuary estate and passes to Mildred.[267] Where, however, the dividend relates to a period partly before but partly after death, it must be apportioned in accordance with section 2 of the Apportionment Act 1870,[268] unless this enactment has been expressly excluded. Section 2 provides:

> "All rents, annuities, dividends, and other periodical payments in the nature of income ... shall, like interest on money lent, be considered as accruing from day to day, and shall be apportionable in respect of time accordingly."

Thus if a dividend is declared on Tom's shares in respect of a period which overlaps the time of his death, and the Apportionment Act has not been excluded,[269] that dividend must be apportioned on a daily basis. The part which relates to the time before death forms part of the capital of the estate and falls into residue; the part which relates to the time thereafter goes to Maud, the legatee. If the Act has been excluded, or if it is inapplicable, the specific legatee is entitled to the entire income including that accruing before death.

12.134 The Apportionment Act applies to most income of a continuing nature (dividends, rent, interest etc). However, it does not apply to the profits of the testator's business, whether he was a sole proprietor or was carrying on business in partnership, since these are considered to accrue entirely on the final day of the period for which they are declared. Therefore if a testator bequeaths his business to Maud, and his residue to Mildred, Maud is entitled to any profits arising after his death and there is no element of apportionment.

---

[267]*Lock* v *Venables* (1860) 27 Beav 598.

[268]*Re Edwards* [1918] 1 Ch 142.

[269]S 7 of the 1870 Act provides for exclusion of apportionment. This can be by an express clause to that effect in the will, or by implication - *Re Lysaght* [1898] 1 Ch 115.

REMUNERATION OF PERSONAL REPRESENTATIVES

12.135 The general rule is that a personal representative, being in a fiduciary position, is not entitled to any remuneration for the work which he does in connection with the administration of the estate.[270] He is, however, entitled to reimbursement from the estate of any out-of-pocket expenses which he properly incurred in the course of his office.[271]

Obviously most professional executors and administrators would be unwilling to provide their services gratuitously and there are a number of exceptions to the general rule.

Authority in the will

Legacy in favour of an executor
12.136 A testator may reward his executor(s) with a legacy. There is a rebuttable presumption that any legacy given to an executor is conditional upon him accepting office,[272] so in order to avoid confusion the will should make it clear whether the legacy is conditional (ie only payable if the executor acts) or unconditional (payable independent of accepting office).

It should be remembered that a legacy to an executor is treated as any other pecuniary legacy and there is the risk that the estate will not be sufficiently solvent to meet it in full (or indeed even at all).

Charging clause
12.137 Where a professional executor is to act it is common for the will to contain an express clause permitting him to charge. Care must be taken when drafting such a clause to ensure that it is sufficiently wide to allow a professional executor to charge for *all* services rendered in the administration of the estate, and not just those which a qualified or professional person is required to do.[273]

A charging clause is construed as a legacy. This has two important practical implications:

---

[270]*Robinson v Pett* (1734) 3 P Wms 249.
[271]*Re Grimthorpe* [1958] Ch 615.
[272]*Re Appleton* (1885) 29 Ch D 893.
[273]*Re Chalinder and Herington* [1907] 1 Ch 58.

(a)   The remuneration will fail where the executor (or his spouse) also witnesses the will, [274] and;

(b)   There is a risk that the estate will not contain sufficient assets to pay the amount due under the charging clause which rates as any other pecuniary legacy.[275]

Authority from beneficiaries

12.138 Where all the beneficiaries entitled under the will or the distribution on intestacy are *sui juris* they may agree to award remuneration to the personal representative(s). If minors or persons of unsound mind are involved, some or all of the adult beneficiaries may be willing to authorise payment out of their own share of the estate.

Authority from the court

12.139 The court always has an inherent jurisdiction to authorise reasonable remuneration to personal representatives[276] and, unlike payments authorised by the will, such authorisation is binding on the creditors of the estate.[277] However, the court will not exercise its powers lightly.[278]

Under the rule in *Cradock* v *Piper*

12.140 Under the anomalous rule in *Cradock* v *Piper*[279] a personal representative who is a solicitor is entitled to charge in respect of litigation done on behalf of himself and a co-representative. The rule does not extend to non-litigious work and its scope is therefore of relatively narrow ambit.

LIABILITY OF THE PERSONAL REPRESENTATIVES

12.141 This chapter concludes with a brief examination of the principles which govern the liability of the personal representatives during the course of the administration of the estate. Most aspects of this topic have warranted some consideration earlier in this chapter, but it was thought appropriate to bring all these strands together by way of an overview.

---

[274]Art 8 of the Wills and Administration Preceedings (NI) Order 1994 - see para 3.43 *supra*. This is unless the permission of the beneficiaries is obtained.

[275]*Re White* [1898] 1 Ch 297.

[276]First exercised in *Brocksopp* v *Barnes* (1820) 5 Madd 90.

[277]See *Re Duke of Norfolk's Trusts* [1982] Ch 61 in which this power was extensively reviewed by the English Court of Appeal.

[278]See the dictum of Upjohn J in *Re Worthington* [1954] 1 WLR 526 at 530.

[279](1850) 1 Mac & G 664.

Law Reform (Miscellaneous Provisions) Act (NI) 1937

12.142 By virtue of the Law Reform (Miscellaneous Provisions) Act (NI) 1937 the personal representatives inherit most of the liabilities incurred by the deceased during his lifetime.[280] This liability is *representative* rather than personal and is met entirely out of the assets of the estate.

Difference between personal and representative liability

12.143 The personal representatives are *personally* liable for any contracts which they enter into during the course of the administration. If, however, they have acted properly and within the scope of their authority they will be indemnified out of the estate.[281] This concept has already been illustrated in connection with a personal representative carrying on the deceased's business.[282] It should be remembered that if expenditure incurred by the personal representatives was unauthorised they are liable to make it good out of their own pockets.

Leases

12.144 Leases warrant special consideration. A distinction must be made between the representative liability and the personal liability of the personal representative, although, as shall be seen, it is of less practical significance in Northern Ireland.

12.145 When a leasehold estate devolves upon the personal representatives they become liable, in their representative capacity, for the payment of rent and for any breaches of covenant. This liability is met entirely out of the assets of the estate. If they then actually take possession of the demised property, they may be personally liable as an assignee under the doctrine of privity of estate.

12.146 A measure of statutory protection is afforded to personal representatives who are liable for rent or other covenants under a lease by section 27(1) of the Trustee Act (NI) 1958. This provision extends to both representative and *personal* liability, and is therefore wider than its English counterpart, section 26(1) of the Trustee Act 1925, which only applies where a personal representative is liable "as such", that is, to representative liability alone. By virtue of section 27 a personal representative who has satisfied all the existing liabilities, made provision by way of a fund to meet any future claims in respect of agreed fixed sums to be laid out on the property, if any, and

---

[280]See para 12.32 *supra*.
[281]Even if the estate is insolvent these will take priority as "administration expenses" - see para 12.69 *supra*.
[282]See para 12.36 *supra*.

assigned the lease to a purchaser or the person entitled to it, can safely distribute the residue of the estate without fear of liability under the lease.[283]

Devastavit

12.147 Personal representatives are liable in *devastavit*[284] where their failure to administer the estate properly in accordance with law has caused a pecuniary loss to the estate. Examples of *devastavit* mentioned earlier in this chapter include the personal representatives causing loss while carrying on the deceased's business without authority; by not paying the creditors in the correct order; by misapplying the estate in an unreasonably expensive funeral or by paying a debt which has become statute-barred.

Breach of trust

12.148 Since the personal representatives occupy a fiduciary position they may also be liable for breach of trust. There is considerable overlap between this and *devastavit* and the same behaviour can amount to both a breach of trust and a *devastavit*. However, breach of trust extends to accounting for a *profit* made from the estate and is therefore wider than *devastavit*. The standard works on trusts should be consulted.

---

[283]Compare England where, as has been noted, s 26 of the 1925 Act does not extend to personal liability. There personal representatives would be advised to retain a fund to meet any further liability. This fund would then be transferred to the residuary beneficiaries when all potential claims are statute-barred - see *Re Lewis, Jennings v Hemsley* [1939] Ch 232.

[284]Literally, the wasting of the estate.

APPENDIX A

Note: completely new provisions are in bold; provisions which amend the former position are marked with an asterisk (*). Additions and amendments are marked with the following symbols:

Ω   amendments etc only apply to wills made on or after 1 January 1995

amendments etc only apply to wills of testators who died on or after 1 January 1995

■   amendments etc apply whenever will made

"1837 Act" refers to Wills Act 1837.

Provision of 1994 Order	Description in Brief	Previous legislative provision, if any	Equivalent English provision, if any	Further Ref. Para No.
ARTICLE				
3	power to dispose of estate by will	s3 of 1837 Act	s3 of 1837 Act	1.01
4(1)	minors cannot generally make a will	s7 of 1837 Act as amended by s2(1)(a) Age of Majority Act (NI) 1969	s7 of 1837 Act as amended by s3(1)(a) Family Law Reform Act 1969	2.03 - 2.05
4(3)Ω	**Married minors power to make will**	NONE	NONE	2.05
5* Ω	Formalities for execution	s9 of 1837 Act as amended by s1 of Wills Act Amendment Act 1852	s9 of 1837 Act as amended by s17 of Administration of Justice Act 1982	3.04 - 3.55
6	Power of appointment of will	s10 of 1837 Act	s10 of 1837 Act	
7	Incompetency of witnesses	s14 of 1837 Act	s14 of 1837 Act	
8(1)	Gift to witness or his spouse void	s15 of 1837 Act	s15 of 1837 Act	3.43 - 3.47, 3.76, 7.86, 12.137

Provision of 1994 Order	Description in Brief	Previous legislative provision, if any	Equivalent English provision, if any	Further Ref. Para No.
ARTICLE				
8(2)	Interested witness still capable of giving evidence	s15 of 1837 Act	s15 of 1837 Act	3.45
8(3) #	**Supernumerary Witnesses**	NONE	**s1 of Wills Act 1968**	3.52
9	Creditor witness	s16 of 1837 Act	s16 of 1837 Act	
10	Executor witness	s17 of 1837 Act	s17 of 1837 Act	
11	Alteration of a Will	s21 of 1837 Act	s21 of 1837 Act	3.75, 4.39 - 4.66
12(1)	Will revoked by marriage	s18 of 1837 Act	s18 of 1837 Act	3.74, 4.05, 4.10
12(2) * ■	Exception relating to powers of appointment	s18 of 1837 Act	s18 of 1837 Act	4.22 - 4.33
12(3) * Ω	Wills in expectation of marriage	s1 of Wills Act (Amendment) Act (NI) 1954	s177 of Law of Property Act 1925	4.10 - 4.16
12(4) Ω	**Gifts in expectation of marriage**	NONE	**s177 of Law of Property Act 1925 as amended by s18(1) of 1982 Act**	4.10 - 4.17
13 #	**Termination of marriage**	NONE	**s4 of Law Reform (Succession) Act 1995**	6.84, 7.51 - 7.59, 9.40
14(1)	Methods of revocation	ss18 and 20 of 1837 Act	ss18 and 20 of 1837 Act	4.02, 4.32, 4.45
14(2)	No revocation presumed by changed circumstances	s19 of 1837 Act	s19 of 1837 Act	4.46

Provision of 1994 Order	Description in Brief	Previous legislative provision, if any	Equivalent English provision, if any	Further Ref. Para No.
ARTICLE				
15	Revival	s22 of 1837 Act	ss22 of 1837 Act	4.68 - 4.77
16	Effect of re-execution of codicil	s34 of 1837 Act	s34 of 1837 Act	4.76
17	Will speaks from death	s24 of 1837 Act	s24 of 1837 Act	5.11
18 * #	Fee simple passes	s28 of 1837 Act	s28 of 1837 Act	5.17
19	Failure into residue	s25 of 1837 Act	s25 of 1837 Act	
20	Property subject to a general power	s27 of 1837 Act	s27 of 1837 Act	5.19 - 5.20, 12.78
21 * #	Gifts carrying intermediate income	NONE (authorities non-statutory)	s175 of Law of Property Act 1925	
22 * #	Statutory exception to lapse	s33 of 1837 Act	s33 of 1837 Act as amended by s19 of Administration of Justice Act 1982	7.39 - 7.47, 10.12
23 #	**Presumption spouse takes absolute gift**	NONE	**s22 of Administration of Justice Act 1982**	5.18
24 #	**Abolition of rule in** *Lawes* v *Bennett*	NONE	NONE	7.70
25 #	**Extrinsic evidence to aid construction**	NONE	**s21 of Administration of Justice Act 1982**	5.33 - 5.39, 9.13
26 Ω	**Meaning of certain words**	None, although see s1 of 1837 Act		5.32

Provision of 1994 Order	Description in Brief	Previous legislative provision, if any	Equivalent English provision, if any	Further Ref. Para No.
ARTICLE				
27	Failure of Issue	S29 of 1837 Act	s29 of 1837 Act	5.22
28 ■	**law leans against intestacy**	**NONE**	**NONE**	5.10, 5.16
29 #	**Rectification of Wills**	**NONE**	**s20 of Administration of Justice Act 1982**	2.47 - 2.49
30 ■	**Commorientes of Executors**	**NONE**	**NONE**	9.19

NOTE: Articles 32-35 contain various powers of the High Court relating to the administration of estates and trusts. These correspond to sections 47-50 of the Administration of Justice Act 1985 and are not yet effective.

APPENDIX B

This is designed as a quick reference table. For further detail see Table at page 115.

INTESTACY RIGHTS OF SURVIVING SPOUSE

This is designed as a quick reference table. For further detail see Table at page 115.

SPOUSE AND ISSUE

Personal chattels plus whole of remaining estate where net value of remaining estate is not greater than that appearing in Column 2. Where it exceeds that amount, then that amount plus interest thereon and a half or one-third share of residue.

SPOUSE - NO ISSUE (But other near relatives)

Person chattels plus whole of remaining estate where net value of remaining estate is not greater than that appearing in Column 3. Where it exceeds that amount, then that amount plus interest thereon and a half share of residue.

DATE	SPOUSE AND ISSUE	SPOUSE - NO ISSUE	REFERENCE
1.1.56	£1,500	£5,000	S 7 Administration of Estates Act (NI) 1955
20.3.70	£2,250	£7,500	Family Provision Act(Northern Ireland) 1969
02.8.73	£7,500	£20,000	Art 2 Administration of Estates (Rights of Surviving Spouse) Order (NI) 1973
01.01.77	£25,000	£55,000	Art 2 Administration of Estates (Rights of Surviving Spouse) Order (NI) 1977
01.6.81	£40,000	£85,000	Art 2 Administration of Estates (Rights of Surviving Spouse) Order (NI) 1981
01.12.87	£75,000	£125,000	Art 2 Administration of Estates (Rights of Surviving Spouse) Order (NI) 1987
01.01.94	£125,000	£200,000	Art 2 Administration of Estates (Rights of Surviving Spouse) Order (NI) 1993

APPENDIX C

ATTESTATION CLAUSES

Standard Clause

Long form:
Signed and acknowledged by the said testator as and for his last will in the presence of us both present at the same time who at his request in his presence and in the presence of each other have hereunto subscribed our names as witnesses.

Short form:
Signed by the testator in our joint presence and then by us in his.

Attestation clause to a codicil:

Signed and acknowledged by the said testator as a codicil to his will made on the ... day of .... 19.. in the presence of us both present at the same time who at his request in his presence and in the presence of each other have hereunto subscribed our names as witnesses.

Will which has been altered before it was executed:

Signed and acknowledged by the said testator as and for his last will in the presence of us both present at the same time who at his request in his presence and in the presence of each other have hereunto subscribed our names as witnesses the alteration [or erasure or interlineation] on page ....hereof having been made previously hereto.

Will in which testator has made his signature by way of a mark because he was unable to write:

Signed and acknowledged by the said testator with his mark (he being unable to read or write) as and for his last will (the same having been previously read over to him by [name] [me the undersigned - name] when he seemed thoroughly to understand the same) in the presence of us both present at the same time who at his request in his presence and in the presence of each other have hereunto subscribed our names as witnesses.

Will in which testator directs another to make his signature:

Signed by [name of person signing] with the name of the above-named [testator] as and for his last will (the same having been previously read over to him by [name] [me the under signed - name] when he seemed thoroughly to understand the same) in his presence and by his direction and in the presence of us both present at the same time who at his request in the presence of him and of each other have hereunto subscribed our names as witnesses.

Testator blind:

This will having first been read over to the above-named [testator] (who is blind) [in our presence] by me the under signed [name] in the presence also of me the undersigned [name] when the said [testator] appeared thoroughly to understand the same and to approve the contents thereof was signed by the said [testator] as and for his last will in the presence of us present at the same time who at his request in his presence and in the presence of each other have hereunto subscribed our names as witnesses.

APPENDIX D

VOID AND VOIDABLE MARRIAGES

Void

The following marriages celebrated on or after 18 April 1979 are void (article 13 of the Matrimonial Causes (NI) Order 1979):

- where the parties are within the prohibited degrees of relationship;
- where one or more of the parties is under the age of marriage;
- if there is non-compliance with the legal formalities required for the formation of marriage;
- if either of the parties is already lawfully married;
- if the parties are not respectively male and female;
- in the case of a polygamous marriage entered into outside Northern Ireland, one of the parties was at the time domiciled in Northern Ireland.

Voidable

The following marriages celebrated on or after 18 April 1979 are voidable (article 14 of the Matrimonial Causes (NI) Order 1978);

- marriages which are unconsummated owing either to the incapacity of either party to consummate them or to the wilful refusal of the respondent to do so;
- marriages in which either party did not consent whether in consequence of duress, mistake, unsoundness of mind or otherwise;
- marriages where, although the party was capable of giving consent he or she was suffering from a mental disorder within the meaning of the Mental Health (NI) Order 1986 of such a kind or such an extent to be unfitted for marriage;
- if at the time of the marriage the respondent was either suffering from venereal disease in a communicable form or was pregnant by some person other than the petitioner.

Note that in the last instance the petitioner must have been ignorant of the facts at the time of the marriage.

APPENDIX E

NOTICE OF APPLICATION

IN THE HIGH COURT OF JUSTICE IN NORTHERN IRELAND

(PROBATE)

CHANCERY FAMILY DIVISION

PROBATE AND MATRIMONIAL OFFICE

TO THE MASTER OF PROBATE AND MATRIMONIAL OFFICE

TAKE NOTICE that I/we apply for Grant* ....

in the Estate of ....

late of ....

County of ...., deceased,

who died on the .... day of ...., 19........,

at ....

on behalf of† ....

....

....

Dated this   day of   **19**

Filed by ....*Solicitor(s)*

....Belfast.

* Describe whether Probate, Administration Intestate, or Administration Will annexed.

⁺ State interest of Applications for such Grant (as Executor, Residuary Legate or Next-of-kin).

OATH FOR EXECUTOR

IN THE HIGH COURT OF JUSTICE IN NORTHERN IRELAND

FAMILY DIVISION
PROBATE AND MATRIMONIAL OFFICE

In the Estate of   I/We

(a) Place of abode and description of Deponent/s

(b) The Commissioner and the Deponent to put their initials only on the Will and Codicils.

of (a)

(c) If there be codicils specify the number

Deceased   in the County of

(d) Place of abode and description of Testator.

Aged 18 years and upwards, make oath and say that   believe the paper writing hereunto annexed and marked by (b)   to contain the true and original last Will (c)
of
late of (d)

(e) The relationship of the Executor to the deceased (if any), e.g., I am a lawful brother of the said Testator.

in the County of   Deceased
that same was made by the said   after attaining
the full age of eighteen years, and that   he did not intermarry with any person after the making of same, that (e)

(f) (1) that I am the sole Executor or one of the Executors saving the rights of A.B., etc.

(f)   therein named
that I/we will

     (i)   collect and get in and administer all the estate of the said deceased according to law;

(2) That we are the Executors or two of the Executors, saving, etc., or the other Executors having renounced. The renunciation should be marked as an exhibit by the Deponent.

     (ii)   when required to do so by the High Court, exhibit on oath in the High Court a full inventory of the estate and when so required render an account of the administration of the estate to the High Court;

     (iii)   when required to do so by the High Court, deliver up the grant of representation to that Court.

that the

(3) That I am the surviving executor, or that we are the surviving Executors.

Testat   died at
domiciled in (g)   on the   day of   19

(g) State country of domicile

aged
And I/we further make Oath and say that to the best of My/our knowledge, information and belief the gross estate passing under the grant does not exceed / amounts to *£

*Delete as appropriate.

and that the net estate does not exceed / amounts to *£
and that this is not a case in which an Inland Revenue Account is required to be delivered*

Signed ....

Filed by .... Solicitor(s)

....

....Belfast

Sworn at
in the County of
this   day of   19
by the said

before me, a Commissioner / Solicitor Empowered to Administer Oaths for the Supreme Court of Judicature in Northern Ireland in and for said County.

.... Commissioner / Solicitor

OATH FOR ADMINISTRATOR
IN THE HIGH COURT OF JUSTICE IN NORTHERN IRELAND

FAMILY DIVISION
PROBATE AND MATRIMONIAL OFFICE

In the Estate of   I(a)

of

(a) Insert the
name, residence
and title or
addition of the
Deponent.

Deceased.   in the County of

aged 18 years and upwards, make Oath and

say that

(b) Place of   late of (b)
abode and
description of   in the County of
Intestate.
                      Deceased, died Intestate (c)

(c) State here
whether Bachelor,
etc.; and clear of
all other Parties
entitled to Grant
in priority to Ap-
plicant, and state
capacity in which
Applicant seeks
Administration.

that I/we will

  (i) collect and get in and administer all the estate of the said deceased according to law;

  (ii) when required to do so by the High Court, exhibit on oath in the High Court a full
inventory of the estate and when so required render an account of the administration
of the estate to the High Court;

  (iii) when required to do so by the High Court, deliver up the grant of representation to
that Court.

that the deceased died at

domiciled in (d)   on the   day of   19

(d) State country   aged
of domicile.
                         And I Further make Oath and say that to the best of my knowledge, information and belief
(e) Here state
gross amount of   the gross estate passing under the grant does not exceed/amounts to *£
Assets without
any deductions   and that the net estate does not exceed/amounts to *£
for Debts, etc.

Delete as   and that this is not a case in which an Inland Revenue Account is required to be delivered
appropriate.

                                Sworn at

                                in the County of

                                this   day of   19

Signed...   by the said

Filed by .... Solicitor (s)

                                before me, a Commissioner/Solicitor Em-

....   powered to Administer Oaths for the Supreme

                                Court of Judicature in Northern Ireland in and

....Belfast   for said County.

                       .... Commissioner/Solicitor

APPENDIX F

INHERITANCE (PROVISION FOR FAMILY AND DEPENDANTS) (NI) ORDER 1979

Interpretation

2.-(2) In this Order

"child" includes an illegitimate or adopted child and a child en ventre sa mère at the death of the deceased;

"former wife" or "former husband" means a person whose marriage with the deceased was during the deceased's lifetime dissolved or annulled by a decree of divorce or of nullity of marriage granted under the Matrimonial Causes (Northern Ireland) Order 1978 or the statutory provisions repealed by that Order;

"full valuable consideration" means such valuable consideration as amounts or approximates to the value of that for which it is given;

"net estate", in relation to a deceased person, means-

(a) all property of which the deceased had power to dispose by his will (otherwise than by virtue of a special power of appointment) less the amount of his funeral, testamentary and administration expenses, debts and liabilities, including any capital transfer tax payable out of his estate on his death;

(b) any property in respect of which the deceased held a general power of appointment (not being a power exercisable by will) which has not been exercised;

(c) any sum of money or other property which is treated for the purposes of this Order as part of the net estate of the deceased by virtue of Article 10 (1) or (2);

(d) any property which is treated for the purposes of this Order as part of the net estate of the deceased by virtue of an order made under Article II

(e) any sum of money or other property which is, by reason of a disposition or contract made by the deceased, ordered under Article 12 or 13 to be provided for the purpose of the making of financial provision under this Order;

"reasonable financial provision" -

(a) in the case of an application made by virtue of Article 3(1)(a) by the husband or wife of the deceased (except where the marriage with the deceased was the subject of a decree of judicial separation and at the date of death the decree was in force and the separation was continuing), means such financial provision as it would be reasonable in all the circumstances of the case for a husband or wife to receive, whether or not that provision is required for his or her maintenance;

(b)   in the case of any other application made by virtue of Article 3 (1), means such financial provision as it would be reasonable in all the circumstances of the case for the applicant to receive for his maintenance;

Powers of court to order financial provision from deceased's estate
Application for financial provision from deceased's estate
3.-(1)   Where after the commencement of this Order a person dies domiciled in Northern Ireland and is survived by any of the following persons:-
   (a)   the wife or husband of the deceased;
   (b)   a former wife or former husband of the deceased who has not remarried;
   (c)   a child of the deceased;
   (d)   any person (not being a child of the deceased) who, in the case of any marriage to which the deceased was at any time a party, was treated by the deceased as a child of the family in relation to that marriage;
   (e)   any person (not being a person included in sub-paragraphs (a) to (d)) who immediately before the death of the deceased was being maintained, either wholly or partly, by the deceased;
that person may apply to the court for an order under Article 4 on the ground that the disposition of the deceased's estate effected by his will or the law relating to intestacy, or the combination of his will and that law, is not such as to make reasonable financial provision for the applicant.

(2)   For the purposes of paragraph (1)(e), a person shall be treated as being maintained by the deceased, either wholly or partly, as the case may be, if the deceased, otherwise than for full valuable consideration, was making a substantial contribution in money or money's worth towards the reasonable needs of that person.

Powers of court to make orders
4.-(1)   Subject to the provisions of this Order, where an application is made for an order under this Article, the court may, if it is satisfied that the disposition of the deceased's estate effected by his will or the law relating to intestacy, or the combination of his will and that law, is not such as to make reasonable financial provision for the applicant, make any one or more of the following orders.-
   (a)   an order for the making to the applicant out of the net estate of the deceased of such periodical payments and for such term as may be specified in the order;
   (b)   an order for the payment to the applicant out of that estate of a lump sum of such amount as may be so specified;
   (c)   an order for the transfer to the applicant of such property comprised in that estate as may be so specified;
   (d)   an order for the settlement for the benefit of the applicant of such property comprised in that estate as may be so specified;
   (e)   an order for the acquisition out of property comprised in that estate of such property as may be so specified and for the transfer of the property so acquired to the applicant or for the settlement thereof for his benefit;

(f) an order varying any ante-nuptial or post-nuptial settlement (includine such a settlement made by will) made on the parties to a marriace to which the deceased was one of the parties, the variation being for the benefit of the surviving party to that marriage, or any child of that marriage, or any person who was treated by the deceased as a child of the family in relation to that marriage.

(2) An order under paragraph (1)(a) providing for the making out of the net estate of the deceased of periodical payments may provide for -

(a) payments of such amount as may be specified in the order,

(b) payments equal to the whole of the income of the net estate or of such portion thereof as may be so specified,

(c) payments equal to the whole of the income of such part of the net estate as the court may direct to be set aside or appropriated for the making out of the income thereof of payments under this Article,

or may provide for the amount of the payments or any of them to be determined in any other way the court thinks fit.

(3) Where an order under paragraph (1) (a) provides for the making of payments of an amount specified in the order, the order may direct that such part of the net estate as may be so specified shall be set aside or appropriated for the making out of the income thereof of those payments; but no larger part of the net estate shall be so set aside or appropriated than is sufficient, at the date of the order, to produce by the income thereof the amount required for the making of those payments.

(4) An order under this Article may contain such consequential and supplementary provisions as the court thinks necessary or expedient for the purpose of giving effect to the order or for the purpose of securing that the order operates fairly as between one beneficiary of the estate of the deceased and another and may, in particular, but without prejudice to the generality of this paragraph -

(a) order any person who holds any property which forms part of the net estate of the deceased to make such payment or transfer such property as may be specified in the order;

(b) vary the disposition of the deceased's estate effected by the will or the law relating to intestacy, or by both the will and the law relating to intestacy, in such manner as the court thinks fair and reasonable having regard to the provisions of the order and all the circumstances of the case;

(c) confer on the trustees of any property which is the subject of an order under this Article such powers as appear to the court to be necessary or expedient.

(5) Where -

(a) the deceased is survived by a wife or husband ("the surviving spouse") and is also survived by children who are either issue of the deceased and the surviving spouse or children adopted by the deceased and the surviving spouse jointly; and

(b) the surviving spouse becomes entitled under the deceased's will or the law relating to intestacy, or a combination of his will and that law, to the net estate of the deceased or to an interest in the estate which amounts to reasonable financial provision for both the surviving spouse and the children,

the court shall not make an order under this Article on the application of any of the children who is a minor.

Matters to which court is to have regard in exercising powers under Article 4

5.-(1) Where an application is made for an order under Article 4, the court shall in determining whether the disposition of the deceased's estate effected by his will or the law relating to intestacy, or the combination of his will and that law, is such as to make reasonable financial provision for the applicant and, if the court considers that reasonable financial provision has not been made, in determining whether and in what manner it shall exercise its powers under that Article, have regard to the following matters:-

(a) the financial resources and financial needs which the applicant has or is likely to have in the foreseeable future;

(b) the financial resources and financial needs which any other applicant for an order under Article 4 has or is likely to have in the foreseeable future;

(c) the financial resources and financial needs which any beneficiary of the estate of the deceased has or is likely to have in the foreseeable future;

(d) any obligations and responsibilities which the deceased had towards any applicant for an order under Article 4 or towards any beneficiary of the estate of the deceased;

(e) the size and nature of the net estate of the deceased and the likely effect on any business undertaking included in the estate of an order resulting in the division of property;

(f) any physical or mental disability of any applicant for an order under Article 4 or any beneficiary of the estate of the deceased:

(g) any other matter, including the conduct of the applicant or any other person, which in the circumstances of the case the court may consider relevant.

(2) Without prejudice to the generality of sub-paragraph (g) of paragraph (1), where an application for an order under Article 4 is made by virtue of Article 3(1) (a) or (b), the court shall, in addition to the matters specifically mentioned in sub-paragraphs (a) to (f) of that paragraph, have regard to-

(a) the age of the applicant and the duration of the marriage:

(b) the contribution made by the applicant to the welfare of the family of the deceased, including any contribution made by looking after the home or caring for the family;

and, in the case of an application by the wife or husband of the deceased, the court shall also, unless at the date of death a decree of judicial separation was in force and the separation was continuing, have regard to the provision which the applicant might reasonably have expected to receive if on the day on which the deceased died the marriage, instead of being terminated by death, had been terminated by a decree of divorce.

(3) Without prejudice to the generality of sub-paragraph (g) of paragraph (1), where an application for an order under Article 4 is made by virtue of Article 3(1) (c)

or (d), the court shall, in addition to the matters specifically mentioned in sub-paragraphs (a) to (f) of that paragraph, have regard to the manner in which the applicant was being or in which he might expect to be educated or trained, and where the application is made by virtue of Article 3(l)(d) the court shall also have regard-

    (a)   to whether the deceased had assumed any responsibility for the applicant's maintenance and if so, to the extent to which and the basis upon which the deceased assumed that responsibility and to the length of time for which the deceased discharged that responsibility;

    (b)   to whether in assumine and discharging that responsibility the deceased did so knowing that the applicant was not his own child;

    (c)   to the liability of any other person to maintain the applicant.

    (4) Without prejudice to the generality ef sub-paragraph (g) of paragraph (1), where an application for an order under Article 4 is made by virtue of Article 3 (1)(e), the court shall, in addition to the matters specifically mentioned in sub-paragraphs (a) to (f) of that paragraph, have regard to the extent to which and the basis upon which the deceased assumed responsibility for the maintenance of the applicant and to the length of time for which the deceased discharged that responsibility.

    (5) In considering the matters to which the court is required to have regard under this Article, the court shall take into account the facts as known to the court at the date of the hearing.

    (6) In considering the financial resources of any person for the purposes of this Article the court shall take into account his earning capacity and in considering the financial needs of any person for the purposes of this Article the court shall take into account his financial obligations and responsibilities.

Time-limit for applications

6. An application for an order under Article 4 shall not, except with the permission of the court, be made after the end of the period of six months from the date on which representation with respect to the estate of the deceased is first taken out.

Interim orders

7.-(l) Where on an application for an order under Article 4 it appears to the court-

    (a)   that the applicant is in immediate need of financial assistance, but it is not yet possible to determine what order (if any) should be made under that Article; and

    (b)   that property forming part of the net estate of the deceased is or can be made available to meet the need of the applicant;

the court may order that, subject to such conditions or restrictions, if any, as the court may impose and to any further order of the court, there shall be paid to the applicant out of the net estate of the deceased such sum or sums and (if more than one) at such intervals as the court thinks reasonable; and the court may order that, subject to the provisions of this Order, such payments are to be made until such date as the court may specify, not being later than the date on which the court either makes an order under Article 4 or decides not to exercise its powers under that Article.

(2) Paragraphs (2), (3) and (4) of Article 4 shall apply in relation to an order under this Article as they apply in relation to an order under that Article.

(3) In determining what order, if any, should be made under this Article the court shall, so far as the urgency of the case admits, have regard to the same matters as those to which the court is required to have regard under Article 5.

(4) An order under Article 4 may provide that any sum paid to the applicant by virtue of this Article shall be treated to such an extent and in such manner as may be provided by that order as having been paid on account of any payment provided for by that order.

Variation, discharge, etc., of orders for periodical payments
8.-(1) Subject to the provisions of this Order, where the court has made an order under Article 4 (1) (a) (in this Article referred to as "the original order") for the making of periodical payments to any person (in this Article referred to as "the original recipient"), the court, on an application under this Article, shall have power by order to vary or discharge the original order or to suspend any provision of it temporarily and to revive the operation of any provision so suspended.

(2)   Without prejudice to the generality of paragraph (1), an order made on an application for the variation of the original order may -
(a) provide for the making out of any relevant property of such periodical payments and for such term as may be specified in the order to any person who has applied, or would but for Article 6 be entitled to apply, for an order under Article 4 (whether or not, in the case of any application, an order was made in favour of the applicant);
(b) provide for the payment out of any relevant property of a lump sum of such amount as may be so specified to the original recipient or to any such person as is mentioned in sub-paragraph;
(c) provide for the transfer of the relevant property, or such part thereof as may be so specified to the original recipient or to any such person as is so mentioned.

(3)   Where the original order provides that any periodical payments payable thereunder to the original recipient are to cease on the occurrence of an event specified in the order (other than the remarriage of a former wife or former husband) or on the expiration of a period so specified, then, if, before the end of the period of six months from the date of the occurrence of that event or of the expiration of that period, an application is made for an order under this Article, the court shall have power to make any order which it would have had power to make if the application had been made before that date (whether in favour of the original recipient or any such person as is mentioned in paragraph (2) (a) and whether having effect from that date or from such later date as the court may specify).

(4) Any reference in this Article to the original order shall include a reference to an order made under this Article and any reference in this Article to the original recipient shall include a reference to any person to whom periodical payments are required to be made by virtue of an order under this Article.

(5) An application under this Article may be made by any of the following persons, that it so say -

(a)   any person who by virtue of Article 3 (1) has applied, or would but for Article 6 be entitled to apply, for an order under Article 4,

(b)   the personal representative of the deceased,

(c)   the trustees of any relevant property, and

(d)   any beneficiary of the estate of the deceased.

(6)   An order under this Article may only affect -

(a)   property the income of which is at the date of the order applicable wholly or in part for the making of periodical payments to any person who has applied for an order under this Order, or

(b)   in the case of an application under paragraph (3) in respect of payments which have ceased to be payable on the occurrence of an event or the expiration of a period, property the income of which was so applicable immediately before the occurrence of that event or the expiration of that period, as the case may be,

and any such property as is mentioned in sub-paragraph (a) or (b) is in paragraphs (2) and (5) referred to as "relevant property".

(7)   In exercising the powers conferred by this Article the court shall have regard to all the circumstances of the case, including any change in any of the matters to which the court was required to have regard when making the order to which the application relates.

(8)   Where the court makes an order under this Article, it may give such consequential directions as it thinks necessary or expedient having regard to the provisions of the order.

(9)   No such order as is mentioned in Article 4(1)(d), (e) or (f), 11, 12 or 13 shall be made on an application under this Article.

(10)   For the avoidance of doubt it is hereby declared that, in relation to an order which provides for the making of periodical payments which are to cease on the occurrence of an event specified in the order (other than the remarriage of a former wife or former husband) or on the expiration of a period so specified, the power to vary an order includes power to provide for the making of periodical payments after the expiration of that period or the occurrence of that event.

Payment of lump sums by instalments

9.-(1) An order under Article 4 (1)(b) or 8(2)(b) for the payment of a lump sum may provide for the payment of that sum by instalments of such amount as may be specified in the order.

(2)   Where an order is made by virtue of paragraph (1), the court shall have power, on an application made by the person to whom the lump sum is payable, by the personal representative of the deceased or by the trustees of the property out of which the lump sum is payable, to vary that order by varying the number of instalments payable, the amount of any instalment and the date on which any instalment becomes payable.

Property available for financial provision

Property treated as part of "net estate"

10.-(l) Where a deceased person has in accordance with any statutory provision nominated any person to receive any sum of money or other property on his death and that nomination is in force at the time of his death, that sum of money, after deducting therefrom any capital transfer tax payable in respect thereof, or that other property, to the extent of the value thereof at the date of the death of the deceased after deducting therefrom any capital transfer tax so payable, shall be treated for the purposes of this Order as part of the net estate of the deceased; but this paragraph shall not render any person liable for having paid that sum or transferred that other property to the person named in the nomination in accordance with the directions given in the nomination.

(2) Where any sum of money or other property is received by any person as a donatio mortis causa made by a deceased person, that sum of money, after deducting therefrom any capital transfer tax payable thereon, or that other property, to the extent of the value thereof at the date of the death of the deceased after deducting therefrom any capital transfer tax so payable, shall be treated for the purposes of this Order as part of the net estate of the deceased; but this paragraph shall not render any person liable for having paid that sum or transferred that other property in order to give effect to that donatio mortis causa.

(3) The amount of capital transfer tax to be deducted for the purposes of this Article shall not exceed the amount of that tax which has been borne by the person nominated by the deceased or, as the case may be, the person who has received a sum of money or other property as a donatio mortis causa.

Property held on a joint tenancy

11.-(l) Where a deceased person was immediately before his death beneficially entitled to a joint tenancy of any property, then, if, before the end of the period of six months from the date on which representation with respect to the estate of the deceased was first taken out or 18 months from the date of the death (whichever first occurs), an application is made for an order under Article 4, the court for the purpose of facilitating the making of financial provision for the applicant under this Order may order that the deceased's severable share of that property, at the value thereof immediately before his death, shall, to such extent as appears to the court to be just in all the circumstances of the case, be treated for the purposes of this Order as part of the net estate of the deceased.

(2) In determining the extent to which any severable share is to be treated as part of the net estate of the deceased by virtue of an order under paragraph (1) the court shall have regard to any capital transfer tax payable in respect of that severable share.

(3) Where an order is made under paragraph (1), the provisions of this Article shall not render any person (other than a surviving joint tenant) liable for anything done by him before the order was made.

(4) For the avoidance of doubt it is hereby declared that for the purposes of this Article there may be a joint tenancy of a chose in action.

Special Provisions relating to cases of divorce, separation, etc.

Provision as to cases where no financial relief was granted in divorce proceedings, etc

16.-(1) Where, within twelve months from the date on which a decree of divorce or nullity of marriage has been made absolute or a decree of judicial separation has been granted, a party to the marriage dies and-

    (a) an application for a financial provision order under Article 25 of the Matrimonial Causes (Northern Ireland) Order 1978 or a property adjustment order under Article 26 of that Order has not been made by the other party to that marriage, or

    (b) such an application has been made but the proceedings thereon have not been determined at the date of the death of the deceased,

then, if an application for an order under Article 4 is made by that other party, the court shall, notwithstanding anything in Article 3 or 5 have power, if it thinks it just to do so, to treat that party for the purposes of that application as if the decree of divorce or nullity of marriage had not been made absolute or the decree of judicial separation had not been granted, as the case may be.

    (2) This Article shall not apply in relation to a decree of judicial separation unless at the date of the death of the deceased the decree was in force and the separation was continuing.

Restriction imposed in divorce proceedings, etc., on application under this Order

17.-(1) See Matrimonial and Family Proceedings (NI) Order 1989.

    (2) In the case of a decree of divorce or nullity of marriage an order may be made under paragraph (1) before or after the decree is made absolute, but if it is made before the decree is made absolute it shall not take effect unless the decree is made absolute.

    (3) Where an order made under paragraph (1) on the grant of a decree of divorce or nullity of marriage has come into force with respect to a party to a marriage, then, on the death of the other party to that marriage, the court shall not entertain any application for an order under Article 4 made by the first-mentioned party.

    (4) Where an order made under paragraph (1) on the grant of a decree of judicial separation has come into force with respect to any party to a marriage, then, if the other party to that marriage dies while the decree is in force and the separation is continuing, the court shall not entertain any application for an order under Article 4 made by the first-mentioned party.

Variation and discharge of secured periodical payments orders

18.(1) Where an application for an order under Article 4 is made to the court by any person who was at the time of the death of the deceased entitled to payments from the deceased under a secured periodical payments order made under the Matrimonial Causes (Northern Ireland) Order 1978, then, in the proceedings on that application, the court shall have power, if an application is made under this Article by that person or by the personal representative of the deceased, to vary or discharge that periodical payments order or to revive the operation of any provision thereof which has been suspended under Article 33 of that Order.

(2) In exercising the powers conferred by this Article the court shall have regard to all the circumstances of the case, including any order which the court proposes to make under Article 4 or Article 7, and any change (whether resulting from the death of the deceased or otherwise) in any of the matters to which the court which made the secured periodical payments order was required to have regard when making it.

(3) The powers exercisable by the court under this Article in relation to an order shall be exercisable also in relation to any instrument executed in pursuance of the order.

Provisions as to personal representatives, etc.

22.-(1) The provisions of this Order shall not render the personal representative of a deceased person liable for having distributed any part of the estate of the deceased, after the end of the period of six months from the date on which representation with respect to the estate of the deceased is first taken out, on the ground that he ought to have taken into account the possibility -

(a)   that the court might permit the making of an application for an order under Article 4 after the end of that period, or

(b)   that, where an order has been made under Article 4 the court might exercise in relation thereto the powers conferred on it by Article 8,

but this paragraph shall not prejudice any power to recover, by reason of the making of an order under this Order, any part of the estate so distributed.

(2) Where the personal representative of a deceased person pays any sum directed by an order under Article 7 to be paid out of the deceased's net estate, he shall not be under any liability by reason of that estate not being sufficient to make the payment, unless at the time of making the payment he has reasonable cause to believe that the estate is not sufficient.

(3) Where a deceased person entered into a contract by which he agreed to leave by his will any sum of money or other property to any person or by which he agreed that a sum of money or other property would be paid or transferred to any person out of his estate, then, if the personal representative of the deceased has reason to believe that the deceased entered into the contract with the intention of defeating an application for financial provision under this Order, he may, notwithstanding anything in that contract, postpone the payment of that sum of money or the transfer of that property until the expiration of the period of six months from the date on which representation with respect to the estate of the deceased is first taken out or, if during that period an application is made for an order under Article 4, until the determination of the proceedings on that application.

(4) For the purposes of this Order where -

(a)   an assent or transfer by a personal representative relating to registered land, or

(b)   an application by a surviving joint tenant for his registration as owner of registered land, is presented to the Registrar of Titles for registration, the Registrar shall, notwithstanding any provision of this Order, be entitled to assume that, as the case may be,-

(i)   the personal representative is acting correctly and within his powers, or

(ii)   the surviving joint tenant is entitled to be registered as owner of the land.

ADMINISTRATION OF ESTATES (NI) ORDER 1979

Jurisdiction of High Court

Power of High Court to grant probate and letters of administration

4.-(1) The High Court has power-

(a)   to grant probate of the will of a deceased person to one or more than one of his executors; and

(b)   to grant administration of the estate of a deceased person, or of any part of his estate, to such person as the High Court may determine in accordance with rules of court.

(2) Paragraph (1) does not prejudice the discretion conferred on the High Court by Article 5 or the provisions of Article 10 relating to the grant of administration to a nominee of the Crown where an intestate's estate devolves on the Crown.

(3) A grant may be limited in any way the High Court thinks fit.

(4) The High Court has jurisdiction-

(a)   to make a grant in respect of a deceased person notwithstanding that he left no estate in Northern Ireland;

(b)   to make a *de bonis non* or other form of grant in respect of unadministered estate notwithstanding that there is no unadministered estate of the deceased person in Northern Ireland.

Discretionary power to appoint administrator in certain cases

5.-(1) Where-

(a)   a person has died, and

(b)   by reason of any circumstances it appears to the High Court necessary or expedient to appoint an administrator under this Article,

the High Court may grant administration of the deceased person's estate, appointing as administrator such person as the High Court in its discretion thinks fit.

(2) Administration under this Article -

(a)   may be granted whether the deceased person died before or after the end of the year 1955

(b)   may be limited as the High Court thinks fit.

(3) On administration being granted under this Article no person shall be or become entitled to administer the estate of the deceased person by virtue of the chain of representation.

Administration pendente lite

6.-(1) Where any legal proceedings are pending touching the validity of the will of a deceased person, or for obtaining or revoking any grant, the High Court may grant administration of the estate of the deceased to an administrator, who shall have all the rights and powers of a general administrator, other than the right or distributing the estate of the deceased.

(2) Every person to whom administration is so granted shall be subject to the immediate control of the High Court and act under its direction.

(3) The High Court may, out of the estate of the deceased person, assign to an administrator appointed under this Article such reasonable remuneration as the High Court thinks fit.

(4) This Article does not prejudice the power of a county court judge to grant limited administration under section 18 of the County Courts Act (Northern Ireland) 1959 (death of a person concerning whose property proceedings are pending in a county court).

Administration during minority of executor
7.-(1) Where a minor is sole executor of a will, administration with the will annexed shall be granted to his guardian, or to such other person as the High Court thinks fit, until the minor attains the the the age of 18 years and applies for and obtains a grant of probate, and on the minor attaining that age, and not before, probate of the will may be granted to him.

(2) Where a testator by his will appoints a minor to be an executor, the appointment shall not operate to transfer any interest in the property of the deceased to the minor or to constitute him a personal representative for any purpose unless and until probate is granted to him under this Article.

Grant of special administration where personal representative is abroad
8.-(1) If at the expiration of 12 months from the death of a person any personal representative of his to whom a grant has been made is residing out of the jurisdiction of the High Court, the High Court may, on the application of any creditor or person interested in the estate of the deceased person, grant to him in such form as the High Court thinks fit special administration of the estate of the deceased person.

(2) The High Court may, for the purpose of any legal proceedings to which the administrator under the special administration ("the special administrator") is a party, order the transfer into the Supreme Court of any money or securities belonging to the estate of the deceased person.

(3) If the special administrator becomes aware that a personal representative capable of acting as such has returned to reside within the jurisdiction of the High Court while any legal proceedings to which the special administrator is a party are pending, he shall apply to have that personal representative made a party to the proceedings.

(4) The costs of and incidental to the special administration and any legal proceedings to which the special administrator is a party shall be paid by such person or out of such fund as the court in which the proceedings are pending may direct.

Grant of representation to *trust corporation*
9.-(1) The High Court may-

(a) where a trust corporation is appointed by a will as executor, whether alone or jointly with another person, grant probate to the corporation either solely or jointly with another person, as the case may require; and

(b) grant administration to a trust corporation, either solely or jointly with another person;

and the corporation may act accordingly as executor or administrator, as the case may be.

(2) Representation shall not be granted to a nominee on behalf of a trust corporation.

(3) Any officer authorised for the purpose by a trust corporation or the directors or governing body thereof may, on behalf of the corporation,-

(a) swear affidavits, give security and do any other act or thing which the court may require with a view to the grant to the corporation of representation, or

(b) renounce the corporation's right to a grant, and the acts of an officer so authorised shall be binding on the corporation.

(4) In this Article, "trust corporation" means -

(a) a corporation appointed by the High Court in any particular case to be a trustee; or

(b) a corporation which -

(i) is constituted under the law of the United Kingdom or any part of it, or under the law of any other Member State of the European Economic Community or any part of it; and

(ii) is empowered by its constitution to undertake in Northern Ireland the business of acting as trustee under wills and settlements and as executor and administrator; and

(iii) has one or more places of business in the United Kingdom; and

(iv) is -

(aa) a company incorporated by special Act or Royal Charter, or

(bb) a company registered (with or without limited liability) in the United Kingdom under the Companies Acts (Northern Ireland) 1960 and 1978 or the corresponding law in Great Britain (or under any earlier corresponding Act or law), or in another Member State of the European Economic Community, and having a capital in stock or shares for the time being of not less than £250,000 (or its equivalent in the currency of the State where the company is registered), of which not less than £100,000 (or its equivalent) has been paid up in cash, or

(cc) a company which is registered without limited liability in the United Kingdom under the Companies Acts (Northern Ireland) 1960 and 1978 or the corresponding law in Great Britain (or under any earlier corresponding Act or law), or in another Member State of the European Economic Community, and of which one of the members is a corporation within any of the previous provisions of this sub-paragraph; or

(c) a corporation which is constituted under the law of the United Kingdom or any part of it, or under the law of any other Member State of the European

Economic Community or any part of it, and which satisfies the Lord Chief Justice -

(i) that it undertakes the administration of any charitable, ecclesiastical or public trust without remuneration, or

(ii) that by its constitution it is required to apply the whole of its net income for charitable, ecclesiastical or public purposes and is prohibited from distributing, directly or indirectly, any part thereof by way of profit,

and which is authorised by the Lord Chief Justice to act in relation to any charitable, ecclesiastical or public trust (as the case may be) as a trust corporation.

(5) This Article has effect whether the deceased person died before or after the end of the year 1955.

Administration of the intestates' estates devolving on the Crown

10.-(1) Where Her Majesty is entitled in right of the Crown to any estate in Northern Ireland of an intestate, the High Court shall, on application being made in that behalf, grant administration of the estate to a nominee of Her Majesty.

Revocation of grants

11.-(l) The High Court has power-

(a)   to recall any grant;

(b)   to revoke any grant.

(2) Without prejudice to paragraph (1), where it appears to the High Court that a grant either ought not to have been made or contains an error, the High Court may call in the grant and, if satisfied that it would be revoked at the instance of a party interested, may revoke it.

(3) A grant may be revoked under paragraph (2) without being called in, if it cannot be called in.

PART III
POWERS AND PROCEDURE OF COURTS

Powers of High Court preliminary or incidental to
grants of probate or administration

Citation to prove will or renounce probate

13. The High Court may cite any person appointed executor by a will to prove or renounce probate of the will.

Caveat against grant

14.-(l) Subject to rules of court under section 55(1)(e) of the Judicature (Northern Ireland) Act 1978 (rules as to practice and procedure in non-contentious probate business)-

(a)   a caveat against a grant may be entered in the Probate and Matrimonial Office; and

(b)   no grant shall be made while a caveat so entered has effect.

(2) Such rules shall make provision about the warning of caveators and the circumstances in which caveats cease to have effect.

Power to require administrators to produce sureties

17.-(1)   Where the High Court grants to a person ("the administrator") administration of the estate of a deceased person, the High Court may -

(a)   as a condition of making the grant, and

(b)   subject to the following provisions of this Article, and subject to and in accordance with rules of court,

require one or more than one surety to guarentee that he will make good, within any limit imposed by the High Court on the total liability of the surety or sureties, any loss which any person interested in the administration of the estate may suffer in consequence of a breach by the administrator of his duties as such.

17.-(2) A guarantee given in pursuance of a requirement under paragraph (1) shall enure for the benefit of every person interested in the administration of the deceased person's estate-

(a)   as if the guarantee were contained in a contract under seal made by the surety or sureties with every such person, and

(b)   where there are two or more sureties, as if the sureties had bound themselves jointly and severally.

(3)   No action shall be brought on any such guarantee without the leave of the High Court.

(4)   Stamp duty shall not be chargeable on any such guarantee.

(5)   This Article does not apply-

(a)   where administration is granted

(i)   to the Treasury Solicitor;

(ii)   to the Crown Solicitor for Northern Ireland;

(iii) to a consular officer of a foreign state to which section 1 of the Consular Conventions Act 1949 applies; or

(b)   in such other cases as may be prescribed by rules of court.

Procedure in relation to representation

Application for grants and revocations

18.-(1) An application for a grant, or for the revocation of a grant, shall be made to the Probate and Matrimonial Office and, where the matter is branch office business, may be made to the appropriate branch office of that Office.

(2) The application may be made either in person or through a solicitor.

Official copies of wills and certificates of grants

25.-(1) An official copy of a will, or a certificate of a grant, may be obtained from the Probate and Matrimonial Office.

(2)   Without prejudice to the provisions of section 4(2)(b) of the Administration of Estates Act 1971 (evidence of Northern Ireland grants in England and Wales and in Scotland), an official copy of a will shall be sufficient evidence of the will, and a certificate of a grant shall be sufficient evidence of the grant.

PART IV
EXECUTORS AND ADMINISTRATORS

Executors

Cesser of right of executor to prove

29.-(1) Subject to Article 30 where a person appointed executor by a will-

(a)   survives the testator but dies without having taken out probate, or

(b)   is cited to take out probate and does not appear to the citation, or

(c)   renounces probate,

his rights in respect of the executorship shall wholly cease, and the representation to the testator and the administration of his estate shall devolve and be committed in like manner as if that person had not been appointed executor.

(2)   Where a person is appointed by the will of a person dying after the commencement of this Article to be both executor and trustee and his rights in respect of the executorship wholly cease under paragraph (1), his rights in respect of the trusteeship shall also wholly cease and the trusteeship shall devolve or be determined as if he had not been appointed as trustee, but nothing in this Article shall prevent his subsequent appointment as trustee.

Withdrawal of renunciation

30.-(1) Notwithstanding anything to the contrary in Article 29, an executor who has renounced probate (whether before or after the commencement of this Article) may be permitted by the court to withdraw the renunciation and prove the will.

(2)   Where an executor who has renounced probate has been permitted to withdraw the renunciation and prove the will,-

(a)   the probate shall take effect and be deemed always to have taken effect without prejudice to the previous acts and dealings of and notices to any other person who has previously proved the will or to whom administration has been granted;

(b)   a memorandum of the subsequent probate shall be endorsed on the original grant; and

(c)   his rights as a trustee which ceased by virtue of Article 29, shall notwithstanding anything to the contrary in that Article, revive, except so far as the court otherwise orders.

Rights of proving executors to exercise powers

31. -(1) When probate is granted to one or some of two or more persons appointed executors by a will, whether or not power is reserved to the other or others to prove, all the powers which are by law conferred on the personal representative may be exercised by the proving executor or executors for the time being and shall be as effectual as if all the persons appointed executors had concurred therein.

(2) This Article applies whether the testator died before or after the commencement of this Article.

Executor of executor represents original testator

32.-(1) An executor of a sole or last surviving executor of a testator shall be the executor of that testator, but -

    (a) this paragraph shall not apply to a person who does not prove the will of his testator, and

    (b) in the case of an executor who on his death leaves surviving him some other executor of his testator who afterwards proves the will of that testator, this paragraph shall cease to apply when probate is granted to that surviving executor.

(2) So long as the chain of representation is unbroken, the last executor in the chain is the executor of every preceding testator.

(3)   The chain of representation is broken by

    (a) an intestacy; or

    (b) the failure of a testator to appoint an executor; or

    (c) the failure to obtain probate of a will; or

    (d) a grant of administration in pursuance of Article 5:

but is not broken by a temporary grant of administration if probate is subsequently granted.

(4) Every person in the chain of representation to a testator-

    (a) has the same rights in respect of the estate of that testator as the original executor would have had if living: and

    (b) is, to the extent to which the estate of that testator has come to his hands, answerable as if he were an original executor.

Administrators

Effect of grant of administration

33.   Every person to whom administration is granted in respect of the estate of a person dying after the end of the year 1955 shall, subject to any limitations contained in the grant, have the same rights and liabilities and be accountable in the same manner as if he were the executor of the deceased; and, where the High Court grants administration with a will annexed, that will shall be performed and observed by the administrator in the same manner as if probate of it had been granted to him as executor.

Executor not to act while administration is in force

34.   "Where administration has been granted to any person, no other person shall be entitled to institute any legal proceedings or otherwise act as executor of the deceased in relation to any estate comprised in or affected by the grant, unless the grant has been revoked or has expired.

Provisions applying to both executors and administrators,
and to persons dealing with them

Duty of personal representative

35.-(1) The personal representative of a deceased person shall be under a duty -

(a) to collect and get in the estate of the deceased and administer it according to law;

(b) when required to do so by the High Court, to exhibit on oath in that court a full inventory of the estate and when so required render an account of the administration of the estate to that court;

(c) when required to do so by the High Court, to deliver up the grant of representation to that court.

(2) In paragraph (1) "personal representative", as regards the duty to exhibit an inventory of the estate of a deceased person or to render an account of its administration, includes an executor in his own wrong.

Debtor who becomes creditor's personal representative to account for debt to estate
36.-(1) Subject to paragraph (2), where a debtor becomes either the executor, by virtue of the chain of representation, or the administrator of his deceased creditor-

(a) his debt shall thereupon be extinguished; but

(b) he shall be accountable for the amount of the debt as part of the creditor's estate in any case where he would be so accountable if he had been appointed as an executor by the creditor's will.

(2) Paragraph (1) does not apply where the debtor's authority to act as executor or administrator is limited to part only of the creditor's estate which does not include the debt; and a debtor whose debt is extinguished by virtue of sub-paragraph (a) shall not be accountable for its amount by virtue of subparagraph (b) of that paragraph in any case where the period of limitation under the Statute of Limitations (Northern Ireland) 1958 in respect of the debt had expired before the debtor became the creditor's executor or administrator.

(3) In this Article "debt" includes any liability, and "debtor" and "creditor" shall be construed accordingly.

Payment of debts by personal representative
37.-(1) A personal representative shall not pay the debt of a creditor (including himself) of the estate of any degree in preference to the debt of any other creditor of the same degree.

(2) Nevertheless a personal representative-

(a) other than one mentioned in sub-paragraph (b) who, in good faith and at a time when he has no reason to believe that the deceased's estate is insolvent, pays the debt of any person (including himself) who is a creditor of the estate; or

(b) to whom administration had been granted solely by reason of his being a creditor and who in good faith and at such a time pays the debt of another person who is a creditor of the estate:

shall not, if it subsequently appears that the estate is insolvent, be liable to account to a creditor of the same degree as the paid creditor for the sum so paid.

(3) This Article has effect only in relation to the estates of persons dying after the end of the year 1971.

Protection of persons acting on invalid or revoked probate or administration

38.-(1) Every person making or permitting to be made any payment or disposition in good faith under any grant shall be indemnified and protected in so doing, notwithstanding any defect or circumstance whatsoever affecting the validity of the grant.

(2) When any grant is revoked, all payments and dispositions made in good faith to a personal representative under it before the revocation are a valid discharge to the person making them; and the personal representative who acted under the revoked grant may retain and reimburse himself in respect of any payments or dispositions made by him which the person to whom a grant is afterwards made might have properly made.

(3) This Article has effect only in relation to the estates of persons dying after the end of the year 1971.

ADMINISTRATION OF JUSTICE ACT 1982

International Wills

27.-(1) The Annex to the Convention on International Wills shall have the force of law in the United Kingdom.

(2) The Annex is set out in Schedule 2 to this Act.

(3) In this Part of this Act-

"intemational will " means a will made in accordance with the requirements of the Annex, as set out in Schedule 2 to this Act; and

"the Convention on International Wills" means the Convention providing a Uniform Law on the Form of an International Will concluded at Washington on 26th October 1973.

28.-(l) The persons authorised to act in the United Kingdom in connection with international wills are -

    (a)   solicitors; and

    (b) notaries public.

(2) A person who is authorised under section 6(1) of the Commissioners for Oaths Act 1889 to do notarial acts in any foreign country or place is authorised to act there in connection with international wills.

(3) An international will certified by virtue of subsection (1) or (2) above may be deposited in a depository provided under section 23 above.

(4) Section 23 above shall accordingly have effect in relation to such international wills.

(5) Subject to subsection (6) below, regulations under section 25 above shall have effect in relation to such international wills as they have effect in relation to wills deposited under section 23 above.

(6) Without prejudice to the generality of section 25 above. regulations under that section may make special provision with regard to such international wills.

(7) In section 10 of the Consular Relations Act 1968 (by virtue of which diplomatic agents and consular officials may administer oaths and do notarial acts in certain cases)-

(a) at the end of subsection (l)(b) there shall be added the words "or (c) in connection with an international will."; and

(b) at the end of subsection (4) there shall be added the words "and "international will" has the meaning assigned to it by section 27 of the Administration of Justice Act 1982".

SCHEDULE 2
THE ANNEX TO THE CONVENTION ON INTERNATIONAL WILLS

UNIFORM LAW ON THE FORM OF AN INTERNATIONAL WILL

ARTICLE I

1. A will shall he valid as regards form, irrespective particularly of the place where it is made, of the location of the assets and of the nationality, domicile or residence of the testator, if it is made in the form of an international will complying with the provisions set out in Articles 2 to 5 hereinafter.

2. The invalidity of the will as an international will shall not affect its formal validity as a will of another kind.

ARTICLE 2

This law shall not apply to the form of testamentary dispositions made by two or more persons in one instrument.

ARTICLE 3

1. The will shall be made in writing.
2. It need not be written by the testator himself.
3. It may be written in any language, by hand or by any other means.

ARTICLE 4

1. The testator shall declare in the presence of two witnesses and of a person authorized to act in connection with international wills that the document is his will and that he knows the contents thereof.

2. The testator need not inform the witnesses, or the authorized persons of the contents of the will.

ARTICLE 5

1. In the presence of the witnesses and of the authorized person, the testator shall sign the will or, if he has previously signed it, shall acknowledge his signature.

2. When the testator is unable to sign, he shall indicate the reason therefor to the authorized person who shall make note of this on the will. Moreover, the testator may be authorized by the law under which the authorized person was designated to direct another person to sign on his behalf.

3. The witnesses and the authorized person shall there and then attest the will by signing in the presence of the testator.

ARTICLE 6

1. The signatures shall be placed at the end of the will.

2. If the will consists of several sheets, each sheet shall be signed by the testator or, if he is unable to sign, by the person signing on his behalf or, if there is no such person, by the authorized person. In addition, each sheet shall be numbered.

ARTICLE 7
1. The date of the will shall be the date of its signature by the authorized person.
2. This date shall be noted at the end of the will by the authorized person.

ARTICLE 8
In the absence of any mandatory rule pertaining to the safekeeping of the will, the authorized person shall ask the testator whether be wishes to make a declaration concerning the safekeeping of his will. If so and at the express request of the testator the place where he intends to have his will kept shall be mentioned in the certificate provided for in Article 9.

ARTICLE 9
The authorized person shall attach to the will a certificate in the form prescribed in Article 10 establishing that the obligations of this law have been complied with.

ARTICLE 10
The certificate drawn up by the authorized person shall be in the following form or in a substantially similar form:

CERTIFICATE
(Convention of October 26th, 1973)

1. I .... (name, address and capacity), a person authorized to act in connection with international wills

2. Certify that on .... (date) at .... (place).

3. (testator) .... (name, address, date and place of birth)
   in my presence and that of the witnesses

4. (a) .... (name, address, date and place of birth)
   (b) .... (name, address, date and place of birth)
   has declared that the attached document is his will and that he knows the contents thereof.

5. I furthermore certify that:

6. (a) in my presence and in that of the witnesses
   (1) the testator has signed the will or has acknowledged his signature previously affixed.

> *(2)   following a declaration of the testator stating that he
> was unable to sign his will for the following reason
>
> ....
> ....
> - I have mentioned this declaration on the will
> *-the signature has been affixed by .... (name, address)

7. (b) the witnesses and I have signed the will;

8. *(c) each page of the will has been signed by .... and
    numbered:

9. (d) I have satisfied myself as to the identity of the testator and of the
    witnesses as designated above;

10. (e) the witnesses met the conditions requisite to act as such
    according to the law under which I am acting;

11. *(f) the testator has requested me to include the following statement
    concerning the safekeeping of his will:

    ....
    ....

12. PLACE

13. DATE

14. SIGNATURE and, if necessary, SEAL
    * To be completed if appropriate.

ARTICLE 11
The authorized person shall keep a copy of the certificate and deliver another to the testator.

ARTICLE 12
In the absence of evidence to the contrary, the certificate of the authorized person shall be conclusive of the fornial validity of the instrument as a will under this Law.

ARTICLE 13
The absence or irregulanty of a certificate shall not affect the formal validity of a will under this law.

ARTICLE 14
The international will shall be subject to the ordinary rules of revocation of wills.

ARTICLE 15
In interpreting and applying the provisions of this law, regard shall be had to its international origin and to the need for uniformity in its interpretation.

THE MATRIMONIAL AND FAMILY PROCEEDINGS (NI) ORDER 1989

11. For paragraph (1) of Article 17 of the Inheritance (Provision for Family and Dependants) (Northern Ireland) Order 1979 (under which the court on the grant of a decree of divorce, nullity or judicial separation has power, if the parties to the marriage agree, to order that one party shall not on the death of the other party be entitled to apply for an order under Article 4 of that Order) there shall be substituted the following paragraph -

"(1) On the grant of decree of divorce, a decree of nullity of marriage or a decree of judicial separation or at any time thereafter the High Court or a divorce county court, if it considers it just to do so, may, on the application of either party to the marriage, order that the other party to the marriage shall not on the death of the applicant be entitled to apply for an order under Article 4.".

THE WILLS AND ADMINISTRATION PROCEEDINGS (NI) ORDER 1994

PART II
WILLS

Scope of, and power to make, will
Power to dispose of estate by will
3. Subject to this Part, a person may dispose of all his estate by a will.

Minority
4.-(1) No will made by a person under the age of 18 years is valid, unless he is or has been married.

(2) No will made before 1st January 1970 by a person under the age of 21 years is valid.

(3) No will made before the commencement of this Order by a person who, at the date of the will, had not attained the age of 18 years is valid, even though he then was or had been married.

Execution of will
Formalities for execution
5.-(1) No will is valid unless it is in writing and is executed in accordance with the following requirements, that is to say,-
  (a) it is signed by the testator, or by some other person in his presence and by his direction; and
  (b) it appears from the will or is shown that the testator intended by his signature to give effect to the will; and
  (c) the signature is made or acknowledged by the testator in the presence of two or more witnesses present at the same time; and
  (d) each witness, in the presence of the testator (but not necessarily in the presence of any other witness), either-
    (i) attests the testator's signature or the testator's acknowledgment of his signature and signs the will; or

(ii) acknowledges his signature.

(2) No form of attestation or acknowledgment is necessary.

Testamentary execution of power

6.-(1) No appointment made by will, in exercise of any power, is valid unless the will is executed in accordance with Article 5.

(2) Paragraph (1) applies notwithstanding anything to the contrary in the instrument creating the power.

(3) A will executed in accordance with Article 5 is, so far as respects the execution thereof, a valid execution of a power of appointment by will, notwithstanding that the instrument creating the power expressly requires that a will made in exercise of such power should be executed with some additional or other form of execution or formality.

Incompetency of witness

7. If a witness to a will is at the time of its execution or becomes at any time afterwards incompetent as a witness to prove its execution, the will is not invalid on that account.

Gift to witness

8.-(1) Subject to paragraph (3), if a witness to a will is a person to whom, or to whose spouse, any property is given by the will (whether by way of gift or by way of exercise of a special power of appointment, but other than by way of a charge or direction for the payment of debts), the gift or appointment is void so far as concerns that witness or his spouse or any person claiming under the witness or spouse.

(2) Notwithstanding that property is given by will as mentioned in paragraph (1), the witness is competent as a witness to prove-

(a) the execution of the will;

(b) the validity or invalidity of the will.

(3) Witnessing by a person to whom, or to whose spouse, property is given as mentioned in paragraph (1) is to be disregarded if the will is duly executed without his signature and without that of any other such person.

Witnessing by creditor

9. Where a will charges any property with a debt, any creditor whose debt is so charged, or the spouse of any such creditor, is not incompetent, on account only of the charge,-

(a) to act as a witness to the will; or

(b) as a witness to prove-

    (i)   the execution of the will; or

    (ii) the validity or invalidity of the will.

Witnessing by executor

10. An executor of a will is not incompetent, on account only of his being an executor,-

(a) to act as a witness to the will; or

(b)   as a witness to prove-
   (i)   the execution of the will; or
   (ii)   the validity or invalidity of the will.

Alteration of will after execution
11.   No obliteration, interlineation or other alteration made in a will, after its execution, is valid or has any effect except so far as the words or effect of the will before the alteration are not apparent, unless the alteration, or a memorandum referring to the alteration and written on the will, is executed in the manner in which a will is required to be executed.

Effect of marriage, divorce, etc.

Effect of marriage
12.-(1) Subject to paragraphs (2) to (4), a will is revoked by the testator's marriage.

(2)   A disposition in a will in exercise of a power of appointment takes effect notwithstanding the testator's subsequent marriage unless the property so appointed would in default of appointment pass to his personal representatives.

(3)   Where it appears from a will that at the time it was made the testator was expecting to be married to a particular person and that he intended that the will should not be revoked by the marriage, the will is not revoked by his marriage to that person.

(4)   Where it appears from a will that at the time it was made the testator was expecting to be married to a particular person and that he intended that a gift in the will should not be revoked by his marriage to that person-
   (a)   that gift takes effect notwithstanding the marriage; and
   (b)   any other gift in the will takes effect also, unless it appears from the will that the testator intended the gift to be revoked by the marriage.

Effect of dissolution or annulment of marriage
13.-(1) Where, after a testator has made a will, his marriage is dissolved or annulled-
   (a)   provisions of the will appointing executors or trustees or conferring a power of appointment, if they appoint or confer the power on the former spouse, take effect as if the former spouse had died on the date on which the marriage is dissolved or annulled, and
   (b)   except as provided in paragraph (2), any property comprising or included in a gift to the former spouse passes as if the former spouse had died on that date.

(2)   Where property comprising or included in a gift to the former spouse is a share of residue, the will takes effect as if the gift of the residue were to the other person or persons entitled thereto (and, if more than one, in such shares as to preserve the ratio of their former shares), to the exclusion of the former spouse.

(3)   Paragraphs (1) and (2) are subject to any contrary intention appearing from the will.

(4)   Paragraph (i)(b) is without prejudice to any rights of the former spouse to apply for financial provision under the Inheritance (Provision for Family and Dependants) (Northern Ireland) Order 1979.

(5) In this Article, "dissolved or annulled" means-
(a) dissolved by a decree of divorce or annulled by a decree of nullity of marriage granted under the law of any part of the United Kingdom or the Channel Islands or under the law of the Isle of Man, or
(b) dissolved or annulled in any country or territory outside the United Kingdom, the Channel Islands and the Isle of Man by a divorce or annulment which is entitled to be recognised as valid by the law of Northern Ireland; and "the former spouse" means the person whose marriage with the testator was so dissolved or annulled.

Revocation, revival and confirmation

Revocation
14.-(1) No will, or any part thereof, is revocable otherwise than-
(a) in accordance with Article 12 (marriage); or
(b) by another will; or
(c) by some writing, declaring an intention to revoke the will, executed in the manner in which a will is required to be executed; or
(d) by the testator, or some person in his presence and by his direction, burning, tearing or otherwise destroying the will, with the intention of revoking it.
(2) No will is revoked by any presumption of an intention on the ground of an alteration in circumstances.

Revival of revoked will
15.-(1) No will, or any part thereof, which has been revoked is revived otherwise than by
(a) re-execution of the revoked will; or
(b) a codicil showing an intention to revive the revoked will.
(2) Where any will which has been, first, partly revoked, and later wholly revoked, is revived, the revival does not extend to the part revoked before the revocation of the whole will unless an intention to revive that part is shown.

Effect of re-execution or codicil
16. Subject to any statutory provision-
(a) every will which is re-executed is made at the time of the re-execution;
(b) every will which is confirmed or revived by a codicil is made at the time of the execution of the codicil.

Gifts

Will speaks from death
17.-(1) Every will is to be construed, with reference to the property referred to in it, to speak and take effect as if it had been executed immediately before the death of the testator, unless a contrary intention appears from the will.
(2) No conveyance or other act, made or done subsequently to the execution of a will, of or relating to any property referred to in the will, prevents the operation of the will with respect to that property to the extent that the testator has power to dispose of that property.

(3) The reference in paragraph (2) to an act does not include an act which revokes the will.

Words of limitation unnecessary
18.-(1) A devise of land passes the fee simple absolute in possession or other the whole estate that the testator had power to dispose of by will.

(2) A devise creating an estate of any kind in land passes the largest estate of that kind which the testator had power to create in the land.

(3) This Article applies whether the devisee takes beneficially or on trust and is subject to any contrary intention which appears from the will.

Residuary dispositions to carry property comprised in lapsed and void gifts
19. Unless a contrary intention appears from the will, if a gift (other than a residuary gift) in a will fails or is void by reason of the death of the intended beneficiary in the lifetime of the testator, by reason of being contrary to law, or otherwise, any property comprised or intended to be comprised in that gift is included in the residuary gift (if any) contained in the will.

Implied execution of general power of appointment
20. A general or residuary gift of property of any description (however expressed) is to be construed to include any property, to which the description extends, which the testator has power to appoint in any manner he thinks proper and operates as an execution of the power, unless a contrary intention appears from the will.

Contingent and future gifts carry the intermediate income
21. A contingent or future specific gift of property, a contingent residuary devise of land and a specific or residuary devise of land to trustees upon trust for persons whose interests are contingent or executory all carry the intermediate income of that property or land from the death of the testator, except so far as that income, or any part of it, is otherwise expressly disposed of.

Gifts to children etc. who predecease testator
22.-(1) Where-
   (a)   a will contains a gift to a child or remoter descendant of the testator; and
   (b)   the intended beneficiary dies before the testator, leaving issue; and
   (c)   issue of the intended beneficiary are living at the testator's death, then, unless a contrary intention appears from the will, the gift takes effect as a gift to the issue living at the testator's death.
   (2) Where-
   (a)   a will contains a gift to a class of persons consisting of children or remoter descendants of the testator; and
   (b)   a member of the class dies before the testator, leaving issue; and
   (c)   issue of that member are living at the testator's death, then, unless a contrary intention appears from the will, the gift takes effect as if the class included the issue of its deceased member living at the testator's death.

(3) Issue take under this Article through all degrees, according to their stock, in equal shares if more than one, any gift or share which their parent would have taken and so that no issue take whose parent is living at the testator's death and so capable of taking.

(4) For the purposes of this Article-

(a)   the illegitimacy of any person is to be disregarded; and

(b)   a person conceived before the testator's death and born living thereafter is to be taken to have been living at the testator's death.

(5)   This Article applies to a devise of an estate tail with the substitution for references to issue of references to issue who would be inheritable under the entail.

Presumption as to effect of gifts to spouses

23.   Except where a contrary intention is shown, it is to be presumed that if, by his will, a testator makes a gift of property to his spouse in terms which in themselves would give an absolute interest to the spouse, but by the same will purports to give his issue an interest in the same property, the gift to the spouse is absolute notwithstanding the purported gift to the issue.

Property subject to an option

24. The exercise after a testator's death of an option to purchase property contained in or comprising his estate does not adeem a gift of the property or, in the case of land, effect a conversion with effect from any time other than that at which the option is exercised.

Interpretation of wills

Extrinsic evidence

25.-(1) This Article applies to a will-

(a)   in so far as any part of it is meaningless;

(b)   in so far as the language used in any part of it is ambiguous on the face of it;

(c)   in so far as evidence, other than evidence of the testator's intention, shows that the language used in any part of it is ambiguous in the light of surrounding circumstances.

(2) In so far as this Article applies to a will extrinsic evidence, including evidence of the testator's intention, may be admitted to assist in its interpretation.

Construction of certain expressions

26.-(1) Unless a contrary intention appears from the will, in a will-

(a)   "month" means calendar month;

(b)   "person" includes a corporation;

(c)   words in the singular include the plural, and words in the plural include the singular;

(d)   words importing the masculine gender include the feminine, and words importing the feminine gender include the masculine;

(e)   "land" includes-

(i)   buildings and other structures;

(ii)   land covered by water;

      (iii) any estate in land;

      (iv) any beneficial interest, of which the testator could dispose by will, in capital money;

      (v) if the testator dies owning no other property passing under a gift of land, any beneficial interest, of which the testator could dispose by will, in proceeds of sale under a trust for sale of land;

  (f) "realty" or any cognate expression includes-

      (i) any beneficial interest, of which the testator could dispose by will, in capital money arising from a legal or equitable fee simple;

      (ii) if the testator dies owning no other property passing under a gift of realty, any beneficial interest, of which the testator could dispose by will, in proceeds of sale under a trust for sale of a legal or equitable fee simple.

(2) In this Article "capital money" means capital money under the Settled Land Acts 1882 to 1890.

Construction and effect of references to failure of issue

27.-(1) Where by a will a person is entitled to any property subject to a condition precedent or subsequent (whether or not giving rise to an executory limitation) importing a default or failure of the issue of any person, whether within or at any specified time or not, in his lifetime, at the time of his death or thereafter (including an indefinite failure of issue), the provisions of this Article apply to that condition.

(2) Unless a contrary intention appears from the will, the words of the condition shall be construed to import a default or failure of the issue of the said person only in the lifetime of that person.

(3) Where the condition gives rise to an executory limitation over, a right of entry or re-entry or any right equivalent thereto, a possibility of reverter or a possibility of a resulting trust on default or failure of any of the said person's issue, whether or not-

  (a) the construction is governed by paragraph (2); and

  (b) the default or failure is to be within any specified period of time,

then, if and as soon as there is living any issue, who has attained age of 18 or married, to whose default or failure the condition relates, a default or failure ceases to be possible and the limitation over, right or possibility, as the case may be, ceases to exist.

(4) This Article does not apply to an estate tail.

Operative meaning to be preferred

28. If the purport of a gift admits of more than one interpretation then, in case of doubt, the interpretation according to which the gift will be operative is to be preferred.

Rectification

Rectification of wills

29.-(1) If a court is satisfied that a will is so expressed that to carry out the testator's intentions, in consequence-

(a) of a clerical error; or

(b) of a failure to understand his instructions,

it may order that the will shall be rectified so as to carry out his intentions.

(2) An application for an order under this Article shall not, except with the permission of the court, be made after the end of the period of six months from the date on which representation with respect to the estate of the deceased is first taken out.

(3) The provisions of this Article do not render the personal representatives of a deceased person liable for having distributed part of the estate of the deceased, after the end of the period of six months from the date on which representation with respect to the estate of the deceased is first taken out, on the ground that they ought to have taken into account the possibility that the court might permit the making of an application for an order under this Article after the end of that period; but this paragraph does not prejudice any power to recover, by reason of the making of an order under this Article, any part of the estate so distributed.

(4) In considering for the purposes of this Article when representation with respect to the estate of a deceased person was first taken out, a grant limited to settled land or to trust property is to be left out of account, and a grant limited to real estate or to personal estate is to be left out of account unless a grant limited to the remainder of the estate has previously been made or is made at the same time.

Personal representatives

Substitute executors: uncertainty about order of deaths

30. Where a will contains a provision for a substitute executor operative if an executor designated in the will-

(a) dies before the testator, or

(b) dies at the same time as the testator,

and the executor so designated dies in circumstances rendering it uncertain which of them survived the other, then, for the purpose of probate, the case for which the will provides is deemed to have occurred.

CHILDREN (NI) ORDER 1995

PART XIV
PARENTS NOT MARRIED TO EACH OTHER

Parents not being married to each other to have no effect in law on relationships

155.-(1) In this Order and in any statutory Provision or any instrument passed or made after the commencement of this Article, references (however expressed) to any relationship between two persons shall be construed without regard to whether or not the father and mother of either of them or the father and mother of any person through whom the relationship is deduced, have or had been married to each other at any time.

(2) In this Order and in any statutory provision passed or made after the commencement of this Article-

(a) references to a person whose father and mother were married to each other at the time of his birth include, and

(b) references to a person whose father and mother were not married to each other at the time of his birth do not include,

references to any person to whom paragraph (3) applies.

(3) This paragraph applies to any person who -

(a) is treated as legitimate by virtue of section 1 of the Legitimacy Act (Northern Ireland) 1961;

(b) is a legitimated person within the meaning of Article 32 of the Matrimonial and Family Proceedings (Northern Ireland) Order 1989;

(c) is an adopted child within the meaning of Part V of the Adoption Order; or

(d) is otherwise treated in law as legitimate.

(4) For the purpose of construing references falling within paragraph (2), the time of a person's birth shall be taken to include any time during the period beginning with-

(a) the insemination resulting in his birth; or

(b) where there was no such insemination. his conception, and (in either case) ending with his birth.

(5) Paragraphs (1) and (2) have effect subject to any contrary intention.

Property rights

157. Schedule 6 (which contains provisions relating to property rights where the parents of a child were not married to each other at the time of his birth) shall have effect.

SCHEDULE 6
PROPERTY RIGHTS WHERE PARENTS NOT MARRIED TO EACH OTHER

Succession on intestacy

1.-(1) In Part II of the Administration of Estates Act (Northern Ireland) 1955 (which deals with the distribution of the estate of an intestate), references (however expressed) to any relationship between two persons shall be construed in accordance with Article 155.

(2) For the purposes of sub-paragraph (1) and that Part of that Act, a person whose father and mother were not married to each other at the time of his birth shall be presumed not to have been survived by his father, or by any person related to him only through his father, unless the contrary is shown.

(3) In section 19(l) of that Act (which relates to the construction of documents), the reference to Part II of that Act, or to the foregoing provisions of that Part, shall in relation to an instrument inter vivos made, or a will coming into operation, after the commencement of this paragraph (but not in relation to instruments inter vivos made or wills coming into operation earlier) be construed as including references to this paragraph.

(4) This paragraph does not affect any rights under the intestacy of a person dying before the commencement of this paragraph.

Dispositions of property

2.-(1) In the following dispositions, namely-

(a)   dispositions inter vivos made after the commencement of this paragraph: and

(b)   dispositions by will where the will is made after the commencement of this paragraph, references (whether express or implied) to any relationship between two persons shall be construed in accordance with Article 155.

(2)   The use, without more, of the word "heir" or "heirs" or any expression which is used to create an entailed interest in real or personal property does not show a contrary intention for the purposes of Article 155 as applied by sub-paragraph (1).

(3)   In relation to the dispositions mentioned in sub-paragraph (1), section 34 of the Trustee Act (Northern Ireland) 1958 (which specifies the trust implied by a direction that income is to be held on protective trusts for the benefit of any person) shall have effect as if any reference (however expressed) to any relationship between two persons were construed in accordance with Article 155.

(4)   Where under any disposition of real or personal property, any interest in such property is limited (whether subject to any preceding limitation or charge or not) in such a way that it would, apart from this paragraph, devolve (as nearly as the law permits) along with a dignity or title of honour, then

(a)   whether or not the disposition contains an express reference to the dignity or title of honour: and

(b)   whether or not the property or some interest in the property may in some event become severed from it, nothing in this paragraph shall operate to sever the property or any interest in it from the dignity or title, but the property or interest shall devolve in all respects as if this paragraph had not come into operation.

(5)   This paragraph is without prejudice to Article 42 of the Adoption Order (construction of dispositions in cases of adoption).

(6)   In this paragraph "disposition" means a disposition, including an oral disposition, of real or personal property whether inter vivos or by will.

(7)   Notwithstanding any rule of law, a disposition made by will executed before the date on which this paragraph comes into operation shall not be treated for the purposes of this paragraph as made on or after that date by reason only that the will is confirmed by a codicil executed on or after that date.

No special protection for trustees and personal representatives

3.   Article 6 of the Family Law Reform (Northern Ireland) Order 1977 (which enables trustees and personal representatives to distribute property without having ascertained that no person whose parents were not married to each other at the time of his birth, or who claims through such a person, is or may be entitled to an interest in the property) shall cease to have effect.

Entitlement to grant of probate, etc.

4.-(1) For the purpose of determining the person or persons who would in accordance with rules of court be entitled to a grant of probate or administration in respect of the

estate of a deceased person, the deceased shall be presumed, unless the contrary is shown, not to have been survived -
   (a)   by any person related to him whose father and mother were not married to each other at the time of his birth; or
   (b)   by any person whose relationship with him is deduced through such a person as is mentioned in head (a).

(2) This paragraph does not apply in relation to the estate of a person dying before the commencement of this paragraph.

THE DRAFT SUCCESSION (NI) ORDER 1996

Distribution of estates on intestacy
3.-(1) In the Administration of Estates Act (Northern Ireland) 1955 ("the 1955 Act"), after section 6 there shall be inserted the following section-

"Spouse dying within 28 days	6A. Where -
	(a) the intestate dies leaving a spouse, but
	(b) the spouse dies before the end of the period of 28 days beginning on (and including) the day on which the intestate died,
	this Part shall have effect as respects the intestate as if the spouse had not survived the intestate.".

(2)   Section 17 of the 1955 Act (advancements to children of intestate to be brought into account) is hereby repealed.

(3)   Paragraphs (1) and (2) have effect as respects an intestate dying after the coming into operation of this Order.

(4)   In section 19(1) of the 1955 Act (construction of documents) the references to Part II of that Act and to the foregoing provisions of that Part shall, in relation to an instrument inter vivos made or a will coming into operation after the coming into operation of this Order (but not in relation to instruments inter vivos made and wills coming into operation earlier), be construed as including references to this Article.

Application for financial provision by person who lived with deceased as husband and wife
4.-(1) The Inheritance (Provision for Family and Dependants) (Northern Ireland) Order 1979 shall be amended as follows.

(2)   In Article 3(1) (persons who may apply for financial provision from deceased's estate) after sub-paragraph (b) there shall be inserted the following sub-paragraph-

   "(ba) any person (not being a person included in sub-paragraph (a) or (b)) to whom paragraph (1A) applies;".

(3)   In that Article after paragraph (1) there shall be inserted the following paragraph-

   "(1A) This paragraph applies to a person if the deceased died after the coming into operation of the Succession (Northern Ireland) Order 1996 and, during the whole of the period of two years ending immediately before the date when the deceased died, the person was living-

    (a)   in the same household as the deceased; and

    (b)   as the husband or wife of the deceased.".

(4) In Article 5 (matters to which the court is to have regard in exercising its power to make orders), after paragraph (2) there shall be inserted the following paragraph-

"(2A) Without prejudice to the generality of sub-paragraph (g) of paragraph (1), where an application for an order under Article 4 is made by virtue of Article 3(1)(ba), the court shall, in addition to the matters specifically mentioned in sub-paragraphs (a) to (f) of that paragraph, have regard to -

    (a)   the age of the applicant and the length of the period during which the applicant lived as the husband or wife of the deceased and in the same household as the deceased; and

    (b)   the contribution made by the applicant to the welfare of the family of the deceased, including any contribution made by looking after the home or caring for the family.".

INDEX